First World War
and Army of Occupation
War Diary
France, Belgium and Germany

61 DIVISION
184 Infantry Brigade
Oxfordshire and Buckinghamshire Light Infantry
2/4th Battalion
1 December 1915 - 30 April 1919

WO95/3067/1

The Naval & Military Press Ltd
www.nmarchive.com
Published in association with The National Archives

Published by

The Naval & Military Press Ltd

Unit 10 Ridgewood Industrial Park,

Uckfield, East Sussex,

TN22 5QE England

Tel: +44 (0) 1825 749494

www.naval-military-press.com

www.nmarchive.com

This diary has been reprinted in facsimile from the original. Any imperfections are inevitably reproduced and the quality may fall short of modern type and cartographic standards.

© Crown Copyright
Images reproduced by permission of The National Archives, London, England, 2015.

Contents

Document type	Place/Title	Date From	Date To
Heading	WO95/3067/1		
Heading	61st Division 184th Infy Bde 2-4th Bn Oxf & Bucks Lt Infy. 1915 Sep-1919 Mar		
Heading	War Diary of 2/4th Battalion Oxfordshire And Buckinghamshire Light Infantry From 1st December, 1915 To 31st December, 1915. Volume 2.		
War Diary	Broomfield	01/12/1915	31/12/1915
Miscellaneous	Appendix A. 184th. Infantry Brigade.	14/12/1915	14/12/1915
Miscellaneous	Appendix B. Report by Captain And Adjutant D.M. Rose on Brigade Exercise in Timing and Clearing Given Points.		
Heading	War Diary of 2/4th Battalion Oxfordshire And Buckinghamshire Light Infantry. From 1st January, 1916 To 31st January, 1916. Volume 3.		
War Diary	Broomfield	01/01/1916	31/01/1916
Miscellaneous	184th Infantry Brigade.	05/01/1916	05/01/1916
Miscellaneous	Appendix 1. Brigade Exercise.	05/01/1916	05/01/1916
Miscellaneous	Appendix 2. 2/4th Oxford And Bucks Light Infantry.	09/01/1916	09/01/1916
Miscellaneous	Appendix C 184th. Infantry Brigade.	12/01/1916	12/01/1916
Miscellaneous	Appendix 4		
Miscellaneous	Appendix 5		
Miscellaneous	War Diary For October.1915.		
Miscellaneous	2/4th Bn. Oxford And Bucks Light Infantry.		
Heading	War Diary of 2/4th Oxfordshire and Buckinghamshire Light Infantry From May 24th, 1916 To May 31st, 1916. (Volume I).		
War Diary		09/05/1916	10/05/1916
War Diary	Parkhouse	24/05/1916	24/05/1916
War Diary	Havre	25/05/1916	25/05/1916
War Diary	Merville	26/05/1916	31/05/1916
Operation(al) Order(s)	Operation Order No. 1.	29/05/1916	29/05/1916
Heading	War Diary of 2/4th Oxfordshire and Buckinghamshire Light Infantry From June 1st To June 30th, 1916. (Volume II).		
Miscellaneous	From Officer Commanding 2/4th Oxf. & Bucks Lt. Infty.	17/07/1916	17/07/1916
War Diary	Laventie	01/06/1916	08/06/1916
War Diary	Arrewage K-10-C	09/06/1916	09/06/1916
War Diary	Laventie	10/06/1916	14/06/1916
War Diary	Fauquissart	15/06/1916	21/06/1916
War Diary	Laventie	22/06/1916	30/06/1916
Heading	War Diary of 2/4th Bn. Oxfordshire and Buckinghamshire Light Infantry From July 1st To July 31st, 1916. (Volume III).		
War Diary	Laventie	01/07/1916	03/07/1916
War Diary	Riez Bailleul	04/07/1916	06/07/1916
War Diary	Croix Barbee	07/07/1916	12/07/1916
War Diary	Ferme Du Bois	13/07/1916	14/07/1916
War Diary	Lestrem	15/07/1916	15/07/1916
War Diary	Rue De La Lys	16/07/1916	19/07/1916

War Diary	Fauquissart	20/07/1916	23/07/1916
War Diary	Moated Grange	24/07/1916	27/07/1916
War Diary	Riez Bailleul	28/07/1916	31/07/1916
Miscellaneous	Appendix A 2/4th Oxfords.		
Miscellaneous	Appendix B 184th. Infantry Brigade Routine Orders	13/07/1916	13/07/1916
Heading	War Diary Of 2/4th Battalion Oxfordshire and Buckinghamshire Light Infantry, 1st August, 1916 To 31st August, 1916 (Volume IV).		
War Diary	Riez Bailleul	01/08/1916	01/08/1916
War Diary	Robermetz	02/08/1916	09/08/1916
War Diary	Fauquissart	10/08/1916	15/08/1916
War Diary	Laventie	16/08/1916	21/08/1916
War Diary	Fauquissart	22/08/1916	27/08/1916
War Diary	Laventie	28/08/1916	31/08/1916
Heading	War Diary Of 2/4th Battalion Oxfordshire and Buckinghamshire Light Infantry, 1st September,1916 To 30th September,1916. (Volume V).		
War Diary	Laventie	01/09/1916	03/09/1916
War Diary	Robermetz	04/09/1916	11/09/1916
War Diary	Moated Grange	12/09/1916	19/09/1916
War Diary	Riez Bailleul	20/09/1916	27/09/1916
War Diary	Moated Grange	28/09/1916	30/09/1916
Miscellaneous	Appendix D 4 Oxfords.	05/09/1916	05/09/1916
Miscellaneous	Appendix E 61st Division.	14/09/1916	14/09/1916
Heading	War Diary Of 2/4th Battalion Oxfordshire & Buckinghamshire Light Infantry. 1st October, 1916 To 31st October, 1916. (Volume VI).		
War Diary	Moated Grange	01/10/1916	03/10/1916
War Diary	Riez Bailleul	04/10/1916	09/10/1916
War Diary	Moated Grange	10/10/1916	15/10/1916
War Diary	Riez Bailleul	16/10/1916	21/10/1916
War Diary	Moated Grange	22/10/1916	28/10/1916
War Diary	Riez Bailleul	29/10/1916	29/10/1916
War Diary	Robecq	30/10/1916	31/10/1916
Heading	War Diary of 2/4th Bn. Oxfordshire and Buckinghamshire Light Infantry From 1st November, 1916 To 30th November,1916 (Vol. VII).		
War Diary	Robecq	01/11/1916	02/11/1916
War Diary	Auchel	03/11/1916	03/11/1916
War Diary	Magnicourt	04/11/1916	04/11/1916
War Diary	Tinques	05/11/1916	05/11/1916
War Diary	Etree-Wamin	06/11/1916	06/11/1916
War Diary	Neuvillette	07/11/1916	16/11/1916
War Diary	Bonneville	17/11/1916	17/11/1916
War Diary	Contay	18/11/1916	18/11/1916
War Diary	Contay Area	19/11/1916	19/11/1916
War Diary	Albert	20/11/1916	21/11/1916
War Diary	Fabick Trench	22/11/1916	24/11/1916
War Diary	Ovillers	25/11/1916	26/11/1916
War Diary	Mouquet	27/11/1916	30/11/1916
Heading	War Diary Of 2/4th Battalion Oxfordshire & Buckinghamshire Light Infantry. 1st December, 1916 To 31st December, 1916. (Volume VIII).		
War Diary	Martinsart	01/12/1916	01/12/1916
War Diary	Hedauville	02/12/1916	11/12/1916
War Diary	Martinsart	12/12/1916	23/12/1916

Type	Description	Start	End
War Diary	Mouquet Farm	24/12/1916	29/12/1916
War Diary	Martinsart	30/12/1916	31/12/1916
Operation(al) Order(s)	Order No. 151 by Lt Col R. Bellamy D.S.O.	23/12/1916	23/12/1916
Operation(al) Order(s)	2/4 Oxford Bucks L I Order No. 152	27/12/1916	27/12/1916
Operation(al) Order(s)	2/4th Oxford and Bucks Light Infantry Order No. 153 by Lt Col R. Bellamy D.S.O.	30/12/1916	30/12/1916
Heading	War Diary Of 2/4th Battalion Oxfordshire and Buckinghamshire Light Infantry. 1st January, 1917 To 31st January, 1917. (Volume IX).		
War Diary	Hedauville	01/01/1917	08/01/1917
War Diary	Martinsart	09/01/1917	15/01/1917
War Diary	Puchevillers	16/01/1917	17/01/1917
War Diary	Longvillette	18/01/1917	18/01/1917
War Diary	Domqueur	19/01/1917	19/01/1917
War Diary	Maison Ponthieu	20/01/1917	31/01/1917
Operation(al) Order(s)	2/4th Oxford and Bucks Light Infantry Order No. 163.	07/01/1917	07/01/1917
Operation(al) Order(s)	2/4th Bn Oxford and Bucks Light Infantry Order No. 164.	14/01/1917	14/01/1917
Operation(al) Order(s)	2/4th Oxford and Bucks Light Infantry Order No. 166 Appendix M	16/01/1917	16/01/1917
Operation(al) Order(s)	2/4th Oxford and Bucks Light Infantry Order No. 167.	17/01/1917	17/01/1917
Operation(al) Order(s)	2/4th Oxford and Bucks Lt Infantry Order No. 168.		
Heading	War Diary Of 2/4th Battalion Oxfordshire and Buckinghamshire Light Infantry. 1st February, 1917 To 28th February, 1917. (Volume X).		
War Diary	Maison Ponthieu	01/02/1917	04/02/1917
War Diary	Brucamps	05/02/1917	13/02/1917
War Diary	Wiencourt	14/02/1917	15/02/1917
War Diary	Rainecourt	16/02/1917	21/02/1917
War Diary	Rainecourt & Herleville	22/02/1917	23/02/1917
War Diary	Ablaincourt	24/02/1917	28/02/1917
Operation(al) Order(s)	2/4 Oxford and Bucks Lt Infty Order No 186	03/02/1917	03/02/1917
Operation(al) Order(s)	2/4 Oxford and Bucks Lt Infty Order No 194.	12/02/1917	12/02/1917
Operation(al) Order(s)	2/4 Oxford and Bucks Lt Infty Order No 195.	14/02/1917	14/02/1917
Operation(al) Order(s)	2/4 Oxford and Bucks Lt Infty Order No 204	22/02/1917	22/02/1917
Heading	War Diary Of 2/4th Battalion, Oxfordshire & Buckinghamshire Light Infantry For Period 1st March 1917 To 31st March 1917. Volume XI.		
War Diary	Ablain-Court	01/03/1917	15/03/1917
War Diary	Framerville	16/03/1917	18/03/1917
War Diary	Tour Carree	19/03/1917	19/03/1917
War Diary	Rainecourt	20/03/1917	22/03/1917
War Diary	Chaulnes	23/03/1917	23/03/1917
War Diary	Marchele-Pot	24/03/1917	25/03/1917
War Diary	Athies	26/03/1917	30/03/1917
War Diary	Tertry	31/03/1917	31/03/1917
Heading	War Diary of 2/4th Battalion, Oxfordshire & Buckinghamshire Light Infantry From April 1st, 1917 To April 30th, 1917. Volume XII.		
War Diary	At Caulaincourt	01/04/1917	03/04/1917
War Diary	Soyecourt	04/04/1917	07/04/1917
War Diary	Caulaincourt	08/04/1917	09/04/1917
War Diary	Marteville	10/04/1917	10/04/1917
War Diary	Monchy-Le-Gache	11/04/1917	12/04/1917
War Diary	Hombleux	13/04/1917	19/04/1917
War Diary	Germaine	20/04/1917	20/04/1917

War Diary	Holnon	21/04/1917	26/04/1917
War Diary	Fayet	27/04/1917	29/04/1917
War Diary	Attilly	30/04/1917	30/04/1917
Miscellaneous	184th Infantry Brigade		
Map	Map		
Operation(al) Order(s)	2/4 Oxford and Bucks Lt Infty Order No 237	03/04/1917	03/04/1917
Operation(al) Order(s)	2/4 Oxford and Bucks Lt Infty Order No 239	06/04/1917	06/04/1917
Operation(al) Order(s)	2/4 Oxford and Bucks Lt Infty Order No 240	07/04/1917	07/04/1917
Operation(al) Order(s)	2/4 Oxford and Bucks Lt Infty Order No 244	11/04/1917	11/04/1917
Operation(al) Order(s)	2/4 Oxford and Bucks Lt Infty Order No 251		
Operation(al) Order(s)	2/4 Oxford and Bucks Lt Infty Order No 253	20/04/1917	20/04/1917
Operation(al) Order(s)	2/4 Oxford and Bucks Lt Infty Order No 255	26/04/1917	26/04/1917
Operation(al) Order(s)	2/4 Oxford and Bucks Lt Infty Order No 256	27/04/1917	27/04/1917
Operation(al) Order(s)	2/4 Oxford and Bucks Lt Infty Order No 258	29/04/1917	29/04/1917
Heading	War Diary Of 2/4th Battalion, Oxfordshire & Buckinghamshire Light Infantry For Period May 1st To May 31st 1917 Volume XIII		
War Diary	Attilly	01/05/1917	02/05/1917
War Diary	Vaux	03/05/1917	13/05/1917
War Diary	Mesnil St Nicaise	14/05/1917	15/05/1917
War Diary	Rivery	16/05/1917	17/05/1917
War Diary	La Vicogne	18/05/1917	21/05/1917
War Diary	Neuvillette	22/05/1917	23/05/1917
War Diary	Barly	24/05/1917	24/05/1917
War Diary	Duisans	25/05/1917	31/05/1917
Operation(al) Order(s)	2/4 Oxford and Bucks Lt Infty Order No 270	12/05/1917	12/05/1917
Operation(al) Order(s)	2/4 Oxford and Bucks Lt Infty Order No 272	14/05/1917	14/05/1917
Operation(al) Order(s)	2/4 Oxford and Bucks Lt Infty Order No 274	16/05/1917	16/05/1917
Operation(al) Order(s)	2/4 Oxford and Bucks Lt Infty Order No 278	20/05/1917	20/05/1917
Operation(al) Order(s)	2/4 Oxford and Bucks Lt Infty Order No 280	22/05/1917	22/05/1917
Operation(al) Order(s)	2/4 Oxford and Bucks Lt Infty Order No 282	23/05/1917	23/05/1917
Operation(al) Order(s)	2/4 Oxford and Bucks Lt Infty Order No 290	30/05/1917	30/05/1917
Heading	War Diary of 2/4th Battalion, Oxfordshire & Buckinghamshire Light Infantry From June 1st, 1917 To June 30th, 1917. (Volume XIV).		
War Diary	Tilloy	01/06/1917	01/06/1917
War Diary	Monchy	02/06/1917	10/06/1917
War Diary	Tilloy	11/06/1917	11/06/1917
War Diary	Berneville	12/06/1917	23/06/1917
War Diary	Noeux	24/06/1917	30/06/1917
Operation(al) Order(s)	2/4 Oxford and Bucks Lt Infty Order No 292	01/06/1917	01/06/1917
Operation(al) Order(s)	2/4 Oxford and Bucks Lt Infty Order No 293	06/06/1917	06/06/1917
Operation(al) Order(s)	2/4 Oxford and Bucks L I Order No 294	07/06/1917	07/06/1917
Operation(al) Order(s)	2/4 Oxford and Bucks L I Order No 295	09/06/1917	09/06/1917
Operation(al) Order(s)	2/4 Oxf and Bucks Lt Infty Order No. 296	11/06/1917	11/06/1917
Operation(al) Order(s)	2/4 Oxford and Bucks Lt Infty Order No. 307	22/06/1917	22/06/1917
Heading	War Diary of 2/4th Battalion, Oxfordshire & Buckinghamshire Light Infantry From 1st July,1917 To 31st July,1917. (Volume XV)		
War Diary	Noeux	01/07/1917	26/07/1917
War Diary	Broxeele	27/07/1917	31/07/1917
Operation(al) Order(s)	2/4 Oxford and Bucks Lt Infty Order No 339	25/07/1917	25/07/1917
Heading	War Diary of 2/4th Battalion, Oxfordshire & Buckinghamshire Light Infantry From 1st August,1917 To 31st August,1917 (Volume XVI)		
War Diary	Broxeele	01/08/1917	15/08/1917

War Diary	Watou	16/08/1917	18/08/1917
War Diary	Ypres	19/08/1917	20/08/1917
War Diary	St Julien	21/08/1917	23/08/1917
War Diary	Ypres	24/08/1917	25/08/1917
War Diary	Brandhoek	26/08/1917	30/08/1917
War Diary	Ypres	31/08/1917	31/08/1917
Operation(al) Order(s)	2/4 Oxford and Bucks Lt Infty Order No 359	14/08/1917	14/08/1917
Diagram etc	Formation For Attack		
Operation(al) Order(s)	Battalion Attack Order No 1	19/08/1917	19/08/1917
Heading	War Diary of 2/4th Battalion Oxfordshire And Buckinghamshire Light Infantry. From 1st September, 1917 To 30th September, 1917 (Volume XVII.)		
War Diary	Ypres	01/09/1917	07/09/1917
War Diary	Wieltje	08/09/1917	09/09/1917
War Diary	St. Julien	10/09/1917	10/09/1917
War Diary	Ypres	11/09/1917	12/09/1917
War Diary	Brandhoek	13/09/1917	13/09/1917
War Diary	Watou	14/09/1917	16/09/1917
War Diary	Wormhoudt	17/09/1917	18/09/1917
War Diary	Gouves	19/09/1917	23/09/1917
War Diary	Arras	24/09/1917	30/09/1917
Operation(al) Order(s)	2/4 Oxford And Bucks Light Infantry Order No. 380.	09/09/1917	09/09/1917
Operation(al) Order(s)	Battalion Attack Order No. 2.		
Operation(al) Order(s)	2/4 Oxford And Bucks Light Infantry Order No. 382.	12/09/1917	12/09/1917
Operation(al) Order(s)	2/4th Bn Oxford And Bucks Light Infantry Order No. 383	12/09/1917	12/09/1917
Operation(al) Order(s)	2/4th Bn Oxford And Bucks Light Infantry Order No. 386.	16/09/1917	16/09/1917
Operation(al) Order(s)	2/4th Oxford And Bucks Light Infantry Order No. 388.	18/09/1917	18/09/1917
Operation(al) Order(s)	2/4th Bn Oxford And Bucks Light Infantry Order No. 385	23/09/1917	23/09/1917
Heading	War Diary of 2/4th Battalion, Oxfordshire & Buckinghamshire Light Infantry From 1st October To 31st October,1917. Volume XVIII.		
War Diary	St Nicholas	01/10/1917	04/10/1917
War Diary	Greenland Hill	05/10/1917	28/10/1917
War Diary	Arras	29/10/1917	31/10/1917
Operation(al) Order(s)	2/4th Bn Oxford And Bucks Light Infantry Order No. 405.	03/10/1917	03/10/1917
Operation(al) Order(s)	2/4th Bn Oxf And Bucks Lt Infty Order No. 406.	09/10/1917	09/10/1917
Operation(al) Order(s)	2/4th Oxford And Bucks Light Infantry Order No. 409	15/10/1917	15/10/1917
Operation(al) Order(s)	2/4th Oxford And Bucks Light Infantry Order No. 410.	21/10/1917	21/10/1917
Operation(al) Order(s)	2/4th Oxford And Bucks Light Infantry Order No. 411.	27/10/1917	27/10/1917
Heading	War Diary of 2/4th Battalion Oxfordshire & Buckinghamshire Light Infantry. From 1st November, 1917, To 30th November, 1917. (Volume XIX).		
War Diary	Arras	01/11/1917	09/11/1917
War Diary	Chemical Works Sector	10/11/1917	28/11/1917
War Diary	Arras	29/11/1917	30/11/1917
War Diary	Bertincourt	30/11/1917	30/11/1917
Operation(al) Order(s)	2/4th Bn Oxford And Bucks Light Infantry Order No. 422.	08/11/1917	08/11/1917
Operation(al) Order(s)	2/4th Oxford And Bucks Light Infantry Order No. 423.	14/11/1917	14/11/1917
Miscellaneous	App B.8		
Map	Map		
Miscellaneous	To Headquarters 184th Infantry Brigade.	20/11/1917	20/11/1917

Type	Description	Start	End
Operation(al) Order(s)	Raid Order No. 1.	13/11/1917	13/11/1917
Operation(al) Order(s)	2/4th Oxford And Bucks Light Infantry Order No. 424.	20/11/1917	20/11/1917
Operation(al) Order(s)	2/4th Oxford And Bucks Light Infantry Order No. 426.	27/11/1917	27/11/1917
Operation(al) Order(s)	2/4th Oxford And Bucks Light Infantry Order No. 428.	29/11/1917	29/11/1917
Heading	War Diary of 2/4th Battalion, Oxfordshire & Buckinghamshire Light Infantry From 1st December To 31st December,1917 Vol. XX.		
War Diary	Bertincourt Fins	01/12/1917	02/12/1917
War Diary	N.E Of Metz	03/12/1917	05/12/1917
War Diary	La Vacquerie Sector	06/12/1917	10/12/1917
War Diary	Havrincourt Wood	11/12/1917	16/12/1917
War Diary	N.W. of La Vacquerie	17/12/1917	19/12/1917
War Diary	Havrincourt Wood	20/12/1917	22/12/1917
War Diary	Lechelle	23/12/1917	24/12/1917
War Diary	Suzanne	25/12/1917	31/12/1917
Operation(al) Order(s)	2/4th Oxford And Bucks Lt Infty Order No 431	10/12/1917	10/12/1917
Operation(al) Order(s)	2/4th Oxford And Bucks Light Infantry Order No 434.	15/12/1917	15/12/1917
Operation(al) Order(s)	2/4th Oxford And Bucks L I Order No 439	21/12/1917	21/12/1917
Operation(al) Order(s)	2/4th Oxford And Bucks L I Order No 435	19/12/1916	19/12/1916
Operation(al) Order(s)	2/4th Oxford And Bucks L I Order No 440	23/12/1917	23/12/1917
Operation(al) Order(s)	2/4th Bn Oxford And Bucks Lt Infty Order No 447.	30/12/1917	30/12/1917
Heading	War Diary of 2/4th Oxfordshire & Buckinghamshire Light Infantry. From 1st January 1918-31st January 1918. (Volume XXI.)		
War Diary	Caix	01/01/1918	07/01/1918
War Diary	Voyennes	08/01/1918	09/01/1918
War Diary	Attilly	10/01/1918	10/01/1918
War Diary	Gricourt	11/01/1918	14/01/1918
War Diary	Maissemy	15/01/1918	18/01/1918
War Diary	Gricourt	19/01/1918	22/01/1918
War Diary	Fresnoy-Le-Petit	23/01/1918	26/01/1918
War Diary	Holnon	27/01/1918	31/01/1918
Operation(al) Order(s)	2/4th Bn Oxford And Bucks Light Infantry Order No. 454.	06/01/1918	06/01/1918
Operation(al) Order(s)	2/4th Bn Oxford And Bucks Light Infantry Order No. 456	08/01/1918	08/01/1918
Operation(al) Order(s)	2/4th Oxford And Bucks Lt Infty Order No. 458	09/01/1918	09/01/1918
Operation(al) Order(s)	2/4th Oxford And Bucks Light Infantry Order No. 460.	13/01/1918	13/01/1918
Operation(al) Order(s)	2/4th Oxford And Bucks Light Infantry Order No. 462.	17/01/1918	17/01/1918
Operation(al) Order(s)	2/4th Oxford And Bucks L I Order No. 464	25/01/1918	25/01/1918
Operation(al) Order(s)	2/4th Oxford And Bucks Lt Infty Order No. 463	21/01/1918	21/01/1918
Heading	War Diary of 2/4th Battalion, Oxfordshire & Buckinghamshire Light Infantry From 1st Feb.1918 To 28th Feb.1918. Volume XXII.		
War Diary	Holnon	01/02/1918	03/02/1918
War Diary	Fayet	04/02/1918	07/02/1918
War Diary	Holnon	08/02/1918	11/02/1918
War Diary	Fayet	12/02/1918	15/02/1918
War Diary	Holnon	16/02/1918	19/02/1918
War Diary	Vaux	20/02/1918	22/02/1918
War Diary	Fresnoy Quarry	23/02/1918	28/02/1918
Operation(al) Order(s)	2/4th Bn Oxford And Bucks Light Infantry Order No. 471.	02/02/1918	02/02/1918
Operation(al) Order(s)	2/4th Bn Oxford And Bucks Lt Infty Order No. 472.	06/02/1918	06/02/1918
Operation(al) Order(s)	2/4th Bn Oxford And Bucks Light Infantry Order No. 475.	10/02/1918	10/02/1918

Type	Description	Start	End
Operation(al) Order(s)	2/4th Bn Oxford And Bucks Light Infantry Order No. 476.	14/02/1918	14/02/1918
Operation(al) Order(s)	2/4th Bn Oxford And Bucks Light Infantry Order No. 481.	18/02/1918	18/02/1918
Operation(al) Order(s)	2/4th Bn Oxford And Bucks Light Infantry Order No. 483.	21/02/1918	21/02/1918
Heading	War Diary of 2/4th Battalion, Oxfordshire & Buckinghamshire Light Infantry From 1st March 1918 To 31st March 1918. Volume XXIII		
Heading	War Diary of 2/4th Battalion Oxfordshire & Buckinghamshire Light Infantry From 1st March, 1918 To 31st March 1918. (Volume XXIII)		
War Diary	Fresnoy Quarry	01/03/1918	02/03/1918
War Diary	Ugny	03/03/1918	10/03/1918
War Diary	Attilly	11/03/1918	18/03/1918
War Diary	Fayet	19/03/1918	21/03/1918
War Diary	Attilly	22/03/1918	22/03/1918
War Diary	Beauvois	23/03/1918	23/03/1918
War Diary	Languevoisin	24/03/1918	24/03/1918
War Diary	Hombleux	25/03/1918	25/03/1918
War Diary	Fresnoy-La-Chaussee	26/03/1918	26/03/1918
War Diary	Le Quesnil	27/03/1918	27/03/1918
War Diary	Marcelcave	28/03/1918	31/03/1918
Operation(al) Order(s)	2/4th Oxford And Bucks Lt Infty Order No 484	02/03/1918	02/03/1918
Operation(al) Order(s)	2/4th Bn Oxford And Bucks Light Infty Order No. 493.	09/03/1918	09/03/1918
Operation(al) Order(s)	2/4th Bn Oxford And Bucks Light Infantry Order No. 500	17/03/1918	17/03/1918
Heading	2/4th Battalion Oxford & Bucks Light/infantry April 1918.		
War Diary	Gentelle	01/04/1918	03/04/1918
War Diary	Mericourt	04/04/1918	06/04/1918
War Diary	Avesne	07/04/1918	10/04/1918
War Diary	In The Train	11/04/1918	11/04/1918
War Diary	Robecq	12/04/1918	16/04/1918
War Diary	St. Venant	16/04/1918	19/04/1918
War Diary	Robecq	20/04/1918	24/04/1918
War Diary	St Venant	25/04/1918	28/04/1918
War Diary	Robecq	29/04/1918	30/04/1918
Operation(al) Order(s)	2/4th Battn Oxford And Bucks Light Infty Order No. 509.	10/04/1918	10/04/1918
Operation(al) Order(s)	2/4 Oxford & Bucks Lt Infty Operation Order No 2	15/04/1918	15/04/1918
Operation(al) Order(s)	2/4th Bn Oxford & Bucks L.I. Operation Order No 1.	12/04/1918	12/04/1918
Heading	War Diary of 2/4th Battalion Oxfordshire And Buckinghamshire Light Infantry From 1st. May 1918 To 31st. May 1918. (Volume XXV)		
War Diary	Robecq	01/05/1918	06/05/1918
War Diary	St. Venant	07/05/1918	10/05/1918
War Diary	Robecq	11/05/1918	18/05/1918
War Diary	St. Venant	19/05/1918	22/05/1918
War Diary	Robecq	23/05/1918	29/05/1918
War Diary	La Pierriere	30/05/1918	31/05/1918
Diagram etc	Diagram		
Operation(al) Order(s)	Operation Order No 17. by Lieut Col C.R.C. Boyle D.S.O. Commdg 2/4th Oxf and Bucks Lt Infty	13/05/1918	13/05/1918
Operation(al) Order(s)	Operation Order No 4 by Major R. R. Will Cmdg 256 Bde R.F.A.	13/05/1918	13/05/1918

Operation(al) Order(s)	C Coy 61st Batt M.G.C. Operation Order No. 80	13/05/1918	13/05/1918
Map	Information Obtained From Air Photographs. Taken On 3. May 1918		
Miscellaneous	App. P.10.	13/05/1918	13/05/1918
Map	Map		
Heading	War Diary of 2/4th Battalion Oxfordshire And Buckinghamshire Light Infantry From 1st June 1918 To 30th June 1918. Volume XXVI		
War Diary	La Pierriere	01/06/1918	02/06/1918
War Diary	Robecq	03/06/1918	10/06/1918
War Diary	La Pierriere	11/06/1918	14/06/1918
War Diary	Robecq	15/06/1918	22/06/1918
War Diary	La Pierriere	23/06/1918	30/06/1918
Heading	War Diary of 2/4th.Bn. Oxfordshire & Buckinghamshire Light Infantry. From 1st July 1918 To 31st July 1918 (Volume 27.)		
War Diary	La Pierriere	01/07/1918	10/07/1918
War Diary	Liettres	11/07/1918	17/07/1918
War Diary	Cottes	18/07/1918	19/07/1918
War Diary	Warne	20/07/1918	22/07/1918
War Diary	Pont Asquin	23/07/1918	31/07/1918
Miscellaneous	Appendix "A" 2/4 Oxford & Bucks Lt. Infty.		
Heading	War Diary Of 2/4th Battalion Oxfordshire & Buckinghamshire Light Infantry. 1st August, 1918 To 31st August,1918. (Volume XXVIII).		
War Diary	Cottes	01/08/1918	04/08/1918
War Diary	Thiennes	05/08/1918	05/08/1918
War Diary	Arrewage	06/08/1918	14/08/1918
War Diary	S Presiano Camp	15/08/1918	20/08/1918
War Diary	Chapelle Boom	21/08/1918	24/08/1918
War Diary	Neuf Berquin	25/08/1918	29/08/1918
War Diary	Les Puresbecques	30/08/1918	31/08/1918
Miscellaneous	Operation Order by Major G.K. Rose M.C. Commanding 2/4 Oxf Bucks Lt Infty		
Heading	War Diary of 2/4th Battalion Oxfordshire & Buckinghamshire Light Infantry. From 1st September 1918 To 30th September 1918 (Volume 29)		
War Diary	Rue Montigny	01/09/1918	01/09/1918
War Diary	Chappelle Duvelle	02/09/1918	03/09/1918
War Diary	Estaires	04/09/1918	10/09/1918
War Diary	Laventie	11/09/1918	13/09/1918
War Diary	Sailly	14/09/1918	17/09/1918
War Diary	Linghem	18/09/1918	24/09/1918
War Diary	Le Crusecbeau	25/09/1918	27/09/1918
War Diary	Laventie	28/09/1918	30/09/1918
Heading	War Diary of 2/4th Battalion, The Oxfordshire & Buckinghamshire Light Infantry From 1st Oct. 1918 To 31st Oct. 1918. Vol XXX.		
War Diary	Laventie East	01/10/1918	01/10/1918
War Diary	Rouge De Bout	02/10/1918	02/10/1918
War Diary	Croix Marechal	03/10/1918	03/10/1918
War Diary	Thiennes	04/10/1918	06/10/1918
War Diary	Beauval	07/10/1918	09/10/1918
War Diary	Hermies	10/10/1918	10/10/1918
War Diary	W. Of Bourlon Wood	11/10/1918	17/10/1918
War Diary	Cantaing	18/10/1918	18/10/1918

War Diary	Cagnocles	20/10/1918	23/10/1918
War Diary	St. Aubert	24/10/1918	24/10/1918
War Diary	Bermerain	25/10/1918	25/10/1918
War Diary	Sepmeries	26/10/1918	26/10/1918
War Diary	Bermerain	27/10/1918	28/10/1918
War Diary	Vendegies	29/10/1918	29/10/1918
War Diary	Bermerain	30/10/1918	31/10/1918
Miscellaneous	Appendix "A" 2/4th Oxf. & Bucks Lt. Infty.		
Heading	War Diary of 2/4th Battalion, Oxfordshire & Buckinghamshire Light Infantry. From 1st Nov.1918 To 30th Nov.1918 Vol. XXXI.		
War Diary	Bermerain	01/11/1918	01/11/1918
War Diary	Maresches	02/11/1918	02/11/1918
War Diary	Bermerain	03/11/1918	03/11/1918
War Diary	Avesnes-Lez-Aubert	04/11/1918	05/11/1918
War Diary	Bermerain	06/11/1918	08/11/1918
War Diary	Maresches	09/11/1918	14/11/1918
War Diary	Haussy	15/11/1918	15/11/1918
War Diary	Cagnoncles	16/11/1918	16/11/1918
War Diary	Cambrai	17/11/1918	27/11/1918
War Diary	Lourques	28/11/1918	28/11/1918
War Diary	Domart	29/11/1918	30/11/1918
Miscellaneous	Divisional Routine Orders By Major General F.J. Duncan C.M.G. D.S.O. Commanding 61st Division	18/11/1918	18/11/1918
Miscellaneous	Special Order Of The Day By Marshal Foch Commander-In-Chief Of The Allied Armies		
Heading	War Diary of 2/4th Battalion Oxfordshire And Buckinghamshire Light Infantry. From 1st December, 1918 To 31st December 1918 (Volume 32)		
War Diary	Domart	01/12/1918	31/12/1918
Miscellaneous	2/4th Oxf. & Bucks Lt. Infty		
Heading	War Diary of 2/4th Battalion Oxfordshire And Buckinghamshire Light Infantry. From 1st January 1919 To 31st January 1919 (Volume 33)		
War Diary	Domart	01/01/1919	31/01/1919
Miscellaneous	2/4th Oxf. & Bucks Lt. Infty.		
Heading	War Diary Of 2/4th Battalion Oxfordshire & Buckinghamshire Light Infantry. 1st February,1919 To 28th February, 1918 (Volume XXXIV).		
War Diary	Domart-En-Ponthieu	01/02/1919	01/02/1919
War Diary	Cucq	02/02/1919	06/02/1919
War Diary	Etaples	07/02/1919	28/02/1919
Miscellaneous	2/4th Bn. Oxf. & Bucks Lt. Infty		
Heading	War Diary of 2/4th Battalion Oxfordshire And Buckinghamshire Light Infantry From 1st March, 1919 To 31st March, 1919 (Volume XXXV.)		
War Diary	Etaples	01/03/1919	29/03/1919
War Diary	Le Treport	30/03/1919	31/03/1919
Miscellaneous	2/4th Bn. Oxf. & Bucks Lt. Infty.		
Heading	War Diary of 2/4th. Battalion Oxfordshire & Buckinghamshire Light Infantry. From 1st April, 1919 To 30th April 1919 (Volume XXXVI)		
War Diary	Le Treport	01/04/1919	30/04/1919
Miscellaneous	2/4th. Oxford & Bucks Light Infantry.		

was 3067 1 1

61ST DIVISION
184TH INFY BDE.

2-4TH BN OXF. & BUCKS LT INFY.

MAY 1916 - MAR 1919

1916 SEP — ~~1917 JAN~~
~~1917 MAY~~ — 1919 MAR

(FEB & MAR APR. DIARIES MISSING)

3(IND). DIV 9 BDE

C O N F I D E N T I A L.

War Diary of

2/4th Battalion Oxfordshire and Buckinghamshire Light Infantry.

from 1st December, 1915 to 31st December, 1915.

Volume 2.

Page 1

Army Form C. 2118

WAR DIARY
~~or~~ INTELLIGENCE SUMMARY
(Erase heading not required.)

Instructions regarding War Diaries and Intelligence Summaries are contained in F. S. Regs., Part II. and the Staff Manual respectively. Title Pages will be prepared in manuscript.

Place	Date	Hour	Summary of Events and Information		Remarks and references to Appendices
BROOMFIELD	1/12/15	—	(1)	NIL	
			(2) In Billets at BROOMFIELD GREAT WALTHAM & LITTLE WALTHAM.	(5) Operations NIL	
			(3) MAJOR G.W. SEYMOUR member of Quartering Committee & Billet Officer to Bttn.	(6) NIL	
				(7) NIL	
			(4) NIL	(8.9.10) NIL	
BROOMFIELD	2/12/15	—	(1) NIL	(5) Operations NIL	
			(2) In Billets at BROOMFIELD ETC.	(6,7) NIL	
			(3) NIL	(8.9.10)	
			(4) NIL		
BROOMFIELD	3/12/15	—	(1) NIL	(5) Operations NIL	
			(2) In Billets at BROOMFIELD ETC	(6,7) NIL	
			(3) NIL	(8.9.10)	
			(4) NIL		

1875 Wt. W593/826 1,000,000 4/15 J.B.C. & A. A.D.S.S./Forms/C. 2118.

Page 2

Army Form C. 2118

WAR DIARY
INTELLIGENCE SUMMARY
(Erase heading not required.)

Instructions regarding War Diaries and Intelligence Summaries are contained in F. S. Regs., Part II. and the Staff Manual respectively. Title Pages will be prepared in manuscript.

Place	Date	Hour	Summary of Events and Information	Remarks and references to Appendices
BROOMFIELD	4/12/15	—	(1) NIL (2) In Billets at BROOMFIELD ETC. (6,7,8,9,10) (3) NIL (4) NIL (5) operations NIL	[signature]
BROOMFIELD	5/12/15	—	(1) NIL (2) In Billets at BROOMFIELD, ETC. (6,7,8,9,10) (3,4) NIL (5) operations NIL	[signature]
BROOMFIELD	6/12/15	—	(1) 61st Division order received, no special leave to be granted at Christmas. (2) In Billets at BROOMFIELD ETC. (6,7,8,9,10) (3) NIL (4) Working Party, 2 Officers 200 other Ranks at BOREHAM RANGE. (5) operations NIL	[signature]

1875 Wt. W593/826 1,000,000 4/15 J.B.C. & A. A.D.S.S./Forms/C. 2118.

Page 3

Army Form C. 2118

WAR DIARY
or
INTELLIGENCE SUMMARY

(Erase heading not required.)

Instructions regarding War Diaries and Intelligence Summaries are contained in F.S. Regs., Part II. and the Staff Manual respectively. Title Pages will be prepared in manuscript.

Place	Date	Hour	Summary of Events and Information	Remarks and references to Appendices
BROOMFIELD	7/12/15	—	(i) NIL (v) Operations NIL (ii) In Billets at BROOMFIELD ETC. (vi) Lieut G.H. SIMPSON HAYWARD Returned to unit for duty from 1845 Infty Bepe: (iii) NIL 14 Recruits arrived from OXFORD noted to "C" Company. (iv) Working Party 2 Officers 200 other Ranks at BOREHAM RANGE. 6 L.D. MULES transferred to R.F.A at GALLEY WOOD by 1843 Infty Bepe orders. (vii, viii, ix, x) NIL	
BROOMFIELD	8/12/15	—	(i) Southern Command order 2624 Super "DISCIPLINE" received & published. (v) Operations NIL (ii) In Billets at BROOMFIELD ETC. (vi) 5 N.C.Os & MEN Report to M.T at GROVE PARK. (all Returned). (iii) Regimental Count of Enrolment - Losses & deficiencies. (vii, viii, ix, x) NIL (iv) Working Party 2 Officers + 200 other Ranks at BOREHAM RANGE.	

Page 45

Army Form C. 2118

WAR DIARY
INTELLIGENCE SUMMARY

(Erase heading not required.)

Instructions regarding War Diaries and Intelligence Summaries are contained in F. S. Regs., Part II. and the Staff Manual respectively. Title Pages will be prepared in manuscript.

Place	Date	Hour	Summary of Events and Information	Remarks and references to Appendices
BROOMFIELD	9/12/15	—	i. NIL V operations NIL	
			ii. In Billets at BROOMFIELD ETC (vi, vii, viii, ix)	1/
			iii. NIL NIL	
			iv. Working Party, 2 officers 200 other Ranks at BOREHAM RANGE.	
BROOMFIELD	10/12/15	—	i. orders to carry out Reduction of Stores (II part II.) V operations NIL	
			ii. In Billets at BROOMFIELD ETC. vi, vii, viii, ix, x	2/
			iii. NIL NIL	
			iv. Working Party 2 officers 200 other Ranks at BOREHAM RANGE.	
BROOMFIELD	11/12/15	—	i. NIL V operations NIL	
			ii. In Billets at BROOMFIELD ETC vi, vii, viii, ix, x	3/
			iii. NIL	
			iv. Working Party, 2 officers 200 other Ranks at BOREHAM RANGE.	

Page 5.
Army Form C. 2118

WAR DIARY
INTELLIGENCE SUMMARY
(Erase heading not required.)

Place	Date	Hour	Summary of Events and Information	Remarks and references to Appendices
BROOMFIELD	12/2/15	—	i. NIL ii. In Billets at BROOMFIELD ETC. iii. Brigade Field Officer, Capt. H.N. DAVENPORT iv. NIL	V OPERATIONS. NIL Brigade Guards & Observation Post occurrences — NIL. vi, vii, viii, ix, x — NIL	JwR
BROOMFIELD	13/2/15	—	i. NIL ii. In Billets at BROOMFIELD ETC. iii. NIL iv. NIL	V Operations. — NIL Brigade Guards & Observation Post occurrences — NIL vi. 4 Officers, 2nd Lieuts. J.C. COOMBES. CAREW HUNT FREAKE A. BIANCHI. 49 other Ranks. Transferred to 3rd Bn. this unit. vii, viii, ix, x — NIL	JwR

Page 6

Army Form C. 2118

WAR DIARY
INTELLIGENCE SUMMARY
(Erase heading not required.)

Place	Date	Hour	Summary of Events and Information	Remarks and references to Appendices
BROOMFIELD	14/12/15		i. NIL ii. In Billets at BROOMFIELD ETC. iii. NIL iv. NIL V. Operations :- NIL Brigade Guards & Observation Post occurrences — NIL VI. 2/Lt T. NEWMAN-HALL " MORDEN WRIGHT 50 other Ranks Transferred to 3rd Line Unit at OXFORD VII, VIII, IX, X. NIL	[signature]
BROOMFIELD	15/12/15		i. NIL ii. In Billets at BROOMFIELD ETC. iii. NIL iv. NIL v. Operations — NIL Brigade Guards & Observation Post occurrences — NIL vi. MAJOR G.W. SEYMOUR, 2/Lt J.L. ETTY 2/Lt F.E. SMITH, 2/Lt J.S. ROFFEY, 2/Lt F.L. BREEY 2/Lt J.G. SHEPHERD, 2/Lt H.S. TAYLOR, Transferred to 3rd Line Unit at OXFORD 48 other Ranks. " " VII VIII IX } NIL X	[signature]

Page 7
Army Form C. 2118

WAR DIARY
INTELLIGENCE SUMMARY
(Erase heading not required.)

Place	Date	Hour	Summary of Events and Information	Remarks and references to Appendices
BROOMFIELD	16/12/15	—	i. NIL ii. in Billets at BROOMFIELD ETC. iii. NIL iv. NIL V. Operations — NIL Brigade Guards & Observation Post occurrences. NIL	
BROOMFIELD	17/12/15	—	i. NIL ii. in Billets at BROOMFIELD ETC. iii. NIL iv. NIL V. Operations NIL Brigade Guards & Observation Post occurrences. NIL VI. . NIL VII. VIII. IX. X } NIL VI. 6 N.C.O's & NEN Transferred to 83rd Provisional Battalion at BURNHAM-ON-CROUCH. VII. VIII. } NIL IX. X.	

Page 8

Army Form C. 2118

WAR DIARY
INTELLIGENCE SUMMARY

(Erase heading not required.)

Instructions regarding War Diaries and Intelligence Summaries are contained in F.S. Regs., Part II and the Staff Manual respectively. Title Pages will be prepared in manuscript.

Place	Date	Hour	Summary of Events and Information	Remarks and references to Appendices
BROOMFIELD	18/12/15	—	i. NIL ii. Billets at BROOMFIELD ETC. iii. MEDICAL Lieut. BANNERMAN, R.A.M.C.(T), attached as M.O. i/c replacing Lt SMALLWOOD O.M.P. iv. NIL v. Operation NIL Brigade Guards & Section, OBSERVATION POST, manoeuvres — NIL vi. Lieut. BANNERMAN R.A.M.E.(T) attached vii.⎫ viii.⎬ NIL ix.⎪ x.⎭	Q.L.
BROOMFIELD	19/12/15	—	i. NIL ii. Billets at BROOMFIELD ETC. iii.⎫ NIL iv.⎭ v.⎫ vi.⎪ vii.⎬ NIL viii.⎪ ix.⎭ x.	Q.L.
BROOMFIELD	20/12/15	—	i. NIL ii. BILLETS AT BROOMFIELD ETC. iii.⎫ NIL iv.⎭ v.⎫ vi.⎪ vii.⎬ NIL viii.⎪ ix.⎪ x.⎭	Q.L.

WAR DIARY or INTELLIGENCE SUMMARY

Army Form C. 2118
Page 9

Place	Date	Hour	Summary of Events and Information	Remarks and references to Appendices
BROOMFIELD	21/12/15	—	i Nil ii In Billets at BROOMFIELD ETC. iii Nil iv Transport Received of E.S. Limbered Wagon from BIRMINGHAM. V. Operations Nil. VI. 2 L.D. Mules sent CHELMSFORD. Cart. VII } VIII } Nil IX } X }	SR
BROOMFIELD	22/12/15	—	i Nil ii In Billets at BROOMFIELD. ETC iii Nil iv MAJOR GENERAL R. BANNATYNE-ALLASON. C.B assumes command of the 61st Division. T.F. Vice BRIGADIER GENERAL THE MARQUIS OF SALISBURY. G.C.V.O. C.B. T.D. V. Operations Nil VI. Christmas leave until Dec. 26th 60 other Ranks. 3 officers VII. Trenches in Camp Field for Grenadier instruction Course worked at by K Co. & Companies	SR
BROOMFIELD	23/12/15	—	i Nil ii In Billets at BROOMFIELD. ETC iii Nil iv Nil V Operations Nil VI. Trenches in Camp Field continued	SR

Page 10
Army Form C. 2118

WAR DIARY
INTELLIGENCE SUMMARY
(Erase heading not required.)

Place	Date	Hour	Summary of Events and Information	Remarks and references to Appendices
BROOMFIELD	24/12/15	—	i. Nil ii. In Billets at BROOMFIELD ETC. iii. Promotion to complete establishment of M.G.'s. New C.S.M's as follows:- 1815 Sgt. WITNEY to "A" Vice C.S.M. MOORE 17.12.15. 3330 Sgt. CAMPION to "C" — — WILLIAMS 17.12.15. 3352 L/Sgt. DOUGLAS to "D" — — BASSETT 17.12.15. V. operations Nil. VI. Nil VII. Trenches in Camp Field Continued. Trenches at CHIGNAN ST JAMES dismantled.	Sgd/
BROOMFIELD	25/12/15	—	i. Nil ii. In Billets at BROOMFIELD ETC. V. operations Nil	Sgd/
BROOMFIELD	26/12/15		ii. In Billets at BROOMFIELD ETC.	Sgd/

Army Form C. 2118

Page 11.

WAR DIARY
or
INTELLIGENCE SUMMARY
(Erase heading not required.)

Place	Date	Hour	Summary of Events and Information	Remarks and references to Appendices
BROOMFIELD	27/12/15	—	Individual Training. Trench digging Exercises in Camp Field. Col. W.H. AMES proceeded on leave of absence. Major G.P.R. BEAMAN assumed command of the Battalion. Confidential letter respecting keeping of WAR DIARIES received. New Machine Gun class formed under M/G officer. Certificate from M/G Course held at BISLEY 24/11/15 to 15/12/15 received. Classification "Distinguished". First Party of 60 N.C.O.s & men proceeded on Five Days leave with Free Warrants by 12.50 p.m. Train. They return by 9.30 p.m. Train from LIVERPOOL ST. on 2/1/16.	
BROOMFIELD	28/12/15	—	Individual Training. Trench digging Exercises in Camp Field. L.D. Mans transferred to 2/15 GLOUCESTER REGT. CHELMSFORD. Received Confidential memo. (C.174) Subject "Report on Sniping & Trench Warfare" (C.XV) ". Appendix to III Army memo 3A/C.R./228 H.Q.	"A"
BROOMFIELD	29/12/15	—	Received Confidential Circular memo: (C160) Subject "Duties of Regimental Staff Officer". 9. G.S. Wagons transferred to No. 4 Coy A.S.C. CHELMSFORD. Brigade Exercise in Route marching in Two Columns. Lecture by Signal officer at Chelmford 5.30 p.m. Sgt Officer & Signal N.C.Os. Orders conveying Brigade Worthy Park's leave of absence 20/12/15 to 4/1/16, 2/L ieut. R.L. ABRAHAM proceed on leave of absence 20/12/15 to 4/1/16, 2/L ieut. J.H. ZEDER taken over duties of Transport Officer.	Appendix "A" ". "B"

1875 Wt. W593/826 1,000,000 4/15 J.B.C. & A. A.D.S.S./Forms/C. 2118.

WAR DIARY or INTELLIGENCE SUMMARY

Army Form C. 2118

Place	Date	Hour	Summary of Events and Information	Remarks and references to Appendices
BROOMFIELD	30/12/15	—	Individual Training and Trench Digging Exercise in Camp Field. Major General R. BANNATINE-ALLASON called at Orderly Room & visited Camp Field. CAPT H.N. DAVENPORT PROCEEDED on leave of absence from 30/12/15 to 6/1/16.	1/
		3-30 p.m.	Lecture of Officers at Chelmsford at 5-30. p.m. By R.E. on Engineer Services Abroad. Riding Class for Officers who 2nd Lieut J.H. 2EDER Commanded. Commanding Officers meeting at Brigade Headquarters.	
BROOMFIELD	31/12/15		Individual Training and Trench Digging by Party of 2 Officers, 6 N.C.O 60 men 2/Lt K.E. Brown in charge of work. Notes on Interviews with G.O.C. issued by Brigade & Communicated to all Officers.	2/

W. N. Ames Lt.

2/4TH BN OXFORDSHIRE & BUCKS LT INFY

APPENDIX A.

184TH INFANTRY BRIGADE.

OBJECT OF EXERCISE   PRACTICE OF TIMING & CLEARING GIVEN POINT

MARCH ORDER NO. 1.   Copy No.2.

Ref. $\frac{1}{2}$" O.S. 30.   14/12/15.

RIGHT COLUMN.
Col. Ames. 2/4th
Ox. & Bucks L.I.

2/4th Ox. & Bucks)   Will report to Col.Ames. 2/4th Ox. & Bucks L.I.
  L.I.   )   at Starting Point at 10 a.m.
2/5th Gloucester Regt.)

1. ROUTE.   BEDELL'S END- WRITTLE- OXNEY GREEN- MONTPELLIER'S
                            FARM- EDNEY COMMON- Pt.241 - SMITHY-WRITTLE-
                            CHELMSFORD.

2. STARTING POINT.   Junction CHELMSFORD-ROXWELL-CHELMSFORD-BROOMFIELD
                            Roads.

3.   Col.Ames Column will be clear of Road Fork S.
                            of 1. in 24<u>1</u> at 12 noon.

LEFT COLUMN
Lt. Col. Wheeler,
2/4th R. Berks Regt.

2/4th R. Berks Regt.)   Will report to Lieut. Col. Wheeler, 2/4th Royal
2/1st Bucks Battalion.)   Berks Regt at Starting Point.   Time to be fixed
                            by Lieut. Col.Wheeler and notified by him to O.C.
                            2/1st Bucks Battalion.

1. ROUTE.   WRITTLE-OXNEY GREEN-NEWNEY GREEN-COOKSMILL GREEN-
                            INN-FORK ROAD S.of 4 in 24<u>1</u>- EDNEY COMMON-WRITTLE-
                            CHELMSFORD.

2. STARTING POINT.   Road junction NEW LONDON-OAKLANDS-WRITTLE ROADS.

3.   The left column will be clear of Road Fork South
                            of 2nd <u>N</u> in OXNEY GREEN at 10-45 a.m. and clear
                            of Road Fork N. of 2 in Pt. 24<u>1</u> at 12-5 p.m.

4. TRANSPORT.   No transport.

5. RATIONS.   Haversack Ration.

6. REPORTS.   Staff Officers will time column at above
                            mentioned points.

                                            R. W. HARLING. Major.
                                                Brigade Major.
                                            184th Infantry Brigade.

APPENDIX B.

REPORT BY CAPTAIN AND ADJUTANT D.M.ROSE ON BRIGADE EXERCISE IN TIMING AND CLEARING GIVEN POINTS.

(1)   The Right Column was 10 minutes early at Road Fork N of 1 in Pt. 24$\underline{1}$.

(2)   The Left Column took wrong Road at OXNEY GREEN, and was late at Road Fork N of 2 in Pt. $\underline{2}$41.

　　　1 man in "A" Company fell out with sore heel.

　　　2 men in "D" Company required treatment on line of march for sore feet.

　　　Company Commanders failed to carry the Adhesive Plaster ordered.

CONFIDENTIAL.

War Diary of

2/4th Battalion Oxfordshire and Buckinghamshire Light Infantry.

from 1st January, 1916 to 31st January, 1916.

Volume 3.

Ref. 1"/2 O.S. 30

Army Form C. 2118

WAR DIARY
or
INTELLIGENCE SUMMARY
(Erase heading not required.)

Instructions regarding War Diaries and Intelligence Summaries are contained in F. S. Regs., Part II. and the Staff Manual respectively. Title Pages will be prepared in manuscript.

Place	Date	Hour	Summary of Events and Information	Remarks and references to Appendices
BROOMFIELD	1/1/16		Battalion Route March. Broads Green, Chignalls.	
"	2/1/16		Church Parade at Broomfield. Great Waltham & Little Waltham. 2nd Leave Party on Free Warrant departed 12.50 p.m. Train. L.D. Mule died.	
"	3/1/16	3.15 p.m.	Commenced Grenadier Class under 2/Lt PROCTOR using new Trenches in CAMP FIELD. One man Range Finder class under Lt G. SIMPSON HAYWARD.	
"		7.30 p.m.	Arrival. 2/Lt. MILLER from M/C Course BISLEY, takes up duty with "D" Coy.	
"		5.30 p.m.	Lecture to N.C.O.s of "C" and "D" Coy at Gt WALTHAM	
"	4/1/16		Individual Training. Working Party from "B" Coy on New Trenches.	
"	5/1/16		Brigade Exercise in Timing & Passing Points. Capt H. J. BENNETT proceeded on Leave.	APPENDIX #
"		10.15 p.m.	Practice Alarm. Message sent from 164th Brigade by Arrangement.	
"	6/1/16	9.30 a.m.	Col: W.H. AMES returned from leave of absence. Individual Training. Commenced Wind Cutanglement class at 2/Lt W.H. MOBERLY. Capt H.N. DAVENPORT returned from Leave. G.O.C called at Headquarters & visited Companies morning & afternoon	
"	7/1/16		Individual Training. 2nd Leave Party Returned.	
"	8/1/16	9.30 p.m.	Battalion Route March. Springfield. Boreham. Russells Green. Waltham S. Practice Cooking at Halt. Lieut. MARSDEN proceeded on Special Leave	

1875 Wt. W593/826 1,000,000 4/15 J.B.C. & A. A.D.S.S./Forms/C. 2118.

Army Form C. 2118

WAR DIARY
or
INTELLIGENCE SUMMARY
(Erase heading not required.)

Instructions regarding War Diaries and Intelligence Summaries are contained in F. S. Regs., Part II. and the Staff Manual respectively. Title Pages will be prepared in manuscript.

Place	Date	Hour	Summary of Events and Information	Remarks and references to Appendices
BROOMFIELD	9/1/16	-	Church Parade at BROOMFIELD, GREAT WALTHAM & LITTLE WALTHAM. 3rd Leave Party on Home Warrant departed 12-50 Train. Commenced Brigade Duties.	
BROOMFIELD	10/1/16	-	Individual Training. Class in Knotting & Lashing Commenced under LIEUT. W.D.SCOTT. 2/LIEUT. C.R. PARSONS proceeded on 7 days leave. Brigade Duties.	
"	11/1/16	-	Individual Training. Brigade Duties. Quarterly Audit Board met 2.30 p.m. CAPT. H.J. BENNETT Returned from leave. Acting Bombard returned to their Company Billets Areas.	
"	12/1/16	-	Brigade Exercise in the attack. Flagged Enemy in position South of HYLANDS PARK. Brigade Duties. CAPT. R.F. CUTHBERT proceeds on 7 days Special Leave.	Appendix 3
"	13/1/16	-	Individual Training. Brigade Duties.	
"	14/1/16	-	Individual Training. Brigade Duties. LIEUT. C.S.W. MARCON Returned from Special Leave. Divisional Sanitary Officer called & inspected Sanitary Stand and Water Carts. BRYANT	
"	15/1/16	-	Individual Training. Brigade Duties. Wire Entanglement Class Ends. 2/Lieut Bryant R.E. Returned to WITHAM.	
"	16/1/16	-	Church Parade at BROOMFIELD, GREAT WALTHAM & LITTLE WALTHAM. Received orders CAPT. W.T. GRAY to be posted to 83rd PROVISIONAL BATTALION.	

1875 Wt. W593/826 1,000,000 4/15 J.B.C. & A. A.D.S.S./Forms/C. 2118.

WAR DIARY or INTELLIGENCE SUMMARY

Army Form C. 2118

Place	Date	Hour	Summary of Events and Information	Remarks and references to Appendices
BROOMFIELD	17/1/16		Individual Training. Brigade Intelle Review to 1 p.m. (Chelsea in consequence of 5 Glors Reg: Working Party, BOREHAM RANGE. 2 Officers 10 N.C.O. 190 Privates being inspected). 2/Lt C.R. PARSONS returned from Special Leave. Medical Examination of all Officers will exception CAPTS DAVENPORT, CUTHBERT and 2/LT PARSONS, by Divisional Standing Medical Board. New Water Cart arrived.	Appendices
"	18/1/16		Individual Training. Inspection of Battalion by MAJOR GENERAL DICKSON at 2.30 p.m. work on the Various Parade Grounds.	
"	19/1/16	10.35 a.m	Individual Training. 4th Leave party. CAPT R.F. CUTHBERT returned from Special Leave.	
	3.30 pm	Draft of 242 Recruits from 3rd & 4th Line Units arrived from OXFORD, under MAJOR SEYMOUR 3/4 STAFF. Two Certificated Bayonet Instructors & party of 20 men inspected in Bayonet Fighting & Physical	
	2.45 pm	Exercises by CAPT. SHARPE, THE BUFFS, of ALDERSHOT GYMNASTIC STAFF. General Vaccination again. "A" Coy.	
"	20/1/16	5.30 pm	Individual Training. Three Officers absent on 17th inst went before Divisional Standing Medical Board at HQ.s of Bucks Battn. 10.15 a.m. Lecture by Col. H.M. WILLIAMS. Subject "Notes of a visit to the front in Flanders". CAPT W.T. GRAY posted to 1/3RD PROV: BATTN. CAPT R.F. CUTHBERT assumed Command of "D" Company.	
"	21/1/16	9.30 a.m	Battalion Route March. Route - Roman Rd, CHATLEY(Inn), FAIRSTEADS, TERLING. Practical Cooking.	
"	22/1/16		Individual Training. Brigadier (Col.W.R.LUDLOW. C.B.T.D) visited Headquarters & inspected Rations. CAPT. DAVIS, 61st Divisional Staff called & inspected new Draft of Recruits. S.A.A arrived. 229, 510 '303 Mark VI	

1875 Wt. W593/826 1,000,000 4/15 J.B.C. & A. A.D.S.S./Forms/C. 2118.

WAR DIARY
or
INTELLIGENCE SUMMARY

(Erase heading not required.)

Army Form C. 2118

Place	Date	Hour	Summary of Events and Information	Remarks and references to Appendices
BROOMFIELD	23/1/16		Church Parade at BROOMFIELD, GT WALTHAM & LT WALTHAM. 100 Short Lee Enfield Rifles arrived.	GPB
"	24/1/16		Individual Training. 2/LT. G.H. SHEPHERD proceeded on leave. 2nd Class in Entanglements & obstacles under 2/LT. W.H. MOBERLEY commenced.	GPB
"	25/1/16		Individual Training. 5th Leave Party by ordinary Train. 10-30 a.m. LIEUT. Q. SIMPSON HAYWARD appointed Musketry Officer vice CAPT R.F. CUTHBERT.	GPB
"	26/1/16		Brigade Exercise A.G, R.G and F.O Formation & marches in neighbourhood of PLESHEY. APPENDIX	GPB
"	27/1/16		Individual Training. Sent 37 · 256 Carbines and 4 Fop: Bayonets to 5th Prov. Brigade GORLESTON	GPB
"	28/1/16		Individual Training.	GPB
"	29/1/16		Individual Training. MAJOR W.T. HOYTEN visited Headquarters Ref: to Civilian Case of Cerebro-Spinal Meningitis. COL. W.H. AMES models on week end leave MAJOR G.P.R. BEAMAN carries command of Batt.	GPB
"	30/1/16		Church Parade at BROOMFIELD, GT WALTHAM & LT WALTHAM.	GPB
"	31/1/16		Individual Training. Working Party to BOREHAM 1 officer. 3. M.C.O5 and 47 men. 2/LT A.W. PROCTOR proceeds on leave 31/1/16 to 6/2/16.	GPB

G.P.R. Beaman Maj
2/4TH BN OXFORDSHIRE & BUCKS LT INFY

184th Infantry Brigade.

Copy No. 3.

MARCH ORDERS.

Ref. O.S. ½" No. 30.   BY COL. W.R. LUDLOW CB   January 5th, 1916.

Battalions will march by following routes <u>clearing</u> points specified at the times shown in brackets.

2/4th Oxf. & Bucks L.I.

Starting Point.   1.   Point 141.
Time   2.   8-40 a.m.
Route.   3.   Road Fork NNW of B in BROOMFIELD   (8-52 a.m.)
                        Road Junction E of M in CHELMER   (9-14 a.m.)
                        Road Junction S of 1st A in LITTLE WALTHAM (9-40 a.m.
                        Road Junction W of W in LITTLE WALTHAM   (9-47 a.m.)
                        CHATHAM GREEN - LYONS HALL - road fork S of LYONS
                        HALL (rendezvous).

2/4th R.Berks Regt.

Starting Point   1.)
Time   2.)   at discretion of O.C.
Route   3.   N.LONDON ROAD - TINDAL STREET - KING EDWARDS AVENUE.
                      Fork Roads NNW of B in BROOMFIELD   (9-12 a.m.)
                      Road Junction E of M in CHELMER   (9-24 a.m.)
                      Road Junction S of 1st A in LITTLE WALTHAM (9-50 a.m.)
                      Road junction S of Point 129   (10-13 a.m.)
                      GREAT WALTHAM - road fork E of 2nd T in HOW STREET
                      (rendezvous)

2/5th Gloucester Regt.

Starting Point   1.)
Time   2.)   at discretion of O.C.
Route   3.   SHIRE HALL   (8-15 a.m.)
                      NAVIGATION ROAD   (8-22 a.m.)
                      NABBOTTS FARM   (9-8 a.m.)
                      Road junction E of M in CHELMER   (9-17 a.m.)
                      Road fork NNW of B in BROOMFIELD -
                      Road form S of Point 129 (10-5 a.m.)
                      LITTLE WALTHAM - HILL'S FARM - Road junction
                      E of T in HOW STREET   (rendezvous)

2/1st Bucks Battalion.

Starting Point   1.   QUEENS PARK.
Time   2.   at discretion of O.C.
Route   3.   SHIRE HALL (8-7 a.m.) SUPPLY DEPOT - RECTORY LANE
                      Road junction NNW of B ib BROOMFIELD. (9-3 a.m.)
                      Road junction W of W in LITTLE WALTHAM (9-35 a.m.)
                      Road junction S of 1st A in L. WALTHAM (9-43 a.m.)
                      Point 213 - ALSTEADS FARM - Road fork S of LYONS
                      HALL (rendezvous).

On arrival at points marked Rendezvous, the senior Officers of the two Battalions will assume command, and the two columns thus formed will concentrate as under:-
        (2/4th R.Berks Regt.
         2/5th Gloucester Regt.
will march to starting point via Great Waltham.)
Starting Point   Road fork S of 2 in Point 129.
Time   12 noon.
Headquarters   1.
2/1st Bucks Bn.   Both columns in column of route facing
2/4th R.Berks Regt.   E. & W. respectively.
2/5th Gloster Regt.   Order of march as per margin.
2/4th Oxf. & Bucks L.I.

Reports   2. to Headquarters.

Transport   a. all available transport less cookers
Rations   b. a haversack ration will be carried
                  c. Parade as strong as possible.

                                        R.W. Harling, Major,
                              Brigade Major, 184th Infantry Brigade.

"The Vineyards",
Great Baddow.
January 3rd, 1916.

From Headquarters,
     184th Infantry Brigade.

To O.C.   2/5th Gloucester Battn.
  "   2/4th Oxford & Bucks L.I.
  "   2/1st Bucks Battalion
  "   2/4th Royal Berkshire Regt.

          Reference March Orders for January 5th 1916, it has been found necessary to make the following corrections in times shown thereon:-

2/4th Oxford & Bucks L.I.

Time 2.   8-38 a.m. (instead of 8-40 a.m.)
Route 3.   Road fork NNW of B in BROOMFIELD.(8-50 a.n.)
           Road junction E of M in CHELMER (9-12 a.m.)
           Road junction S of 1st A in L. WALTHAM (9-38 a.m.)
           Road junction W of W in L. WALTHAM (9-45 a.m.)

2/1st Bucks Battalion.

           Road junction S of 1st A in L.WALTHAM (9-42 a.m.)

          O's.C. Units are reminded that Clock Hour halts must be observed in every case, i.e. from 50 minutes past the hour until the hour.

                                        Cecil Bartram, Major,
                              for Brigade Major, 184th Infantry Brigade.
Gt.Baddow,
4/1/16.

                    184TH INFANTRY BRIGADE.
                                                  Copy No. 3.
                    FURTHER MARCH ORDERS No. 2.
Ref.March Orders 5/1/16.   5th January, 1916.

TRANSPORT.   The following Transport per Battalion will be taken as far as
available:-   Water Carts   Ammunition and Tools will be
               4 S.A.A.Wagons   carried in Wagon.
               2 Limbered Wagons with Tools
               Pack Animals will be loaded with Ammunition as well.
               A Note will be added to the parade state showing (A) amount
               of Ammunition carried on (1) Wagons, (2) Pack Animals, and
               (B) No. of Tools carried.

                                        R.W.HARLING, Major,
                                             Brigade Major,
                                             184th Infantry Brigade.

Gt. Baddow.
4/1/16.

APPENDIX
1.

BRIGADE EXERCISE.

5/1/16

Report on 2/4th Oxford & Bucks Lt. Infy. by Capt F.L. Hadden

---

1. Point 141 cleared — 8-39 a.m.
2. Road fork NNW of B in BROOMFIELD cleared — {8-47 a.m. / 8-50 a.m.}
   Halt — 8-50 a.m. to 9-0 a.m.
3. Road Junction E of M in CHELMER cleared — {9-10 a.m. / 9-12 a.m.}
4. Road junction S of 1st A in L.WALTHAM cleared — {9-37 a.m. / 9-38 a.m.}
5. Road junction W of W in L.WALTHAM. cleared — {9-44 a.m. / 9-45 a.m.}
   Halt — 9-50 a.m. to 10-0 a.m.
6. CHATHAM GREEN cleared — 10-34 a.m.
   Halt — 10-50 a.m. to 11-0 a.m.
7. LYONS HALL cleared — 11-3 a.m.
8. Road fork S of LYONS HALL reached (rendezvous) — 11-7 a.m.
9. Brigade Starting Point (road fork S of 2 in Point 129) reached — {11-53 a.m. / 11-50 a.m.}

There was no halt at the rendezvous as the Bucks Battalion had turned about and moved off as the Oxfords came up.

5.1.1916.

(Sgd) F.L.HADDEN, Captain,
2/4th R.Berks Regiment.

Ordered times in red.

The fact of these points being cleared too early by 1-2 minutes is accounted for by the fact that 5 minutes was allowed for the time of passing of column. This allowance was rather too much for the actual length of the 2/4th. Oxfords. (Sgd) R.W.H.

The timing was based at 100 yards per minute + clock hour halt + 5 minutes for battalion & transport passing a given point.

APPENDIX B 2.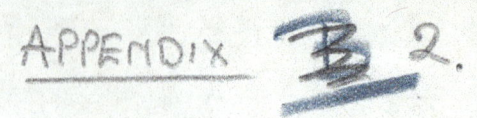

2/4TH OXFORD AND BUCKS LIGHT INFANTRY.

REMARKS ON ALARM PARADE 5.1.16.

By MAJ. B.P.R. BEAMAN

At 10.15 p.m. orders were received for the Battalion to parade immediately and proceed to Chelmsford to entrain, Ball ammunition to be issued, Great coats to be carried, orders for Transport to follow.

The following order was issued to Companies:-

"Battalion parades at once on BROOMFIELD CHURCH GREEN, men carry great coats and 100 rounds Ball ammunition, orders for Horses and Pack animals follow AAA Bring ammunition for your Transport men, carry best rations obtainable quickly."

x The Transport men of A & B were ordered to fetch their ammunition; this was not satisfactory. In future Companies will bring ammunition for any such details on parade and issue at first opportunity.

x Waited too long on their Coy. Alarm post before proceeding to parade ordered.

A Coy. reported at 11-53 p.m.
B Coy.   "   at 11-58 p.m.
D Coy.   "   at 12 ~~midnight~~ -20 a.m.
C Coy.   "   at 1.10 a.m.

WARNING FOR PARADE.

Orderlies at Battalion Headquarters must have their equipment with them.

At Battalion Orderly Room one of the two orderlies was away on an errand and not available when wanted urgently

The Pioneers were not warned at all, the Band was not warned immediately, orders for stretchers were not given at once; the whereabouts of the stretchers was not known to the Quartermaster or at the Battalion Orderly Room.

Officers who were absent from their quarters had not taken steps to acquaint their Company Orderly Rooms as to their movements.

One Company had to be marched in by an Officer temporarily attached, no Officer of the Company being available.

B2

Officers' Servants must be taught their duties; they should be billeted near their Officers and know exactly what to do in rousing & getting their Officer on parade quickly.	Officers were not roused by orderlies owing to want of arrangement for such a contingency.

One Officer returned from a Course had not joined his new Company, consequently was not warned at all.

Some Officers who were warned late failed to report. They should report personally even if too late to parade with their Companies. |
| The message should have ended "Acknowledge" and acknowledgment sent by "D" Coy. | No Telephone Orderly was available at LITTLE WALTHAM Post Office to take message. Signal Message Book A.F. C.2121 must be used and kept ready. |
| ˣRegimental Bicycles must be kept ready for use with lamps filled. | Message was sent to GREAT WALTHAM by Cyclist Orderly on ˣPrivate bicycle; this was satisfactory, and receipt on A.F. C.398 was in Adjutant's hands by 11-30 p.m. |
| On Service orderlies from each Coy. would always be available at Battalion Headquarters. They take rations and blankets and can be relieved at the discretion of their Company Commanders. | There was not sufficient method in the rousing of the men, too much dodging from house to house; some billets being missed.

A system whereby certain individuals systematically rouse an area is recommended, all N.C.O's and men in such area being warned irrespective of their being in a certain Company, or Specialists, Transport etc. |

TURN OUT.

A large number of men and some N.C.O's paraded deficient in Equipment, entrenching tools helves were missing frequently, also some waterbottles.

Waterbottles in many cases were not filled, some claimed as being filled contained merely the water left from the Route March.

Several mess tins were deficient.

ˣIf returned to Store these should be drawn again.	ˣWire Cutters were not carried in some Companies.

The Barr and Stroud Rangefinders were not brought on parade by those who had them in charge.

Identity discs were deficient in a great many cases and one third of those on parade were not properly worn.

A few men paraded without their puttees on and had not put them in their packs.

O.C. Coys must impress upon their men the importance of being prepared to move off suddenly with proper kit on them. Haversacks should be used for food only. On service the Iron Ration and unexpended day's ration will completely fill.

Kits were not systematically inspected but only a small proportion of some Companies appeared to be complete. One Company was very good in this respect.

INTERPRETATION OF ORDER.

The orders were "men carry Great Coats" this meant that Great coats would not be worn. Some appear to have considered that this order meant that nothing besides great coat need be carried. In many cases men paraded wearing great coat.

The two outlying Companies misunderstood the order as to pack animals and horses.

GENERALLY.

Discipline was good and there was no noise, the issue of ammunition was quickly and well carried out. One Company reports losing 40 rounds which indicates carelessness. Responsibility for this loss cannot be fixed owing to lack of system in the return of ammunition to Company Store.

The Company Commander must stay at his Headquarters and not run about rousing the men.

Outlying Companies should have sent an Orderly with message to Battalion Headquarters stating time they moved off and numbers on parade.

Arrangements are necessary as to the charge of Company Orderly rooms and documents, an orderly room clerk with men selected from those unable to march can be left in charge if no specific orders are issued on the subject.

RATIONS.

Men must be prepared with food on a sudden emergency.

(Company Commanders must not forget Field Kitchens and Cooks. The Second Captains are responsible.)

On service the soldier carries the unexpended portion of the day's ration. On Wednesday night he would have brought the ration issued to him for Thursday.

(signed) G.P.R.BEAMAN,
Major,
Commdg. 2/4th Oxf. & Bucks Lt. Infty.

Broomfield.
9/1/16.

COPY.   184TH INFANTRY BRIGADE.   Copy No. 3.

APPENDIX

Ref. ½" O.S. 30.   *operation orders*   Date 12.1.16.
Col. W.R. LUDLOW. CB.

1. INFORMATION.   No information to hand as to enemy dispositions. The Brigade is to be imagined to have advanced from HIGH ONGAR, and to have reached starting point (as given herein) in A.G. Formation.

2. INTENTION.   To seek out the enemy and to attack him.

3. STARTING POINT.   Road Junction W. of I in INN W. of EDNEY COMMON.

4. TIME.   10 a.m.

5. V.G.)
)
   Col. Ames,)
   2/4th Oxford &)
   Bucks L.I.) 2
   2/4th Oxford &)
   Bucks L.I.)

6. HEADQUARTERS.
   2/5 Gloucester Regt.   Main Body
   2/1st Bucks Bn.   Column of Route facing S.E.
   2/4th R. Berks Regt.   as per margin.
   Bde. S.A.A. Reserve
   2 Ambulance Wagons.

7. AMMUNITION.   10 rounds of Blank per man to be carried.

8. RATIONS.   Haversack Rations will be taken.

9. TRANSPORT.   (Less Cookers). The O.C. 2/4th Oxford & Bucks L.I. will bring Cookers at his discretion.

10. REPORTS.   To Headquarters.

The O.C. 2/4th Royal Berks Regt. will detail 1 Officer and 20 men with flags and 10 rounds of blank ammunition per man, and will provide White Tape or String with Pegs to represent entrenchments to meet a Staff Officer at 9-30 a.m. at the Bridge over the Stream just S. of Pt. 144 HYLANDS PARK on the CHELMSFORD-BRENTWOOD ROAD.

R.W. HARLING, Major,
Brigade Major,
184th Infantry Brigade.

Gt. Baddow.   Issued as per Distribution list.
January 11th, 1916.

APPENDIX "D"

Daily Parade State.   Army Form B. 237.

Unit ~~2/4TH BN OXFORDSHIRE & BUCKS LI INFTY~~

_____ Squadron, Battery, or Company

Place _Broomfield_   Date _18th Jany. 1916_

Distribution	Officers	Other Ranks	Horses	Remarks
On parade	23	446		Includes all classes of instruction and Regimental Courses shown on back of State.
Signallers				
Riding school				
⁂ Regimental and garrison employ	1	110*		
Hospital		5		
Sick in quarters		12		⁂ Includes 39 Transport
Absent, with leave	2	11		
Absent, without leave				
Detention				
~~Guard~~		30		
Command	3	7		
Recruits at drill				
~~Gymnasium~~ Munition Works		7		
Total	29	628		

J. H. Rose Capt & ADJUTANT
2/4TH BN OXFORDSHIRE & BUCKS LI INFTY

Absentees from Gymnasium.

(To be filled in only when form is used as a gymnastic state.)

Name	No.	Cause
Garrison & Reg.tl Employ.		Instructional Courses in progress.
61st S.M. Division	6	
184th Infy. Brigade	4	Grenadiers
Regimental Police	8	Entanglements
Transport	39	Water duties
Cooks	4	Stretcher bearers.
Postmen	2	Signalling
Clerks { Br. O Room	4	Machine gun
Clerks { Company	8	Scouts & Snipers
Clerks { Q.M. office	1	Sanitary Squad.
Orderlies { Day	4	Transport drivers
Orderlies { Night	4	
Officers Mess	4	
Shoemakers	4	
Tailors	2	
Med officers orderlies	2	
Butchers	4	
Master Cook	1	
Storemen	3	
Fatigue parties	6	
Total	110	

APPENDIX E 5

Notes on Exercise 26/1/16 by
MAJOR HARLING Brigade Major
184th Infy. Bde

From :- Headquarters,
    184th Infantry Brigade.

To :- O.C.
    2/4th Oxford & Bucks L.I.

    The following notes on Exercise 26/1/16 are forwarded for your information:-

Transport.   Inventory boards were not in all cases carried on Wagons.

Harness.   G.O.C. called attention to several cases where sufficient attention has not been paid to fitting same, specially breeching.

Water Carts.   A copy of instructions must be carried on each Water Cart.

    It is the duty of all Officers in command of A.G.F.G. & R.G. to acquaint themselves with orders as to route, action etc. If these orders are insufficiently explained, Officers must call attention of their C.O. or of the Staff to this and request further explanation before moving off. Yesterday the O.C. R.G. mistook his orders and deviated from the route laid down in orders, followed the Cookers which were sent on a different route, as this Officer was mounted it would have been a simple matter for him to have ridden forward and ascertained his correct route. The lack of a little foresight had the operations been actually in face of the enemy might have resulted in most serious consequences. At the same time it is realized that this does not absolve the staff for failing to provide the O.C. R.G. with Cyclist Orderlies for the purpose of keeping touch or the Officer acting as S.O. and conducting the cookers for permitting the R.G. to follow him. The fact remains that all Officers are responsible for the proper conduct of their share in the operations and the staff in war from may be casualties, and therefore officers must use their own initiative.

The movement of troops from resting fields to starting point at 3 p.m. was too slow. Orders were dictated to Adjutants at 2-35 p.m. 25 minutes therefore should have sufficed for Units to have moved from a central place of assembly to S.P. It was 3-10 p.m. before the column moved off.

Officers sent on to choose positions for R.G. action should ascertain probable direction of enemy attack. It is not necessary for such officers in a tactical exercise to work together and choose the same position. Officers should be guided in choice of position by their own individual opinion and report accordingly. They thereby gain instruction in criticism of several positions.

R.W. Harking.

Major.
Brigade Major.
184th Infantry Brigade.

Gt. Baddow.
28/1'16.

UNIT.   2/4th Oxf. & Bucks Lt. Infty.

BRIGADE.   184th Infantry Brigade.

DIVISION.   61st (South Midland) Division.

MOBILIZATION CENTRE.   Oxford.

TEMPORARY WAR STATION.   Broomfield.

STATIONS SINCE OCCUPIED   (1) Northampton, (2) Writtle,
SUBSEQUENT TO CONCENTRATION.   (3) Hoddesdon, (4) Broomfield,
                               (5) Epping, (6) Broomfield.

(a) MOBILIZATION.   Nil.

(b) CONCENTRATION AT WAR STATIONS

     Moved into Camp at Broomfield on Saturday August 21st.

(c) ORGANIZATION FOR DEFENCE.

     2 officers and 50 men on Springfield Picquet for 7 days.

(d) TRAINING.   Battalion Training. Entraining & detraining practice, Sunday August 8th.

(e) DISCIPLINE.   Nil.

(f) ADMINISTRATION.

     1. Medical Services.   Nil.

     2. Veterinary Services.   Nil.

     3. Supply Services.   Nil.

     4. Transport Services.   Transport used for 1 week by A.S.C. for moving units to camp at Epping.

                                 9 limber wagons.
                                 4 Field Kitchens.   issued Aug.11th
                                 2 Maltese carts.   & 12th.

     5. Ordnance Services.   Nil.

     6. Billeting & Hutting.   Billets vacated except a few sick men on August 21st.

     7. Channel of correspondence   Nil.
        in routine matters.

     8. Range Construction.   2 fatigue parties supplied to dig fire trenches & latrines at Boreham Range.

     9. Supply of Remounts.   13 Mules, 3 Light Draught horses.

(g) REORGANIZATION OF T.F. INTO   Nil.
    HOME & IMPERIAL SERVICE.

(h) PREPARATION OF UNIT FOR IMPERIAL SERVICE.
                                 Capt. Doyne & 2/Lt. Bridges posted to 1/4th Oxf. & Bucks Lt. Infty.

WAR DIARY FOR OCTOBER, 1915.

PLACE	DATE	HOUR	SUMMARY OF EVENTS AND INFORMATION	REMARKS AND REFERENCES TO APPENDICES
			UNIT 2/4th Oxford and Bucks Lt. Infy.	
			BRIGADE 184th Infantry Brigade.	
			DIVISION 61st (South Midland) Division.	
Broomfield	26.10.15.	6 p.m.	BILLETING AND HUTTING. Returned to Billets	
Do.	28.10.15.		RANGE CONSTRUCTION. Miniature Range at Brookland, Broomfield, completed and in use.	

Broomfield,
5. 11. 15.

[signature] Colonel,
Commanding 2/4th Oxford and Bucks Lt. Infy.

WAR DIARY FOR PERIOD FROM 1ST TO 16TH NOVEMBER, 1915.

PLACE	DATE	TIME	SUMMARY OF EVENTS AND INFORMATION	REMARKS AND REFERENCES TO APPENDICES
			UNIT 2/4th Oxford and Bucks Lt. Infy. BRIGADE 184th Infantry Brigade DIVISION 61st (South Midland) Division	
Broomfield	11.11.15.	11-58 a.m.	PREPARATION OF UNIT FOR IMPERIAL SERVICE. 50 men sent to 3rd Line.	

W. H. Ames
Colonel,
Commanding 2/4th Oxford and Bucks Lt. Infy.

Broomfield,
3. 12. 15.

2/4TH BN. OXFORD AND BUCKS LIGHT INFANTRY.

MARCHING OUT STATE, 24TH MAY, 1916.

OFFICERS: 34, plus 1 Officer in advance.

OTHER RANKS: 956 (includes 6 attached).

LEWIS GUNS: 4.

HORSES: 64.

TWO-WHEELED: 4.

FOUR-WHEELED: 17.

                    (signed) D.M.ROSE,
              Major and Adjutant,
                    for O.C.,
         2/4th Oxf. & Bucks Lt. Infty.

NOMINAL ROLL OF OFFICERS.

Lieut.Col. W.H.Ames
Major G.P.R.Beaman
Major D.M.Rose
Capt. H.J.Bennett
Capt. H.N.Davenport
Capt. A.H.Brucker
Capt. R.F.Cuthbert
Capt. H.T.Harris
Capt. G.H.Simpson-Hayward
Capt. W.D.Scott.
Capt. R.F.R.Boyle.
Capt. Rev. W.B.Buggins
Lieut. R.L.Abraham.
Lieut. C.S.W.Marcon
Lieut. J.G.Stockton.
Lieut. W.A.Hobbs
Lieut. A.Worsley, R.A.M.C.(T).

Lieut. R.J.E.Tiddy
Lieut. K.E.Brown
Lieut. J.G.R.Miller (Advance Officer)
Lieut. A.W.Proctor
Lieut. G.H.G.Shepherd.
Lieut. R.A.Asser
Lieut. E.I.Powell
Lieut. L.L.Loewe
2/Lieut. C.R.Parsons
2/Lieut. J.H.Zeder
2/Lieut. W.H.Moberly
2/Lieut. H.E.Coombes
2/Lieut. J.S.Roffey
2/Lieut. E.A.Bianchi
2/Lieut. R.E.Roche
2/Lieut. J.Hopkinson
2/Lieut. J.L.Bulmer
2/Lieut. E.O.R.Byworth

WAR DIARY FOR SEPTEMBER 1915.

UNIT	2/4th Oxford and Bucks Lt. Infty.
BRIGADE	184th Infantry Brigade
DIVISION	61st. (South Midland) Division.
MOBILIZATION CENTRE	Oxford
TEMPORARY WAR STATION	Broomfield
STATIONS SINCE OCCUPIED SUBSEQUENT TO CONCENTRATION	(1) Northampton (2) Writtle (3) Hoddesdon (4) Broomfield (5) Epping (6) Broomfield
(a) MOBILIZATION	Nil
(b) CONCENTRATION AT WAR STATIONS	Nil
(c) ORGANIZATION FOR DEFENCE	2 Officers and 50 men on Springfield Picquet for 7 days. Orders issued in case of aircraft raids.
(d) TRAINING	Brigade Training
(e) DISCIPLINE	Nil
(f) ADMINISTRATION	
1. Medical Services	Nil
2. Veterinary Services	Nil
3. Supply Services	Nil
4. Transport Services	Nil
5. Ordnance Service	1914 Equipment issued
6. Billeting and Hutting	Nil
7. Channel of Correspondence in routine matters	Nil
8. Range Construction	Negotiations for Miniature Range at Brookland, Broomfield
9. Supply of Remounts	5 Mules issued 23.9.15.
(g) REORGANIZATION OF T.F. INTO HOME AND IMPERIAL SERVICE	Nil
(h) PREPARATION OF UNIT FOR IMPERIAL SERVICE	Nil

CONFIDENTIAL.

War Diary

of

2/4th Oxfordshire and Buckinghamshire Light Infantry

from May 24th, 1916 to May 31st, 1916.

(Volume I).

WAR DIARY
or
INTELLIGENCE SUMMARY

(Erase heading not required.)

Army Form C. 2118

REF. HAZEBROUCK SHEET 5A.

Place	Date	Hour	Summary of Events and Information	Remarks and references to Appendices
PARK HOUSE	24/5/16		1ST Train, Headquarters A & B Coys. left TIDWORTH STATION 2 P.M. 1ST Train arrived SOUTHAMPTON 3.40 P.M. 4.30 P.M. 2nd Train Major G.R.R. BEAMAN, C & D Coys - 3 P.M. Lwd	APPENDIX 1
			Headquarters A, B, C, & Part of D Coy Entrained on S.S. ARUNDEL Sailing at 9-15 P.M. (16 Officers 740 O.R.) TRANSPORT & Coy Entrained on S.S. CITY OF DUNKIRK, Sailing at 7-0 P.M. (7 " 215 OR) Major G.R. BEAMAN, Part of D Coy	
HAVRE	25/5/16		S.S. ARUNDEL arrived HAVRE at 3.G.a.m. followed by S.S. CITY OF DUNKIRK at 3-40 a.m. Headquarters "A", "B", "C" & Part of "D" marched to No. 2. Rest Camp & Remained There until 5.30 P.M. Transport & Part of "D" Remained at Docks and joined Battalion at Entraining Point. Headquarters B, C, & Part D left Rest Camp and marched to GARE DU MARCHANDISE for Entrainment, leaving Capt. H.T. BENNETT & 200 of "A" at Rest Camp to follow next day. Entrainment of Battn. (less A) complete at 8.0 P.M. Train left Station at 9-50 P.M.	
MERVILLE	26/5/16		Battn: (less "A") detrained at MERVILLE at 6-50 p.m. & marched to Billets 3 miles N.W. of Town situated on S.E. Boundary FORÊT DE NIEPPE. Headquarter details joined into HQ Coy under General Supervision of 2nd in Command. MARCHED IN. 29 Officers. 850 O.R.	
MERVILLE	27/5/16		Battn: in Billets. Capt. H.T. Bennett with "A" Coy arrived from HAVRE reaching Billets at 7-15 p.m. MARCHED IN. 4 Officers 155 OR.	
MERVILLE	28/5/16		Battn: in Billets. Lieut. T.G.R. MILLER Joined from Landing Details under 6/25 Div. at HAVRE. Lieut. R.A. ASSER " " having travelled from SOUTHAMPTON with 2/4 ROYAL BERKS REGT.	

WAR DIARY or **INTELLIGENCE SUMMARY.**

Army Form C. 2118.
Page 60

Hour, Date, Place	Summary of Events and Information	Remarks and references to Appendices
13th May (continued)	Message from R. Glow Kavure enemy on the line sent to protect left flank of 6th Cav Bde. Message from 27th Bn. 10 Car Force & 3rd Car 8.20 p.m. Bn resting for 2 Sqn R.R.G. who seem on high our reported fresh mile were began. 9.10 p.m. Message from 27th Bn. Cavalry chief on Divn is to take over the line from Lake to Railway from 6th Cav Bde. 9.30 Orders sent to 9 Yorks Regt to move to WITTE POORT FM. 10.10 Orders to R.J. Kreiler Krake on line from line closing 16th to BELLEWAARDE FM with 3 Coy U's Coy to fill gap between line closing and Railway road. 10.20 Orders to 3 KRR to take over the line between BELLEWAARDE FM and the Lake. 10.35 Message to 17th Bn pointing out all left/flank Bde be on Ghain leaving of 7 Cav Bde N of Railway. Intend to do anything tonight. Meanwhile were getting 3rd Car but nothing was seen upon Weewerfill. Further work be served.	Appendices 70 CE 70 DD 70 EE 70 FF 70 GG 70 HH 70 II 70 JJ

WAR DIARY
or
INTELLIGENCE SUMMARY
(Erase heading not required.)

Army Form C. 2118

Place	Date	Hour	Summary of Events and Information	Remarks and references to Appendices
MERVILLE	29/5/16	—	Battⁿ in Billets. Training. Capt. G. Simpson Hayward attached to H.Q. 61st Div. at St Venant for attachment. Readiness in 6 hours ordered.	
MERVILLE	30/5/16	—	Battⁿ in Billets. Training. Officers addressed by Lieut. Gen. Sir R. Haking K.C.B. Commanding XI Corps, at Salles des Fetes, Merville.	
MERVILLE	31/5/16		Battⁿ (less Part Transport, sick + details) marched 8.G.L. to Laventie for instruction in Trenches. attached 114th INF. BDE. Lieut J. Hopkinson sick, remained behind.	APPENDIX 2

W. H. Ames Colonel
Comndg. 2/4ᵀᴴ Bⁿ Oxfordshire & Bucks Lᵀ Infᵀʸ

SECRET.   COPY NO. 10

OPERATION ORDER NO. 1.   May 29th, 1916.

1. The Battalion will be attached to 114 and 115 Infty.Bdes. for instruction from May 31st - June 8th and will move by Road, Route MERVILLE - LA GORGUE - BELLECROIX - LAVENTIE LEVEL CROSSING on 31st inst.

2. Starting Point Cross Roads W of V in VIEUX BERQUIN. Time 8 a.m. Order:- H.Q.Details, A,B,C,D Coys, Lewis Guns, M/G Limbers, Maltese Cart, 2 Water Carts, Officers' Mess Cart, Cookers, 2 Supply Wagons empty, 1 Baggage Wagon.

3. Dinners will be cooked on the march and be ready for issue at 1 p.m. Tea Rations will be carried on the Cookers and Wagons.

4. Detailed orders will be issued as to the evacuation of Company Billets. Billets will be left entirely clean, blankets rolled in tens, and Officers' Valises will be collected by Wagon in the case of A,B, and D Coys at 6 a.m. on 31st inst.

5. ATTACHMENT.
	Battalion to which attached.
Battalion Headquarters and Signallers.	14th Welsh Regiment. (Right Reserve Battalion)
"A" Company	15th Welsh Regiment (Right Front Battalion)
"B" "	10th Welsh Regiment (Left Front Regiment)
"C" "	14th Welsh Regiment (Right Reserve Battalion)
"D" "	13th Welsh Regiment. (Left Reserve Battalion)

6. DISTRIBUTION. Each Battalion of this Brigade will distribute one Platoon of the attached Company to one of its own Companies again sub-dividing the platoon one section to each Platoon.

7. BILLETS. Battalion H.Q., Signallers and companies for attachment to the Right and Left Reserve Battalions respectively, will proceed to Billets.
"A" Company will be conducted to the Billeting area of the 14th Battalion Welsh Regiment where the men will be accommodated until evening.
"B" Company will be conducted to the Billeting area of the 13th Battalion Welsh Regiment. The Officers Commanding the 13th and 14th Battalions Welsh Regiment respectively will arrange for their accommodation. "A" and "B" Companies will proceed to the Trenches after dark.

8. OFFICERS. Officers attached will mess with the Officers of the Companies to which they are attached. They will bring with them cups, plates, knives, forks and spoons; a cooking pot per platoon and mess stores.

9. BOMBING. Officers Commanding Battalions in Reserve Billet will arrange demonstration and lectures on Bombing attacks to be given to Officers, N.C.O's and Bombers of Companies attached.

10. STORAGE. Officers Commanding Battalions will arrange for the storing of packs, blankets and Officers' kits of the attached Companies when in the Trenches.

11. MAPS AND ORDERS. The attached Battalion will be shewn all maps and Standing Orders.

12. MACHINE GUNS. The Machine Guns of the attached Battalion will be distributed one to each of their Companies. Captain A.SINCLAIR will arrange to have these guns placed and will supervise their instruction.

CONFIDENTIAL.

War Diary

of

2/4th Oxfordshire and Buckinghamshire Light Infantry

from June 1st to June 30th, 1916.

(Volume II).

From Officer Commanding,
2/4th Oxf. & Bucks Lt. Infty.

To D.A.G.,
G.H.Q.,
3rd Echelon,
BASE.

        Herewith War Diary of this Unit for the month of June, 1916.

                                        W. H. Ames
                                                      Colonel,
        Commdg. 2/4th Oxf. & Bucks Lt. Infty.

17/7/16.

War Diary or Intelligence Summary

Army Form C. 2118

(Erase heading not required.)

Place	Date	Hour	Summary of Events and Information	Remarks and references to Appendices
LAVENTIE	1/6/16	—	attached 114th Brigade. A & B Coys in Trenches in Right Sub-Section FAUQUISART SECTOR. "B" Coy attached 15th WELSH REGT in Left Sub-Section. "C" & "D" Coys and Battn Headquarters in Reserve Billets at LAVENTIE.	Ref. CONSIGNED SHEET 36 36a
"	2/6/16	—	A & B Coys Relieved by C & D Coys. "C" Coy attached 14th WELSH REGT. "D" to 13th WELSH REGT. 2 O.Rs Raids Wounded at B.[?] attached 14th Welsh Right Sub-section.	
"	3/6/16	—	136 Steel Helmets issued. 2 O.Rs Raids Wounded.	
"	4/6/16	—	5.a.t. Enemys Trenches shelled by R.F.A & TRENCH MORTAR BATTERIES and Wire cut ready for night operations. Slight retaliation by Enemy. 11 P.M. The Whole of "B" 38th DIVISIONAL ARTILLERY BOMBARDED Enemy Trenches. C. Ts & Support Lines. Two Raiding Parties attacked from the Shelter of Enemys Trench. Slight Artillery Retaliation by Enemy. Raiding Parties Returned one having accomplished objects however 14th WELSH 1 officer Wounded 1 missing. 1 officer Wounded. 1 O.R Killed. During day we lost 1 O.R Killed 3 Wounded.	
"	5/6/16	—	14th WELSH relieved by 17th R.W.F. [?] Command by Lt. Col. J.A. BALLARD. 10th WELSH relieved by 10th S.W.B. 114 BRIGADE was Relieved by 115 BRIGADE on Relief 2 O.R. Wounded. LIEUT F.I. POWELL proceeded to TRENCH MORTAR SCHOOL ST VENANT for Course of Instruction.	

1875 Wt. W503/826 1.000.000 4/15 J.B.C. & A. A.D.S.S./Forms/C. 2118.

WAR DIARY or INTELLIGENCE SUMMARY

Army Form C. 2118

(Erase heading not required.)

Instructions regarding War Diaries and Intelligence Summaries are contained in F.S. Regs., Part II. and the Staff Manual respectively. Title Pages will be prepared in manuscript.

Place	Date	Hour	Summary of Events and Information	Remarks and references to Appendices
LAVENTIE	6/6/16	—	REF. SHEET 36A. "A" & "B" Coys relieve "C" & "D" in Trenches. Quiet Day. Regt. Sergt. Major & 1 O.R. Wounded b. Rifle Grenade. R.S.M. remained at Duty.	O.i.R.
"	7/6/16		In Trenches. Reserve Posts & Billets. 2 O.R. Wounded by Shrapnel. Poison Gas again stood to for ½ an hour. No attack developed. Capt. H.T. Harris Bett. forward to Arrewage to take charge of Details. Stores left by 2/4 Royal Berks Regt. who proceed to trenches tomorrow.	O.i.R.
"	8/6/16		Came out of Trenches. Course of instruction being finalised commenced at 6 a.m. Very useful. Parties to Church Parade for Divine service at 12 noon. Batt. marched to previous Billets at Arrewage (K.10.c.) at 1 P.M. in open Column. Route La Gorgue, Merville, arrived at Arrewage at 5.30 P.M. Casualties on March 5. On return from 2/Lieut. J. Hopkinson returned from Hospital.	O.i.R.
ARREWAGE K.10.c.	9/6/16	—	In Billets. Men generally clean up. Arms & Equipment cleaned & Deficiencies made good. 2 Lieut. E.O.R. Byworth & 12 O.R. proceed to 115 Brigade at Laventie for attachment to Trench Mortar Battery. Steel Helmets issued to Remainder of the Batt. Orders received to move to Laventie tomorrow.	O.i.R.

Army Form C. 2118

WAR DIARY or INTELLIGENCE SUMMARY

(Erase heading not required.)

Instructions regarding War Diaries and Intelligence Summaries are contained in F.S. Regs., Part II. and the Staff Manual respectively. Title Pages will be prepared in manuscript.

Place	Date	Hour	Summary of Events and Information	Remarks and references to Appendices
LAVENTIE	10/6/16	—	Batt: marched from Billets at 9.30 a.m. arrived at LAVENTIE 12.45. Casualties on march. NIL. Capt. H.M. DAVENPORT preceded Batt. & took over Billets from 11th S.W.B. Following Distribution:- "B" Coy at LAVENTIE EAST POST - Y PICANTIN POST & HOUGUMONT POST. "C" Coy at DEAD END POST. 115 BRIGADE Handed over to 184th BRIGADE.	Appx 1
"	11/6/16	—	In Billets & Posts. 3 Platoons of "C" Coy withdrawn from DEAD END to Billets at LAVENTIE. Two A.D. + 3 Platoons "C" Coy in Town. Shrapnel over 2/Lt COOMBES shared duties in Front Line Right Subsector with 2/4 Royal Berks. This arrangement will continue when we relieve the BERKS.	Appx 2
"	12/6/16	—	In Billets + Posts. Supply R.E. Working Parties DAILY. Lieut. E.I. POWELL reported the TRENCH MORTAR BATTERY SCHOOL.	Appx 3
"	13/6/16	—	In Billets + Posts. The large number of Fatigues & Working Parties made it impossible to carry out any musketry training except with 31 miniature 22.	Appx 4
"	—	—	Memorial Service to the late F.M. VISCOUNT KITCHENER & to fallen Comrades of 61st DIVISION.	
"	14/6/16	—	In Billets + Posts. Relieve Royal BERKS REGT tomorrow.	Appx 5

WAR DIARY or INTELLIGENCE SUMMARY

Army Form C. 2118

Place	Date	Hour	Summary of Events and Information	Remarks and references to Appendices
FAUQUISSART	15/6/16		Battⁿ marched from Billets at 8.30 p.m, and relieved R. BERKS in Trenches. Casualties on move. NIL. Relief completed at 12.5 am. Distribution. A Coy. Right and FIREWORKS POST. B Coy Right Centre, C. Coy. Left Centre and FLANK POST. D Coy LEFT and A1 POST. Connection established on RIGHT with 2/5 GLOUCESTERS, and on LEFT with	
"	16/6/16		IN Trenches + Front Posts. Patrols examined ground for 100x in front of our line, and on either side of RHONDDA SAP. WIRING commenced in front of CRATER (Right Coy). Casualties. O.R. 1 WOUNDED.	
"	17/6/16		IN Trenches + Front POSTS. Gas alarms given on Left at 12.40 a.m. and 1.45 a.m. All precautions taken, but as wind was favourable, no action was necessary. Patrols from each Coy examined and reported on enemy wire. Casualties. NIL.	
"	18/6/16		In Trenches + Front Posts. At 1 a.m. bombardment by our artillery and Trench Mortars on selected points. Enemy retaliated on our Support and Communication Trenches. No damage. Rifle Grenades registered on enemy front trench + range observed. Capt DAVENPORT with 1 Corporal went out by day from SALLY PORT YA to see if a day observation post	

Army Form C. 2118.

WAR DIARY
or
INTELLIGENCE SUMMARY
(Erase heading not required.)

2/4th Oxf & Bucks Light Infy

Instructions regarding War Diaries and Intelligence Summaries are contained in F.S. Regs., Part II. and the Staff Manual respectively. Title Pages will be prepared in manuscript.

Place	Date	Hour	Summary of Events and Information	Remarks and references to Appendices
FAUQUISSART			Could be established in NO MAN'S LAND, and reported that no useful purpose could be served thereby. Lt. LOEWE and 1 man went out to right to report on WIRE (enemy) over pond 5.3, and found wire thin, but no gaps. 2/Lt ROFFEY and party occupied crater in front of Right Coy and made emplacement for Lewis Gun. Covering party of 1 officer, 25 ORs provided to Australian Digging party on RHONDDA SAP. Casualties O.R. 1 WOUNDED.	N.F.1
	19/6/16		At In Trenches & Front Posts. At 2.20 am our Artillery and Trench Mortars bombarded enemy Trenches and damaged parapet. Retaliation slight. At 10 a.m. and later enemy dropped shells on left + left Centre Coys and did some damage to support + communication trenches, an aerial Torpedo doing considerable damage to BOND STREET. Crater in front of Right Coy maintained by Lewis gunners + Bombing party. Covering party of 1 officer + 25 men provided to Australian digging party over RHONDDA SAP. Casualties NIL.	P.S.1
	20/6/16		In Trenches & Front Posts. Supported Raid by Right Battⁿ (1/5 Gloucesters), by Rapid fire, T.M. Bombardment + Rifle Grenade. Also by throwing dummies over parapet. Casualties NIL	N.F.1 1051

WAR DIARY
or
INTELLIGENCE SUMMARY

Army Form C. 2118

Place	Date	Hour	Summary of Events and Information	Remarks and references to Appendices
FAUQUISSART	21/6/16		In Trenches & Posts. Patrol of Enemy wire by A + D Coys, and our own wire strengthened in places. Relieved by 1/4 R. Berks at 9.30 p.m. and Batt^n marched back to LAVENTIE and Posts. Casualties in line O.R. 1 killed, 1 wounded. Casualties on march Nil. Distribution A + B Coys + 3 Platoon of D Coy in Billets, C Coy + 1 Platoon D Coy in Posts, 2 Platoon D/Coy (Kompany of Recent Trench)	N.F.1.
LAVENTIE	22/6/16		In Billets + Posts. WORKING PARTIES found to front line and 2 Platoons in reserve Trenches at night. Casualties Nil.	N.F.1.
"	23/6/16		In Billets + Posts. Working Parties + Supports as above. Casualties, O.R. 1 wounded	N.F.1.
"	24/6/16		In Billets + Posts. Working Parties Supports as above Casualties, O.R. 1 killed, 1 wounded	N.F.1.
"	25/6/16		In Billets, Posts. Working Parties Supports as above and R.Berks to reinforced at night by B + D Coys. Capt. DAVENPORT and Platoon of B Coy patrolled Enemy wire. Casualties, 1 killed, 2 wounded	N.F.1.
"	26/6/16		In Billets + Posts. Working Parties + Supports as above. Casualties Nil. Major D.M. ROSE and 11.A.W. Procter to hospital (ill).	102.1

WAR DIARY or INTELLIGENCE SUMMARY

Army Form C. 2118

Place	Date	Hour	Summary of Events and Information	Remarks and references to Appendices
LAVENTIE	27/6/16		Batt'n marched from Billets at 8.27 p.m. and took over the Trenches & Front Posts from R. Berks. Relief completed 9.45. Connection established on Right with 1/5 Gloucesters, on Left with Australians. B Coy unmasked to put out Saps in front of Left Coys lines and extending posts joined at Nieta. Casualties Nil.	N.T.J.
LAVENTIE	28/6/16		In Trenches and Front Posts. Capt. R.F. CUTHBERT assumed the duties of Acting Adjutant. Capt. W.D. SCOTT taking over the command of D Coy. 2/Lt. HOPKINSON to hospital (sick). L'T K.E. BROWN and 2/Lt. W.H. MOBERLY left our lines at about 1 p.m. to make a Reconnaissance of the Enemys wire in view of a raid that Evening. L'T BROWN successful. Accomplished this task, returning about 5.30. 2/Lt. MOBERLY was wounded in left shoulder by a sniper about 2.20 p.m. and remained in NO MANS LAND till dark, when he managed to get back to our Trenches. A raid was carried out by B Coy at night. Orders and Reports are contained at Appendix I. Casualties: Missing (believed killed) 2/Lt. J.H. ZEDER. Wounded Capt. H.N. DAVENPORT. Other Ranks killed 8, wounded 26. Also 2/Lt. MITCHELL, as indicated above.	See Appendix I N.T.J.
LAVENTIE	29/6/16		In Trenches and Front Posts. Work continued on Saps in front of Left of our lines, and Patrols sent out to bring in dead & wounded. No trace could be found of 2/Lt. ZEDER. Casualties Nil.	N.T.J.

WAR DIARY
or
INTELLIGENCE SUMMARY

Army Form C. 2118

Place	Date	Hour	Summary of Events and Information	Remarks and references to Appendices
LAURENTIE	30/6/16		In Trenches. Front Posts. The work of wiring the saps on our left was continued, and D Coy parts came under heavy M.G. fire, in which one man was killed and 3 wounded. The wounded men brought in but one stretcher bearer was killed in this work. Patrols sent out (by night 6ry), and further progress was made to wiring. Casualties (as above). O.R. killed 2, wounded 2.	AAA

Instructor of Front Posts

[signature] Capt.
a/adjt.

CONFIDENTIAL.

War Diary

of

2/4th Bn. Oxfordshire and Buckinghamshire Light Infantry

from July 1st to July 31st, 1916.

(Volume III).

WAR DIARY or INTELLIGENCE SUMMARY

Army Form C. 2118

Place	Date	Hour	Summary of Events and Information	Remarks and references to Appendices
LAVENTIE	1/7/16		In Trenches and Front Posts. Further progress made with the Saps, under considerable fire. Casualties, O.R. Killed 3, Wounded 2.	R.J.
"	2/7/16		In Trenches and Front Posts. Considerable damage done to our Parapet and Communication Trenches by enemy artillery. This was repaired. Work on Saps continued. Casualties, O.R. Wounded 6.	R.J.
"	3/7/16		In Trenches and Front Posts. A good deal of hostile shelling resulted in a good deal of Artillery Bombardment, and further damage was done to our Communication Trenches which we repaired. The Battⁿ was relieved by 2/4 GLOUCESTERS about 10 p.m. and marched to Billets at RIEZ BAILLEUL. Casualties, O.R. Killed 1, Wounded 6. Casualties on march, Nil.	R.J.
RIEZ BAIL-LEUL	4/7/16		In Billets. Training and Re-fitting under Company arrangements. Casualties Nil. Report on fur appendix 2. seconded Battⁿ when attached to 3⁰ Bri.	See appendix R. R.J.
"	5/7/16		In Billets. Training continued under Company arrangements. Casualties Nil.	R.J.

War Diary or Intelligence Summary

Army Form C. 2118

Place	Date	Hour	Summary of Events and Information	Remarks and references to Appendices
RIEZ BAILLEUL	6/7/16		In Billets. During instruction in throwing Live Bombs one Bomb detonated prematurely resulting in 16 Casualties set out below. Lt Powell was attached 68th Bde for the Orders and received to move to Croix Barbée, to take over Billets in Battⁿ in Reserve in the FERME DU BOIS sector. Battⁿ marched to Billets at 6.30 and took over Billets by 8 p.m. Casualties on march NIL. Casualties (accidental), Officers Capt W.D.SCOTT and Lt J. LOEWE, wounded. O.R. killed 1, wounded 2.	N.F.
CROIX BARBEE	7/7/16		In Billets and Posts. Several small recent posts taken over. Parts of S.O. men sent to LECTREM to work under Officer i/c Roads. Front line working parties found by all other available men. Officers reconn^d roads to approaches to front line Trenches. Casualties NIL.	N.F.
"	8/7/16		In Billets and Posts. Working parties found as above. Lt STOCKTON took over (temporary) Command of D Coy, vice Capt. W.D.SCOTT wounded, and following transfers made :- 2/Lt ROFFEY from C to D Coy, Lt AGER from B to D Coy. 2/Lt PARSONS from A to B Coy. Casualties NIL.	N.F.
"	9/7/16		In Billets and Posts. Working Parties found as above. The following officers being attached to the Battⁿ joined for duty and were posted as under :- 2/Lt F.F.MOORAT, C Coy, 2/Lt. M. THORNE, B Coy, 2/Lt E.H.WOOD, D Coy, 2/Lt G.H. DALTON and 2/Lt M. EDEN, A Coy. Casualties NIL.	N.F.

Army Form C. 2118

WAR DIARY
or
INTELLIGENCE SUMMARY
(Erase heading not required.)

Place	Date	Hour	Summary of Events and Information	Remarks and references to Appendices
CROIX BARBÉE	10/7/16		In Billets and Post. Working parties found as before. Casualties NIL.	117
"	11/7/16		In Billets and Posts. Working parties found as before. Casualties NIL.	117
"	12/7/16		In Billets and Posts. At 2 p.m. the Battn. marched to the FERME DU BOIS, reaching and relieving the 1/4th Royal Berks in the Trenches. Casualties on march NIL. Distribution, A Coy on Right, C Coy Centre, D Coy Left in B Coy, ½ Platoon in PORT ARTHUR Post, ½ Platoon in HILL'S POST, 2 Platoons in LANSDOWNE POST and 1 Platoon at Bn. H.Q. Patrols sent out from all Coys in Front Line and Listening Posts established. In response to an T.M. fire, Enemy fired rifle grenades on our Coy, wounding 3 men. 2/Lt ROBINSON being attached joined for duty and was attached to C Coy. Casualties O.R. Wounded 3.	119
FERME DU BOIS	13/7/16		In Trenches and Front Posts. In the early hours of the morning rifle grenades fired by the Enemy on to the left of our line caused several casualties. The rest of the day was quiet. At night a portion of the R Berks line was shelled to enable a company of the R. Berks to carry some TM trench mortars to support a raid. This raid was supported and in its conclusion sent out the grenade patrols to assist in finding and bringing in the Berks wounded. Lieut TEDDY and Lt BROWN went out several times. Also Capt. BENNETT. O.R. killed 4, wounded 11. Casualties.	119 / 112

WAR DIARY or INTELLIGENCE SUMMARY

Army Form C. 2118

Place	Date	Hour	Summary of Events and Information	Remarks and references to Appendices
FERME DU BOIS	14/7/16		In Trenches and front posts. Notification received that the following awards had been made:- MILITARY MEDAL - No. 3794 Sergt. A.H. PRENTICE, No. 1333 Pte. H.F. GARDNER (1/1 Welsh Regt, att'd 2/1 Oxfords) No. 3125 Cpl. A.E. BRERETON. All these awards were for conspicuous gallantry on the occasion of the raid on 28/29 June. See APPENDIX 3. A.M. quiet morning, the enemy fired a lot of Trench Mortars on to our right, doing considerable damage to parapets and dug outs, but causing no casualties. At night the Batt'n was relieved by the 17th K.R.R, and marched to billets at LESTREM. D Coy however remained in occupation of their section of the line. Casualties O.R. wounded 1. D Coy in Trenches, FERME DU BOIS.	See APPENDIX 3B. Nil.
LESTREM	15/7/16	4.30	In Billets. At 4.30 Batt'n marched to billets on the RUE DE LA LYS, between ESTAIRES and SAILLY. Working parties were relieved & joined Batt'n. D Coy were relieved & joined Batt'n. work in front & rear of the FAUQUISSART section. Casualties NIL.	(A.J.)
RUE DE LA LYS	16/7/16		In Billets. The whole Batt'n engaged day and night in trench works parties as above. Casualties NIL.	(S.) 1196

WAR DIARY or INTELLIGENCE SUMMARY

Army Form C. 2118

Place	Date	Hour	Summary of Events and Information	Remarks and references to Appendices
RUE DE LA LYS	17/7/16		In Billets. The whole Batt" engaged in working parties as above, day and night. Casualties, O.R. wounded 3.	M.F.
"	18/7/16		In Billets. Whole Batt" engaged as above. Casualties	M.F.
"	19/7/16		In Billets. A and C Coys moved up at 6 am to the Assembly Trenches behind the left of the FAUQUISSART section. C Coy then provided 1 officer and 80 men to carry up T.M. Amm" to front line and arranged to carry same across NO MAN'S LAND behind an assault on Enemy Trenches by the Berks + 2/1 Bucks. At 7 pm A Coy and remainder of C Coy moved into front trench to reinforce above two Batt"s. At 7.15 pm remainder of Batt". left Billets in motor Lorries and eventually relieved 1/1 Berks and 2/1 Bucks in front line. In the meantime the assault had commenced but neither Batt" succeeded in getting into enemy trenches. A party of "C" Coy carried part nearly succeeded in getting in but were heavily repulsed. After the relief, all Coys were used in the 2/1 Bucks, 2 other Batt"s in the dead and wounded of their own + of the 2 other Batt"s. Orders were received for another assault but were subsequently cancelled. Casualties, O.R. Killed 14, missing 1, Wounded 43.	M.F. 114
FAUQUISSART	20/7/16		In Trenches. The Bombardment by our own Artillery thought the day had produced little attrition. The work of getting in dead + wounded continued and also the work of cleaning up the Trenches was proceeded with. Casualties, O.R. 6	M.F.

WAR DIARY or INTELLIGENCE SUMMARY

Army Form C. 2118

Place	Date	Hour	Summary of Events and Information	Remarks and references to Appendices
FAUQUISSART	21/7/16		In Trenches. Considerable artillery activity throughout the day. The work of repairing parapets and stop butts was continued. 2/Lt. THORNE was twice hit during the day and once by a rifle grenade on both occasions pieces got caught in his equipment after striking and prevented him being severely wounded. Casualties O.R. Wounded 2.	R.J.
"	22/7/16		In Trenches. Several Patrols went out to inspect Enemy's wire & to make sure that he had not repaired any of the damage which had been caused by our bombardment. A strong Patrol under Lt. TIDDY went out to front of the ELBOW, Enemy patrols but on the ELBOW Enemy aware of our patrol, they retired. Casualties NIL.	R.J.
"	23/7/16		In Trenches. The Batt. was relieved by 1/7 Worcesters by 1/2 noon, and marched to the MOATED GRANGE and with one, the left sub-sector from 1/1 E. YORKS. Distribution B Coy on left, D in Centre C on right, A in reserve in WINCHESTER POST. Patrols from front Coys examined Enemy's wire. Casualties. O.R. Wounded 3.	R.J.
MOATED GRANGE	24/7/16		In Trenches and Posts. We replied with Rifle Grenades and sent over a large number on the Enemy front line. Retaliation slight. A mild musis was laid in another Crater formed, Patrols again went out from front Company front. 2/Lt. C.J. BARTON and 2/Lt. J.E. MACKAY attached from 3rd Batt. joined for duty. Casualties O.R. Killed 1. Wounded 1.	115r

Army Form C. 2118

WAR DIARY
or
INTELLIGENCE SUMMARY
(Erase heading not required.)

Instructions regarding War Diaries and Intelligence Summaries are contained in F. S. Regs., Part II. and the Staff Manual respectively. Title Pages will be prepared in manuscript.

Place	Date	Hour	Summary of Events and Information	Remarks and references to Appendices
MOATED GRANGE	25/7/16		In Trenches and Posts. Further considerable activity on our part with Rifle Grenades and L.T.Mortars with some retaliation from Enemy Trench Mortars and Artillery. New Crater examined by patrol. Troops. 3 Company and found to be occupied by Enemy, his is Post 7 on Flap abandoned. Casualties, O.R. Wounded 1.	R.S.J.
"	26/7/16		In Trenches and Posts. Enemy considerably harassed by our Rifle Grenades and L.T.Mortars, and he retaliated with Aerial Torpedoes and Trench Mortars but without much damage. Patrols sent out to Enemy's wiring parties were located and intermittingly fired on. Casualties, O.R. Wounded 3.	R.S.J.
"	27/7/16		In Trenches and Posts. We continued to bombard the Enemy Front Line with Rifle Grenades but in the event 2 entirely went out of our own exploded prematurely causing 2 Casualties (2/Lt THORNE + 1 O.R.) 2/Lt THORNE had shown great activity and enterprise in this form of annoying the Enemy. At 6.45 p.m. the Battn was relieved by 2/R.Berks and marched to Billets at RIEZ BAILLEUL. Casualties Officers Wounded, 2/Lt T.M.THORNE, O.R. Wounded 2.	R.S.J.
RIEZ BAILLEUL	28/7/16		In Billets. In Reserve. Watering parties formed day and night. Front Line Patrol under 2/Lt GUINER sent out from Civil Idees by R.BERKS to examine found with a raid. Casualties, O.R. Killed 1.	R.S.J.

Army Form C. 2118

WAR DIARY
or
INTELLIGENCE SUMMARY
(Erase heading not required.)

Instructions regarding War Diaries and Intelligence Summaries are contained in F.S. Regs., Part II. and the Staff Manual respectively. Title Pages will be prepared in manuscript.

Place	Date	Hour	Summary of Events and Information	Remarks and references to Appendices
RIEZ BAILLEUL	29/7/16		In Billets in Reserve. Working parties as above. Casualties, NIL.	N.T.J.
"	30/7/16		In Billets in Reserve. Working parties as above. Casualties, NIL.	N.T.J.
"	31/7/16		In Billets in Reserve. Working parties as above. Casualties, NIL.	N.T.J.

W.S.P. Brennan Comdg 7/4 Ox & Bucks L.I.

Vere Fullerd
Capt & Adjt
2/4 Oxford & Bucks L.I.

117v

War DIARY
Appendix - A

CONFIDENTIAL   G46.
                                                4.7.16

To :-   2/4th Oxfords.

         The following report has been received on your
Unit, in connection with its attachment to the 38th Div, for
instruction, is forwarded for your information :-

    2/4th Oxfords
         "All ranks showed exceptional interest and keenness
         to learn, and were well grounded before they came
         out to this Country. Men well disciplined, and of
         good physique."

                                    Ec Gepp
                                        Major
                                    Brigade Major
                                    184th Infantry Brigade.

B.H.Q.
4/7/16.

War Diary

Appendix B

184TH INFANTRY BRIGADE ROUTINE ORDERS

By Brigadier-General, C.H.P. Carter. C.B.
C.M.G. Commanding 184th Infantry Brigade.

July 13th, 1916.

65. **AWARDS FOR GALLANTRY.**

The following awards for Gallantry have been made:-

MILITARY MEDAL.

1. No.3174 Sergeant ALBERT HENRY PRENTICE, 2/4th Bn. Ox. & Bucks L.I.

   AT FAUQUISSART on the 28th June 1916, displayed courage of a high order in cutting the enemy's wire whilst under severe machine gun fire some thirty yards to his front.

2. No.1333 Private HARRY VICTOR GARDNER, 1/7th Bn. Welsh Regt. attached 2/4th Bn. Ox. & Bucks L.I.

   AT FAUQUISSART on 28th June, 1916, showed conspicious gallantry in that, after returning unhurt from the raid, he subsequently went out four times under heavy fire and assisted to bring in one dead and three wounded comrades.

3. No.3125 Corporal ALBERT EDWARD BRERETON, 2/4th Bn. Ox. & Bucks L.I.

   At FAUQUISSART on 28th June, 1916, behaved with conspicious gallantry in carrying back, 250 yards from the enemy's trenches, a comrade who had been shot in both legs. This was carried out under very heavy artillery and machine gun fire, the enemy having formed a curtain round the area of withdrawal.

R. W. HARLING. MAJOR
Staff Captain
184th Infantry Brigade.

NOTICE

LOST

Equipment & rifle belonging to No.1791 Pte. Willmott P.H. 2/5th R. Warwicks was left on the Bus which conveyed the Party returning from the Sniping School on the 10th inst. If this was collected by anyone of this Brigade who was dropped at ZELOBES will the finder return same to Camp Commandant, 61st Division.

CONFIDENTIAL.

War Diary

of

2/4th Battalion Oxfordshire and Buckinghamshire Light Infantry,

1st August, 1916 to 31st August, 1916.

(Volume IV).

Army Form C. 2118.

WAR DIARY or INTELLIGENCE SUMMARY

(Erase heading not required.)

Instructions regarding War Diaries and Intelligence Summaries are contained in F.S. Regs., Part II. and the Staff Manual respectively. Title Pages will be prepared in manuscript.

Place	Date	Hour	Summary of Events and Information	Remarks and references to Appendices
RIEZ BAILLEUL	1/8/16		In Billets in Reserve. Batt" marched into Rest Billets at ROBERMETZ, near MERVILLE. Casualties on march, NIL. Col. W.H. AMES, T.D. relinquished command of the Battalion and returned to England, MAJOR G.P.R. BEAMAN assuming temporary command.	
ROBERMETZ	2/8/16		In Rest Billets. Company training. Classes for Bombers, Lewis Gunners and Signallers.	
"	3/8/16		In Rest Billets. Training continued as above.	
"	4/8/16		In Rest Billets. Batt" Route march. Training as above.	
"	5/8/16		In Rest Billets. Training as above. Brigade Sports in afternoon.	
"	6/8/16		In Rest Billets. Church Parade in morning. MAJOR R. BELLAMY D.S.O. joined and assumed command of Batt". Capt" R.E.P. BOYLE to hospital, newlyitis. Casualties, O.R. Wounded 1. (Injured.)	
"	7/8/16		In Rest Billets. Batt" Route march. Brigade Horse show in afternoon.	
"	8/8/16		In Rest Billets. Training as above. Coys marched to baths at LA GORGUE.	

1875 Wt. W593/826 1,000,000 4/15 J.B.C. & A. A.D.S.S./Forms/C. 2118.

Army Form C. 2118

WAR DIARY or INTELLIGENCE SUMMARY
(Erase heading not required.)

Place	Date	Hour	Summary of Events and Information	Remarks and references to Appendices
ROBERMETZ	9/8/16		In Rest Billets. At 9.30 am Battⁿ marched to FAUQUISSART, and thence to take over trenches at FAUQUISSART from 2/4 Gloucester Regt. Relief completed at 5.30 pm. Dispositions D on right, A Right Centre. C. Left Centre. B Left. A.B.+C. each had a platoon in front line posts. Patrols inspected wire. Casualties, O.R Wounded 1.	(Sgd)
FAUQUISSART	10/8/16		In Trenches + Front Posts. Quiet day, with some artillery activity at night. Patrols inspected Enemy wire. Casualties NIL.	(Sgd)
"	11/8/16		In Trenches + Front Posts. Mine inspected wells on left Centre Coy, and section of trench destroyed accordingly. Casualties Officer, 2/Lt R.J.E. TIDDY killed, O.R Wounded 2.	(Sgd)
"	12/8/16		In Trenches + Front Posts. Rifle Grenades fired into Enemy Trenches. Quiet day, and at night T.M's, Rifle Grenades + M.Guns cooperated with artillery in trenching Enemy trenches. Retaliation was slight. Casualties NIL.	(Sgd)
"	13/8/16		In Trenches + Front Posts. Further activity with Rifle Grenades, and bombardment at night with Artillery + T.M's. Enemy retaliation again slight. Casualties. O.R. Wounded 1.	(Sgd)
"	14/8/16		In Trenches + Front Posts. We continued harass the Enemy with Rifle Grenades and Trench Mortars and at night the artillery again cooperated. Casualties, Officer, 2/Lt DALTON wounded by Rifle + M.G. fire, died of wounds same day.	(Sgd)

Army Form C. 2118

WAR DIARY or INTELLIGENCE SUMMARY
(Erase heading not required.)

Place	Date	Hour	Summary of Events and Information	Remarks and references to Appendices
FAUQUISSART	15/8/16		In Trenches & Front Posts. Batt" relieved by 2/4 R Berks. Relief completed at 5.30pm. Marched to LAVENTIE. D Coy to sector line Posts during day & occupied Reserve Trenches by night. Casualties Nil.	G.J.
LAVENTIE	16/8/16		In Reserve Billets & Posts. "A" Coy special training for raid. B and C Coys working parties night and day. D Coy in Posts and Reserve Trenches. Casualties Nil.	G.J.
"	17/8/16		In Reserve Billets & Posts. "A" Company training as above. B & C working parties. C Coy relieved D in Posts & Reserve Trenches. Casualties Nil.	G.J.
"	18/8/16		In Reserve Billets & Posts. A Coy training as above, and at night patrol under 2/Lt. BULMER went out through Boch lines & examined front for trenches raid. B & D working parties. C in Posts & Reserve Trenches. Casualties O.R. Wounded 1.	G.J.
"	19/8/16		In Reserve Billets & Posts. B & D Coy working parties. C in Posts & Reserve Trenches. At 7pm. A Coy proceeded to Trenches to prepare for raid. The party took up position in Bomm ditch and advanced under cover of artillery barrage. It carried bombing posts, reached Enemy parapet without loss & bombed his trenches, after an exchange of bombs the Enemy brought up reinforcements and the whole party had to retire. Capt H.J.BENNETT was in command of the raiding party & 2/Lt BULMER with him. Casualties, O.R. Wounded, 12	G.J.

1375

WAR DIARY or INTELLIGENCE SUMMARY

Army Form C. 2118

Place	Date	Hour	Summary of Events and Information	Remarks and references to Appendices
LAVENTIE	20/8/16		In Reserve Billets & Posts. A Coy. relieving D. Coy. working parties. B relieved C in Posts & Reserve Trenches. Casualties NIL. The following officers joined and were posted as follows: Capt. G.K. ROSE, D Coy (2nd command). 2/Lt. CALLENDER, A Coy; 2/Lt. FOWLER, B Coy.	[sig]
"	21/8/16		In Reserve Billets & Posts. The Battn. (less A Coy) relieved R. Berks in Trenches. Bistrihm, D Right, C Left Centre, B Left. Relief completed at 5.5 p.m. Companies engaged in improving own wire. Casualties, wiring parties from all Companies. O.R. Killed 1.	[sig]
FAUQUISSART	22/8/16		In Trenches & Front Posts. A Coy relieved R. Berks Centre Coy by R. Berks. Relief complete at 4.30 p.m. 2/Lt. HARRINGTON joined and was posted to A Coy. Wiring continued along whole front, and large numbers of Rifle Grenades fired on Enemy Trenches. Casualties, O.R. Wounded 2.	[sig]
"	23/8/16		In Trenches & Front Posts. Enemy replied to our Rifle Grenades with T.M.'s and Artillery and did some damage to our Communication Trenches & Parapet. Casualties, O.R. Wounded 4. 2/Lt. BENSON joined and was posted to C Coy.	[sig]
"	24/8/16		In Trenches & Front Posts. Wiring continued along front, & covering parties for R. Berks who were working on RHONDDA S.A.P. Considerable artillery, T.M. Rifle Grenade & M.G. activity on both sides. Casualties NIL.	[sig]
"	25/8/16		In Trenches & Front Posts. Wiring and covering parties found as above. On T.M.'s engaged on cutting gaps in enemy wire and supported by artillery and Rifle fire. Some retaliation from enemy T.M.'s. 2/Lt. W.H.J.S. LYONS joined and was posted to B. Coy. Casualties. 2/Lt. BENSON Wounded. O.R. NIL.	[sig]

Army Form C., 2118

WAR DIARY
or
INTELLIGENCE SUMMARY
(Erase heading not required.)

Instructions regarding War Diaries and Intelligence Summaries are contained in F. S. Regs., Part II. and the Staff Manual respectively. Title Pages will be prepared in manuscript.

Place	Date	Hour	Summary of Events and Information	Remarks and references to Appendices
FAUQUISSART	26/8/16		In Trenches & Front Posts. Wiring and covering parties as above. also wire cutting by T. Mortars. Casualties Nil.	(Sgd)
"	27/8/16		In Trenches & Front Posts. Relieved by 4 R. Berks and marched to Billets at LAVENTIE. Relief complete at 7 pm. A Coy to Posts. Casualties, Officers wounded, 2/Lt E.M.WOOD 1, 2/LT R.E. ROCHE (at duty). O.R. Wounded. 2.	(Sgd)
LAVENTIE	28/8/16		In Reserve Billets & Posts. B. Coy provided wiring party in RHONDDA SAP. C & D Coy working parties. Casualties Nil	(Sgd)
"	29/8/16		In Reserve Billets & Posts. B. Coy relieved A in Pots. C and D working parties, Casualties Nil	(Sgd)
"	30/8/16		In Reserve Billets & Pots. A. C. and D Coys working parties. Casualties Nil.	(Sgd)
"	31/8/16		In Reserve Billets & Posts. D. Coy relieved B Coy in Posts. C Coy found wiring party for RHONDDA SAP. A Coy working parties, Casualties Nil.	(Sgd)

1-9-16.

R. Bellamy Lt Col
Comdg 2/4 Bn Oxf & Bucks L.I.

C O N F I D E N T I A L.

War Diary

of

2/4th Battalion Oxfordshire and Buckinghamshire Light Infantry.

1st September, 1916 to 30th September, 1916.

(Volume V).

WAR DIARY or INTELLIGENCE SUMMARY

Army Form C. 2118

Place	Date 1916	Hour	Summary of Events and Information	Remarks and references to Appendices
LAVENTIE	Sept 1		In Billets and Posts. Working parties found day and night. One Officer and 30 men go up at night to wire RHONDDA S.A.P. Casualties NIL.	N.T.R.
"	2		In Billets and Posts. The same working and wiring parties. Casualties NIL.	N.T.R.
"	3		In Billets and Posts. Brigade goes into Reserve, and we march to billets at MERVILLE. Casualties NIL.	N.T.R.
ROBERMETZ	4		In Billets in Reserve. Company training, refitting and equipping. Casualties NIL.	N.T.R.
"	5		In Billets in Reserve. Training Continued and classes formed for instruction in Bombing, Lewis Gun and Signalling. Letter of Appreciation received from G.O.C. Division. Casualties NIL.	APPENDIX D
"	6		In Billets in Reserve. Training continued. Casualties NIL.	N.T.R.
"	7		In Billets in Reserve. Training continued. In afternoon Brigade Sports were held. Casualties NIL.	N.T.R.
"	8		In Billets in Reserve. Training continued. Battn. inspected by the General Officer Commanding XIth Corps. Casualties NIL.	N.T.R.
"	9		In Billets in Reserve. Training continued. Battn. paraded at 4 pm for inspection by Maj. Gen. ANDERSON, commanding XI TH CORPS. Casualties NIL.	N.T.R.
"	10		In Billets in Reserve. Church parade in morning. Brigade Sports continued in afternoon. Casualties NIL.	

WAR DIARY or INTELLIGENCE SUMMARY

Army Form C. 2118

Place	Date 1916	Hour	Summary of Events and Information	Remarks and references to Appendices
ROBERMETZ	Sep. 11		In Billets in Reserve. At 8 am Battⁿ marched to relieve 2/6th Gloucesters in left Subsector of MOATED GRANGE section. Relief complete at 6 pm. Distribution, A Coy on left, D Centre, C Right, B in Posts. Letter of Congratulations from G.O.C. 1st Army received. Casualties NIL.	APPENDIX E. R.S.J.
MOATED GRANGE	12		In Trenches & Front Line Posts. Enemy very quiet, and there is not much response to our Rifle Grenades and T.M. Bombardment. Casualties O.R. 1 killed, 2 wounded	R.S.J.
"	13		In Trenches & Front Line Posts. The O.C. 2/4 R Berks having proceeded on leave, Major BEAMAN left to take on the temporary command of that Unit. Fighting Patrols out by night to try to capture a German Patrol but on first none. Casualties, 2/Lt BULMER, wounded. O.R. NIL.	R.S.J.
"	14		In Trenches & Front Line Posts. The second Anniversary of the formation of this Battⁿ. The wire in this section is front & to the rear, and wiring parties go out from each Company to Front line every night. Captⁿ H.J. BENNETT proceeds to England on Court. Casualties. Cannuthier NIL.	R.S.J.
"	15		In Trenches & Front Line Posts. Wiring parties all along the Front. Casualties, O.R. wounded, 1.	R.S.J.
"	16		In Trenches & Front Line Posts. Wiring parties and Patrols as usual. Lt. K.E. BROWN received the MILITARY CROSS for good work on 13th July last. Casualties. O.R. wounded, 1.	R.S.J.

Army Form C. 2118

WAR DIARY
or
INTELLIGENCE SUMMARY
(Erase heading not required.)

Instructions regarding War Diaries and Intelligence Summaries are contained in F. S. Regs., Part II. and the Staff Manual respectively. Title Pages will be prepared in manuscript.

Place	Date 1916	Hour	Summary of Events and Information	Remarks and references to Appendices
MORTED GRANGE	Sep. 17		In Trenches and Front Line Pots. Wiring continued. Casualties O.R. wounded 1.	R.F.J.
"	18		In Trenches and Front Line Pots. Weather very wet. Wiring continued. Casualties Nil.	R.F.J.
"	19		In Trenches and Front Line Pots. Weather still bad. Relieved by 2/4 R. Berks. At 11.30 a.m. and marched to Billets at RIEZ BAILLEUL. Casualties Nil.	R.F.J.
RIEZ BAILLEUL	20		In Reserve Billets. Company training. Corals for Lewis Gunners, Bombers and Signallers. Casualties Nil.	R.F.J.
"	21		In Reserve Billets. Company training. Casualties Nil.	R.F.J.
"	22		In Reserve Billets. Company training. Lt. & Q.M. HOBBS to England on leave. Casualties Nil. Assault on trenches under supervision of Brigadier practised.	R.F.J.
"	23		In Reserve Billets. Working parties found by whole Batn. and C. Co. relieved 2/1 Bucks in Pots. In entrainment in A.D.M.S. working parties 2 Officers and 116 O.R. in ½ Billets at PONT DU HEM. Casualties Nil.	R.F.J.
"	24		In Reserve Billets & Pots. Working parties day and night. Church Parade in morning. Capt. BENNETT returned from leave. Casualties Nil.	R.F.J.
"	25		In Reserve Billets & Pots. Working parties as above. Major BEAMAN returned to Batn. from 2/4 R. Berks. Casualties Nil.	R.F.J.
"	26		In Reserve Billets & Pots. Working parties as above. Casualties Nil.	R.F.J.

WAR DIARY or INTELLIGENCE SUMMARY

Army Form C. 2118

Place	Date 1916	Hour	Summary of Events and Information	Remarks and references to Appendices
RIEZ BAILLEUL	July 27		In Reserve Billets & Posts. Lt. Col. R. BELLAMY proceeded to England on leave. At 12 noon Batt'n marched to relieve 2/1 R.Berks in left subsection of MOATED GRANGE Section. Relief complete by 3 p.m. Distribution C. Coy. on Right, A Coy. Centre, B on Left. D in Posts. Casualties NIL.	W.J.
MOATED GRANGE	28		In Trenches & Front Line Posts. Patrols sent out from Companies in front line. Wiring carried out by all Companies in Line. Rifle Grenades were freely fired, with but slight retaliation. Casualties O.R. killed 1.	W.J.
"	29		In Trenches & Front Line Posts. Patrolling and Wiring carried out as usual. Slight hostile bombardment in morning. Casualties 2/Lt C.B. HUNT and 2/Lt T.W.P. HAWKE's joined for duty and were posted to D and C Companies respectively. Casualties NIL.	W.J.
"	30		In Trenches & Front Line Posts. Patrolling and Wiring as usual. Slight Fighting Patrol. Day in night for German Patrol but none came. Casualties, O.R. Wounded 1.	W.J.

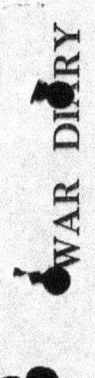

1/10/16.

G.P.P. Brannan Major
Commanding 2/4th Oxford & Bucks L.I.

APPENDIX D

4 Oxfords.	184 M.G.C.	5 Cornwalls.
4 Royal Berks.	184 L.T.M.B.	
5 Glosters.	2 Fld Coy.	
2 Bucks R.	3 Fld Coy.	

The following letter from Divisional Headquarters is forwarded for your information.

"The G.O.C. is very pleased with the report on work done in the FAUQUISSART Section, 9th August to September 3rd. He considers it reflects great credit on all concerned. The result is apparent."

E. Gepp Major.
Brigade Major.
184th Infantry Brigade

5.9.16.

APPENDIX E

SECRET.   XIth Corps.
                                       R.H.S.676/82.

61st Division.
─────────────

    The following correspondence between 1st Army and G.H.Q
is forwarded with reference to your C.4/6(1) of 22nd August 1916,
reporting on raid carried out by 184th Inf Bde on the night 19th/
20th August.

                        (1).

    To Adv G.H.Q.

"   This was a well organised raid, prepared throughout on sound
"   lines. Its success id encouraging. I should like to call
"   particular attention to the great care displayed by the
"   responsible officers in arranging all the details. I think
"   that the fighting efficiency of both battalions who that had
"   companies engaged will be greatly improved by the operation.

                                    (sd) R.HAKING, General
    25.8.16.   commanding 1st Army.
                        (2)   G.H.Q.No. O.B. N/8813.

"   To First Army (thro M.S.)

"   The Commander in Chief has noted this favourable report
"   with satisfaction.

                                    (sd) L.E.KIGGELL-C.G.S.
    5th Sept 1916.

                    ─────────────

    XIth Corps.   W.H.ANDERSON
    14.9.16.   B.G.,G.S.,

                        2.

    4 Oxfords.
    5 Glosters.
    ──────────

                For information. The Brigadier General wishes
    to congratulate Lt Colonel P. Bellamy & the 4/Oxfords on the
    good work done.

                        E.C. Gepp, Major.
    15.9.16.   Brigade Major.
                                    184th Infantry Brigade.

C-O-N-F-I-D-E-N-T-I-A-L.

War Diary

of

2/4th Battalion Oxfordshire & Buckinghamshire Light Infantry.

1st October, 1916 to 31st October, 1916.

(Volume VI).

Army Form C. 2118

WAR DIARY or INTELLIGENCE SUMMARY
(Erase heading not required.)

Place	Date 1916	Hour	Summary of Events and Information	Remarks and references to Appendices
MOATED GRANGE	Oct. 1st		In Trenches and Frontline Posts — Wiring carried out. Evening quiet. Casualties OR 1 wounded	C.S.W.M.
"	2nd		In Trenches and Frontline Posts. Good deal of rain during day. Patrols out at night. Wiring continued. Casualties Nil.	C.S.W.M
"	3rd		In Trenches and Frontline Posts. Battalion relieved by 2/4 R.BERKS 3.0 P.M. and marched to Billets at RIEZ BAILLEUL. Casualties Nil	C.S.W.M
RIEZ BAILLEUL	4th		In Billets (Res) & Posts — Working Parties found by men killed at RMT Du HEM; Companies carried out parties; attention being paid to cleaning of equipment and clothes in morning. Men bathed. Cos (Commanding Officers?) Casualties Nil	C.S.W.M
"	5th		In Res. Billets & Posts — Companies received in Route March, Bayonet Fighting etc. Demonstration in wiring by Capt WHITWELL R.E.- classes of instruction in Bombing LEWIS guns & Signalling carried on. Casualties Nil.	C.S.W.M
"	6th		In Res. Billets & Posts Companies continued Training. Demonstration in wiring. Casualties — O.R. 1 wounded (Died of wounds 7.10.16)	C.S.W.M
"	7th		In Res. Billets & Posts — Training continued. LT-Col Bellamy DSO returned from leave proceeding direct on course at BOULOGNE. Casualties Nil	C.S.W.M
"	8th		In Res. Billets & Posts — Church Parade in morning. Casualties Nil	C.S.W.M
"	9th		In Res. Billets & Posts at 12 noon Battn. marched to relieve 2/4 R.Berks in MOATED GRANGE Section. Relief complete by 3 P.M. Left 1 Subsection MOATED GRANGE. Distribution D.Coy 2 right A subsection Right C.in Posts. Crest 1 Casualties OR wounded 1 (Died 11.10.16)	C.S.W.M

1875 Wt. W593/826 1,000,000 4/15 J.B.C. & A. A.D.S.S./Forms/C. 2118.

Army Form C. 2118

WAR DIARY
or
INTELLIGENCE SUMMARY
(Erase heading not required.)

Place	Date 1916	Hour	Summary of Events and Information	Remarks and references to Appendices
MOATED GRANGE	Oct. 10th		In Trenches and Front Line Posts. Wiring carried out by all Companies. Night very quiet. Casualties NIL	CWM
"	11th		In Trenches & front line Posts. L.T.M.Bs fired morning and afternoon — little retaliation. Raid by 2/4 BERKS postponed, at last moment — Casualties ML	CWM
"	12th		In Trenches & front line Posts. Wiring by all Coys — especially good work by Right Coy. Casualties OR. 3 wounded.	CWM
"	13th		In Trenches & front line Posts. Demonstration at DDE of Box Respirator, attended by representatives of all Coys. Wiring continued. Night very quiet. Casualties OR. 1. wounded.	CWM
"	14th		In Trenches & front line Posts. Centre Coy turned HQRS back to BLASS Hn. w R.BERKS. 2 A.M.— Successful Raid by 2/4 R.BERKS. 2 T.M.s were out of action. Support line. Little hostile shelling. Casualties NIL	CWM
"	15th		In Trenches & front line Posts. Battalion relieved 3 P.M. by 2/4 R.BERKS, and marched to billets in RIEZ BAILLEUL. C. Coy remained for another day. Men billeted in PONT DU HEM to provide all working parties. Casualties NIL	CWM

135

WAR DIARY or INTELLIGENCE SUMMARY

Army Form C. 2118

(Erase heading not required.)

Place	Date 1916	Hour	Summary of Events and Information	Remarks and references to Appendices
RIEZ BAILLEUL	Oct 16.		In Res. Billets & Posts. Equipment & clothes of men attended to, in morning. Training carried on in afternoon. Lewis Gun class started. "C" Coy relieved in morning from front line Post. Demonstration in co-operation between Infantry & aeroplane by Brigade Signals. Lt-Col BELLAMY DSO returned to Battalion. Casualties OR 1 wounded. MAJOR BEAMAN, Capt CUTHBERT proceed on leave.	CSUM
	Oct 17th		In Res. Billets & Posts. Training continued under Coy arrangements. Casualties NIL	CSUM
	Oct 18th		In Res. Billets & Posts. Training continued. Capt DAVENPORT proceeds on leave. Casualties OR 1 wounded.	CSUM
	19th		In Res. Billets & Posts. Inspection by GOC 184 Brigade in morning. Casualties NIL	CSUM
	20th		In Res. Billets & Posts. Training continued. Battalion Route march in morning	CSUM
	21st		In Res. Billets & Posts. Battalion relieved 2/4 R. BERKS in left subsector MOATED GRANGE. Relief complete 3 P.M. 2/Lt COOMBES to Hospital. Casualties OR 1 wounded. 2/Lt BENSON (attached MTB) wounded.	CSUM
MOATED GRANGE	22nd		In Trenches & Front Line Posts. L.T.M's laid in morning little. Practically no reply except for a few 10 pdrs on left Coy front. 2 Lt BROWN proceeds on leave. Casualties NIL C(right) D.B. Coys in frontline, A posts indicated.	AWM
	23rd		In Trenches & Frontline Posts. Y quiet position still retained. Many dove in himself by all Coys. Quiet day - Nothing to report	CSUM

WAR DIARY
or
INTELLIGENCE SUMMARY
(Erase heading not required.)

Army Form C. 2118

Place	Date 1916	Hour	Summary of Events and Information	Remarks and references to Appendices
MOATED GRANGE	Oct 24th		In Trenches of front line Posts - Gas alert withdrawn. Dummy screen erected by C Coy near RUE TILLELOY to draw enemy's fire: result Nil. Firing at Battn. Coy at night. Casualties Nil.	C.8.S.M.
"	25th		In Trenches of front line Posts - Gas alert ordered in the night. withdrawn during the day. Wiring generally at night. L.T.M.B. shoot being used principally as retaliation. 6/16 India order Troops; cup attachments from No mans Land on enemy wire & putting, in cooperation with a Lewis gun. Casualties Nil	C.O.S.M.
"	26		In Trenches of front line Posts - Officers of 8th MIDDLESEX reconnoitre Trenches. Wiring & patrolling carried out at night. Casualties O.R. 2 wounded (attd. L.T.M.B)	C.S.O.M.
"	27th		In Trenches of front line Posts - One officer per Coy. Specialists of 8TH MIDDLESEX come up to line to stay 24 hours. MAJ. BEAMAN, CAPT CUTHBERT, 2/Lt COOMBES return to Battalion. Casualties NIL.	C.O.S.M.
"	28.		In Trenches of front line Posts. Battalion relieved by 8TH MIDDLESEX REGT. Relief complete 5 P.M. Every guide a front line Battalion marches to billets in RIEZ BAILLEUL. Causing casualties! Casualties Nil.	C.O.S.M.
RIEZ BAILLEUL	29th		In Rue Billets. Battalion marches from RIEZ BAILLEUL goes to billets at ROBECQ - which marched 3 P.M. after a start at 9. A.M. - Casualties NIL	C.O.S.M.
ROBECQ	30th		In Coys Rest Billets - Morning spent in cleaning up, receiving feldetter etc. Casualties NIL	C.O.S.M.
"	31st		In Coys Rest Billets - Training in morning. Special church service Gunners, he work after. Casualties NIL	C.O.S.M.

Lt Col DAVENPORT returned to Battalion in 30th
R. Williamson Lt Col. 2/4 R Fusiliers

Vol 7

WAR DIARY

OF

2/4th Bn. Oxfordshire and Buckinghamshire Light Infantry

From 1st November, 1916 to 30th November, 1916

(Vol.711)

WAR DIARY
or
INTELLIGENCE SUMMARY.

(Erase heading not required.)

Army Form C. 2118.

Place	Date	Hour	Summary of Events and Information	Remarks and references to Appendices
ROBECQ	1st		In Corps Rest Billets. Training in morning. No work in afternoon. Casualties NIL.	N.F.
"	2nd		" Battalion marched from ROBECQ to AUCHEL, starting at 8.10 A.M. & reached billets in AUCHEL at 1.30 P.M. Casualties NIL.	N.F.
AUCHEL	3rd		Battalion marched from AUCHEL to MAGNICOURT-EN-COMTE, starting at 9.25 A.M. & reached billets at MAGNICOURT at 2 P.M. Casualties NIL	N.F.
MAGNICOURT	4th		Battalion marched from MAGNICOURT-EN-COMTE to TINQUES, starting at 11.0 A.M. & reached TINQUES at 1 P.M. Casualties NIL.	N.F.
TINQUES	5th		Battalion marched from TINQUES to ETREE-WAMIN, starting at 7.15 A.M. & reached ETREE-WAMIN at 2.0 P.M. Casualties NIL.	N.F.
ETREE-WAMIN	6th		Battalion marched from ETREE-WAMIN to NEUVILLETTE, starting at 9 A.M. & reached NEUVILLETTE at 1.30 P.M. Draft of 100 O.R. joined for duty.	N.F.
NEUVILLETTE	7th		Companies handed for re-fitting, equipping &c, in morning. Platoon drill & Bayonet fighting in afternoon. 2 men for duty continued to G. Cross. Casualties NIL.	N.F.
"	8th		Firing carried out for both rifles & Lewis Guns.	N.F.
"	8th		General training throughout the day. Firing continued. Casualties NIL	N.F.
"	9th		Party of R.E's gave instruction in extension for working Parties. 12 Offrs. 32 N.C.Os. + 48 men attended. Firing continued. Casualties NIL.	N.F.
"	10th		Battalion handed for practice in the attack. Moved off at 9.30 A.M & returned to billets at 4 P.M. Military Medal awarded to No.958 4C.T.A.ROWBOTHAM. Draft of 5 O.R. joined. Casualties NIL.	N.F.

Army Form C. 2118.

WAR DIARY
or
INTELLIGENCE SUMMARY.
(Erase heading not required.)

Instructions regarding War Diaries and Intelligence Summaries are contained in F. S. Regs., Part II. and the Staff Manual respectively. Title pages will be prepared in manuscript.

Place	Date	Hour	Summary of Events and Information	Remarks and references to Appendices
NEUVILLETTE	11th		In Corps Reset Billets. Battalion practised in wave attack. Paraded at 7.45 A.M. + returned to Billets for dinner at 1 P.M. No parade in afternoon. Casualties NIL.	NA
"	12th		Divine Service in morning. Regimental baths available. Reman's tailors in morning. improvising pack saddlery for Company Commanders. Casualties NIL.	NA
"	13th		Physical training 7 to 7.30 A.M. Practice in cover in + shelter in fire position, working through woods + maintaining communication, firing, +c. All Companies paraded at 5 P.M. for practice in the extension of working parties. 2/Lt. R.AITKEN joined for duty. Casualties NIL.	NA
"	14th		Moving parades as yesterday. "B" Coy filled in trenches in afternoon. Casualties NIL.	NA
"	15th		Special training for all Coys in morning. New L.G. Bns. commenced. Casualties NIL.	NA
"	16th		Battalion marched to billets at BONNEVILLE. Moved off at 10 A.M. + arrived at BONNEVILLE at 3.45 P.M. Dinner en route. Casualties NIL.	NA
BONNEVILLE	17th		Battalion marched to Huttments in CONTAY AREA. Moved off at 8.5 A.M. + arrived in Huts at 3. P.M. Casualties NIL.	NA
CONTAY	18th		Battalion found working party of 500 O.R. for work at ALBERT. Also B.E. of 400 R. for work in M.49. G.C.S. Medical Officer proceeded on leave. CAPT STOBIE joined unit temporarily. Casualties NIL.	NA

WAR DIARY
or
INTELLIGENCE SUMMARY

(Erase heading not required.)

Army Form C. 2118.

Instructions regarding War Diaries and Intelligence Summaries are contained in F.S. Regs., Part II. and the Staff Manual respectively. Title Pages will be prepared in manuscript.

Place	Date	Hour	Summary of Events and Information	Remarks and references to Appendices
PONTAY AREA	19th		Battalion marched to billets in ALBERT, arriving in ALBERT at 11.45 A.M. Casualties NIL.	N.A.
ALBERT	20th		Battalion in billets, moving off at 8.10AM & arriving in ALBERT. 2/Lts H.JONES, E.S.FOLD, O.K.HATHORN, & T.A.COFFIN joined for duty. Casualties NIL.	N.A.
"	21st		Battalion less C & D Coys marched to Tarakan, H.Q. & B Coy. to FABICK Trench. A Coy to MOUQUET FARM. C & D Coys to huttments at OVILLERS. Lt C.S.W. MARCON + 7 O.R. proceeded on leave. Casualties NIL.	N.A.
FABICK TRENCH	22nd		In line. Working parties found. Casualties NIL.	N.A.
"	23rd		Working parties found. Battalion Hdqrs moved into huttments at OVILLERS at 9 P.M. Casualties NIL.	N.A.
"	24th		Working parties found. A & B Coys joined battalion in huttments at 7 P.M. Casualties NIL.	N.A.
OVILLERS	25th		In huttments. Working parties found. Battalion moved into WELLINGTON huts in evening. Casualties 1 O.R. killed.	N.A.
"	26th		In front line Trenches. Relieved R. Bn in MOUQUET L Sector Trenches. Relief complete at 11.40 pm. Distribution A & B Coys and Batt H.Q. in HESSIAN TRENCH, C & D Coys in REGINA Trench with 2 platoons of D in DESIRE & ZOLLERN Gum in front with 2 in reserve. Patrols out and about STUMP ROAD and along left of DESIRE. Casualties O.R. wounded 1.	N.A.

Army Form C. 2118.

WAR DIARY
or
INTELLIGENCE SUMMARY
(Erase heading not required.)

Instructions regarding War Diaries and Intelligence Summaries are contained in F. S. Regs., Part II. and the Staff Manual respectively. Title Pages will be prepared in manuscript.

Place	Date	Hour	Summary of Events and Information	Remarks and references to Appendices
MOUQUET FARM	27		In front line Trenches. Fairly heavy shelling on both sides all day and night. The work of Communicating Trenches in front of REGINA was commenced, and the whole of clearing up trenches, burying dead, was carried on. Patrols from 2 front companies sent out. Nil. Casualties Nil.	N.A.
"	28		In front line Trenches. Work continued as above and troops in Post established in front of right companys lines. Artillery active on both sides. Patrols as above. Casualties Nil.	N.A.
"	29		In front line Trenches. Work continued as above. Strong points constructed in front of REGINA. Patrols as above. Enemy put a barrage on our front (right) at 4.30 p.m. which our own artillery stopped by 5.25. Casualties, O.R. killed 1, wounded 2. (1 accidental).	N.A.
"	30		In front line Trenches. Work continued as above. Batt: was relieved by 4" Gloucesters at 10 p.m. and marched to bivouacs at MARTINSART. Casualties Nil.	N.A.

30/11/16

[signature]
Lt Col.
Commanding 2/4" Oxford & Bucks L.I.

CONFIDENTIAL.

War Diary
of
2/4th Battalion Oxfordshire & Buckinghamshire Light Infantry.

1st December, 1916 to 31st December, 1916.

(Volume VIII).

Army Form C. 2118

WAR DIARY
or
INTELLIGENCE SUMMARY
(Erase heading not required.)

Instructions regarding War Diaries and Intelligence Summaries are contained in F.S. Regs., Part II. and the Staff Manual respectively. Title Pages will be prepared in manuscript.

Place	Date	Hour	Summary of Events and Information	Remarks and references to Appendices
MARTINSART	DEC 1	In support Hutments	Arrival of Battn. at Martinsart Wood at 2 a.m. Casualties Nil	N.T.R.
HEDAUVILLE	2	—	Battn. marched to billets at HEDAUVILLE, moving off 10.30 am arriving HEDAUVILLE 2 pm. Casualties Nil	N.T.R.
	3	In reserve billets	All Coys at disposal of their Commanders for cleaning Kit, equipment, etc. Battn. parade for Divine Service 3 pm. Casualties Nil	N.T.R.
	4	—	Battn. practised in wave attack. Paraded 8.30 am & returned to billets for dinner 1 pm. No parade afternoon. Casualties Nil	N.T.R.
	5	—	All Coys exercised in Physical Training, Bayonet fighting, Musketry, Night patrolling, etc. Special class commenced in Bombing under Lieut. C.R. Parsons. Casualties Nil	N.T.R.
	6	—	Training as above continued. Parade 9 am to 1 pm. Casualties Nil	N.T.R.
	7	—	do	N.T.R.

WAR DIARY or INTELLIGENCE SUMMARY

Army Form C. 2118

Place	Date	Hour	Summary of Events and Information	Remarks and references to Appendices
HEDAUVILLE	8		In reserve billets. Training by all Coys continued (as before) Casualties Nil	N.F.
	9		Training continued. Battn. found working party of 50 O.R. for work under 9th Labour Battn. Casualties 1 O.R. wounded (accidentally) one.	N.F.
	10		Battn. paraded 9.30 am for Kit Inspection. Battn Parade drill with Box Respirators. Battn. Parade for Divine Service at 11.30 am. Casualties O.R. Wounded one	N.F.
	11		Coys paraded 9am to 1pm for Physical Training, Bayonet fighting etc. A Court of Enquiry assembled at Battn. H.Q. 10am President Captn. L.H. R Davenport. C.O.i Conference at H.Q. meet with O/C Coys at 12 noon. Bombing Competition held 2:30 pm. Casualties Nil	N.F.
MARTINSART	12		In support Hutments. Battn. found working parties of 100 O.R. Battn. marched to MARTINSART WOOD HUTS – moved off at 2pm arrived in Hutments at 3.30p – 2pt HUNT left behind to settle claims for damages etc. Casualties Nil	N.F.

Army Form C. 2118

WAR DIARY
or
INTELLIGENCE SUMMARY
(Erase heading not required.)

Instructions regarding War Diaries and Intelligence Summaries are contained in F. S. Regs., Part II. and the Staff Manual respectively. Title Pages will be prepared in manuscript.

Place	Date	Hour	Summary of Events and Information	Remarks and references to Appendices
MARTINSART	13		In support trenches. Working parties found by Battn.	171.
	14		do	171.
	15		do	171.
	16		do	171.
	17		do	171.
	18		do. At Staff Captains Office at 10am. 2/Lt Taylor attended for Instruction.	171.
	19		Working parties found by Battn. F.G.C.M. assembled. Member Captn H.N Davenport	171.

WAR DIARY
or
INTELLIGENCE SUMMARY
(Erase heading not required.)

Army Form C. 2118

Place	Date	Hour	Summary of Events and Information	Remarks and references to Appendices
	20		In line. Battn. less A B & H Coys. attached to Frencher, C & D Coys relieving 2 Coys of 5 Warwicks - 2 Platoons D Coys to MOUQUET FARM. A.B.S. H.Q. Coys covered in Wellington Huts.	P.J.
	21		Working parties found by A & B Coys. Casualties O.R. Killed 1 Wounded 1.	C P.J.
	22		Working parties found by A & B Coys. Casualties O.R. Wounded 2.	P.J.
	23		— do — Casualties NIL.	P.J. appendix G. B.
MOUQUET FARM	24		In front line trenches. Relieved 4 R Berks at 9 pm. Distribution, A Coy right front, B left front, C left rear D right rear. Patrols went out from each front Company carried on the wiring of front line. Snipers continued post in advance of front line Casualties NIL	P.J.

WAR DIARY
or
INTELLIGENCE SUMMARY

Army Form C. 2118

Place	Date	Hour	Summary of Events and Information	Remarks and references to Appendices
MOUQUET FARM	25		In front line Trenches. Our artillery periodically shelled enemy this on Enemy. We captured a prisoner who wandered in to our lines at 10.30 am. Patrols and wiring as before. Casualties NIL.	W.J.
	26		Patrols and wiring as above. A German Patrol was engaged by our snipers with result that one prisoner was captured. Casualties O.R. wounded one.	W.J.
	27		Patrols and wiring as above. A fighting patrol under LT. BROWN M.C. went out to examine and if necessary clean trench in advance of enemy this evident then unoccupied patrol proceeded to within sight of GRANDCOURT TRENCH. Casualties NIL.	W.J.
	28		A German patrol was engaged by one of our front posts, and L/Cpl STURGESS and 3 O.R. went out and captured 3 German prisoners. Battn was relieved by 2/6 Gloucesters. Casualties O.R. wounded one.	W.J.

1875 Wt. W593/826 1,000,000 4/15 J.B.C. & A. A.D.S.S./Forms/C. 2118.

Army Form C. 2118

WAR DIARY
or
INTELLIGENCE SUMMARY
(Erase heading not required.)

Place	Date	Hour	Summary of Events and Information	Remarks and references to Appendices
MOUQUET FARM	29		In Front line Trench. Relief commenced last night was completed at 1:45 a.m. and Battⁿ marched to support hutments near MARTINSART. Casualties NIL.	Appendix to R.S.F.
MARTINSART	30		In Support hutments. Battⁿ marched to Reserve billets at HEDAUVILLE, arriving at 12.30 p.m. A draft of 102 O.R. arrived. Casualties NIL.	Appendix to R.S.F.
"	31		In Reserve hutments. Companies at disposal of their Commanders for cleaning and refitting. Casualties NIL.	

F. D. Newey
Lt. Col.
Commᵈᵍ 2/4 OXFORD & BUCKS L.I.

War Diary appendix C.

ORDERS NO. 131   Lt.Col. R. BELLAMY, D.S.O.
                                                  23rd December 1916

1. The Battalion will relieve the 4th R.BERKS in the line tomorrow.

2. The following will be the dispositions of Companies and they will relieve in the order named.
   Right Front Company   —   A Coy.
   Left Front Company   —   B Coy.
   Right Rear Company   —   D Coy.
   Left Rear Company   —   C Coy.
   Guides from the 4th R.BERKS will meet Companies as above at GRAVEL PIT at 4.30, 5.0, 5.30, and 6 p.m. respectively. Guides for Signallers at 12 noon.

3. Blankets, Great Coats in sacks, Valises and Mess Boxes will be stacked in the Storage hut (under the supervision of 2/Lt. MARTYN) by 2 p.m. A batman from each Company will be left in charge.

4. Gum boots will be drawn from Crucifix Corner in the course of the morning, and carried up to the trenches slung.

5. Feet will be oiled in the morning. A certificate will be sent in that this has been done in the case of every man and also that each man is in possession of a tin of oil. Whilst in the line a certificate will be sent every 24 hours that each man has had his feet rubbed daily, and has put on a pair of dry socks.

6. C and D Companies will each detail 1 Corporal, 1 L/Corporal, and 10 men for the carrying party. These men will report to the R.S.M. at the Gravel Pit at 12 noon.

7. Hot food will be served to every man daily, and a report sent in every 24 hours as to the condition in which food reaches the line.

8. In addition to above, the following reports will be sent in and the times given being those by which they reach Battalion H.Qrs.
   Situation Report   —   9 a.m. and 3 p.m.
   T.M. Report   —   9 a.m.
   Casualty Report   —   10 a.m.
   Situation and Casualty Reports may be wired, provided that the regulations regarding sending messages by wire are complied with.

9. Snipers will join their Companies. Those of C and D Companies will meet their Companies at the GRAVEL PIT at 5 p.m. and 5.45 p.m. respectively.

10. The unconsumed portion of the days rations will be carried by the men, water bottles must be filled before leaving the huts.

11. Relief complete will be reported by wire, the code being "BACK RECEIVED".

12. Disposition sketches will be sent to Battalion Hdqrs by 10 p.m. C and D Coys will each send a Lewis Gun and complete team to A. They will report to O.C. A Coy at GRAVEL PIT at 4.30 p.m.

13. Battalion H.Qrs will close at BLIGHTY HUTS at 4 p.m. and open at ZOLLERN REDOUBT at 6 p.m.

                                               (sd) R.F.CUTHBERT
Battalion Headquarters.   Captain and Adjutant.
Issued at 9.15 p.m.   6 OXFORDS

Copy No. 1 – 3   Battalion Hdqrs   Copy No. 10   O.C. D Coy
         4   184th Inf Bde   11   Quartermaster
         5   4th R.BERKS   12   Transport Officer
         6   War Diary   13   Medical Officer
         7   O.C. A Coy   14   Lewis Gun Officer
         8   O.C. B Coy   15   Signalling Ofcr
         9   O.C. C Coy   16   Sniping Officer
                                                17
                         M.G.   R.S.M.

SECRET   2/4 OXFORD & BUCKS L.I.   COPY NO. 1
ORDER NO. 52

1. The Battalion will be relieved by the 2/6th GLOUCESTER REGT on 28th December 1916.

2. Guides from all Platoons will meet Platoons of the Incoming Unit at GRAVEL PIT at the following times, and Companies will be relieved in the order named:-
   A, Right Front,   4.30 pm.
   B, Left   "   5.0   "
   D Right Rear   5.30 "
   C Left   "   6.0   "
A guide for the Incoming H.Q'rs will be at GRAVEL PIT at 5 pm.

3. Completion of Relief will be notified by wire, the code being "PLUM PUDDINGS ARRIVED."

4. On completion of relief, all Companies will march independently to Huts at W.9.d.5.5. A halt will be made at CRUCIFIX CORNER where GUM BOOTS will be handed in and tea or soup served. O.C. Companies will

ensure that every man carries his GUM BOOTS out of the line.

5. In the event of any outgoing Platoon meeting an Incoming Platoon on the Duckboards, they will stand clear, and allow the latter to pass.

6. Sick men, or men with bad feet will be sent down early to report to M.O. at GRAVEL PIT. They will be collected and despatched by 2 p.m. to the HUTS. Care must be taken that they go in parties of not more than five, N of the THIEPVAL - POZIERES road, at intervals of not less than 150 yards.

7. A N.C.O. from each Company will report to Capt H.J. BENNETT at GRAVEL PIT at 9 a.m. This party will proceed to the new huts for taking over.

8. Separate orders have been issued to Signallers.

3

9. North of the THIEPVAL – POZIERES road an interval of 150 – 200 yards will be kept between platoons.

10. Receipts for Trench Stores will be sent in duplicate to Batt. H.Q. as early as possible. It will facilitate the handing over for all stores such as Petrol Tins, food containers and other articles usually kept at GRAVEL PIT, to be sent there as soon as possible.

11. Limbers will be at the usual place on NAB ROAD for carrying Lewis Guns and STORES.

12. The R.S.M. will be responsible for ~~obtaining~~ assembling the Guides and allotting them to incoming Companies.

13. Batt. Headquarters will move on completion of Relief to W.9.d.5.5.

Batt. H.Q.
Issued at 10 p.m.
27th Decr 1916

Robert F. Jutters
Capt. - or/jt
40xxxxxxx

Copy No. 1. H.Q. + War diary
       2. 184 Brigade
      3-6. O/C Companies
       7. Capt Bennett & M.O
       8. Transport Officer
       9. Lewis Gun Sergeant

SECRET 2/4th Oxford and Bucks Light Infantry COPY NO. 4

ORDER NO. 153   BY   LT.COL. R.BELLAMY, D.S.O.
30th December, 1916.

1. The Battalion will move tomorrow in accordance with Table A, March Table, at foot.

2. Companies will move in the order H.Q. C, D, A, B. Distances of 200x will be maintained between Companies. Quarter hour halts at 15 minutes to clock hour.

3. Lewis Guns under 2/LT. TAYLOR will move one hour in advance of the Battalion. Details for this move will be arranged by 2/LT. TAYLOR in conjunction with the Lewis Gun Sergeant.

4. A N.C.O. from each Company (including H.Q.) will report to CAPT. H.J. BENNETT outside the Chateau at HEDAUVILLE at 10 a.m.

5. Breakfasts will be served at 7 a.m. punctually. Blankets will be ready by that hour and will be carried down and loaded on the G.S.Wagons as soon as the latter arrive. Valises and Mess Boxes will be ready by 8 a.m.

6. Tools, Bombs and Ammunition will be exchanged with 182nd Bde., and receipts given and taken. Lewis Gun Ammunition will not be exchanged. A Guard will be posted by the R.S.M. over the Battn. Ammunition and Tools until the Incoming Unit arrives.

7. Dinners will be served on arrival in Billets.

8. Battalion Headquarters will close at W.9.d.5.5. at 9 a.m. and open at HEDAUVILLE at 12 noon.

(sd) R.F.CUTHBERT,
Captain and Adjutant
4 OXFORDS.

Battalion Headquarters
Issued as 6.15.p.m.

Table A, March table issued with above order

Starting Point	Time	Route	To
W.9.d.5.5.	9.20 a.m.	ENGLEBELMER	HEDAUVILLE

Copy No. 1 – 3   Battalion Headquarters
        4   War Diary
        5   184th Bde.
     6 – 9   O's C. Companies
       10   Transport Officer
       11   Medical Officer
       12   Quartermaster
       13   Signalling Officer
       14   Lewis Gun Officer
       15   R.S.M.

CONFIDENTIAL.

War Diary
of
2/4th Battalion Oxfordshire and Buckinghamshire Light Infantry.

1st January, 1917 to 31st January, 1917.

(Volume IX).

WAR DIARY or INTELLIGENCE SUMMARY

Army Form C. 2118

(Erase heading not required.)

Instructions regarding War Diaries and Intelligence Summaries are contained in F.S. Regs., Part II. and the Staff Manual respectively. Title Pages will be prepared in manuscript.

Place	Date 1917	Hour	Summary of Events and Information	Remarks and references to Appendices
HEDAUVILLE	Jan 1		In active billets. Company training, and classes for specialists formed. Casualties NIL.	N.f.
"	2		Training continued as above. Casualties NIL.	N.f.
"	3		Do. Do. Do.	N.f.
"	4		Do. Do. Do. Lt. Col. BELLAMY proceeded on leave. Capt. H.N. DAVENPORT assumed command of the Batt. Christian burns for Batt. Casualties NIL.	N.f.
"	5		Training continued as above. Casualties NIL.	N.f.
"	6		Do. Do. Do.	N.f.
"	7		Do. Do. Do.	N.f.
"	8		Batt. marched to support trenches near MARTINSART. Casualties NIL.	Appendix
MARTINSART	9		In support trenches. Worked parties in forward area formed day and night. Casualties NIL.	N.f.
"	10		Do. Do. as above. Casualties NIL.	N.f.
"	11		Do. Do. Do.	N.f.
"	12		Do. Do. Do.	N.f.
"	13		Do. Do. Brig. RUTHVEN arrived and Lt. Col. BELLAMY. Command is returned to Lt. Col. BELLAMY. Casualties NIL.	N.f.

WAR DIARY
or
INTELLIGENCE SUMMARY

(Erase heading not required.)

Army Form C. 2118

Place	Date 1917	Hour	Summary of Events and Information	Remarks and references to Appendices
MARTINSART	Jan 14		In support huts & inlets. Working parties in tunnel aux. day and night. Casualties Nil.	R.F.
"	15		" Batt" moved to billets at PUCHEVILLERS.	appendix L ref.
PUCHEVILLERS	16		In Billets. Batt" moved to billets at PUCHEVILLERS. Casualties Nil.	N.F.
"	17		" Cleaning up and refitting. Remainder of day available for rest.	appendix M. R.F.
LONGUEVILLETTE	18		" Batt" marched to billets at LONGUEVILLETTE. Casualties Nil.	appendix N R.F.
DOMQUEUR	19		" Batt" marched to billets at DOM QUEUR. Casualties Nil.	appendix O R.F.
MAISON PONTHIEUX	20		In Rest Billets. Batt" marched to billets at MAISON PONTHIEUX. Lt Col BELLAMY rejoined from leave. Casualties Nil.	R.F.
"	21		" Cleaning up and refitting. Casualties Nil.	R.F.
"	22		" do	R.F.
"	23		" do	R.F.
"	24		" Platoon training and sectional training	R.F.
"	25		" do	R.F.
			do Capt C. Cuthbert proceeded on leave.	N.F.

Army Form C. 2118

WAR DIARY
or
INTELLIGENCE SUMMARY
(Erase heading not required.)

Place	Date	Hour	Summary of Events and Information	Remarks and references to Appendice
MAISON PONTHEVIL	JAN. 1917 26th		In Rest Billets Platoon training in morning, recreational training in afternoon	C.S.W.M.
"	27th		Practice platoon attack — Platoon recreational training.	C.S.W.M.
"	28th		Medical inspection. Church parade. Recreational training in afternoon	C.S.W.M.
"	29th		Platoon & Company Training. Recreational training, Night work.	C.S.W.M.
"	30th		Platoon practice attacks & training.	" C.S.W.M.
"	31st		Coy. attack practice & training. Recreational training in afternoon. Nightwork.	C.S.W.M.

[signature] Lt. Col.
Commanding 2/4 Oxford & Bucks
L.I.

Appendix K.

SECRET.
COPY NO. 4

2/4TH OXFORD AND BUCKS LIGHT INFANTRY.
ORDER NO. 163.
7/1/17.

1. The Battalion will move tomorrow as per Table "A", March Table at foot.

2. Companies will move in the order D,A,B,C. Cookers and pack ponies in rear of Companies. Remainder of Transport in rear of Battalion. Distances of 200X will be maintained between Coys.

3. Blankets will be rolled by 7-30 A.M. Mess boxes and Valises ready by 8-15 A.M.

4. Halts will be made at 15 minutes to clock hour, and the march resumed at the clock hour.

5. The Lewis Guns, under 2/Lt. MATTHEWS, will move one hour in advance of the Battalion. 2/Lt. MATTHEWS will arrange for the necessary assistance in pushing the handcarts.

6. One N.C.O. from each Coy. (including H.Q.) will report to Lieut. MARCON outside Brigade H.Q. at 7-30 A.M. for billeting.

7. The leave party will report to Lt. BARTON at the huts at 9 A.M. They will hand over to the incoming Unit and be responsible for the cleanliness of the Camp. They will also find a guard over the ammunition until taken to by the incoming Unit.

8. Ammunition, bombs, etc. will be exchanged as hitherto.

9. Q.M. Stores and Transport Lines at MARTINSART will be taken over from the 4TH GLOUCESTERS.

10. Battalion Headquarters will close at HEDAUVILLE at 9 A.M, after which reports to head of column.

(sd) R.F.CUTHBERT,
Captain and Adjutant,
4 OXFORDS.

Battalion Headquarters.
Issued at 2-30 P.M.

TABLE "A". March Table issued with above Order.

From.	To.	Starting Point.	Time.	Route.
HEDAUVILLE.	Huts at W.9.D.5.5.	X Roads at P.34.C.8.3.	9-25 A.M.	BOUZINCOURT - NORTHUMBERLAND AVENUE.

Copy No. 1 - 3. Battalion Headquarters.
4. War Diary.
5. 184th Infantry Brigade.
6 - 9. Os.C. Companies.
10. Quartermaster.
11. Transport Officer.
12. Medical Officer.
13. Lewis Gun Officer.
14. Signalling Officer.
15. Regimental Sergeant Major.

Appendix L.

COPY NO. 4

2/4TH BN. OXFORD AND BUCKS LIGHT INFANTRY.

14-4-17.

Ref. Map 57.D.   ORDER NO.
        40000

1.   The Battalion will march tomorrow as per Table A, March Table, at foot.

2.   A distance of 200x will be maintained between Coys. and between the rear Coy. and the Transport. Pack animals and cookers in rear of Coys.

3.   The Battalion will parade at 7-35 A.M. on road running S from the balloon, in the order H.Q.,A,B,C,D, in line, facing West.

4.   Blankets must be rolled tightly in tens, and be ready for loading by 6 A.M. Mess Boxes and valises by 6-30 A.M. It is of the greatest importance that these times are punctually observed.

5.   Halts will be made at 15 minutes to the clock hour and the march resumed at the clock hour.

6.   Haversack rations will be carried, and consumed during a half-hour halt from 11-45 A.M. to 12-15 P.M. Dinners on arrival in billets.

7.   Billet stores will be carefully checked and handed over to arrangements advance parties of the incoming Unit, proper receipts being taken.

8.   All secret maps, prepared by Division or Brigade, will be sent in to Orderly Room by 5 P.M. to-day.

9.   All huts (including Officers' Mess huts) will be inspected by an Officer from each Coy. half an hour before the time fixed for parade.

10. Battalion Headquarters will close at W.9.D.5.5. at 7-15 A.M., after which reports to head of Column.

                                    (sd) R.F.CUMBERLY
                                    Captain and Adjutant,
                                    4 OXFORDS.

Battalion Headquarters.
Issued at 2-30 P.M.

Table A, March Table, issued with above order.

FROM	TO	STARTING POINT.	TIME OF PASSING STARTING POINT.	ROUTE
Huts W.9.D.5.5.	PUCHEVILLERS	Road Junction W.3.D.4.2.	8 A.M.	NORTHUMBERLAND AVENUE — BOUZINCOURT — HEDAUVILLE — VARENNES — HARPONVILLE.

Copy No. 1 - 3. Battalion Headquarters.
         4.   War Diary.
         5.   184th Infantry Brigade.
         6 - 9. Os. C. Coys.
         10.   Quartermaster & Transport Officer.
         11.   Medical Officer.
         12.   Signalling Officer.
         13.   Lewis Gun Officer.
         14.   Regimental Sergeant Major.

SECRET   Appendix M.   Copy No. 4

2/4th Oxford & Bucks Light Infantry

Order No. 166

Ref. Map 1/100000 LENS   16-1-17.

1. The Battalion will march tomorrow as per TABLE 'A', March Table at foot.

2. Companies will move in the order H.Q., B, C, D, A. The Battalion will be closed up, but an interval of 200x will be maintained between the rear Company and the Transport. All Transport will be in rear of the Battalion in the normal order of march as laid down by Divisional Standing Orders.

3. Companies will be responsible for reaching their position at the starting point at 10-15 A.M.

4. All Blankets will be properly rolled and stacked at a central point in Company Areas by 8 A.M. Valises, mess boxes by 9 A.M.

5. All Companies will detail an Officer to inspect billets and ensure that they are left thoroughly clean.

6. Halts will be made at 15 minutes to the clock hour and the march resumed at the clock hour. Haversack rations will be carried and consumed at a halt from 1-15 P.M. to 2 P.M.
Dinners on arrival at Billets.

7. Separate orders have been issued to the billeting party.

8. Sick parade at 8-15 A.M.

9. Battalion Headquarters will close at PUCHEVILLERS at 9-30 A.M. after which reports to head of column.

(Sd.) R.F. CUTHBERT
Captain & Adjutant,
4 OXFORDS.

Battalion Headquarters,
Issued at 8-15 P.M.

Table A. March Table issued with above order

From	To	Starting Point	To	Route
PUCHEVILLERS	LONGUEVILLETTE	Road Junction 2000x W. of PUCHEVILLERS CHURCH	10-22 A.M.	VAL DE MAISON - FME DU ROSEL, BEAUVAL Road, then 300x S.W. STA. Road parallel to Railway, GEZINCOURT, S. Road to LONGUEVILLETTE

Copy No. 1-3   Battn. H.Q.
     4   War Diary
     5   184 Inf. Bde.
     6-9   O.C. Coys
     10   Quartermaster & Transport Officer
     11   Medical Officer
     12   Signalling Officer
     13   L.G. Officer
     14   R.S.M.

Secret.   Appendix N   Copy No. 4.
                 2/4 Oxford and Bucks Light Infantry
                         Order No. 164
Ref. Map Lens 1/100,000.   17/1/17

1. The Battalion will march tomorrow as per Table A, March Table, at foot.

2. Companies will move in the order H.Q, C, D, A, B. A distance of 200 yards will be maintained between Companies, and between the rear Company and the Transport.

3. Pack animals and Cookers will march in rear of Companies. Company Commanders will be responsible that Cookers keep up with Companies.

4. The Battalion will be formed up ready to move in the above order with head on 'B' Company's Headquarters by 8-45 A.M.

5. Blankets properly rolled to be dumped at a central point in Company Billeting area by 7-30 A.M. Valises and mess boxes by 8 A.M.

6. The usual quarter hour halts will be observed, and there will be a halt from 12-30 P.M. - 1-15 P.M. during which haversack rations will be consumed.

7. The Billeting party as detailed for to-day will hold themselves ready to move at 7 A.M. Further orders will be issued when particulars are received from Brigade.

8. Instructions for leave party will be given on arrival at new billets.

9. Battalion Headquarters will close at LONGUEVILLETTE at 8-30 A.M. after which reports to head of column.

                                          (sd.) R.F. CUTHBERT,
Battalion Headquarters.   Captain and Adjutant,
Issued at 11-30 P.M.   4 OXFORDS

        Table A, March Table, referred to in above order.

FROM	TO	Starting Point	Time	Route
LONGUEVILLETTE	DOMQUER	Cross Roads 1100x S. of O in LONGUEVILLETTE	9-17 A.M.	FIENVILLERS -BERNAVILLE -LONGVILLERS

    Copy No. 1-3   Battalion Headquarters
          4   War Diary
          5   184th Inf. Bde.
          6-9   Os. C. Coys.
          10.   Quartermaster & Transport Officer.
          11.   Medical Officer.
          12.   Signalling Officer.
          13.   R.S.M.

CONFIDENTIAL.

War Diary

of

2/4th Battalion Oxfordshire and Buckinghamshire Light Infantry.

1st February, 1917 to 28th February, 1917.

(Volume X).

WAR DIARY or INTELLIGENCE SUMMARY

Army Form C. 2118

Place	Date 1917	Hour	Summary of Events and Information	Remarks and references to Appendices
MAISON PONTHIEU	FEB. 1st	-	In Rest Billets. Coy. attacks and Training. Recreation in afternoon. Range practices in morning. Casualties NIL	C.S.W.M.
"	2ND	-	Do. Casualties NIL	C.S.W.M.
"	3RD	-	Battalion attack - witnessed by Brigadier - all Area billet Stores sent to HERMONT - Lieuts STOCKTON & LOEWE returned from leave. Casualties NIL	C.S.W.M.
"	4TH	-	Battalion marched to rest billets at BRUCAMPS arriving 2.15 P.M. Casualties NIL	Appendix P C.S.W.M.
BRUCAMPS	5TH	-	Coy. attacks and Training. Marching Order parade in afternoon. Lecture in evening. Casualties NIL	C.S.W.M.
"	6TH	Night	Coy. attacks and Training - do. Work. Casualties NIL	C.S.W.M.
"	7TH	-	Battalion attack - witnessed by G.O.C. Division in morning Lecture in evening. Casualties NIL	C.S.W.M.
"	8TH	-	Coy. attacks and training. Range practices. Casualties NIL	R.J.
"	9TH	-	Battalion practised the attack. Regimental Transport inspected by Colonel HARRISON, O.C. 61st Divisional Train. Casualties NIL	R.J.
"	10TH	-	Coy. attacks and training. Range practices in morning. Casualties NIL	R.J.

Army Form C. 2118

WAR DIARY
or
INTELLIGENCE SUMMARY
(Erase heading not required.)

Instructions regarding War Diaries and Intelligence Summaries are contained in F.S. Regs., Part II. and the Staff Manual respectively. Title Pages will be prepared in manuscript.

Place	Date 1917	Hour	Summary of Events and Information	Remarks and references to Appendices
BRUCAMPS	FEB 11th	–	In Rest Billets. Church parade and Medical Inspection. Regimental Transport moved at 9 A.M. for new area. Casualties NIL.	NIL
"	12th	–	" Company attacks and training. Casualties NIL.	NIL
"	13th	–	" Battalion moved to LONGPRÉ by route march, where they entrained at 11 A.M., detraining at 3 P.M. at MARCELCAVE. Marched to hutments at WIENCOURT, which were taken over from FRENCH troops. Casualties NIL.	Appendix Q
WIENCOURT	14th	–	In Hutments. Cleaning and refitting. Casualties NIL.	NIL
"	15th	–	" Battalion moved by route march at 10-30 A.M. to Reserve Billets at RAINECOURT. Remainder of the Brigade taking over from the French in the line. Working parties for the line found by 'C' and 'D' Coys. Casualties NIL.	Appendix R
RAINECOURT	16th	–	In Reserve Billets. Company and Specialist training. Casualties NIL.	NIL
"	17th	–	" do. do. do.	NIL
"	18th	–	" do. do. do.	NIL

Army Form C. 2118

WAR DIARY
or
INTELLIGENCE SUMMARY
(Erase heading not required.)

Instructions regarding War Diaries and Intelligence Summaries are contained in F.S. Regs., Part II. and the Staff Manual respectively. Title Pages will be prepared in manuscript.

Place	Date 1917	Hour	Summary of Events and Information	Remarks and references to Appendices
RAINECOURT	FEB 19th	—	In Reserve Billets. Company and Specialist Training. Casualties Nil.	N.T.J.
"	20th	—	do. The following working parties were attached for work in the line :— (a) 45 O.R. from 'B' Coy under Lieut. G.H.G. SHEPHERD. (b) 45 O.R. from 'A' 'C' + 'D' Coys. under 2/Lieut. H. JONES. Casualties NIL.	N.T.J.
"	21st	—	Company and Specialist Training. 'C' and 'D' Coys. moved at 1-30 p.m. by route march to billets at HERLEVILLE. Casualties NIL.	N.T.J.
" HERLEVILLE	22nd	—	Commanding Officer, Adjutant, Medical Officer, Company Commanders + Specialist Officers reconnoitred the line previous to taking over. Casualties NIL.	N.T.J.
"	23rd	—	Batt. relieved 2/4 R. Berks in the left subsection of the ABLAINCOURT sector. Relief not complete until 5 a.m. next morning. Disposition A Left, C. Centre, D right, B in support. Casualties NIL.	Appendix S. N.T.J.

1875 Wt. W593/826 1,000,000 4/15 J.B.C. & A. A.D.S.S./Forms/C. 2118.

WAR DIARY or INTELLIGENCE SUMMARY

Army Form C. 2118

(Erase heading not required.)

Instructions regarding War Diaries and Intelligence Summaries are contained in F.S. Regs., Part II. and the Staff Manual respectively. Title Pages will be prepared in manuscript.

Place	Date 1915	Hour	Summary of Events and Information	Remarks and references to Appendices
ABLAIN-COURT	Sep 24		In front line Trenches. Most of the trenches being deep in mud or water, parties engaged along and nights by all cleaning. Patrols sent out at night by all Companies in the line. Casualties Nil.	N.F.
"	25		Work and patrols as above. Casualties O.R. Killed 1. Wounded 5.	R.F.
"	26		do. do. Our artillery cured out bombardment on German front line but so retaliation was indulged in. Casualties Nil	N.F.
"	27		Work and patrols as above. Enemy bombarded our trenches for two hours. Casualties, Officers Wounded 2/Lt EDY. O.R. wounded 2.	N.F.
"	28		Work and patrols as above. Enemy again bombarded our lines, with exception of trenches for 3½ hours, and at 6.15 p.m. raided our trenches, penetrating the Centre Company front. Counter attack was organised and the enemy driven out, but not before they inflicted them Casualties - on follows - Officers Wounded 2/Lt CONSTABLE missing 2/Lts. GUILDFORD and HUNT. O.R. Killed 6, Wounded 18, missing 19. 2/Lt FRY reported as died from wounds.	N.F.

Commdg 2/4 OXFORDS
R.P. Kennedy, Lt Col

Secret
Ref Map
LENS 1/100000

App. P. ~~About Others~~ Chaoups

2/4 Oxford & Bucks Lt Infty
Order No 186

Copy No 4
3rd February 1917

1. The Battalion will move tomorrow as per Table A, march table at foot.
2. Companies will move in the order H.Q. A.B.C.D, distance 200ˣ will be maintained between Companies and between rear Company and transport. All transport in rear of Battalion.
3. Blankets properly rolled and tied will be dumped at a Central billet in Company areas by 7.45 a.m. Valises and mess boxes to be outside Officers billets by 8.15 a.m.
4. Billets to be left thoroughly clean and to be inspected by Company Officers before the Battalion moves off.
5. Dinners on arrival at billets. Haversack rations to be carried.
6. Usual 15 minute halts will be made.
7. Sick parade 7.30 a.m.
8. Battalion Headquarters will close at MAISON PONTHIEU at 9 a.m., after which reports to head of column.

(Signed) C.S.W. MARCON
Lieut & A/Adjt
4 Oxfords

Battalion Headquarters
Issued at 6 p.m.

Table A. March Table Issued with above order

FROM	TO	STARTING POINT	TIME	ROUTE
MAISON PONTHIEU	BRUCAMPS	Cross Roads 700ˣ S of second 1 in MAISON PONTHIEU	9.36 a.m.	YVRENCH DOMQUEUR GORENFLOS

No 1-3. Battalion Headquarters
4. War Diary
5. 184 Inf Bde
6-9. O/C Coys
10. Quartermaster
11. 2/Lt Hathorn
12. Medical Officer
13. R.S.M.

SECRET. 2/4TH. OXF. AND BUCKS LT. INFTY. COPY NO. 4
REF. MAPS ORDER NO. 194. 12-2-17.
LENS 1/100000 + ABBEVILLE 1/100000.

Appendix R

1. The Battalion will march to LONGPRE Station tomorrow. Route LA FOLIE — ETOILE.

2. Coys will move in the order H.Q. B, C, D, A. The leading Coy. will pass the starting point, 200x S of BRUCAMPS CHURCH at 7-35 A.M. A distance of 200x will be maintained between Coys.

3. Halts will be made at 15 minutes to the clock hour, and the march resumed at the clock hour.

4. Rations will be so distributed as to enable the dinner ration to be consumed in the train.

5. 2/Lt. ALLDEN and a platoon of D Coy. will proceed ½ hour in advance of the Battalion for loading the baggage on to the train. The same party will unload on arrival at the Detraining Station.

6. All men must be warned that strict silence is to be observed during entraining and detraining.

7. Reveille at 5 A.M. Blankets properly rolled and tied must be dumped by 6 A.M. as follows —
B + C at Quartermaster's Stores, A + D at a central point in Coy. billeting areas. Valises, Mess Boxes

and Dixies outside Orderly Room by 6-45 A.M. Platoon Commanders must supervise the rolling of blankets, which must be most carefully done, owing to shortage of space in the lorries.

Sick parade at 6 A.M.
Breakfasts at 6-15 A.M.

Battalion Headquarters will close at BRUCAMPS at 7 A.M. and open in the new area at 5 P.M.

(sd) R. F. CUTHBERT,
Captain and Adjutant,
4 OXFORDS.

Battalion H.Q.
Issued at 7 P.M.

1-3 Battalion H.Q.
4 War Diary.
5 184 Inf. Bde.
6-9 Os. C. Coys.
10 Quartermaster.
11 Medical Officer.
12 R.S.M.

SECRET.   App. R
2/4 Oxford & Bucks Lt. Infty   Copy No. 4
Order No. 195.   14.2.17.

1. The Battalion will march tomorrow to billets at RAINECOURT. Route: WIENCOURT – GUILLAUCOURT – HARBONNIERES – VAUVILLERS.

2. Coys. will parade on their own grounds and will be ready to move in the order H.Q, C, D, A, B by 10-10 A.M.

3. Lieut. SHEPHERD with the 5 Coy. Q.M Sgts will draw bicycles at Q.M. Stores at 8.15 A.M. and will meet the Staff Captain at X roads at FRAMERVILLE for the purpose of taking over billets at RAINECOURT.

4. Field Kitchens, Water carts, Mess cart and baggage wagons will march behind the Battn. The remainder of the Transport will be brigaded, and will pass the LEVEL CROSSING 400 yds north of present lines, in the following order and at the following times.

   Bde. H.Q.   10.25 A.M.
   2/1 BUCKS   10.28 A.M.
   2/4 ROYAL BERKS   10.31 A.M.
   2/5 GLOSTERS   10.34 A.M.
   2/4 OXFORDS   10.37 A.M.
   479 Field Co. R.E. 10.40 A.M.

5. Halts will be made at 15 minutes to the clock hour & the march will be resumed at the clock hour

6. A distance of 200x will be maintained between Coys.

7. Blankets properly rolled will be dumped at Q.M. Stores by 8.30 A.M. Valises & Mess boxes by 9 A.M.

8. Dinners on arrival at Billets.

9. In taking over billets from the French, all damage must be reported at once. Coys will furnish a report by 6 P.M tomorrow of the condition of billets, all existing damage being shown in detail.

10. Sick parade will be at 7.30 A.M.

11. Battn H.Q. will close at WIENCOURT at 10 A.M. and open at RAINECOURT at 2 P.M.

Battn. H.Q.   (Sd) R.F. CUTHBERT
Issued at 10.45 P.M.   Capt & Adjt
                                   4 Oxfords.

Copy No 1 - 3   Battn. H.Q.
            4   War Diary
            5   184 Inf. Bde
      6 - 9   O's C. Coys
           10   Quartermaster & T.O
           11   Medical Officer
           12   R.S.M.

Order No 204   1/4 Oxf & Bucks Lt Infty   Copy No 4
SECRET   22-2-17

App. S

1. The Battn will relieve the 1/4 R. Berks in the line tomorrow. Disposition A Coy, left, C, Centre, D, right, B in support

2. Guides from the 1/4 R. Berks will meet Coys at the ESTREES X roads M.30.c.4.4 in the following order, commencing at 6 p.m.

         D
         A
         C
         B
        H.Q.

3. A distance of 200x will be maintained between Coys up to FOUCAUCOURT, beyond that point 200x will be maintained between platoons.

4. Completion of relief will be reported by wire the code being "N'IMPORTE"

5. Gum boots will be drawn from RAINECOURT dump in the morning & put on at a halt just before reaching the trenches.

6. Rations for the following day will be carried on the man. Tea will be served on the march in or near FOUCAUCOURT.

7. Reports are required daily as follows:—
   SITUATION (by wire) 2 A.M. 2 P.M.
   T. P.   (by runner) 6.30 A.M.
   Casualty   (by wire) 11. A.M.
Certificate that every man has had his feet rubbed & put on dry socks, by 2 am Commencing 25th inst.

8. Disposition Sketches & receipt for trench stores will be sent in by 12 noon. on 24th inst.

9. DRESS Fighting Kit only, greatcoats with packs will be stored at Q.M. Stores.

Battn H.Q.   (Sd) R F CUTHBERT
Issued at 9.45 pm.   Capt & Adjt
                                 4 Oxfords

Copy Nos 1-3 Battn H.Q.
         4 War Diary
         5 Bde H.Q.
       6-9 the Coys
        10 Bomb & T.O.
        11 M.O.
        12 R.S.M.

Vol XI

CONFIDENTIAL.

WAR DIARY

--- of ---

2/4TH BATTALION, OXFORDSHIRE & BUCKINGHAMSHIRE
LIGHT INFANTRY

for period

1ST MARCH 1917 to 31ST MARCH 1917.

VOLUME XI.

WAR DIARY or INTELLIGENCE SUMMARY

Army Form C. 2118

Place	Date 1917	Hour	Summary of Events and Information	Remarks and references to Appendices
ABLAIN-COURT	March 1		In Front line Trenches. Posts re-occupied and damage done on previous nights raid made good. Casualties NIL.	N.F.
"	2		Do. Batt relieved at night by 1/4 R. Berks and marched to Support trenches. Casualties NIL.	N.F.
"	3		In Support Trenches. Day and night working parties found by all Companies. Casualties NIL.	N.F.
"	4		Do. Working parties as above. Casualties. O.R. wounded 1	N.F.
"	5		Do. Casualties NIL.	N.F.
"	6		Do. Do.	N.F.
"	7		Do. Do.	N.F.
"	8		Do. Casualties O.R. wounded 2	N.F.
"	9		Do. Batt relieved R. Berks in front line trenches. Distribution A, left front, B right front, C right support, D left support. Casualties NIL.	N.F.
"	10		In Front line Trenches. Patrols and not by Trench Corps and wiring? carried out. Casualties NIL.	N.F.
"	11		Do. Patrols and wiring as above. Casualties. Killed O.R. 1 (9m), Wounded, O.R. 3 (290).	N.F.
"	12		Do. Patrols and wiring as above. Casualties NIL.	N.F.

WAR DIARY or INTELLIGENCE SUMMARY

Army Form C. 2118

Place	Date 1917	Hour	Summary of Events and Information	Remarks and references to Appendices
ABLAIN-COURT	13		In front line Trenches. Patrols and wiring as above. Casualties O.R. Wounded, 1.	N.F.I.
"	14		Do. Patrols and wiring as above. Casualties, O.R. Killed, 1.	N.F.I.
"	15		Do. Batt: relieved by 2/6 R. Warwicks, and marched to billets at FRAMERVILLE which were reached about 6 a.m. next morning. Casualties NIL.	N.F.I.
FRAMER-VILLE	16		In Billets in Reserve. Resting, refitting &c Casualties NIL.	N.F.I.
"	17		Do. Do.	N.F.I.
"	18		Do. Batt: marched to TOUR CARREE for work on old trenches. Casualties NIL.	N.F.I.
TOUR CARREE	19		Bivouac. Batt: marched to Reserve billets at RAINECOURT. Working parties found for work on roads &c destroyed by the Enemy who had retired. Casualties NIL.	N.F.I.
RAINECOURT	20		In Billets in Reserve. Working parties found as above. Casualties NIL.	N.F.I.
"	21		Do. Do.	N.F.I.
"	22		Do. Batt: marched to CHAULNES. Dug outs - ruined houses &. watering parties on roads. Casualties NIL.	N.F.I.

WAR DIARY
or
INTELLIGENCE SUMMARY

Army Form C. 2118

Place	Date 1917	Hour	Summary of Events and Information	Remarks and references to Appendices
CHAULNES	March 23		In Recent dug outs and cellars. Batt. marched to MARCHELEPOT. Working parties on roads at Casualties NIL.	
MARCHELE- POT	24		Do. Working parties on roads. Casualties NIL.	
"	25		Do. Batt. marched to ATHIES, in support. Working parties on roads in support. Casualties NIL.	
ATHIES	26		In support billets Batt. working parties on roads. Supports dug out begun support line held and trench patrolled. Casualties NIL.	
Do.	27		Do. Working parties on about. Pignats and patrols as about. Casualties NIL.	
Do.	28		Do. Do. Casualties NIL	
Do.	29		Do. Do. Do.	
Do.	30		Do. Batt. marched to support billets at TERTRY	
TERTRY	31		Do. Batt. marched to support billets at CAULAIN-COURT. Outpost line held and roads patrolled. Casualties NIL	

In the field
1-4-17

R. Dulwich Col.
Commd g. 2/4 Oxford Bucks L.I.

CONFIDENTIAL

61/184

Vol/2

12.T.
30 sheet

WAR DIARY

of

2/4TH BATTALION, OXFORDSHIRE & BUCKINGHAMSHIRE LIGHT INFANTRY

from

April 1st, 1917 to April 30th, 1917.

VOLUME XII.

****

Army Form C. 2118

WAR DIARY
or
INTELLIGENCE SUMMARY
(Erase heading not required.)

Map. 62 C. SE

Place	Date	Hour	Summary of Events and Information	Remarks and references to Appendices
at CAULAINCOURT	APRIL 1ST		The Battalion in support. 2 Coys (C. & D.) (Ref 62.C.SE) moved up to SAILORS WOOD in close support to 2/1st BUCKS - A&B Coys at work on roads - Casualties NIL	C.S.W.M
"	2ND		Battalion in support. Work on roads by A&B Coys. Casualties NIL	C.S.W.M (app. M)
"	3RD		Line reconnoitred in morning. The Battalion relieved 2/1 Bucks in the line during the night in the sector E. of SOYECOURT. HQRS in SOYECOURT. Disposition of Coys: "D" Coy frontline posts; "C" Coy in closesupport; "B" Coy at Rly.embankment of MONTOLU WOOD. "A" Coy at SOYECOURT - Relief complete 6 a.m. Casualties NIL [Appendix M]	C.S.W.M (app. M)
SOYECOURT	4TH		In frontline. Snowed all day. Outposts were heavily shelled during the morning. Casualties Killed O.R. 1 - Wounded O.R. 2.	C.S.W.M
"	5TH		In frontline. Trenches improved. Enemy's artillery less active. Casualties Wounded O.R. 1	C.S.W.M
"	6TH		In frontline - Brigade attacked enemy's trenches. 2/5 GLOUCESTERS on right, OXFORDS on left. ZERO time midnight. "A" Coy was the attacking Coy. Wire found uncut, 2 attempts being made to break through - but without success. The attacking Coy of bttn Bathalion withdrew - withdrew. Casualties - Killed officers 1 (Lieut C.J. BARTON) - O.R. 8. Wounded officers 3 (2/Lts. J.P. WAYTE, R. AITKEN, A.H. TILLEY (afterwards died of wounds)) O.R. 21. [Appendix. N]	C.S.W.M (app. N)

Army Form C. 2118

WAR DIARY
or
INTELLIGENCE SUMMARY
(Erase heading not required.)

Place	Date	Hour	Summary of Events and Information	Remarks and references to Appendices
SOYECOURT	APRIL 7TH		In front line. Battalion relieved by 2/1 BUCKS on night 7th and marched to billets in CAULAINCOURT — except B. Coy. who proceeded to SAILORS WOOD in support to 2/1 BUCKS. Relief complete 10.30 P.M. Casualties NIL. [Appendix O]	C.S.M. (App O)
CAULAINCOURT	8TH		In support billets. Cleaning up and checking of men rations etc, carried out. Capt. H. J. BENNETT posted to Battalion and 2nd in command vice MAJ. W. L. RUTHVEN. Casualties NIL.	C.S.M.
"	9TH		In support billets. The Battalion moved up into area of 182nd BDE. to consolidate and hold a line of trenches W. of HORNON WOOD in Trenches dug wired by all Coys. Casualties NIL.	C.S.M.
MARTEVILLE	10TH		Work on trenches and wire continued till mid-day. The Battalion then marched back to new billets in MONCHY-LE-PACHE via CAULAINCOURT. Casualties NIL.	C.S.M.
MONCHY-LE-PACHE	11TH		In reserve billets. Cleaning up, kit inspections etc. carried out, together with wash on roads by a number of all Coys. Billetting party left for HOMBLEUX. Casualties NIL.	C.S.M.
"	12TH		In reserve billets. The Battalion marched to rest billets at HOMBLEUX arriving 3.30 P.M. Casualties NIL	C.S.M. (App. P)

WAR DIARY or INTELLIGENCE SUMMARY

Army Form C. 2118

(Erase heading not required.)

Place	Date	Hour	Summary of Events and Information	Remarks and references to Appendices
HOMBLEUX	APRIL 13TH		In rest billets. Cleaning up, refitting etc. Casualties Nil.	CSWM
"	14TH		Training commenced. Steady drill, drill in extended order with special classes for Lewis gunners. Casualties Nil.	CSWM
"	15TH		In rest billets. Training in morning till 12.30 p.m. Casualties Nil.	CSWM
"	16TH		Training continued in morning. Casualties Nil.	CSWM
"	17TH		" " and afternoon. Drill and attack practices. Casualties Nil.	CSWM
"	18TH		In rest billets. Training continued morning and afternoon. Casualties Nil	CSWM
"	19TH		In rest billets. The battalion marched to reserve billets at GERMAINE arriving 12.30 P.M. Casualties Nil.	CSWM (App Q)
GERMAINE	20TH		In reserve billets. The battalion moved up to HOMBON to relieve 16TH NORTHUMBERLAND FUSILIERS (32nd DIV) in Support line - in left Subsection. "A" Coy came under orders of O.C. 7/5 GLOS. being placed in close support. The battalion arrived in HORNON S.p.m. Casualties Nil.	CSWM (App R)

Army Form C. 2118

WAR DIARY
or
INTELLIGENCE SUMMARY
(Erase heading not required.)

Place	Date	Hour	Summary of Events and Information	Remarks and references to Appendices
HOLNON	APRIL 21st		In support trenches. Work on BROWN LINE (line of resistance) carried on by B. C. and D. Coys - improvement of trench and erection of wire. Casualties NIL. HOLNON shelled during night, HQRS. being compelled to move out during early hours of the morning.	C.W.M.
"	22nd		In support trenches. Work on BROWN LINE carried on by all 3 Coys day and night. Casualties. Wounded O.R. 1.	C.W.M.
"	23rd		In support trenches. Work on BROWN LINE continued. Casualties NIL. A. Coy return to HOLNON. Strong points	C.W.M.
"	24th		" " " " " Casualties NIL. dug and wired.	C.W.M.
"	25th		In support trenches. Work on BROWN LINE and strong points. HOLNON shelled as usual. Casualties Wounded O.R. 1.	C.W.M.
"	26th		In support trenches. The Battalion relieved the 2/1 BUCKS - the line relief being complete 2.30. A.M. Disposition A Coy Right B " centre C " Left D Reserve in support Casualties. Wounded. O.R. 4. BN. HQRS at FAYET	C.W.M. (Ap. S)

Place	Date	Hour	Summary of Events and Information	Remarks and references to Appendices
FAYET.	April 27th		In front line. Enemy artillery active at times on Coy front & HQrs. – FAYET received usual amount of attention. Casualties. Wounded O.R. 4	CRCM
"	28th		In front line. "D" Coy. plus 2 platoons of "C" Coy raided enemy's trenches in morning. (Zero 4.20. a.m.) and after capturing 2. M.Gs. & 1 man, the party returned to our lines about 5.15. a.m. Casualties rather heavy. The 2nd objective was reached – Casualties Killed Officers. 1. (2/Lt. T.H. ALLDEN) – O.R. 16. Wounded and missing Officers 1. (2/Lt H.S. TAYLOR) O.R. Wounded 42. Missing 9.	CRCM (App. T)
"	29th		In front line. The Battalion was relieved by 2/4 R.BERKs. and marched to reserve billets. Relief complete 1.30.a.m. – CEPY F.M. entered by "B" Coy. & one or two encounters with enemy took place – 9 some enemy killed. Identifications obtained Casualties Wounded O.R. 2	CRCM (App. U)
ATTILLY	30th		In reserve billets. Cleaning & refitting. Casualties Nil	CRCM

B. Bennett Lt-Col
Comdg. 2/4 Oxford & Bucks L.I.

During the month of May the following report of the raid on 28th April was rec'd.

IV Corps No. 17/1 (G).

REPORT ON THE RAID ON THE ENEMY'S TRENCHES
FROM ABOUT M.36.central to M.30.b.5.4.
CARRIED OUT ON APRIL 28th, 1917 BY 2/4th
BATTALION, OXFORDSHIRE & BUCKINGHAMSHIRE
LIGHT INFANTRY, 184th INFANTRY BRIGADE.

1. On taking over the line from the 96th Infantry Brigade, 32nd Division, I received orders from G.O.C. 61st Division to be prepared to carry out an enterprise against the enemy on my front at an early date. The enemy were at that time known to be the 451st I.R. of the 234th Division. Troops who had already, when engaged with the 32nd Division, failed signally to exhibit any fighting qualities.

2. I decided that the plan which presented the greatest chances of success was to deploy at about M.36.central where there was a gap between the enemy's posts, and by forming to a flank in this gap, roll up his line from left to right. There appeared to be sufficient space in the gap to allow of the deployment of a small force without attracting attention, though it was quite clear that this delicate operation would require very careful forethought.

3. Energetic patrol work, carried out by the 2/1st Bucks Battalion, O.B.L.I. during their period in the front line enabled me to gather some further information on the points above mentioned.
It appeared that the enemy held his line lightly, and that the Troops holding it were of the unenterprising character already referred to.

4. I decided therefore to carry out this enterprise as soon as possible, so as not to allow the enemy time to strengthen his defences; 4.20 a.m. was selected as the hour and April 28th the date.

5. The O.C. 2/4th Oxfords (Lieut.-Col. Bellamy., D.S.O.) in Command of the Outpost Line, decided to use for the scheme "D" Coy. (Capt G.K.ROSE., M.C.) plus 2 platoons "C" Coy. Two parties were specially detailed, one as Moppers-Up, the other as Wire-cutters.

6. The orders for the enterprise were, briefly, that deployment should take place at the time and place already stated; the Company to be formed up in normal attack formation with the Wire-cutting and Mopping-Up parties echeloned in depth to its left rear; while on the right rear the 2 extra Platoons were to be similarly echeloned. The Company followed by the 2 special parties was to advance at ZERO and roll up the enemy's line; and while the Moppers-Up cleared the trench behind the advancing Company, the Wire-cutters were ordered to halt at about M.36.a.9.8. and there cut a gap through the wire on the W. of the enemy's trench, through which the Company, the Moppers-Up, and one of the extra Platoons will eventually withdraw.

The /

The tasks allotted to the 2 platoons were as follows:-
The leading platoon was to rush the crater at M.36.b.9.6. at ZERO covered by an intense bombardment for 2 minutes by 1 section R.F.A. It was then to secure the Crater, the ST QUENTIN - LE CATELET Road on each side of it and cover the withdrawal of the whole force; eventually itself withdrawing along the FAYET Road. It was thought that the Crater was very lightly held or not held at all. This was probably correct as regards the unenterprising Troops of the 234th Division, but, as a fact, it was found to be held strongly. The success of the whole enterprise largely depended on securing this objective.

The rear platoon was to support the leading platoon, if necessary, in its attack on the Crater, and then wheel to its left and advance N. astride the ST QUENTIN - LE CATELET Road, thereby protecting the right flank of the Company, and cutting off any enemy who might attempt to run away in that direction.

7. The Company detailed for the enterprise was stationed in the SUNKEN ROAD near the MONUMENT in M.34.d. Previous to moving off from this place to the place of deployment, the enemy's artillery shelled this road with 5.9s causing several casualties, and trying very highly the endurance of the party. Nevertheless, Capt ROSE brought his Company up to the place of deployment in good order and up to time, an achievement as difficult as it was creditable, and completed the deployment by 4.15 a.m.

8. At 4.20 a.m. the Bombardment commenced. An Artillery programme had been arranged which dealt thoroughly with the enemy's advance and support positions, as well as with the Crater. It was carried out with great accuracy and success under the direction of Lt.-Col. A.S.COTTON, D.S.O., R.F.A. who had left nothing undone to ensure complete co-operation with the infantry. During the whole operation there was not a single instance of a short shell as far as can be ascertained.

The Infantry advanced at the same moment. The leading platoon rushed the Crater and captured a Machine Gun there. Another gun which had also occupied the Crater was carried away by its team in a N.E. direction. This gun halted and opened fire on our men, but was at once engaged, and put out of action in about two minutes by 2 Machine guns of the 184th Machine Gun Company.

The rear platoon advanced astride the ST QUENTIN - LE CATELET Road for about 100 yards bombing three dugouts full of the enemy, and killing others who tried to escape. One prisoner was captured and sent back. More prisoners might have been taken, but, unfortunately, the situation did not allow of this and they had to be dealt with in the usual manner. The Lewis Gun of the platoon fired down the road along which several Germans were running with useful results. It was however, unable to subdue the enemy's fire further up the road although a German Machine Gun which attempted to engage the Lewis Gun was put out of action by the Rifle Grenade Section without much difficulty.

Meanwhile the main body had made considerable progress. After reaching the S.E. corner of the CURATES GORSE the enemy was encountered in the trench running in N.W. direction through that Wood. It was evident that they thought the attack to be coming from the W. instead of the S.E. on their flank, as they fired to their front, instead of towards the attackers.

The enemy on the ST QUENTIN - LE CATELET Road however saw our men as they crossed the Road running from the Crater towards FAYET, and opened rifle and machine gun fire on them. This fire, which in spite of the action of the platoon astride the road continued to be troublesome throughout, did not stop the attack or cause serious loss, at least at first.

The bombing

The bombing section of the left platoon cleared the trench in the CURATE, dealing with 3 shelters full of the enemy. The rifle section captured 2 machine guns, killing most of the gun teams, and bombed about 20 more Germans so vigorously that they fled up the trench towards CREAM GORSE after suffering a loss of 1 man killed.

On reaching the trench junction N.E. of the CURATES GORSE the enemy's resistance in front, and his fire from the right front on the ST QUENTIN - LE CATELET Road, grew more and more pronounced. Two Lewis Guns and the Rifle Sections of the Company engaged in a short struggle for fire superiority. The enemy's fire lessened, and the bombing section of the right platoon entered the cross trench running N.E. towards ST QUENTIN - LE CATELET Road, after forcing its way through some thin wire in front of it. This trench had been abandoned by the enemy. The Company continued the attack along the trench up to CREAM GORSE. The enemy again opened fire on the right front. The three Lewis Guns of the Company were brought into action, and produced some effect; but by this time they had begun to run short of ammunition, and the supply of bombs and rifle grenades also threatened to give out. Capt. ROSE therefore decided to carry out the withdrawal in the manner previously arranged. The Wire-cutting party specially detailed for the task had cut a wide gap in the enemy's wire near the point where his trench entered the CURATES GORSE; through this the Company withdrew, covered by the fire of 2 Lewis Guns. The withdrawal was carried out steadily, and only one casualty was sustained in passing through the enemy's barrage, which had been put down on the general line of the GRICOURT - ST QUENTIN Road, and on localities W. of it. The last party to withdraw were the platoon in occupation of the CRATER. While doing so at about 5.30 a.m. they came under M.G. fire from the enemy. This M.G. was located and put out of action by 2 of our machine guns, which had been detailed to cover the withdrawal.

A Contact Aeroplane which flew along the line at about 5.35 a.m.

dropped a message at Brigade Headquarters at 5.55 a.m., which stated that it had been fired on by the enemy from the CURATES GORSE. This shows that the enemy occupied his trenches at once after our withdrawal.

Our casualties were :-

	Offrs.	O.R.
Killed	1	10
Missing	1	2
Wounded	2	41

The enemy lost 3 Machine Guns - two of which were carried back, one prisoner, and certainly an equal number of killed and wounded as ourselves - probably more. He held the position in considerable strength with the 3rd JAEGER Regiment, and not, as had been supposed the 451st Regt troops of an inferior quality. The 3rd JAEGERS on the contrary fought hard, and counter-attacked vigorously. Their demoralization at first, due to the heavy Artillery fire and to the effect of surprise, only makes their subsequent action more creditable.

(Sgd) G. MOORE, Capt.
Brigade-Major.
for G.O.C., 184th Infy. Bde.

P.T.O.

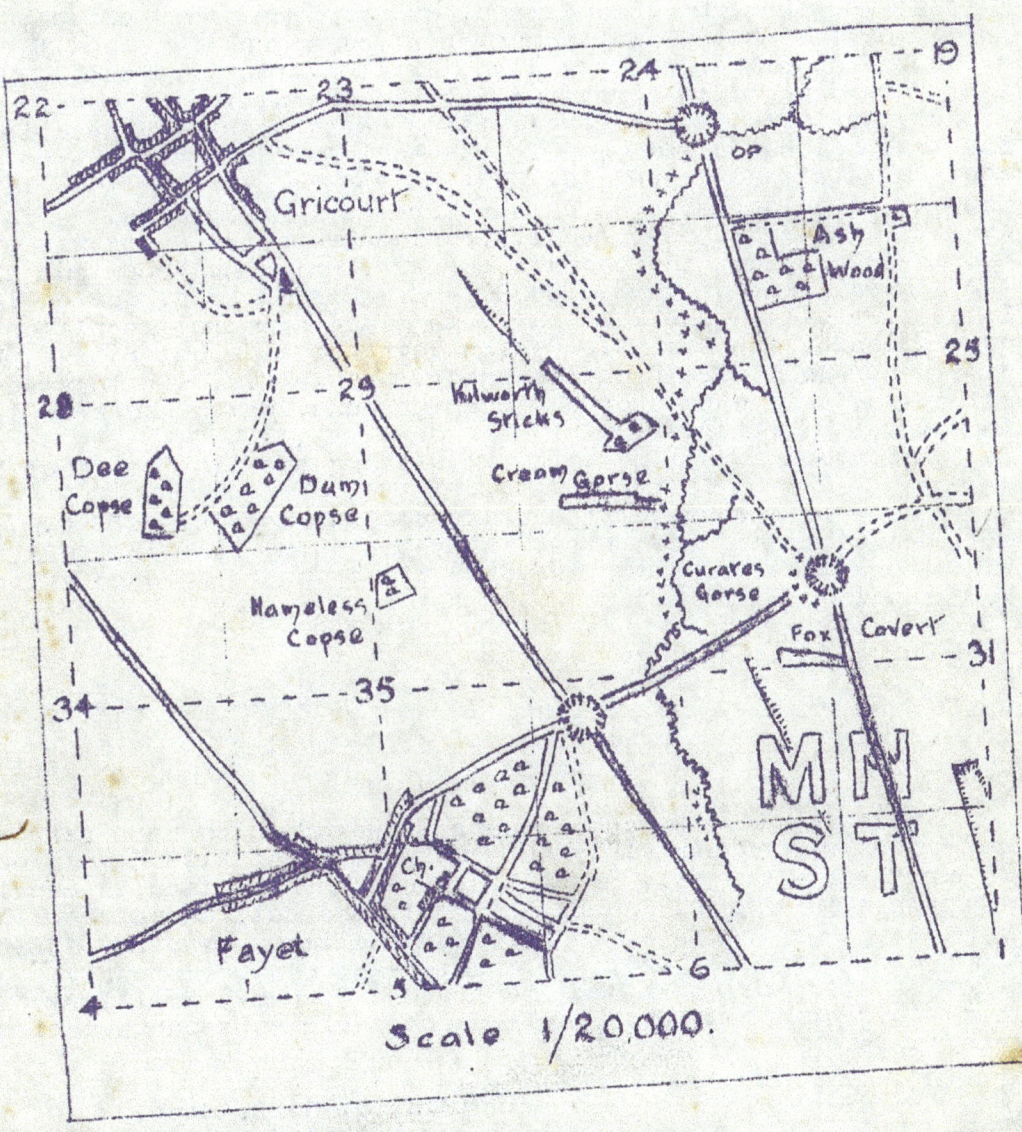

SECRET 2/4 Oxford & Bucks Lt Infty Copy No
Appendix "M" Order No 237   3 April 1917

1. The Battalion will relieve the 2/1 BUCKS Battalion in the line during the night of 3/4 April
Relief to be completed by 5 A.M

2. Disposition.
D Coy in front line posts.
C Coy in trenches behind No 5 Wood
B Coy Ry Embankment in MONTOLU WOOD
BATTN: H Q & A Coy   SOYECOURT

3. Guides for D Coy will be at Ry Embankment at 3 A.M
Guides for other Coys will be at SOYECOURT as under.
    C Coy 2-30 A.M.
    B "   3 - - A.M
    A "   3 - - A.M

4. Lewis Guns with 24 magazines per Gun will be loaded on transport and conveyed to SOYECOURT from which point they will be carried.

5. Tools & reserve Ammunition will not be taken but an exchange will be made with the 2/1 BUCKS

Coys will send to H.Q tomorrow, duplicate receipts for all stores taken over.

6. Rations will be carried on the man.

7. A Coy & H.Q will carry packs. Remainder of Battn in fighting kit.

8. Mess boxes may be taken if desired, but must be man handled from SOYECOURT

9. Officers chargers if taken will return to Transport lines at CAULAINCOURT

10. Battn H.Q. will close at CAULAINCOURT at 2 A.M & open at SOYECOURT at 3.30 A.M.

Battn H.Q   (Sd) R.F. CUTHBERT
Issued 6.15 p.m   Captn & Adjt

No 1-4   O/C Coys
     5   War Diary
     6   184 Inf Bde
     7   Medical Officer
     8   O/mr & Transport Officer
     9   Lewis Gun Sergeant
 10-11   Battn H.Q.

SECRET 2/4 Oxford & Bucks Lt Infty Copy No
Appendix Order No 239 6 April 1917

1. Enemy holds line of trenches from R.12.c.8.4. R.12.a.0.0. R.11.b.5.5. R.11.b.3.9. R.5.d.0.6. thence along W of ridge to S.W. corner of LE VERGUIER

2. The Battalion (in conjunction with 2/5 GLOUCESTERS) will attack this line tonight 6/7th April.

3. <u>Objectives</u>
   (1) GLOUCESTERS from R.11.b.7.5 to R.5.c.9.2.
   [exclusive
   OXFORDS from R.5.c.9.2 inclusive to R.5.c.6.9.
   (2) GLOUCESTERS will endeavour to extend their right so as to include MAREVAL COPSE and the trenches S.W. of it. OXFORDS will conform to this movement by supporting the left of the GLOUCESTERS and closing on it as far as R.5.d.4.0. The line of resistance will be approximately the old German trenches.

4. On reaching the first objective.
   (a) Patrols will at once be sent out to keep in touch with the enemy & protect consolidation & further movement.

(b) For the purpose of refusing the left flank a double block or strong point will be constructed at about R.5.C.6.9, a strong point at about R.5.C.4.8 and another strong point at about R.5.C.1.7. These points should be made as strong as possible and furnished with Lewis Guns.

(c) The front line will consist of strong points with Lewis Guns sited for mutual support. It is essential that observation beyond the crest of the ridge should be held & O.P's must be established should the front line not suffice for this purpose.

(d) As a counter attack is possible all ranks must be prepared to resist it.

5. With reference to above, the attack will be carried out by A Coy, with B Coy in close support, two platoons on each flank.
A Coy will advance in line of columns of half platoons at about 50^x intervals. Connecting files will keep touch between columns & maintain direction by the right.
B Coy will have two platoons in support of the right half of A Coy & two in support of the left half.

These will move in two waves, 100ˣ behind A Coy & at 50ˣ distance, in columns of half platoons at 30ˣ intervals.

6. The left of the GLOUCESTERS will direct, & O.C A Coy will be responsible for keeping touch with them.

7. Deployment of the attacking Coy. will be carried out on the line of the road from R.10.C.7.3. inclusive to R.10.C.0.9. & will be completed one hour before ZERO. B Coy will deploy 100ˣ in rear of A at the same hour.

8. ZERO will be at midnight at which hour the artillery bombardment will commence on the line of the trench from R.11.b.5.5. towards LE VERGUIER along the line to be attacked. The bombardment will be moderate for 25 minutes, then quicker for 10 minutes & intense for 5 minutes. From 0.40 to 0.60 it will creep 100ˣ every 4 minutes to road running through R.6.c and R.5.b. It will remain as a barrage on this line from 0.60 to 1.30 at which hour fire will cease, except for S.O.S.

9. D Coy will be in position to the right rear of No 5 Copse, on the reverse slope by 11.30 p.m.

At 0.10 they will move forward and two platoons will take up a position behind No 3 Copse, the remaining two & Coy H.Q behind No 4.

C Coy will remain in their present position as Coy in reserve.

10. Flares will be lit when the contact aeroplane sounds it KLAXON horn.

11. O.C Coys will arrange that the correct proportion of Officers N.C.O's & Specialists are not taken into action.

12. The two left platoons of B Coy will be responsible for digging the strong points referred to in para 4 (b) above, under orders from O.C A. Coy

13. A & B Coys will carry 50 shovels each and a small proportion of picks.

14. A M. Gun will be in position at No 3 Copse & 3 guns will be in the vicinity of advanced Battn H.Q. Further dispositions of M. Guns will be notified later.

15. Reports to advanced Battn H.Q at about R.10.C 7.3

16. These orders will on no account be taken into action.

Battn H.Q
Issued at 6.30pm

(Sd) R.F CUTHBERT
Captn & Adjt

No 1-4   O.C Coys.
     5   War Diary
     6   184 Inf Bde
  7-8   Battn H.Q
     9   Gloucesters

SECRET   2/4 Oxford & Bucks Lt Infty   Copy No
Appendix   Order No 240   7 April 1917
O/

1. The Battalion will be relieved by the 2/1 BUCKS BATTN. tonight.

2. C Coy will send guides to meet D Coy of the BUCKS at the Ry Embankment at 8 p.m.
Guides for other Coys will not be required.
D Coy will vacate their position at 8 p.m. without waiting for relief.

3. On relief A C & D Coys will march to billets at CAULAINCOURT & B Coy to SAILORS WOOD.
All Coys will send representatives this afternoon to take over & guard billets & billet stores.
C Coy will occupy their former billets & D Coy will occupy those previously occupied by A Coy.

4. All trench stores will be collected & properly handed over, duplicate receipts being sent to Battn H.Q. tomorrow
NOTE Petrol tins are Battalion Stores

and it is most important that every tin is sent to the R.S.M by 6 pm this evening.

Tools, Bombs and Ammunition will be handed over at each end

5. Code for completion of relief:-
"RUM RATION REQUIRED"

6. Battalion H.Q will close at SOYECOURT at 10 P.M. and open at CAULAINCOURT at 11 pm

Battn H.Q　　　　　　　　(Sd) R.F. CUTHBERT
Issued at 4 pm　　　　　　　　Captn & Adjt

No 1-4　O.C Coys
　　5　War Diary
　　6　184 Inf Bde
　7-8　Battn H.Q.
　　9　Medical Officer
　10　R.S.M.

SECRET   2/4 Oxford & Bucks Lt Infty   Copy No
Ref Maps 62c   Order No 244   11 April 1917
66D 1/40000

1. app: p. The Battalion will march tomorrow to billets at HOMBLEUX.
   Route LANCHY, UGNY, DOUILLY, TOUILLE, OFFOY,

2. Companies will be ready to move from V.18.a.6.5. at 9.20 A.M. Order H.Q. C.D.A.B. 100ˣ distance will be maintained between Coys & between last Coy & Transport H.Q & C will move as one Company

3. The usual ten hour halts will be made with a 1/2 hour halt at 1.30 p.m when haversack rations will be consumed.

4. Valises and Mess Boxes will be collected at 8.30 A.M. _punctually._

5. Battn H.Q. will close at MONCHY LAGACHE at 9 a.m. after which reports to head of column.

Battn H.Q   (Sd) R.F. CUTHBERT
Issued 9.15 p.m   Captn & Adjt

No 1-4   O/C Coys
    5   War Diary
    6   184 Inf Bde
    7   Medical Officer
    8   Qmr & Transport
    9   Battn H Q
   10   R.S.M.

SECRET   2/4 Oxford & Bucks Lt Infty   Copy No
                    Order No 251

Ref: Map
66D 1/40000. Appendix Q.

1. The Battalion will march to GERMAINE tomorrow. Route main HOMBLEUX-HAM Road to CANIZY, OFFOY Bridge, TOULLE, DOUILLY, FORESTE.

2. Coys will march in the order H.Q D.A.B.C. The head of the column will move from Road Junction S.32.b.6.7 near CALVAIRE FARM at 8am. A distance of 100ˣ will be maintained between Coys & between the last Coy and the Transport. H.Q & D will march as one Company.

3. Dinners will be served on arrival in billets.

4. Valises & mess boxes will be ready for collection by 7.15 am punctually.

5. Each Coy will detail an Officer to inspect billets & ensure that same are left clean & report to Captn Bennett before moving off.

6. One N.C.O. from each Coy for billeting will draw a bicycle and report to Lieut MARCON at Battn H.Q at 6.45 a.m.

7. Battn H.Q will close at HOMBLEUX at 7.30 a.m, after which reports to head of column.

Battn HQ
Issued 8.15 am

(Sd) R. F. Cuthbert
Captn & Adjt

Nos 1-4 O/c Coys
     5 War Diary
     6 184 Inf Bde
     7 Medical Officer
     8 Qmr & Transport Officer
     9 R.S.M.
    10-11 Battn H.Q.

SECRET   2/4 Oxford & Bucks Lt Infty   Copy No

App. D.   Order No 253   20 April 1917

1.   The Battalion (less A Coy) will relieve the 16th Northumberland Fusiliers in the support line (left subsection) today.

2.   Companies will march in the order B.C.D. with head of column at E.17.b.7.9. (Map 66 D 1/40000) at 1 pm.   200x will be maintained between Coys & between rear Coy and Transport.
Route via VAUX ETREILLERS, SAVY
Dress F.S. Marching Order   Steel Helmets

3.   Valises & mess boxes (reduced in weight as far as possible) will be ready for loading at 12-30 pm.

4.   As many Maps & full patrol times as possible will be taken over from the relieved Battn.

5.   A report of work done will be sent to Battn H.Q by 12 noon daily. The first report by 12 noon on 21st inst.

6. Battn H.Q will close at GERMAINE at 12.30 pm today, after which report to head of column.

7. From 12.30 pm and until further notice A Coy will come under the orders of O.C. 2/5 Gloucester Regt.

Battn H.Q
Issued 11.20am

(Sd) R. F. Cuthbert
Captn & Adjt

1 - 4	O.C. Coys
5	War Diary
6	184 Inf Bde
7	Q'mr & Transport Officer
8	Medical Officer
9 - 10	Battn H.Q

SECRET   2/4 Oxford & Bucks Lt Infty   Copy No
App 5   Order No 255   26 April 1917

1. The Battalion will relieve the 2/1 Bucks Battn in the line tonight.
Dispositions:-
     A Coy   right
     B "   right centre
     C "   left centre
     D "   left.

2. Guides will meet Coys at the Crucifix at 8.30 pm. Coys will move in the order to be notified later, by platoons at 50^x, care being taken to keep connection between platoons.

3. Rations for tomorrow will be carried on the man, waterbottles will be filled & 12 petrol cans (filled) per Coy will be carried, & 5 for H.Q.

4. Dress Fighting kit. Officers may carry packs.

5. Company Commanders may send back to the Q'mr Stores all officers in excess of 3 per Coy, if they wish. The names

of those to be sent back must be sent to Battn H.Q by 3 pm.

6. French shelters will be handed over this afternoon to representatives of the 2/5 Gloucester Regt & receipts taken.

7. Disposition sketches & receipts for stores and ammunition taken over will be sent in to Battn H.Q. by 10 pm. tomorrow.

8. A Company of the 2/5 Gloucester Regt will be in close support of the Battn & will undertake the carrying of rations & water on the nights of 27 & 28th inst.

9. Situation reports and I.P. reports will be sent in at the usual times.

10. Battn H.Q. will close at HOLNON at 8-30 pm and will open at FAYET at 10 pm.

Battn H.Q. (Sd) R. F. Cuthbert
Issued at 1 pm   Captn & Adjt

No 1-4 O/C Coys
5 War Diary
6 184 Inf Bde
7 Transport Officer & Ann
8 Medical Officer
9 Btn H.Q

SECRET   2/4 Oxford & Bucks Lt Infty   Copy No
           Order No 256   27 April 1917
Ref Map. 1/20000. 62 B.S.W. and Sketch Map.

1. D Coy, plus two platoons of C Coy
will raid the enemy's trench running from
M.36. central as far as M.30.b.5.4.
Two special parties (a) MOPPERS UP
                    (b) WIRECUTTERS
will be found by D Coy.
The two platoons of C Coy will for the purpose
of these orders be designated Y and Z platoons.

2. D Coy will deploy in normal attack
formation on the line M.36.d.0.8 to
about M.36.d.4.7. Y & Z platoons will
deploy echeloned to the right rear of D
Company.
The two special parties will deploy echeloned
to the left rear of the Company, the
MOPPERS UP in front, & the ~~wirecutters~~
WIRECUTTERS in rear.
The utmost care will be exercised to make
the deployment as noiseless as possible.

3. ZERO will be at 4.20 am on the
28th April.

4. DIRECTION & OBJECTIVES

D Coy will advance at ZERO, keeping its left on the S.E corner of the CURATE. At this point it will incline slightly to its left and continue to advance up the East side of the CURATE, and thence along the enemy trench, on both sides of it as far as the wire on the West side will permit, up to the line of the final objective.

The MOPPERS UP will follow the left of the Coy. They will take care that no enemy in the trench are left to shoot into the back of the Coy.

They will continue to work along the Trench, partly in it, partly on top, as parapet parties, up to the final objective.

The WIRECUTTERS will follow the Company, and will halt on reaching M.36.b.0.7, at which point the enemy trench bends N.E. from the CURATE. Here they will cut a gap in the enemy's wire along the West front of the trench, from M.36.b.0.7. NORTHWARDS through which the Company and Z platoon will eventually withdraw. The WIRECUTTERS will remain at about this point, to cover the withdrawal of the Company and the MOPPERS UP.

Y platoon will advance straight to the Crater at M.36.b.9.5 which it will occupy together with the ST QUENTIN - LE CATELET road on each side of it, for a distance of 100 yards facing EAST. A patrol will be sent along the track leading from this crater to N.35.c.5.0 for a distance of 50 yards.

Z platoon will follow Y platoon as far as the crater, and will support Y platoon in case strong resistance is encountered there.

It will then turn N.W. and follow the ST QUENTIN - LE CATELET road, keeping slightly in advance of the Company, proceeding along the enemy's trench, and keeping its own centre on the road, until the line of the final objective is reached.

Z platoon will protect the right flank of D Coy, and will also cut off any enemy who attempt to escape EAST from the trench. It will also send out a patrol east of the ST QUENTIN - LE CATELET road to protect its own right flank. Any enemy M.G. found E of the road will be dealt with by Rifle Grenades, Lewis Guns etc.

5   WITHDRAWAL. This will be carried out steadily and in good order as follows:-

(A) By D Company & MOPPERS UP - via the Gap cut by the WIRECUTTERS about

M.36.b.0.7, thence through about M 35 central to M.34.d.9.6. along the road S.E of the MONUMENT.

(B) By Z platoon, by the same route as above, following the Coy.

(C) By the WIRECUTTERS by the same route as above, following the Z platoon.

(D) By Y platoon from the CRATER straight back along the road through M.36. central to the CRATER at M.36.c.w.7. thence to M.34.d.9.6.

It must be impressed on all ranks that wide extensions must be maintained during the withdrawal. All bunching must be avoided. D Company and Y & Z platoons will each detail a small rear guard to cover their own withdrawal.

The word RETIRE will not be used during these operations. Anyone so doing will be treated as an enemy.

6. REORGANIZATION. On reaching the road near the MONUMENT the whole force will be re-organized, and will remain there in support.

7. ARTILLERY will co-operate - a programme is issued separately.

8. M.G. will fire as follows:—
2 guns in position about M.36.d.3.5. engaging ground lying in M.31.a and C throughout.
4 guns in position about M.29.c.9.8 ZERO to ZERO PLUS 10 engaging KILWORTH STICKS and trench from M.30.d.1.3. to M.30.d.u.9. and ground in M.25.a. ZERO PLUS 10 - onwards - enfilade barrage from M.30.a.u.8. to M.25.a.5.9.

9. DRESS. Men should be equipped as lightly as possible, and everything likely to rattle during deployment left behind.
MOPPERS UP will wear white arm bands others white material as already arranged. All titles, cap badges, paybooks, identity discs and documents affording any clue to the identity of the Battn. and all shoulder patches (red) will be removed before dusk tonight.

10. Reports to C Coys Signal Station at M.36.c.5.u. whence they will be transmitted by wire or runners to Battn. H.Q.

Battn H.Q.   (Sd) R F Cuthbert
Issued at 11:30am   Captain & Adjt

Copy No 1. Battn H.Q.
     2 18th Inf Bde.
     3 O/c D Coy
     4 O/c C Coy
     5 O/c 2/5 Gloucester Regt

SECRET   2/4 Oxford & Bucks Lt Infty   Copy No 7
          Order No 258   30/4-17

1. The Battn will be relieved by the BERKS tonight

2. One guide per platoon and one guide from Bn H.Q. will meet incoming Units at 9 p.m. at the gap in wire on BROWN LINE about S.4.a.0.5. on N side of old German wire running to FAYET.
Company Commanders will make the necessary arrangements for guides to the POSTS.

3. Coys will be relieved in the order A.B.C.D., and on relief will march to Billets at Ry Embankment E of ATTILLY Platoons at intervals of not less than 50ˣ

4. Great care must be taken that all trench stores, tools, ammunition, S.O.S. signals, wiring materials &c are properly handed over.
Receipts must be sent in to Btn H.Q as soon as possible.

5. All petrol tins in Company lines must be collected & numbers checked. Coy commanders will be responsible that every tin is brought out of the line and carried to Billets.

6. Arrangements are being made for the Q.M. Serjeants of Coys to take over billets and billet stores.

7. The supporting platoons of the Gloucesters will be relieved by the BUCKS, under arrangements to be made between Units concerned.

8. Codes for completion of Relief
A Coy "Pte ATKINS"
B " "Pte BLOGGINS"
C " "Pte COLLINS"
D " "Pte DOBBINS"

Batln HQ   (Sd) R. F. Cuthbert
Issued at 2pm   Captn & Adjt

Nor to 4 O.C. Coys
       5 War Diary
       6 184 Inf Bde
       7 Batln HQ
       8 R Berks

CONFIDENTIAL

WAR DIARY - VOLUME XIII

of

2/4TH BATTALION, OXFORDSHIRE & BUCKINGHAMSHIRE LIGHT INFANTRY

----- For -----

PERIOD MAY 1ST to MAY 31ST

1917

****

WAR DIARY or INTELLIGENCE SUMMARY

Army Form C. 2118

Place	Date	Hour	Summary of Events and Information	Remarks and references to Appendices
ATHIES	MAY 1ST		Training and refitting. Casualties NIL.	CSWM
	2ND		Battalion was relieved by 2/8. WORCESTERS and marched into Divisional Reserve to billets at VAUX and ETREILLERS relieving the 2/6 GLOSTERS. Bil.ts reached 2.30 p.m. 9 Coys distributed as follows :- HQRS and A. at VAUX, B.C.D at ETREILLERS. Casualties NIL	CSWM
VAUX	3RD		Rest day - Spent in cleaning up and bathing. Casualties NIL	CSWM
"	4TH		Battalion on working parties, repairing roads. Military Medal awarded to S/20084 Sgt. BUTCHER G.W. 201069 Cpl SLOPER A.E. Casualties NIL. Capt ABRAHAM and CUTHBERT proceeded on Paris leave.	CSWM
"	5TH		Training and shooting on Range. Also bathing. Bee H.(Temp Lt.) acting Capt. BROWN .K.E. awarded Bar to M.C. Casualties 2. Accidental: Fracture of arm (?) & burnt.	CSWM
"	6TH		Parade Service at VAUX Medical Inspection. Shooting on Range in evening. Casualties NIL	CSWM

Army Form C. 2118

WAR DIARY or INTELLIGENCE SUMMARY
(Erase heading not required.)

Place	Date MAY	Hour	Summary of Events and Information	Remarks and references to Appendices
VAUX	7TH		Training and firing on Range carried out. Casualties NIL	C.S.M.
"	8TH		Battalion on working parties. Casualties NIL	C.S.M.
"	9TH		Training in the morning. Brigade parade and presentation of parchments by G.O.C. Division in field between GERMAINE and VAUX in afternoon. Casualties NIL	C.S.M.
"	10TH		Firing on Range in afternoon after parade. 1 Coy on working parties. Training & bathing. Transport (1st line) inspection by Maj. Gen. Commanding	R.S.
"	11th		at GERMAINE. Capt.ns ABRAHAM and CUTHBERT returned from leave. Casualties NIL	R.S.
"			staff of 80 men arrived	
"	12		Training continued. Casualties NIL	R.S.
"	13		do. do. Casualties NIL	Appendix 'A' R.S.
"			Batt.n marched to billets at MESNIL ST NICAISE. Casualties NIL	
MESNIL ST NICAISE	14.		Companies refitting or Transport started on march to RIVERY. Casualties NIL	R.S.
"	15		Batt.n marched to NESLE and entrained, detrained at LONGUEAU and marched to RIVERY. Casualties NIL	Appendix 'B' R.S.

Army Form C. 2118

WAR DIARY
or
INTELLIGENCE SUMMARY
(Erase heading not required.)

Place	Date May	Hour	Summary of Events and Information	Remarks and references to Appendices
RIVERY.	16		Company training continued. Capt. H.J.BENNETT appointed acting Major while acting as 2nd in Command. Casualties Nil.	R.J.C.
"	17.		Batt'n. marched to LA VICOGNE. Casualties Nil.	Appendix C¹ R.J.C.
LA VICOGNE	18.		Training continued. Capt. G.K. ROSE M.C. awarded bar to M.C. 2/Lt. H JONES awarded M.C. Casualties Nil.	R.J.C.
"	19		Training continued. Brigade paraded for presentation of Ribbons by G.O.C. Division. Casualties Nil.	R.J.C.
"	20		Training continued. Casualties Nil.	R.J.C.
"	21		Batt'n. marched to billets at NEUVILLETTE. Casualties Nil.	Appendix D¹ R.J.C.
NEUVILLETTE	22.		Training continued and gas appliances tested in Gas Chamber. Casualties Nil.	R.J.C. Appendix E¹
"	23		Batt'n. marched to Billets at BARLY. Casualties Nil.	R.J.C.
BARLY	24		Batt'n. marched to Huts at DUISANS. Casualties Nil.	Appendix F¹ R.J.C.
DUISANS	25		Training continued. Lt. Col. R. BELLAMY DSO relinquished command of 1st Bn 8 Transy ?Regt Command of 1st Bn. 8 Transy? Regt. Casualties Nil.	R.J.C.

1875 Wt. W593/826 1,000,000 4/15 J.B.C. & A. A.D.S.S./Forms/C. 2118.

Army Form C. 2118

WAR DIARY
or
INTELLIGENCE SUMMARY

(Erase heading not required.)

Instructions regarding War Diaries and Intelligence Summaries are contained in F. S. Regs., Part II. and the Staff Manual respectively. Title Pages will be prepared in manuscript.

Place	Date May	Hour	Summary of Events and Information	Remarks and references to Appendices
DUISANS	26		Training continued. Lt. Col. M.E. de R. WETHERALL M.C. joined and assumed Command 2/4th Batt. Casualties NIL.	N.T.R.
"	27		Training Continued. Casualties NIL.	N.T.R.
"	28		Do Do Do	N.T.R.
"	29		Do Do Do	N.T.R.
"	30		Do Do Do	N.T.R.
"	31		Battn. marched to TILLOY and proceeded to bivouac. Casualties NIL.	appendix G1, N.T.R.

In the field
1st June 1917.

M.E. Wetherall Lt. Col.
Commanding 2/4 Oxford S.

SECRET   2/4 Oxford & Bucks Lt Infty   Copy No 5
          Order No 270   12-5-17

1. The Battn will march tomorrow to NESLE (Mesnil St Nicaise) via FORESTE, DOUILLY, MATIGNY, VOYENNES

2. Coys will move in the order C.D.A.B. from VAUX X roads at 5 a.m. A distance of 200ˣ will be maintained between Coys.

3. Cookers will march in rear of Coys. One water cart in rear of each half Battn. Remainder of Transport in usual Echelon.

4. There will be a halt at 6.30 a.m. till 7.15 a.m. for breakfast.

5. All billets will be left thoroughly clean, & will be handed over to Officers of the 2/7 Worcesters who have arrived at VAUX and ETREILLERS respectively for the purpose. Clean certificates will be obtained from these officers

6. Valises & Mess boxes must be ready for collection as under:—
       ETREILLERS   3 a.m.
          VAUX   3.30 a.m.

7.   Battn. H.Q. will close at VAUX at 4.30 a.m. & reopen at NESLE on conclusion of the march.

Battn. H.Q.   (Sd)   R. F. Cuthbert
Issued at 6 p.m.   Captn & Adjt

            1-4   O/C Coys
             5   War Diary
             6   18th Inf Bde
             7   Qmr & Transport Officer
             8   Medical Officer
            9-10 Battn H.Q.

SECRET. 4th Oxford & Bucks Lt Infty   Copy No 5
                Order No 272   14-5-17

1. The Battalion will march to NESLE STATION tomorrow and will entrain there for LONGUEAU

2. Coys will move in the order H.Q. D A.B.C. from x roads by MESNIL CHURCH at 7.20am. A distance of 200ˣ will be maintained between Coys.
There will be no halts on the march.

3. All valises & mess boxes must be dumped at Bn H.Q. by 6.30am. Drums stacked in fours, and covered over with canvass, will be dumped at the same time and place.

4. The R.S.M. will detail 1 N.C.O. & 6 men to load above stores on to a lorry.

5. The following parties will also be detailed —
(1) A Coy 1 N.C.O. & 8 men to report to Q.M. at NESLE STATION at 7.15am for loading stores.
(2) The post orderlies for loading mails

(5) A party to be detailed by Q.M. for
loading rations.
The same parties will unload on arrival at
LONGUEAU.

6. All men must be reminded that
entraining and detraining must be carried
out in silence.

7. Water bottles must be filled before
marching off and O.C. Coys are responsible
for seeing that all water has been
previously boiled.

8. Billets must be left clean & one Officer
per Coy detailed to inspect them & report to
Captn H.J. BENNETT before moving off.

9. After detraining the Battn will march
to Billets, the location of which will be
announced later.

10. Sick parade will be at 6.30 a.m.

Battn H.Q.   (Sd) R F CUTHBERT
Record & Supn   Captn , Adjt

1-4 O.C. Coys
5   War Diary
6   18th M.G. Bde
7   Area Commander
8   Medical Officer
9-10 Battn H.Q.
10   R.S.M.

SECRET   2/4 Oxford & Bucks Lt Infty   Copy No 5
            Order No 274   15-5-17

Ref Maps 1/100000
AMIENS & LENS

1. The Battn will march tomorrow to LA VICOGNE, via POULAINVILLE and VILLERS-BOCAGE.

2. Coys will move in the order H.Q. A.B.C.D. from the x roads 500ˣ due E of final E in CITADELLE at NW exit of RIVERY at 4.20.am.
A distance of 200ˣ will be maintained between Coys.

3. The usual halts will be observed, and there will be a halt from 6.30 am to 7.30 am for breakfast.

4. Cookers in rear of Coys, 1 water cart in rear of each ½ Battn. Remainder of transport in rear of Battn in usual Echelon.

5. Valises & mess boxes must be stacked at x roads S of H.Q. mess by 3.15 am punctually.

6. Billets and huts must be left thoroughly clean, and an officer per Coy detailed to inspect & report on same before moving off.

7. Battn HQ will close at RIVERY at 3.30 am, after which reports to head of column.

Battn H.Q.
Issued 7.30 pm

(Sd) R.F. Cuthbert
Captn & Adjt

1-4 O/c Coys
5 War Diary
6 184 Inf Bde
7 Q'mr & T.O.
8 Medical Officer
9-10 Battn H.Q.
11 R.S.M.

Ref above orders, the Battn starting point tomorrow will be at the Bridge under AMIENS Road facing N. Time 4 am

(Sd) R.F. Cuthbert

SECRET   2/4 Oxford & Bucks Lt Infty   Copy No 5
            Order No 278   20-5-17

1. The Battn will march to billets at NEUVILLETTE tomorrow, via DOULLENS, and will be formed up in the order H.Q. A,B,C,D, with head at Road Junction 500x N of LA VICOGNE at 4.50 am.

2. A distance of 10x will be maintained between Coys. Cookers, followed by Water Carts in rear of Battn with remainder of transport in usual Echelon.

3. The halts will be for 10 mins, the march being resumed at the clock hour. At 6.50 there will be a halt of one hour for breakfasts.

4. Billets must be thoroughly cleaned & inspected by a Coy Officer who will report to Major Bennett before moving off.

5. Valises & mess boxes must be ready for collection by 3.45 am.

6. Battn H.Q will close at LA VICOGNE at 4 am after which reports to head of column.

7.   While the Battn is in 3rd Army Area, all officers & soldiers on duty will wear iron helmets.
   This order will come into force from the commencement of the march tomorrow 21st May.

Battn H.Q.   (Sd) R F Cuthbert
Issued 7.30p   Captain & Adjt

        No 1-4 O/c Coys
            5   War Diary
            6   18th Inf Bde
            7   Qm & T.O.
            8   Medical Officer
          9-10 Battn H.Q.
           11   R.S.M.

SECRET   2/4 Oxford & Bucks Lt Infty   Copy No 5
          Order No 280   22-5-17

1. BARLY The Battalion will march tomorrow to FOSSEUX, via LE SOUICH, MAISON FORESTIERE SUS ST LEGER, SOMBRIN, and will be formed up ready to move from the X roads DOULLENS - FREVENT and NEUVILLETTE - LE SOUICH at 6 a.m.   Order of March HQ. B.C.D.A.

2. Breakfasts at 4:15 a.m.
Haversack rations will be carried.

3. A distance of 10 yards will be maintained between Coys. Transport in usual Echelon, but with Cookers in front of 1st Line Transport, followed immediately by Water Carts.

4. There will be a halt of 10 minutes before each clock hour.

5. Valises & mess boxes will be dumped ready for collection by 5 a.m as under
A.C. & H.Q. at CHATEAU GATES
B & D at Quartermaster's Stores

6. Billets will be thoroughly cleaned and an Officer per Coy detailed to inspect them & to report to Major Bennett before moving off.

7. - Battn H.Q will close at NEUVILLETTE at 5.30 am after which reports to head of column.

Battn H.Q.   (Sd) R.F. Cuthbert
Issued at 7.15 pm   Captn & Adjt

Nos 1-4   O/c Coys
      5   War Diary
      6   184 Inf Bde
      7   Transport Officer & Qmr.
      8   Medical Officer
  9-10   Battn H.Q.

SECRET   2/4 Oxford & Bucks Lt Infty   Copy No 5
           Order No 282   23-5-17

Refer Map.
LENS 1/100 000.

1. The Battalion will march to the DUISANS area tomorrow via WANQUETIN, WARLUS and C in GIMRE and will be ready to move from Road Junction 200x NE of Y in BARLY at 8.40 a.m.
Order H.Q. C.D.A.B.

2. 100x will be maintained between Coys. Transport in the usual Echelon.

3. Valises & men's boxes will be ready for collection at 8 a.m. punctually.

4. Billets will be thoroughly cleaned and an Officer will be detailed by each Coy to inspect billets & report to Major Bennett before moving off. Four men per Coy will be left to carry out any cleaning that Major Bennett may direct.

5. Sick parade at 7.30 a.m.

6. Battn. H.Q. will close at BARLY at 8.30 a.m., after which reports to head of column.

Battn. H.Q. (Sd) R. F. Cuthbert
Issued 6.15 pm Captain & Adjt

Nos. 4 O/C Coys
5 War Diary
6 18th Inf Bde
7 F.O. & Gnr
8 Medical Officer
9-10 Battn H.Q.

SECRET   2/4 Oxford & Bucks Lt Infty   Copy No
           Order No 290   30 May 1917

Ref Maps
1/40000, 51B, 51C,

1. The Battn will march tomorrow to rest trenches in S and of THE HARP, S of TILLOY. Route via ARRAS, and main CAMBRAI road.

2. Coys will be ready to move in the order HQ. A. B. C. D. from the road junction at S.E. corner of Camp at 10.56 a.m.

3. Distances of 200ˣ will be maintained between Coys W of ARRAS ~~distances of~~. In and E of ARRAS distances of 200ˣ will be maintained between platoons.
The necessary connecting files will be detailed before moving off.

4. Cookers will march in rear of Companies. One water cart in rear of Band one in rear of D Coy.
The mess cart, Medical Cart and 1 Baggage wagon will march in rear of Battn. Remainder of transport will march brigaded to its destination

in G.33.d. Details will be furnished to the Transport officer.

5. The usual 10 mins halts will be observed.

6. Billeting representatives from B.C.D & H.Q will draw Bicycles and report to 2/Lt A.V. SMILTON at 8 am. The party will meet a representative of the Staff Captn at 65th Bde H.Q at H.31.d.1.9. at 10 am. Guides will be found by this party for the Unit

7. Dixies & mess boxes will be ready for collection at 10 am.

8. Dinners will be served at the end of the march.

9. The huts and the lines will be left thoroughly clean. One officer per Coy will be detailed to inspect huts and report to the Adjutant before moving off. The R.S.M. will detail the necessary party for cleaning up of latrines, ablution places, etc.

10.   Battn H.Q will close at DUISANS at 10.30 am, after which reports to head of column.

Battn H.Q.   (Sd) R. F. Cuthbert
Issued 5.45 pm   Captn & Adjt

    No 1-4 O/c Coys
       5   War Diary
       6   184 Inf Bde
       7   T.O & Qmr
       8   Medical Officer
      9-10 Battn H.Q.

CONFIDENTIAL

WAR DIARY

**** of ****

2/4th BATTALION, OXFORDSHIRE & BUCKINGHAMSHIRE LIGHT INFANTRY

**** from ****

June 1st, 1917 to June 30th, 1917.

(VOLUME XIV)

****

WAR DIARY
or
INTELLIGENCE SUMMARY
(Erase heading not required.)

Army Form C. 2118

Place	Date 1917 June	Hour	Summary of Events and Information	Remarks and references to Appendices
TILLOY	1		In Bivouacs. Relieved 13th Battn. 60th Rifles in Reserve Line trenches, MONCHY Sector.	Appendix M1
MONCHY	2		In Reserve Trenches. Carrying parties found by whole Battn. to Front Line. Casualties, 2/Lt LINDSEY killed, 2/Lt HERBERT and 10 O.R. Wounded 1 O.R.	R.F.J.
"	3		Do. Carrying and working parties found for front line. Casualties Killed 3 O.R, Wounded 5 O.R.	R.F.J.
"	4		Do. Carrying and working parties found as above. Casualties, Killed 1 O.R. Wounded 2 O.R.	R.F.J.
"	5		Do. Carrying and Working parties found as above. Casualties, Wounded, 3 O.R.	R.F.J.
"	6		Do. Relieved 2/4 R.BERKS in front line trenches, dispositions A Coy. left front, C Right front, B + D in support. Casualties, Wounded 3 O.R.	Appendix M 2.

Army Form C. 2118.

WAR DIARY
or
INTELLIGENCE SUMMARY.
(Erase heading not required.)

Place	Date	Hour	Summary of Events and Information	Remarks and references to Appendices
MONCHY	1917 June 7		In front line trenches. A Coy on left pushed forward their front line about 100x, occupied a line of shell holes under cover of darkness and connected to Consolidated them and to dry communication trenches. The operation was successful, carried out without being observed by the enemy. Casualties Wounded 2 O.R.	Appendix M. 3.
"	8		Do. The work of consolidating the advanced line was continued. A patrol of 5 Germans surprised at first on advanced position, was captured and taken prisoner. Casualties Wounded 2 O.R.	N.g.
"	9		Do. The Batt. less C Coy was relieved, and withdrew to Reserve line trenches Canaletta, N14.	Appendix M. 4.

Army Form C. 2118.

WAR DIARY
or
INTELLIGENCE SUMMARY.
(Erase heading not required.)

Instructions regarding War Diaries and Intelligence Summaries are contained in F.S. Regs., Part II. and the Staff Manual respectively. Title pages will be prepared in manuscript.

Place	Date	Hour	Summary of Events and Information	Remarks and references to Appendices
	1917			
MONCHY	Jun 10		In Front & Reserve Trenches. The Batt was relieved and marched to Bivouac at TILLOY. Casualties Killed 1 O.R. Wounded 2 O.R.	R.J.J.
TILLOY	11		In Bivouac. Batt marched to billets at BERNEVILLE. Casualties NIL	appendix M.5.
BERNEVILLE	12		In Billets. Rest and Refitting. Casualties NIL.	R.J.J.
"	13		"	D⁰	R.J.J.
"	14		"	D⁰	R.J.J.
"	15		"	Batt and Company training. Casualties Nil.	R.J.J.
"	16		"	D⁰	R.J.J.
"	17		"	D⁰	R.J.J.
"	18		"	D⁰	R.J.J.
"	19		"	D⁰	R.J.J.
"	20		"	D⁰	R.J.J.
"	21		"	D⁰	R.J.J.
"	22		"	D⁰	R.J.J.

Army Form C. 2118.

WAR DIARY
or
INTELLIGENCE SUMMARY.
(Erase heading not required.)

Instructions regarding War Diaries and Intelligence Summaries are contained in F.S. Regs., Part II, and the Staff Manual respectively. Title pages will be prepared in manuscript.

Place	Date	Hour	Summary of Events and Information	Remarks and references to Appendices
	1917			
BERNEVILLE	July 23		In Billets. The Batt: marched to GOUY EN ARTOIS and entrained, detrained at AUXI-LE-CHATEAU and marched to billets at NOEUX. Casualties NIL.	Appendix M.6.
NOEUX	24		Rest & Refitting Casualties NIL.	R.I.C
"	25		Batt: Company Training. Casualties NIL	R.I.C
"	26		Do Do Do	R.I.C
"	27		Do Do Do	R.I.C
"	28		Do Do Do	R.I.C
"	29		Lt Col WETHERALL, M.C. proceeded to England on leave. Announcement of award of Victoria Cross to Cpl Sept-hrjn E. BROOKS, D Coy, for gallantry in action at FAYET. Casualties NIL.	R.I.C
"	30		Batt: Company Training. Casualties NIL.	
In the field				

30-6-17.

[signature] Major
Comm.y 2/4 Oxford & Bucks L.I.

App. M.1.

SECRET   1/4 Oxford & Bucks Lt Infty   Copy No 5
           Order No 292   1 June 1917

Ref. Map.
1/10000, 51 B. S.W.

1. The Battn will relieve the 13th Battn. 60th Rifles in the Reserve line tonight.

2. All Coys will parade in F.S. marching order at 10.15 pm.

3. The relief will be carried out in the order H.Q. A, D, B, C. Platoons at 50x distance.

4. 1 Guide per platoon & 1 per Coy H.Q. will meet Battn at road junction N.8.d.6.8. at 11 pm.

5. Rations will be carried on the Cookers. H.Q. rations on the mess.

6. Relief complete will be reported by wire, the code being "Rations Up".

7. Valises & kit not required in the line will be packed ready for loading by 8.30 pm.

8. Attention is drawn to the orders as to wearing of equipment, and as to Gas precautions circulated to coys today.

9. All paper and refuse must be collected and burnt by 9 p.m., & the lines left thoroughly clean.

10. Battn HQ will close at TILLOY at 10.15 p.m., after which reports to head of column.

Battn HQ.
Issued 2.30 pm

(Sd) R. F. Cuthbert
Captain & Adjt

1-4 O/C Coys
5 War Diary
6 18th Inf Bde
7 Qmr & T.O
8 Med. Officer
9-10 Battn HQ.

App. M.2

SECRET   2/4th Oxford & Bucks Lt. Infty.   Copy No 5

Ref. Maps.   Order No 293   6-6-17.
GUEMAPPE. 1/10,000 & 51.B.S.W. 1/20,000.

1. The Battn. will relieve the 2/4 R. BERKS in the left front sub-sector tonight.

2. On completion of relief the disposition of Companies will be as follows.
"A" plus 2 L.G. teams of "D" Coy.   Left front.
"C" " 2 L.G. teams of "D" Coy.   Right front.
"B"   FOSSES FARM.
"D" (less 4 L.G. sections)   FOSSES FARM. Of these sections 3 men go to the line as above, remainder to SPADE TRENCH under 2/Lt. PEAL.

3. Guides will be at N.10.c.8.b. at 9.45 P.M. Companies will move in the following order:- "B", "D" (less L.G. Sections), "A" (via PICK TRENCH), "C" (via GORDON ALLEY). Men of H.Q. Coy. not detailed for the line will be attached to "B" Coy. The first company will be ready to move at 10.15 P.M., by platoons at 100x distance.

4. Rations for tonight will be carried on the man. Field Petrol tins will be carried up as under:-
"A" Coy. 22.   "C". 23.
4 L.G. Sections of "D". 5
H.Q. 10.

5. Packs will be stored by platoons, clear of the

road behind Coy. lines, ready for collection by Transport at dusk. Mess boxes will be ready at same place.

6. Water bottles will be filled by 6 P.M. and the contents not to be touched until completion of relief.

7. Company commanders will see that all men are complete with 120 rounds S.A.A. Any deficiencies to be made up from Battn. reserve behind "D" Coys lines at once.

8. O.C. "D" Coy. will detail a party to load the ammunition reserve on to the returning ration limbers this afternoon.

9. "A" and "C" Coys. will each arrange to carry up 40 boxes MILLS bombs to be dumped at suitable spots to be selected by O's C. Coys. "B" Coy will carry up 20 boxes of Rifle Grenades to FOSSES FARM, from which place they will be sent forward tomorrow night.

10. The Officer of "A" Coy going up at 5 P.M. tonight will take a representative of each of the 6 L.G. teams attached to that Coy. If a guide is required, O.C. Coy. will inform Battn. H.Q. A representative of each of the 6 teams attached to "C" Coy. will report to Battn. H.Q. at 5.30 P.M.

where a guide will be allotted to them.

11. Receipts for all trench stores, photos, S.O.S. signals, etc., will be forwarded to H.Q. as soon as possible after relief.

12. Completion of relief will be reported by wire the code being "PIPE".

13. Battn. H.Q. will close in the reserve line at 10 P.M. and will open at O.7.b.6½.2. at 1 A.M.

Battn. H.Q.
Issued at 12.15 P.M.

(Sd) R. F. Cuthbert
Capt & Adjt.

1 - 4.	Coys.
5.	War Diary
6.	184 Inf. Bde.
7.	M.O.
8.	Qr Mr and T.O.
9 - 10.	Battn. H.Q.

SECRET   App. M.3   2/4th Oxford & Bucks L.I.   Copy No. 2
Order No. 294.   7.6.17.

1. 'A' Coy will form a series of 10 posts of 4 men each between a point 20ⁿ S. of the eastern end of GRAPE TRENCH SAP and a broken telegraph pole at O.8.b.3.3.
    2/LT. CALLENDER will place these posts in position commencing from the GRAPE TRENCH SAP end at 10.15 P.M. These posts will consolidate themselves and immediately commence to join up with posts on right and left.

2. The covering party will consist of two patrols of about 10 men and a Lewis Gun, one advancing on the left of the line & the other on the right.

3. Two C.T.s will be dug out to these posts, one leaving ADA Trench at about O.8.a.8.7. and the other at O.8.b.0.4.
    2/LT. TURRELL will be responsible for the construction of these C.T.s

4. At 12 midnight 2/LT. COOMBES will advance our bombing block in O.8.b. 50ⁿ towards HOOK TRENCH. In addition to the bombs already there, five bags of

Sandbags will be at our block before the advance begins.

5. Two Stokes Guns at about O.8.a.7.7. will be in readiness to open fire if ordered to do so by O.C. "A" Coy on the junction of HOOK and LONG Trench.

6. DRESS Fighting kit. In addition each man under 2/Lt. CALLENDER will carry 3 bombs and one tool.

Batt. H.Q.
Issued at 7.10 P.M.

(Sd) R.F. Cuthbert
Capt & Adjt.

Copy No 1   O.C. "A" Coy
       2   War Diary
       3   Bde
       4   O.C. "C" Coy
       5   O.C. 7th Batt. King. Shropshire L.I.

SECRET 2/4 Oxford & Bucks L.I. App. M. 49.   Copy No. 5
            Order No. 295.   9.6.17

1. 'A' Coy. will be relieved tonight by 'B' Coy.
   7th Kings Shropshire L.I.

2. One guide will be at Junction of GRAPE
   TRENCH with front line at 10.15 P.M. This
   guide will conduct the reliefs for the shell
   holes. One guide for Coy. H.Q. will be at same
   rendezvous at same time. At 10.30 P.M, 2
   guides for the two remaining platoons will
   be at the same rendezvous.

3. At 10.15 P.M. No 13 Platoon (complete with L.G.
   team) will move to position now occupied
   by Reserve L.G. teams in PICK TRENCH,
   without waiting for relief. One Guide
   from the Reserve Lewis Gunners will be
   sent to 'A' Coy. H.Q. by 10 P.M. to lead
   this platoon.

4. On arrival of No 13 platoon, the Reserve
   Lewis Gunners will join their own
   sections according to instructions to
   be given to 2/Lt. HILL.

5. On completion of relief 'A' Coy will
   proceed to the position in the WANCOURT
   line occupied by them when the Batt.
   was in Brigade Reserve.

6. "C" Coy will remain in its present position. Capt. BRUCKER will take over command of Nº 13 & 14 platoons, and will come under the orders of the O.C, 2/1 BUCKS.

7. One guide from "C" Coy will be at FOSSES FARM at 10 P.M. to conduct Nº 14 Platoon to a position in the support line.

8. The Signalling Officer will see that a telephone line to H.Q, 2/1 BUCKS, O.13.a.7.5 from "C" Coy's H.Q. is installed by 6 P.M. tonight.

9. "B" Coy, the remainder of "D" Coy, and the R.A.P. will remain at FOSSES FARM. "B" Coy. will be responsible for carrying rations & water to "C" & 2 platoons "D".

10. Receipts for trench stores, maps &c will be obtained by "A" Coy. from relieving Unit in duplicate & will be forwarded to Battⁿ H.Q. by 12 noon tomorrow.

11. Relief complete will be reported by "A" & "C" Coys, the code being "ANGUS".

12. On completion, Battⁿ H.Q. will move to

its former position in WANCOURT line.
   Men of H.Q. Coy. now at FOSSES FARM (except Medical Staff) will move to this position at 10 P.M.

Batt: H.Q.   (Sd) A.F. Cuthbert
Issued at 10.30 A.M.   Capt & Adjt.

      Copy No 1 – 4.   Coys.
                 5.   War Diary
                 6.   184 Inf. Bde.
                 7.   Medical Officer
                 8.   Qr Mr & T.O.
        9 – 10.   Bn. H.Q.

App. M.5.

SECRET   2/4th OXF. + BUCKS LT. INFTY.   Copy No. 5
          Order No. 296   11.VI.17.

Ref. Map LENS 1/100000
1.   The Battalion will march today to BERNEVILLE, via ARRAS, DAINVILLE and WARLUS.
     The ARRAS road will be gained by the road running N.E. through TILLOY.

2.   Coys. will move in the order H.Q., C, A, D, B, and will parade at the following times.
        H.Q.   4 P.M.
        C   4.2 P.M.
        A   4.7 P.M.
        D   4.12 P.M.
        B   4.17 P.M.
     Orders as to the time of moving will be given on parade.
     Mess boxes will be ready by 3 P.M.

3.   Distances of 200x will be maintained in and E. of ARRAS. These may be reduced to 50x W. of ARRAS.

4.   There will be no regular halts until clear of the railway W. of DAINVILLE.
     When an opportunity of halting without blocking other traffic arises the Commanding Officer will order a halt and platoon commanders will be responsible for getting their men clear of the road.

5. Cookers will march in rear of Coys.
Watercarts, Maltese cart & mess cart in rear of the Battn.

6. Orders as to the collection of packs and greatcoats will be issued later.

7. All paper & refuse will be burnt or buried, and latrines filled in by 3.30 P.M.

8. Battn. H.Q. will close at TICLOY at 4 P.M. after which reports to head of column.

9. Teas will be served on arrival at billets.

10. Tomorrow will be a day of rest and will be devoted to the thorough cleaning of all clothing, arms and equipment. Every man must have had his hair cut by 1st parade on Thursday, 14th inst.

11. Orderly Room tomorrow at 12 noon.

(Sd) R.F. CUTHBERT,
Captain & Adjutant

Bn. H.Q.
Issued at 12.30 P.M.
    1-4 O's C. Coys.
    5 War Diary
    6 1st Inf. Bde
    7 M.O.
    8 Q.M. + T.O.
    9, 10 Bn. H.Q.

App. M.6.

SECRET   1/4 Oxford & Bucks Lt Infty   Copy No 5
             Order No 307   22-1-17

Ref Maps 1/40000 51C
and 1/100000 LENS.

1.   The Battn will march to station at GOUY-EN-ARTOIS tomorrow and entrain.
Route BEAUMETZ   MUNCHIET
Dress F.S. Marching order with F.S. Caps.

2.   Coys will move from billets in the order H.Q. B.C.D.A. with distances of 100ˣ between Coys. The leading Coy will be prepared to move at 7.20 am.

3.   15 minute halts will be observed before each clock hour.

4.   The Battn will detrain at AUXI-LE-CHATEAU and march to billets at NOEUX.

5.   Entraining & detraining must be conducted in silence.

6.   Valises, Mess boxes, dixies, signalling and other stores for loading on lorry will be stacked at Q.M. stores by 7 am punctually.

7. All waterbottles will be filled before departure. Rations for tomorrow will be carried on the man & the dinner rations will be consumed on the train.

8. Billets will be left thoroughly clean. An Officer will be detailed by each Coy to inspect billets and to report to Major BENNETT before moving off.

9. Reveille at 5.30 a.m.
Breakfasts at 5.45 a.m.

10. Battn H.Q. will close at BERNEVILLE at 7a.m. and will open at NOEUX on arrival of the Battn.
Reports in the meantime being sent to the Head of the Column.

Battn H.Q.   (Sd) R.H. Cuthbert
Moved at 1.30pm.   Captn & Adjt

   1 - 4   Coys
   5   War Diary
   6   15th Inf Bde
   7   Battn & T.O.
   8   Medical Officer
   9-10   Battn H.Q.

CONFIDENTIAL

WAR DIARY

*** of ***

2/4th BATTALION, OXFORDSHIRE & BUCKINGHAMSHIRE LIGHT INFANTRY

From 1st July, 1917 to 31st July, 1917.

(VOLUME XV)

****

Army Form C. 2118.

WAR DIARY
or
INTELLIGENCE SUMMARY.
(Erase heading not required.)

Instructions regarding War Diaries and Intelligence Summaries are contained in F. S. Regs., Part II. and the Staff Manual respectively. Title pages will be prepared in manuscript.

Place	Date 1917	Hour	Summary of Events and Information	Remarks and references to Appendices
NOEUX les MINES	July 1		Church parade Cavallier N.I.L.	n.f.
"	2		Do. Batt. and Coy training Cavalier N.I.L	n.f.
"	3		Do. Do. Cavalier	n.f.
"	4		Do. Wounded O.R. 1 (accidentally)	n.f.
"	5		Do. Batt. & Coy training Cavalier N.I.L	n.f.
"	6		Do. Do.	n.f.
"	7		Do. Do.	n.f.
"	8		Do. Do.	n.f.
"	9		Church parade	n.f.
"	10		Do. Batt. Coy training	n.f.
"	11		Do. Do.	n.f.
"	12		Do. (Lt. Col. Wetherall M.C. returned from leave) Do.	n.f.
"	13		Do. Do.	n.f.
"	14		Do. Do.	n.f.
"	15		Do. Church parade	n.f.

WAR DIARY or INTELLIGENCE SUMMARY

Army Form C. 2118.

Place	Date 1917	Hour	Summary of Events and Information	Remarks and references to Appendices
NOEUX	Aug 16		In not billets. Batt" and Coy training. Casualties NIL	N.J.
"	17		Do Do Do	N.J.
"	18		Do Divisional Race Meeting; Holiday. Do	N.J.
"	19		Do Batt" and Coy training.	N.J.
"	20		Do Do	N.J.
"	21		Do Do	N.J.
"	22		Do Church parade	N.J.
"	23		Do Batt" and Coy training	N.J.
"	24		Do Do	N.J.
"	25		Do Rest and Refitting	N.J.
"	26		Do Batt" moved to AUXI-LE-CHATEAU and entrained. Detrained at ST OMER and marched to billets at BROXEELE. Casualties NIL	Appendix A.2 N.J.
BROXEELE	27		Do Rest. Inspections &c. Casualties NIL	N.J.
"	28		Do Batt" and Coy" training	N.J.
"	29		Do Parade service (Casualties) during last weeks	N.J.

Army Form C. 2118.

WAR DIARY
or
INTELLIGENCE SUMMARY.
(Erase heading not required.)

Place	Date	Hour	Summary of Events and Information	Remarks and references to Appendices
BROYEELE	1917 July 30		In rest billets. Batt. & Coy training. Casualties Nil.	
"	31		During the month, Lt W.D. SCOTT, and 2/Lts T.H. WEBB, C.H. WALLINGTON, W.A.C. MOORE and W.H. MOBERLY, and drafts amounting to 153 O.R. joined the Batt. Capt. H.N. DAVENPORT M.C. rejoined from senior officer school, ALDERSHOT, but was transferred to 2/6 WARWICKS & 2nd in command.	
			M.J.Wetherall Lt Col Comm'g 2/4 Oxford + Bucks L.I.	

In the field
31 - 7 - 17.

Appendix A

SECRET 1/4 Oxford & Bucks Lt Infty Copy No 5.
Order No 338.   25 July 1917

1. The Battn (less transport) will march to AUXI-LE-CHATEAU tomorrow and entrain. Coys will be ready to move at 7 a.m. in the order H.Q. A.B.C.D. with head of column at cross roads in NOEUX on road to WAVANS. Distances of 50ˣ will be maintained between Coys. DRESS. Full marching order, with steel helmet on the pack.

2. Marching out states (exclusive of transport & transport personnel) will be sent in by 6 p.m. tonight.

3. An advance party, consisting of 2/Lt DUNAND & the C.Q.M.S. or 1 N.C.O. from each Coy will proceed to the Station 1/2 hour in advance of the Battn for marking carriages.

4. Dinner rations will be carried on the man. Waterbottles will be carried full. On arrival at the Station each Coy will send 1 N.C.O. & 4 men to report to the Adjutant and to draw full petrol cans for use on the journey. Cans will be drawn as under:—
    H.Q.   12.
    Each Coy: 17

Coy. O. M. Sergts will be responsible that these cans are handed in on detraining.

5. Rations & men boxes will be ready for loading at the Church at 5.30 a.m. punctually. The transport will be ordered not to wait for any articles which are not ready at the right time.

6. All billets will be left thoroughly clean, an inspected by one officer per Coy who will report to Major BENNETT before moving off.

7. The transport will march at 5.55 a.m. and entrain as above.

8. The Battn will detrain at ST OMER & march to billets in the BROXEELE area. Distance of 200x will be maintained between Coys on this march.

9. No lights will be allowed in the train after dark. The fires of cookers will be drawn before entrainment.

10. Mounted Officers will be notified later as to whether their Chargers will or will not be available for the march to the Station.

11. Sick parade tomorrow at 5.30 a.m.

12. Battn H.Q will close at NOEUX at 6.30 a.m. after which reports to head of column.

Battn H.Q.   (Sd) R.F. CUTHBERT
Issued at Noon.   Captain & Adjt

Roll. 4   O/C Coys.
       5   War Diary
       6   18th Infty. Bde
       7   Arm & Transport officer
       8   Medical officer
       9   R.S.M.
    10-12 Battn H.Q

CONFIDENTIAL.

WAR DIARY

*** of ***

2/4TH BATTALION, OXFORDSHIRE & BUCKINGHAMSHIRE LIGHT INFANTRY

From 1st August, 1917 to 31st August, 1917.

VOLUME XVI.

WAR DIARY or INTELLIGENCE SUMMARY

Army Form C. 2118.

Place	Date 1917	Hour	Summary of Events and Information	Remarks and references to Appendices
BROXEELE	Aug 1		In rest Billets. Batt & Coy training. Casualties NIL	NIL
"	2		d⁰. d⁰ d⁰	R.J.
"	3		d⁰. d⁰ d⁰	R.J.
"	4		d⁰. d⁰ d⁰	R.J.
"	5		d⁰. Church parade	R.J.
"	6		d⁰. Inspection by General HUNTER WESTON d⁰.	R.J.
"	7		d⁰. Batt & Coy training Casualties NIL	R.J.
"	8		d⁰. Brigade practice trench attack d⁰	R.J.
"	9		d⁰. Batt & Coy training d⁰	R.J.
"	10		d⁰. d⁰ d⁰	R.J.
"	11		d⁰. d⁰ d⁰	R.J.
"	12		d⁰. Church parade d⁰	R.J.
"	13		d⁰. Batt & Coy training d⁰	R.J.
"	14		d⁰. d⁰ d⁰	R.J.
"	15		d⁰. Batt marched to ARNEKE and entrained detrained at ABEELE and marched to camp at WATOU Casualties NIL	Appendix A3 R.J.

Army Form C. 2118.

WAR DIARY
or
INTELLIGENCE SUMMARY.
(Erase heading not required.)

Instructions regarding War Diaries and Intelligence Summaries are contained in F.S. Regs., Part II. and the Staff Manual respectively. Title pages will be prepared in manuscript.

Place	Date 1917	Hour	Summary of Events and Information	Remarks and references to Appendices
WATOU	Aug 16		In rest Camp. Battalion and Coy training. Casualties NIL	N.S.J.
"	17		Do. Do. Do.	N.S.J.
"	18		Do. Batt: marched to Camp in reserve in YPRES N area. Casualties NIL	N.S.J.
YPRES	19		In Camp in reserve. Company Commanders reconnoitred line in the ST JULIEN area. Casualties NIL	N.S.J.
Do	20		Do. In the afternoon the Batt: relieved the 2/6 Gloster Regt in the support line. At night the Batt: moved up and relieved the 4th Glosters in the front line trenches. Casualties NIL	N.S.J.
ST JULIEN	21		In front line trenches. Preparing to attack the German position at dawn. Considerable artillery activity on both sides. Casualties 2/Lt J.C. CALLENDER killed. O.R. killed 4. Wounded 31.	N.S.J.
Do	22		Do. At 4.45 a.m. the Batt: attacked the German position on a front of 750". The objective being	

about 900x distant. The 1/5- R. Warwicks attacked on left and the 2/ Bucks on right. The following Officers went into the line H.Q. LT COL WETHERALL M.C, Capt R.F. CUTHBERT, 2/Lt A.J. ROBINSON and 2/Lt T.A. HILL.
A Coy. 2/Lts COOMBES, TURRELL and WEBB. (2/Lt COLLENDER having been killed in previous day). B Coy Capt. J. G. STOCKTON, 2/Lts MOSERLY and GRAY. C Coy Capt. A.H. BRUCKER, 2/LTS MATTHEWS, HAWKES and DUNAND D Coy LT W.D. SCOTT, 2/LTS GUEST, DAWSON SMITH and GASCOYNE.
The assembly for the advance was on a type line, laid out in advance of our line by 2/Lt ROBINSON on night of 21st, and was carried out without the knowledge of the enemy. Two platoons of R.BERKS Co operated with the Batt: for support ups. The disposition of Coys from left to right was A, D, C in front line with B in support. The Batt: advanced under a creeping artillery

WAR DIARY or INTELLIGENCE SUMMARY

Army Form C. 2118.

Barrage, and A and D Coys closely followed by 2 platoons of B reached their Objective and consolidated. C Coy on right, with a platoon of B Coy in support, were held up owing to the failure of the support up platoon to take POND FARM. Owing to casualties amongst Officers, the front line command was assumed by 2/Lt Moseley, and with him were 2/Lt Coombes, (A Coy) and 2/Lt Gresch (D Coy). The 1/5 Warwicks on left failed to reach their Objective and envelope Hotchfolders of the front line were unprotected, but 2/Lt Moseley decided to hold on and arranged his men with their positions as to form, with the assistance of 2 platoons of 2/Lt Gleton in reserve and captured POND FARM. Casualties.

Officer Killed ‡ Capt J.G. STOCKTON, Lt W.D. SCOTT and 2/Lt GASCOYNE. Wounded Capt A.H. BRUCKER, 2/Lt

Place	Date 1917	Hour	Summary of Events and Information	Remarks and references to Appendices
			T.A. HILL, 2/LT H.R. TURRELL, 2/LT E. DAWSON SMITH and 2/LT T.W.P. HAWKES. O.R. killed 26, wounded 74, missing (probably killed & wounded) 44.	99.
ST JULIEN	Aug 23		In front line Trenches. At dawn the enemy rushed out Captured POND FARM, which had been held by a garrison of machine gunners & Ghurkas, assisted by 3 platoon of 2/6 Ghurkas in occupation the farm. The enemy snipers and local counter attacks on our front line, but these were repulsed with heavy loss, owing to the steep slopes about 20 prisoners were taken by us. At nightfall the B.M. was relieved by 2/6 Ghurkas except forty snipers about 3 a.m. next morning. Bn. marched to Camp at YPRES N area. Casualties Officers wounded 2/LT T.H. WEBB and V.C. GRAY. O.R. killed 3, wounded 29.	99.

WAR DIARY
INTELLIGENCE SUMMARY.
(Erase heading not required.)

Army Form C. 2118.

Place	Date 1917	Hour	Summary of Events and Information	Remarks and references to Appendices
YPRES	Aug 24		In Reserve Camp. Refit & cleaning up. Casualties NIL.	R.J.
"	25		Do. Batt marched to Rest Camp at BRANDHOEK. Casualties NIL.	R.J.
BRANDHOEK	26		In Rest Camp. Refit & cleaning up. Casualties NIL.	R.J.
"	27		Do. Coy training. 50 men went up at night as auxiliary Stretcher bearers. Casualties O.R. wounded 1.	R.J.
"	28		Do. Coy training. Do. Casualties O.R. wounded 1.	R.J.
"	29		Do. Do. Casualties NIL	R.J.
"	30		Do. 25 men went up at dawn as auxiliary Stretcher Bearers. Batt. marched to reserve Camp at YPRES N. Casualties NIL.	R.J.
YPRES	31		In Reserve Camp. 25 men found for auxiliary Stretcher bearers in the line. Casualties NIL.	R.J.

M.C. [signature]
Lt Col
Commd'g 2/4 Oxford & Bucks L.I.

SECRET   2/4 Oxford & Bucks Lt Infty   Copy
Appendix A 3   Order No 359   14-8-17

1. The Battn less Transport will march to ARNEKE tomorrow & entrain. Coys will be ready to move at 3 am in the order H.Q. A.B.C.D with head of column at road junction in G.17.d. A distance of 50ˣ will be maintained between Coys. Dress Full Marching order with steel helmets on packs.

2. Marching out states, exclusive of transport & transport personnel will be sent in by 6 pm tonight.

3. An advance party consisting of 2/Lt DUNAND & 1 NCO from each Coy will proceed to the station a 1/4 hour in advance of the Battn for marking carriages. 2/Lt DUNAND will report to the Adjutant at 7 pm tonight.

4. Reveille will be at 12.45 am.
5. First breakfast at 1.30 am. 2nd do on road. Dinners will be carried on the man. Teas on arrival in new area. Waterbottles

will be carried full. S.A.A. in mineboxes will be stacked in 2 dumps before moving off. 1 dump at H.Q. mess, the other at road junction G.22.b.9.7/2.

7 All billets will be left thoroughly clean and inspected by 1 officer per Coy who will report to the Adjutant before moving off.

8 The Battn will detrain at ABEELE & march to billets in the WATOU area.

9 Sick parade will be at 6 pm this evening.

10 Lights out tonight will be at 9 pm when men are to rest & not talk.

11 Lewis guns & Lewis gun teams will be handed in to transport to be loaded by 6.30 pm this evening.

12 All tools will be handed in to HQ Coy billet by 6.30 pm for loading.

13 Transport will pass road junction in S.23.b at 8.45 am.

14. Officers chargers will accompany Battn to ARNEKE where they will rejoin transport.

15. Battn H.Q. will close at BROXEELE at 3 am after which reports to head of column.

Battn H.Q. (Sd) A. J. Robinson
Issued at 3.15 pm Lt & A/Adjt

    Copies 1-4   Companies
            5   War Diary
            6   184 Bde.
            7   Q'mr & T.O.
            8   Medical Officer
            9   Battn H.Q.
           10   —do—

NOTE.

It is hoped to get a lorry from Bde, if so Officers Mess boxes & Officers cooks will go on this lorry.

FORMATION FOR ATTACK.

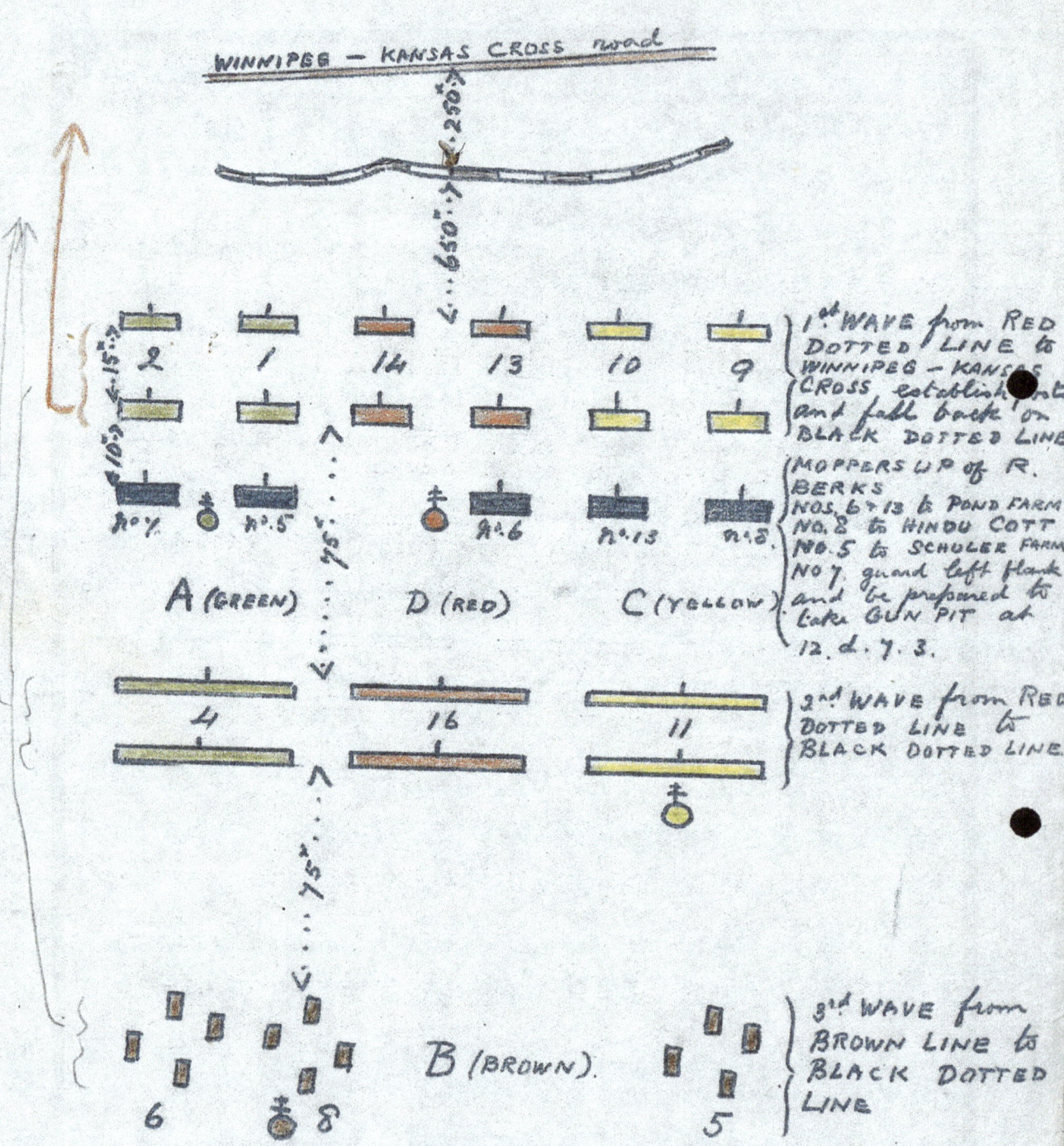

1st and 2nd Waves extended to 8 paces.
3rd Wave to keep in artillery formation
as long as possible

Battalion Attack Order No 1   Copy No 6

SECRET

Ref. Sketch Map 1/10000

1. (a) The Brigade will attack from MARTHA HOUSE to Road junction at C.7.c 2½ 5½ both inclusive

   (b) The Battalion will attack from GUN PIT 36 in C.13.b to Road junction at C.7.c 2½ 5½ both inclusive

   (c) The 1/5 WARWICKS 143rd Bde attack on our left the BUCKS on our Right dividing line green on sketch

2. Objective & Formation as per attached diagram

3. <u>Direction</u> Left of A on a true bearing of 48°
   Right of C   "   "   "   64°

4. <u>Moppers Up</u>
   Found by 5 platoons of R. BERKS. They are to consolidate their objectives as gained.

5. <u>Consolidation</u>
   Outpost line
   'C' Coy No 9 platoon to form a strong point around GUN PIT 36 with a standing patrol across WINNIPEG ROAD
   No 5 Platoon R BERKS at SCHULER FARM with a standing patrol across the road.
   'A' Coy No 1 Platoon at C.D.7.c. 4½. 5½ with a standing patrol near road.

   <u>Main Line of Resistance</u> Black dotted line on sketch.
   'C' Coy No 11 & 10 Platoon from Right to cross tracks at C.13.a. 6½.6. both inclusive
   'D' Coy Nos 13, 14 & 16 platoons from cross tracks at C.13.a. 6½.6. exclusive to C.7.c. 5.0. inclusive.
   'A' Coy No 4 & 2 platoons from D C.7.c.5.0 exclusive to track at C.7.c. 2.2.
   'B' Coy No 6 platoon to continue line to junction with 1/5 WARWICKS.
   No 8 platoon if there is a gap to further prolong our line to the left, otherwise to be behind A Coy at C.D.7.c. 3.0

O.C. A Coy may have this platoon to thicken his line if required.

No 5 platoon will fill any gap there may be between us and BUCKS. If no gap will assist 'C' Coy

No 7 platoon R BERKS to make a strong point around GUN PIT at C.12.d.7.3.

6. **Assembly** Will commence at 10 pm. A tape line will be laid out by that time by S/Lt ROBINSON.

He will move this tape directly after the Battn has assembled. The exact line will be indicated when it is known what the 183rd Bde has done.

'A & C' Coy will simultaneously commence at that hour.

D Coy will not commence until A & C have fixed their inner flanks.

B Coy who on night of 20/21st will be around SETQUES Farm C.22.b will commence to move up at 10.30 pm and form a line 100x behind the tape line.

O/C 'B' Coy is responsible for reconnoitring a way up.

R BERKS (attached platoons) Nos 11 and 13 will be guided up by their platoon commanders.

Guides will be provided for Nos 5, 7 and 8 platoons. They will report at Battn H.Q. R BERKS at 5 pm on the 21st.

All the platoons will move off as soon as possible after dark. All will be finished by 2.45 am when troops will rest.

It must be impressed on all ranks that
(1) Absolute SILENCE must be kept.
(2) The opening of our barrage is the signal to advance.

7. Probable ZERO and Artillery barrage.

ZERO about 4.45 am (Exact time later)

The Infantry will advance and the barrage commence at ZERO.

ZERO to -05.   About 200x in advance of our front line
05 -   Advance by 50x lifts at the rate of 100x in 5 minutes.
               Barrage will halt for 15 minutes 100x E of a line through HINDU COTT - AISNE HO.

The Artillery will bombard the following areas with Smoke Shells.
HILL 37.
GALLIPOLI COPSE
MARTHA HOUSE
WURST FARM
BOETLEER RIDGE

Therefore these smoke screens will form useful directing points.

The 1st Wave must at all costs follow the barrage.

8. <u>Machine Guns and L.T.M.B.</u>
2 V.G.s will be on JEW HILL at ZERO. They will fire towards WINNIPEG.
2 V.G.s about POND FARM to cross fire with them.
1 Section L.T.M.B. will be prepared at ZERO to fire on the GUN PIT immediately to the East of POND FARM.

9. <u>Dumps</u> Position will be notified later. It will contain S.A.A. Bombs, Flares, 100 tins of water, 150 shovels.

10. <u>Flares</u> will be lit only by front line, one to every 40 or 50 yds directly aeroplane calls by a succession of A.A.A. on "Klaxon". The aeroplane is marked by a black oblong on the right lower wing.

11. <u>Synchronisation of Watches</u> 1 Officer per Coy to report to Battn H.Q. at 2.30 am. They will give the time not only to the officers of their own Coys but to the platoons of R BERKS covering them off.

12. <u>S.O.S.</u> Green 1" very lights fired until guns open.

13. <u>Prisoners</u> Over the top direct to Advanced Bde H.Q. at C.23.c.7.8. Usual order as to escorts.

14. <u>Dress</u> Mars fighting order. Officers to wear mens kits.

15. <u>Signalling & Liaison</u> instructions are attached.

16. <u>Tanks</u> 2 Tanks will assist in taking SCHULERS GALLERY and POND FARM.

17. <u>Tank signals</u> Red disc = wire uncut
    Green " = " cut
    Red and Green " = have reached objective

17. Dressing station in RAT Farm.

18. Anybody using the word "RETIRE" will be treated as an enemy & shot.

19. Officers will carry only Sketch Maps, Note Books & Message forms. No Headquarters are to be marked on the sketch maps. No copy of these orders or anything likely to be of value to the enemy will be taken into action.

20. <u>Reports</u> Battn H.Q. in WINE HOUSE where all reports will be sent. Companies will send in short situation reports every ½ hour from ZERO to ZERO + 2½. All captured documents maps etc. will be sent in at once to Battn H.Q.

Issued at 7. pm.
19-8-17

                                                  [signature]
                                                  Capt. Adjt.

Copies 1-4   O/c Coys
        5   War Diary
        6   184 Inf Bde
        7   4 R. BERKS
        8   184 L.T.M.B.
        9   184 M.G. Coy
      10   Battn H.Q.

War Diary

of

2/4TH BATTALION OXFORDSHIRE AND BUCKINGHAMSHIRE

LIGHT INFANTRY.

from 1st September, 1917, to 30th September, 1917.

(Volume XVII.)

WAR DIARY
or
INTELLIGENCE SUMMARY.
(Erase heading not required.)

Army Form C. 2118.

Place	Date	Hour	Summary of Events and Information	Remarks and references to Appendices
Ypres	Sept 1.		In Reserve Camp. Resting and Cleaning up.	
"	2		do. Church Parade	
"	3		do. Company & Specialist training	
"	4		do. do.	
"	5		do. do.	
"	6		do. do. O.R. Wounded 2.	
"	7		In the evening Headquarters with "B" & "C" Companies relieved the 2/6 Royal Warwick Regiment in the Support line at WIELTJE. "A" & "D" Companies remaining in the Reserve Camp.	
WIELTJE	8		"A" & "D" Companies remaining in Support. 2 O.R. wounded.	App. 4.
			The Battalion relieved the 2/1st Bucks Battalion	
	9		In the evening the whole Battalion relieved the 2/1st Bucks Battalion in the Front Line (Right Brigade). Casualties O.R. 5 wounded 3 of whom subsequently died from wounds.	
ST JULIEN	10		At 4.5.p.m. A & D Companies of the Battalion under Captain K.E. Brown M.C. and Captain G.K. Rose M.C. respectively, proceeded to attack certain German gun positions on HILL 35. "A" Company on the Left, "D" Company	App 5.

T/131. Wt. W708-776. 500000. 4/15. Sir J.C. & S.

Army Form C. 2118.

WAR DIARY
or
INTELLIGENCE SUMMARY.
(Erase heading not required.)

Place	Date	Hour	Summary of Events and Information	Remarks and references to Appendices
ST JULIEN	Sept 16		On the Right. The following officers went into the Line :- H.Q. Lt.Col. H.E. M^cR Lethbridge M.C. Captain R. Fletcher, Adjt Captain C.S.W. Mason, 2/Lt. A.J. Robinson. "A" Company Captain K.E. Brown M.C. 2/Lieut H.P. Coombes 2/Lieut W.A.C. Moore. "B" Company 2/Lieut H. Stoehrn (2 in command) 2/Lieut R.S. Roche, 2/Lieut H.F. Ledger "C" Company 2/Lt C.S.S. Matthews (in command) 2/Lieut A.M. Durand, 2/Lieut H.R. Jones, 2/Lieut J.P. CopMarger. "D" Company Captain Fitz Rowe M.C. 2/Lieut P. Little. The two Companies (upper) assembled at dawn in Shell holes about 400 yards from our front line remained there till ZERO. The Companies advanced at 4.50 am under an Artillery Barrage and reached to within 30 + of the Objective, here they were held up by M.G. fire from the fern Pils and by M.G. fire from IBERIAN FM on the Right and AISNE HOUSE on the Left. One Platoon of "C" Company was sent to reinforce "A" Company, but all was still found impossible to advance, and the troops remained in this position until withdrawn under cover of darkness. The Battalion was relieved by the 2/15th Bucks Battalion by 11.30 p.m. that night and	

WAR DIARY or INTELLIGENCE SUMMARY

Army Form C. 2118.

(Erase heading not required.)

Place	Date	Hour	Summary of Events and Information	Remarks and references to Appendices
St JULIEN	10.5.15		returned to the Reserve Camp at YPRES. Casualties: Killed Officers Nil. O.R. 16. Wounded Officers 2/Lieut H. Stocken, 2/Lieut H.R. Priest, 2/Lieut J.P. (of Nurs.) and 2/Lieut H.E. Coombes. Wounded O.R. 34. (includes 2 at Duty).	A.F.B. A.F.B. A.F.B. Apx. 6. A.F.B.
YPRES.	11.5.15		in Reserve Camp. Cleaning up and Resting. Casualties Nil	
"	12.		" Cleaning up and Re-fitting "	
BRANDHOEK/13.			The Battalion marched to a Camp at BRANDHOEK on our right. Casualties Nil.	A.F.B. 0667 A.F.B. A.F.B.
WATOU	14		The Battalion marched to Rex Tree Camp at WATOU Casualties Nil	"
"	15		Battalion and Company Training "	"
"	16		Church Parade "	C.R.E. A.F.B. A.F.B. 0669
WORMHOUDT	17		The Battalion moved to WORMHOUDT into Billets "	
"	18		Cleaning up & Refitting. At 11 p.m. the Battalion marched to ESQUELBEC and Entrained for AUBIGNY reaching that place at 7 a.m. on the 19th. No Casualties.	
GOUVES.	19		The Battalion marched to Billets at GOUVES Casualties Nil	A.F.B.

WAR DIARY
or
INTELLIGENCE SUMMARY.
(Erase heading not required.)

Army Form C. 2118.

Place	Date	Hour	Summary of Events and Information	Remarks and references to Appendices
GOUVES	Sept 20		Company Training. Casualties Nil	
"	21		do do Received a draft of 150 O.R. do do	
"	22		do do do do	
"	23		Church Parade do do	
ARRAS	24		The Battalion marched to GRIMSBY CAMP, St NICHOLAS ARRAS. Casualties Nil	
"	25		Company Specialist Training Casualties Nil	
"	26		do do The following Officers joined the Battalion:-	
"			2/Lieut W.J.C. Ougman, A.P. Stephenson, O.S. Quigley, G. Ostin, P.R. Hare.	
"			C.S.M. Bensum all of the R. West Kent Regt. Casualties Nil	
"	27		Company & Specialist Training " "	
"	28		" " " "	
"	29		Church Parade " "	
"	30		L.G. firing on Range	
			During this month the following Honours were awarded to the Battalion:-	
			D.S.O. Lt Col H.S. de R. Wetherall M.C. 2/Lieut W.H. Quotely	
			M.C. 2/Lieut H.R. Prest	

WAR DIARY
or
INTELLIGENCE SUMMARY.
(Erase heading not required.)

Army Form C. 2118.

Place	Date	Hour	Summary of Events and Information	Remarks and references to Appendices
ARRAS	13/4/30		**D.C.M.** No.201098 C.S.M. Cairns J.C. No.23252 Cpl. Frost J. No.203440 L.Cpl. Allard D.R.	
			M.M. No.201234 Sergt. Arthro J. No.201176 Cpl. Jones Y.S. No.203435 L.Cpl. Dedman D. No.33017 Pte. Moorhead H. No.202136 Pte. Slater W.A. No.9852 Pte. Miles W. No.201337 Pte. Kemp H. No.201713 Pte. Kennett V. No.29015 Pte. Evans G.F. No.202735 Pte. Bond W.	

J.C. Mitchell Lt. Col.
1/4 Oxford & Bucks. N.I.

App. A.4.

SECRET.　　　　　　2/4 OXFORD AND BUCKS LIGHT INFANTRY.　　　Copy No. 6
　　　　　　　　　　　　　　ORDER NO. 380.

Ref. Map FREZENBERG 1/10000　　　　　　　　　　　　　　　　　　9/9/17.

1.　　　The Battalion will relieve the 2/1 BUCKS Battn. in the front line tonight.
　　　Guides will report to Coys. at 7.45 p.m. and Coys. will move in the order B.C.D.A. commencing at 8.30 p.m., and proceeding by No. 5 Track.

2.　　　Dispositions.
　　　OXFORDS.　"B" Coy. relieves BUCKS "C" Coy. in SOMME position.
　　　OXFORDS.　"C" Coy. relieves BUCKS "B" Coy, one platoon forming 3 posts between SOMME and Point 36, relieving No. 6 Platoon BUCKS, one platoon in position round point 39 in C.24. b.
　　　OXFORDS.　"D" Coy. will be led by guides of BUCKS "D" Coy. to assembly positions on the Right.
　　　OXFORDS.　"A" COY, will be led by guides of BUCKS "A" Coy.

3.　　　It is notified that the BUCKS Coys. are composed of two platoons.

4.　　　"B" and "C" Coys. will report relief complete by runners to Point 95.

5.　　　"B" and "C" Coys. will forward reports as under, to reach Battn. H.Q. as under at the following times.
　　　SITUATION. (including Strength and direction of Wind) 2 a.m. and 2 p.m.
　　　INTELLIGENCE AND WORK DONE.　8 a.m.
　　　CASUALTY.　2 p.m.
　　　Reports will not be sent by "A" or "D" Coys.

6.　　　Battn. H.Q. will be at POINT 95.

Battn. H.Q.　　　　　　　　　　　　　　　　　　　　　(sd) R.F. Cuthbert,
Issued at 12 noon.　　　　　　　　　　　　　　　　　Captain and Adjutant,
　　　　　　　　　　　　　　　　　　　　　　　　　　　　　　　4 Oxfords.

　　　　　　　　　Copy No. 1-4 O.C. Coys.
　　　　　　　　　　　　　5 184 Inf. Bde.
　　　　　　　　　　　　　6 War Diary.
　　　　　　　　　　　　　7-8 Battn. H.Q.

App. #5

SECRET.   Battalion Attack Order No.2.   Copy No. 7

Map Reference FREZENBERG. 1/10000 and sketch 61 M. 79.

1. "A" and "D" Coys. will attack German gun positions on HILL 35 on
   the 10th.
   "A" Coy. will attack on the left, "D" Coy. on the Right.

2. **Objectives.**
   "A" Coy. Tree on Left of position and Nos. 1.2. and 3 blockhouses.
   They will form a line 50 yards beyond these blockhouses (ie:- East)
   "D" Coy. No.4, point P, blockhouse 5. They will form a block 20
   yards up QR trench and consolidate round No.5 throwing back their right
   flank.

3. Formation as per diagram.

4. Zero will be at 4 P.M.

5. Artillery barrage will be notified later.

6. **Assembly.**
   "A" and "D" Coys. will be assembled at dawn on the 10th in their
   assault formation from D.19.a.8.5. to D.13.c.5.0.
   Men will not shew themselves on any excuse, but will sit down at
   bottom of shell holes. When Enemy's Aircraft come over they are to
   lie quite still, not to fire and not to look up.
   "B" and "C" Coys. are to open heavy Lewis Gun and rifle fire on any
   Enemy Aircraft.

7. **Vickers Guns.**
   1 Vickers Gun will be attached to "A" Coy. and 1 to "D" Coy.
   Company Commanders concerned will place these guns near their line of
   assembly. These guns will not move forward until objectives have
   been secured.
   1 V.G. will then move to No.1 Blockhouse and be sighted to fire N.E.
   1 Gun will move to NO. 5 and be sighted to fire to the south.

8. **L.T.M.B.**   Will be in position near SOMME but will not fire unless
   (a) the enemy counter-attacks.
   (b) hostile fire interfering with our work of consolidation
   (c) to cover retirement.

9. **R.E.**   4 Sappers carrying charges will follow the moppers-up, 2 will
   go to No.1 Blockhouse and 2 to NO.5.
   2 parties for improving M.G. emplacements, No.1 and No.5.
   Blockhouses, will come up directly it is dark.

10. "B" Coy. will remain in the position it takes over from the ????,
    around SOMME. It will co-operate after ZERO by opening fire on
    AISNE HO. After the attack it will keep special look-out for
    counter-attacks from direction of GALLIPOLI.
    "C" Coy. will be ready to re-enforce as will be explained to O.C.
    Coy. on the ground. He will report at Battn. H.Q. for this purpose
    at 10 A.M. on the 10th.

11. **Signalling arrangements.**
    Visual will be maintained from point 95 and BANK FARM to CALL
    RESERVE. Power buzzer from BANK FARM.
    Synchronization of watches. 1 Officer per Coy. will be sent to Battn.
    H.Q. at 3 A.M. on the 10th. It must be impressed on all ranks that

the real signal for the advance is the opening of our barrage fire.

12 **Medical arrangements.**   Stretcher bearers have been detailed by
Medical Officer for special duties.
Auxy. Aid Post. BANK FARM (for walking cases)
Regtl. Aid Post. PLUM FARM.
16 extra bearers have been attached to the Battalion.

13 **Prisoners.**   Will be brought to Battalion H.Q.

14 **Reports.**   Will be ~~brought~~ sent to Battn H.Q. at point 95.

Battn H.Q.   (sd) R.F. Cuthbert.
Issued at 10 p.m.   Captain and Adjutant.,

          Copy No. 1 to 2 Battn H.Q.
                    3 to 6 O.C. Coys.
                         7 War Diary.
                         8 184 Inf. Bde.

SECRET.   2/4 OXFORD AND BUCKS LIGHT INFANTRY.   Copy No. 5

app. 6

ORDER NO. 382.   12/9/17.

Ref. MAP 1/20000, 28 N.W.

1. The Battalion will march tomorrow to BRANDHOEK NO. 3 Area. Route VLAMERTINGHE-POPERINGHE STATION.

2. Coys. will move in the order H.Q.,D,C,B,A, and a distance of 200 yards will be maintained between Coys. on the march. The Transport will fall in 200 yards in rear of the Battalion on passing H.8.a.4.8.

3. H.Q. and D Coy. will parade at 9.30 a.m.
   C Coy.   9.33.
   B "   9.36.
   A "   9.39.

4. Lewis Guns and other Battalion stores will be loaded by 8.30 a.m. Valises and Mess boxes by 9 a.m.

5. Strict march discipline is to be maintained. The usual 10 minute halt will be observed.

6. The Camp will be left thoroughly clean and an Officer per Coy. will inspect and report on Coys. lines.

7. 2/Lieut. ROBINSON with a N.C.O. from each Coy. will move off at 8.30 a.m. and take over new Camp at G.9.a.2.4.

8. Captain MARCON will hand over the present Camp with tents and shelters to the Area Commandant and obtain receipt.

9. Battalion H.Q. will close at YPRES N. at 9 a.m. after which reports to head of column.

                                    (sd) R.F.Cuthbert,
Battn. H.Q.   Captain and Adjutant,
Issued at 8 p.m.   4 Oxfords.

          Copy 1-4 O.C. Coys.
               5. War Diary.
               6. 183 Inf. Bde.
               7. Quartermaster & T.O.
               8. Medical Officer.
               9. Battalion H.Q.

App. 7

SECRET.   2/4TH BN. OXFORD & BUCKS LIGHT INFANTRY.   Copy No. 5
                    ORDER NO. 383.   13.9.17.

Ref. Map 1/40000,
    Sheet 27.

1.   The Battalion will march tomorrow to Camp at L.8.c.5.5.

2.   Coys. will move in the order H.Q.,C,B,A,D. Until reaching the level crossing in L.17.d. distances of 200 yards will be maintained between Coys. From that point the Battalion will march closed up.

3.   Coys. will parade as under:-
            H.Q. and C.   7.25 a.m.
            B.   7.28 a.m.
            A.   7.31 a.m.
            D.   7.34 a.m.

4.   2/Lieut. ROBINSON and 1 N.C.O. per Coy. will move off at 7 a.m., and report to Staff Captain, 183 Brigade at L.13.b.1.7 at 9 a.m.

5.   The Camp will be left thoroughly clean.   1 Officer per Coy. will inspect and report on Coy. Lines before moving off.

6.   Valises and mess boxes, etc. will be ready for loading by 7 a.m.

7.   Battalion H.Q. will close at present Camp at 7.50 a.m. after which reports to head of column.

                                    (sd) R.F.CUTHBERT,
                                    Captain and Adjutant,
                                    4 OXFORDS.

Battalion H.Q.
Issued at 8 p.m.

            Copy No.1 - 4.   O.C. Coys.
                    5.   War Diary.
                    6.   183rd Infantry Brigade.
                    7.   Quartermaster & T.O.
                    8.   Medical Officer.
                    9.   Battalion H.Q.

SECRET.   2/4TH BN. OXFORD & BUCKS LIGHT INFANTRY.   Copy No. 5
                ORDER NO. 386.   16.9.17.

1. The Commanding Officer is pleased to announce that the MILITARY MEDAL for gallantry and devotion to duty in action has been awarded to the undermentioned N.C.O.s and men:-
   201234 Sgt. ARIS, J.   203435 L/Cpl. DEDMAN, B.
   201176 Cpl. JONES, T.S.   33017 Pte. TOWNSEND, H.
   202025 Pte. BELCHER, G.   200514 L/Cpl. WAGSTAFF, C. (att.L.T.M.B.).

2. The Battalion will march tomorrow to WORMHOUDT, via HOUTKERQUE and HERZEELE.

3. Coys. will move in the order H.Q., B, C, D, A, and will parade at 7 a.m.

4. Transport will march in rear of the Battalion with Cookers leading, followed by Water carts.

5. The usual 10 minute halts will be observed.

6. The Camp will be left thoroughly clean, and one officer per Coy. will inspect and report on Coy. lines before moving off.

7. 2/Lt. JONES, M.C. with one N.C.O. from each A and C Coys. and one from H.Q. will draw bicycles and move off at 6 a.m. for billeting. They will billet as follows:-
   A Coy's N.C.O.   A and B Coys.
   C   "   "   C " D "
   H.Q.   "   H.Q., Q.M. Stores and Transport.

8. 2/Lieut. ROBINSON with one N.C.O. each from B and D Coys, will parade at 6.15 a.m. and proceed to the DUISANS area tomorrow for billeting the Battalion.
   They will carry rations for and including the 20th inst. and will report to Brigade H.Q. by 7 a.m. whence they will go by bus.

9. Valises and mess boxes will be ready for loading by 6.15 a.m.

10. Dinners will be ready for serving on arrival in billets, about 12 noon.

11. Battalion H.Q. will close at WATOU area at 6.30 a.m. after which reports to head of column.

12. Sick parade at 5.15 a.m.

                           (sd) R.F.CUTHBERT,
                           Captain and Adjutant,
                           4 OXFORDS.

Battalion H.Q.
Issued at 10.15 p.m.
                  Copy No. 1 - 4.   O.C. Coys.
                           5.   War Diary.
                           6.   184 Bde.
                           7.   Q.M. & T.O.
                           8.   M.O.
                           9.   O.C. H.Q. Coy.
                          10.   Battn. H.Q.

App. 9

SECRET.   2/4TH OXFORD AND BUCKS LIGHT INFANTRY.   Copy No. 5
           ORDER NO. 122.   19.9.17.

1. The Battalion will march to ESQUELBEC Station tonight and entrain.

2. Coys. will move in the order H.Q.,A,B,C,D. The head of the column will be ready to pass the Area Commandant's office in the Square at 10.40 p.m.

3. The Transport will move at 9.10 p.m. under arrangements to be made by the Transport Officer who will reconnoitre the entraining station this afternoon.

4. Water carts will be entrained full; all water-bottles will be filled by 8 p.m.

5. Hot tea will be issued at the entraining station, but no other ration will be served until breakfast after detraining.

6. Probable time of detraining 8.10 a.m.

7. No lights will be allowed in the train.

8. Great care must be taken to leave billets thoroughly clean. Each Coy. will render a certificate that billets have been examined and found clean in all respects.

9. 2/Lieut. LITTLE with 1 N.C.O. per Coy. will move off at 10 p.m. to mark the carriages.

10. Marching out states will be sent in to Orderly room by 6 p.m. today.

                                    (sd) R.F.CUTHBERT,
                                    Captain and Adjutant,
                                    4 OXFORDS.

Battalion Headquarters,
Issued at 11.45 a.m.

            Copy No. 1 - 4.   O.C. Coys.
                     5.   War Diary.
                     6.   184 Bde.
                     7.   Quartermaster & Transport Officer
                     8.   Medical Officer.
                     9.   R.S.M.
                     10 - 11. Battalion H.Q.

App. 10

SECRET.   Copy No. 5

2/4TH BN. OXFORD AND BUCKS LIGHT INFANTRY.
ORDER NO. 295.   23/9/17.

Ref. Maps 1/40000, 51 B. and 51 C.
---

1.   The Battalion will march tomorrow to BRISBEN Camp C.17.b.
Route: AUBER LES HESDIN, OUTRANS, L.9.a.4.6., C.31.a.5.9., C.15.D.1.2,
C.21.b.4.7., C.13.c.0.8.

2.   Companies will move in the order H.Q.,B,C,D,A. The head of the
column will pass starting point, road junction at L.14.d.0.8 at
2.45 p.m.   Intervals of 200 yards will be maintained between Coys.

3.   F.S.Caps will be worn, the steel helmets being carried on the pack.

4.   The Transport will move behind in two echelons, with intervals
of 200 yards.

5.   The usual 10 minute halts will be observed, except that there
will be no halt at 2.50 p.m.

6.   Valises and Mess boxes will be ready for collection by 2.30 p.m.

7.   All billets will be left scrupulously clean. "No damage"
certificates will be obtained. One Officer per Coy. will inspect
and report on billets before moving off.

8.   Orders for the Advance party will be issued later.

9.   Battalion H.Q. will close at OUTRAN at 2.30 p.m., after which
reports to head of column.

                                        (sd) D.F.GUTHRIE,
                                        Captain and Adjutant,
                                        & OXFORDS.
Battalion H.Q.,
Issued at 1.30 p.m.

                Copy No. 1 - 4.   O.C. Coys.
                         5.   War Diary.
                         6.   184th Infantry Brigade.
                         7.   Quartermaster & Transport Officer.
                         8.   Medical Officer.
                         9.   O.C. H.Q.Coy.
                        10 - 11. Battn. H.Q.

CONFIDENTIAL

WAR DIARY

*** of ***

2/4th BATTALION, OXFORDSHIRE & BUCKINGHAMSHIRE LIGHT INFANTRY

From 1st October to 31st October, 1917.

VOLUME XVlll.

****

Army Form C. 2118.

WAR DIARY
or
INTELLIGENCE SUMMARY.
(Erase heading not required.)

Instructions regarding War Diaries and Intelligence Summaries are contained in F.S. Regs., Part II. and the Staff Manual respectively. Title pages will be prepared in manuscript.

Place	Date 1917	Hour	Summary of Events and Information	Remarks and references to Appendices
ST NICHOLAS	Oct. 1		In Camp in Reserve. Coy Training. Casualties Nil.	N.F.C.
"	2		do. do.	N.F.C.
"	3		do. do.	N.F.C.
"	4		do. do.	Appendix B!
"			Battⁿ relieved 2/7ᵗʰ WORCESTERS in right sub-sector, GREENLAND HILL sector. Disposition: Right Front, B; Centre A; Support C; Left D. Casualties Nil.	N.F.C.
GREENLAND HILL	5		In Front Line Trenches. Patrols sent out by Front Line Companies. Wiring and improving Trenches. Casualties Nil.	N.F.C.
"	6		do. Patrols and work as above. Casualties Nil.	N.F.C.
"	7		do. do. C Coy relieved D Coy in centre of Front Line. Casualties Nil.	N.F.C.
"	8		do. Patrols and work as above. Casualties O.R. Wounded, 1.	N.F.C.
"	9		do. Patrols & work as above. Casualties Nil.	N.F.C.

T2134. Wt. W708—776. 500000. 4/15. Sir J. C. & S.

WAR DIARY
or
INTELLIGENCE SUMMARY.
(Erase heading not required.)

Army Form C. 2118.

Place	Date 1917	Hour	Summary of Events and Information	Remarks and references to Appendices
GREENLAND HILL	Oct 10		In Front Line Trenches. Battⁿ relieved by 2/5 GLOSTERS and moved to Support Trenches. Casualties NIL	Appendix B2, T.O.T.
Do	11		In Support Trenches. Working parties found day and night. Casualties NIL	R.R.R.
Do	12		Do. Working parties as above. Casualties NIL	R.R.R.
Do	13		Do. Do. Do.	T.O.T.
Do	14		Do. Do. Casualties O.R. wounded 1.	T.O.T.
Do	15		Do. Do. Casualties NIL	T.O.T.
Do	16		Battⁿ relieved 2/5 GLOSTERS in front line Trenches. Distribution Right B, Centre D, Left C, Support A. Hand Patrols & work on Trenches. Casualties O.R. wounded 1.	Appendix B3 T.O.T.
Do	17		In Protective Trenches. Patrols & work as above. Casualties NIL	T.O.T.
Do	18		Do. Do. Lt Col WETHERALL, D.S.O., M.C. proceeded on Leave, and Major	

WAR DIARY or INTELLIGENCE SUMMARY

Army Form C. 2118.

Place	Date 1917	Hour	Summary of Events and Information	Remarks and references to Appendices
GREENLAND HILL	Oct. 19		In Front Line Trenches. H.J. BENNETT assumed command of the Batt. Casualties Nil.	N.J.
	20		Do. Patrols out last night as above. Casualties Nil.	N.J.
	21		Do. Do.	R.J.
	22		Do. Do. Appendices	N.J.
			Battn relieved by 2/5 GLOSTERS and moved to Support Trenches. Casualties Nil.	N.J.
	23		In Support Trenches. Working parties found day & night. Casualties Nil.	N.J.
	24		Do. Working parties as above. Casualties Nil.	N.J.
	25		Do. Do.	N.J.
	26		Do. Do.	N.J.
	27		Do. Do.	N.J.
	28		Do. Battn relieved by 2/7 WARWICKS and marched to billets at ARRAS, all Companies being quartered	

WAR DIARY
or
INTELLIGENCE SUMMARY

Army Form C. 2118.

Place	Date	Hour	Summary of Events and Information	Remarks and references to Appendices
ARRAS	Oct 29 1917		in the Prison Casualties Nil.	Appendix AB 5. N.P.
	30		In Billets in Reserve. Capt and Adjutant Cavallie N/K. Lt Col WETHERALL D.S.O. M.C. returned from Leave & assumed Command. 13 Other & Company Training Casualties Nil. do.	R.F.C. [signatures] N.I. N.I.
	31		do. do.	
			During the month, the Military Medal was awarded to R⁰ 202909 Pte FLEMING, R. and R⁰ 202064 " SLOCOMBE, W. Strength comprising 14 Officers and 730 O.R. joined the Batt. during the month.	

[signature] W Wetherall
LT COL
Comm'g 2/4 Oxford & Bucks L.I.

Appendix B.

SECRET.   2/4TH BN. OXFORD & BUCKS LIGHT INFANTRY.   COPY NO. 7
                    ORDER NO. 405.   3.10.17.
              Ref. Map 51 B. N.W. 1/20000.

1. The Battalion (less No.4 Platoons) will relieve the 7th WORCESTERS in the right sub-sector (GREENLAND HILL sector) tomorrow.

2. Distribution of Companies will be as follows:-
   Right Front B, Centre A, Left D, Support C.
   Companies will move in the order H.Q., D,A,B,C at 200^x interval, H.Q. being ready to move at 5 p.m.

3. Tea will be issued before moving off, and meat teas served in CAM VALLEY.

4. N. of H.13.b.3.4 distances of 100^x will be maintained between Platoons.

5. One N.C.O. per platoon will be detailed to meet Company Commanders at CAM VALLEY at 2.30 p.m. for the purpose of taking over. They will move off from the Camp under the senior N.C.O. at 1.30 p.m. 2 runners per Coy. will accompany this party and bring back to CAM VALLEY distribution particulars from Company Commanders.

6. The following advance party will report to Sergt. SHERWOOD at 7.30 a.m. at Battalion H.Q. ready to proceed to the line.
   6 H.Q. Signallers.
   8 Coy. Runners. (2 per Coy.).
   4 Battalion Runners.
   1 Sniper. (L/Cpl. BERRY, "C" Coy).
   1 H.Q. Gas N.C.O.
   3 Water duty men.

7. The dress for the line will be packs slung, containing shaving and washing kit, 3 pairs of socks etc. Great coats optional. Haversacks will not be carried.

8. The Snipers and Observers recently trained will parade with and be attached to H.Q. and rationed by H.Q.

9. Receipts for stores taken over will be sent to Battn. H.Q. by 8.30 a.m. on 5th inst. Disposition sketches will be forwarded by the same time. These will shew garrisons of posts and position of Lewis Guns.

10. Guides will meet Coys. at H.15.a. 9.5. at 7 p.m.

11. Code word for "Relief Complete" will be RATIONS.

12. The Camp will be left thoroughly clean. 2/Lieut. COOMBES will hand over to Area Commandant of relieving unit, obtain receipt in duplicate and "clean certificate" and forward the certificate and 1 copy of the receipt direct to Staff Captain, 184 Brigade.

12. Blankets neatly rolled and tied in tens, surplus kits in sandbags valises and mess boxes will be ready for collection by 4 p.m.

Battalion H.Q.
Issued at 8.30 p.m.
                                         (sd) R.F. CUTHBERT,
                                          Captain and Adjutant,
                                             4 OXFORDS.

Appendix B²

SECRET.   2/4TH BN. OXF. & BUCKS LT. INFTY.   Copy No. 9
                                                9.10.17.
           ORDER NO. 406.

1. The Battalion will be relieved tomorrow by the 2/5th GLOSTERS.

2. Coys. will be relieved as under, and in the following order:-

    OXFORDS.   GLOSTERS.
        D   by   (2 platoons A.
                                (1 platoon B.
        C   "   D.
        A   "   2 platoons B.
        B   "   C.

3. Guides for incoming Unit (1 per platoon & 1 per Coy.H.Q.) will be at the junctions of CHILI and HARRY as under:-
    D Coy.   2.15 p.m.
    H.Q., C,A,B.   5.30 p.m.

4. Front line Lewis Gunners will be relieved in daylight. The necessary guides for this purpose will be at the junction of CHILI and COSTA at 3.30 p.m.

5. Signallers will relieve by 12 noon.

6. 1 Officer per Coy. & 1 N.C.O. per platoon of the incoming unit will arrive at 10 a.m. to take over and sign receipts for trench stores etc.

7. The code for completion of relief will be RITZ.

8. On relief Coys. will take over the positions in the support line as under,
        OXFORDS   GLOSTERS
        D.Coy.   A.Coy.
        C. "   D. "
        A. "   B. "
        B. "   C. "
    OXFORDS D.Coy. will be in EFFIE Trench (CAM VALLEY) the remainder in HUDSON.

9. 1 Officer per Coy. and 1 N.C.O. per platoon (OXFORDS) will report to Battn. H.Q. at 10 a.m. Guides will be allotted to them to take them to their positions in the Support line, where they will take over from the GLOSTERS. They will meet their Coys. on relief as under :-
    D.Coy. - Junction of CABLE Trench and Sunken Road (TANK DUMP)
    Other Coys. - Junction of CHILI and HUSSAR.

10. D.Coy. will send with this advance party, 3 Lewis Gunners, to take over positions and duties of 2 Lewis Guns mounted in CAM VALLEY for A.A.work.
    On arrival of the Coy., these guns will be mounted.

11. O.C.,A.Coy.will hand over to relieving Coy. 1 Lewis Gun at his Coy.H.Q. and obtain receipt.

12. Any Mess kit or stores for the Railway will be taken to Railhead by 7.30 p.m. This will be loaded on the trucks which bring up the GLOSTERS rations, and all trucks(empty or otherwise) will be pushed back by a party of 1 N.C.O. and 10 men to be detailed

by A.Coy. for the purpose. On arrival at new positions, Coys. will send to Railbase(TANK DUMP) to fetch their kit, and A.Coy's party will remain in charge until all is cleared.

13. The Lewis Gunners of A, B & C. Coys. who are relieved early, will report for instructions at Battn. H.Q. on their way out. On arrival at their new positions, they will ascertain from the GLOSTERS, the overland route to TANK DUMP, and they will meet the ration limbers there at 6.30 p.m. and carry rations to their Coys.

14. D.Coy's rations will be brought by limber to the road at CAM VALLEY. They will be there by 5.30 p.m. and D.Coy will send party on arrival in their area.

15. Receipts for Trench Stores etc. will be sent in to Battn. H.Q. by 3.30 p.m. tomorrow.

(sd) R.F.CUTHBERT,
Capt. and Adjt.

Battn. H.Q.
Issued at 5 p.m.

1 - 4. Coys.
5. GLOSTERS.
6. 184 Inf. Bde.
7. Quartermaster.
8. Transport Officer.
9. War Diary.
10. Office.

SECRET.   2/4th. Oxford & Bucks Light Infty.   Copy No. 7
                    ORDER NO. 409.   16.10.17.

Appendix B3

1. The Battn. will relieve the 2/5 GLOSTERS in the Right Sub-Sector tomorrow.

2. Coys will relieve as under and in the following order,

OXFORDS.	GLOSTERS.	PLACE.
B (one platoon) relieves	A (1 platoon)	Right front.
A "	C	Support.
C "	D	Left.
D (2 platoons) "	B (2 platoons)	Centre.
B & D (1 platoon each) "	A (2 platoons)	Right.

3. Guides for A.Coy. will be at Junction CHILI and HUSSAR at 2.30 p.m. Guide for 1 platoon of B.Coy. will be at Junction CHILI and CALDRON at 2.30 p.m. Guides for remainder at Junction CHILI and HUSSAR at 5.15 p.m.

4. Guides for all front line Lewis Gun Teams will be at Junction of CHILI and CALDRON at 2 p.m.

5. Signallers and Snipers will relieve by 12 noon.

6. Coy. Commanders with 1 N.C.O. per platoon will take over Stores etc. in their new area at 10 a.m.

7. Coys. will hand over stores in their present area to representatives who will arrive from the GLOSTERS in the morning.
Receipts will be sent forthwith to Battn. H.Q.

8. Petrol tins will be carefully collected and returned to Water Duty men at the TANK by 4 p.m. A note showing the numbers returned by each Coy. will be sent to H.Q.

9. The Petrol Tins will be collected by the Transport Officer and taken back to Stores.

10. Coys. on completion of Relief will send parties to draw rations at Railhead.

11. On the arrival of 2 men for Water Guard from the GLOSTERS, 2 Water Duty men will proceed to relieve the Water Guard in the Forward area.

12. D.Coy. will take over 1 Lewis Gun from B.Coy. GLOSTERS.

13. Distribution sketches (on the maps issued to Coys. herewith) will be sent in by 3.30 p.m. on 17th.

14. Lewis Gunners (GLOSTERS) will take over the A.A. Gun positions in CAM VALLEY by 11 a.m.

15. The code for completion of relief will be "Private PETER has arrived".

16. All parties relieving in the front line by daylight will be warned not to show themselves, and to carry guns, stretchers etc. below the shoulder.

17. Further orders will be issued as to the platoon and details going to the Brigade School.

Battn. H.Q.
Issued at 4.45 p.m.

(sd) R.F.CUTHBERT,
Capt. and Adjt.

1 - 4. Coys.
5. 2/5 GLOSTERS.
6. 184 Inf.Bde.
7. War Diary.
8. Major H.J.BENNETT.
9. Qr,Mr. and Transport Officer.
10. Battn. H.Q.

SECRET. 2/4th Oxford and Bucks Light Infty. Copy No. 7
ORDER NO. 410. 21.10.17.

Appendix B.4

1. The Battn. will be relieved tomorrow by the 2/5 GLOSTERS.

2. Coys. will be relieved as under in the following order,
   OXFORDS   relieved by   GLOSTERS.
   B.   "   "   B.
   C.   "   "   D.
   D.   "   "   A.(2 platoons)
   A.   "   "   C.(2 "   ) & A.(1 platoon

3. On relief Coys. will proceed to HUDSON and EFFIE trenches as under,
   OXFORDS B. take over from GLOSTERS C. in EFFIE.
      "   C.   "   "   "   "   B.
      "   D.   "   "   "   "   A.
      "   A.   "   "   "   "   D.

4. Front Line Lewis Gun teams will be relieved in daylight.
   Guides for Incoming teams will be sent to Junction of CALDRON
   and CHILI at 2 p.m.

5. One Guide per platoon and one per Coy. H.Q. will be at Junction
   of HUSSAR and CHILI as under,
        B.Coy.   2.30 p.m.
        C.)
        D.)"   5 p.m.
        A.)

6. Signallers and Observers (O.P.) will relieve by 12 noon.

7. O.C., B.Coy. will send 1 L.G. and team to take over A.A. positions
   in CAM VALLEY at 11 a.m.   A second gun and team will be sent there
   by B.Coy. on completion of relief.

8. One Officer per Coy of the GLOSTERS and 1 N.C.O. per platoon will
   arrive at Coy. H.Q. at 12 noon for taking over. Receipts for Trench
   Stores(which will include all Petrol Tins and braziers) will be taken
   and forwarded to Battn. H.Q. by 9 p.m. 22nd.

9. The Trenches and all dug-outs and shelters will be left thoroughly
   clean and tidy.

10. One Officer per Coy, and one N.C.O. per platoon will take over
    their positions in the Reserve line at 12 noon, and will arrange to
    meet their Coys. on completion of relief.

11. The Front Line L.G. teams after ascertaining their Coy. positions
    in the Reserve Line will proceed to TANK DUMP and carry rations and
    water for their Coys.   The Signallers will do the same for H.Q.

12. O.C., D.Coy. will hand over 1 Lewis Gun in CHARLIE to A.Coy.
    GLOSTERS and obtain receipt.

13. The rations for B.Coy. will be taken by limber to the road at
    CAM VALLEY where they will be ready by 5 p.m.

14. Code for completion of Relief "TIRED TIM".

Battn. H.Q.   (sd) R.F.CUTHBERT,
Issued at 5.30 p.m.   Captain and Adjt.

S E C R E T.   2/4th Oxford & Bucks Light Infantry   Copy No. 7

ORDER NO. 411.   27.10.17.

1. The Battn. will be relieved tomorrow by 2/7th WARWICKS, and will march to billets at the PRISON, ARRAS.

2. Coys. will be relieved by Coys. of the R.WARWICKS as under and in the following order,

OXFORDS	by	WARWICKS.
H.Q.	"	H.Q.
D.	"	Z.
A.	"	Y.
C.	"	X.
B.	"	W.

3. Incoming Coys. will arrive via CABLE and HUSSAR. Outgoing Coys. will move by HUDSON, NORTHUMBERLAND AVENUE and CABLE.
   On arrival of the relieving Coy, the Coy. to be relieved will immediately move down the trench, and be ready to march out clear of the next incoming Coy.

4. O.C., B.Coy. will post an Officer in the trench to whom outgoing Coys. will report as they pass. O.C., B.Coy. will report relief complete to Battn. H.Q. by telephone, the code being "BUBBLY".

5. Guides for Incoming Unit (1 per platoon & 1 for Coy. H.Q.) will be at CAM VALLEY end of CASTLE LANE at 2 p.m.
   Ten minute intervals will be maintained between Incoming Coys., so as to prevent congestion on arrival at HUDSON.

6. One Officer and one N.C.O. per Incoming Coy., together with Signallers and garrison for the O.P. will arrive at Junction of NORTHUMBERLAND AVENUE and HUDSON where one guide from H.Q. and 1 guide per Coy. will meet them at 11.30 a.m.

7. Receipts for Trench Stores, documents etc. handed over will be sent to H.Q. before moving off.

8. The L.G. team in CAM VALLEY will be relieved by 12 noon. O.C., B.Coy. will send a guide to ROAD end of CAM VALLEY to meet these teams at 11 a.m.

9. The Signalling Sergt. will arrange the relief of the S.O.S. Signal Station by the advance party of Signallers.

10. The Water Guard (4 men) and the permanent loading party at TANK DUMP (1 N.C.O. & 7 men) will be relieved by 12 noon. The Provost Sergt. will detail a man to meet relieving parties at Junction of CABLE and NORTHUMBERLAND AVENUE at 11.30 a.m. and take them to their respective positions.

11. O.C., Coys will take steps to ensure that all trenches and dug-outs are left in a thoroughly clean condition.

12. W.Coy of R.WARWICKS will find the L.G. party in TRENT (1 N.C.O. & 6 men with 2 guns). O.C., B.Coy. will obtain full particulars of this party from O.C., C.Coy. in order to hand over same to relieving Unit. The relief of this party will be completed by 5 p.m. or as soon as light permits.

13. Billeting parties are being found by Officers and O.R. now at the Brigade School.

14. On relief Coys. will march independently to Billets, 200^x intervals between platoons being maintained E. of the ARRAS – LENS Railway. Guides from the Billeting party will meet their Coys. at the X roads at G.16.d.4.7.

15. O.C., D.Coy. will drop 1 N.C.O. at the CAM VALLEY end of CASTLE LANE. He will ascertain from B.Coy. when they are all clear of the Trench, and inform the 2/5 WARWICKS who will be waiting to enter the trench.

16. Great care must be taken to ensure that all Petrol Tins are taken out. Any that can be spared to-night will be returned by ration parties. The remainder will be carried out to CAM VALLEY tomorrow. Coys. will obtain receipts from the Transport N.C.O. for all tins handed over to-night or to-morrow, and send same to Battn. H.Q.

17. Any other Battn. or private stores that can be spared to-night will be sent out by Ration parties.

18. The Transport Officer will arrange for limbers for Lewis Guns and Stores to be at CAM VALLEY by 3 p.m.

19. Sufficient Cooks will be sent in advance to prepare teas for Coys. on arrival at Billets.

(sd) R.F.CUTHBERT,
Captain and Adjutant.

Battn. H.Q.
Issued at 2 P.M.

1 – 4. Coys.
5. 2/7 R.WARWICKS.
6. 184th Inf. Bde.
7. War Diary.
8. Transport Officer & Qr.Mr.
9. Signalling & Provost Sgts.
10. Office.

CONFIDENTIAL.

WAR DIARY

OF

2/4TH BATTALION OXFORDSHIRE & BUCKINGHAMSHIRE LIGHT
INFANTRY.

From 1st November, 1917, to 30th November, 1917.

(Volume XIX).

Army Form C. 2118.

WAR DIARY
or
INTELLIGENCE SUMMARY.
(Erase heading not required.)

Instructions regarding War Diaries and Intelligence Summaries are contained in F.S. Regs., Part II. and the Staff Manual respectively. Title pages will be prepared in manuscript.

Place	Date 1917	Hour	Summary of Events and Information	Remarks and references to Appendices
ARRAS	Nov 1		In Billets in Reserve. Battalion and Company Training. Casualties NIL.	E.10.13
"	2		Do. Do. Do.	E.10.13
"	3		Do. Do.	E.H.13
"	4		Do. Church Parade. Battalion Transport inspected by	E.10.13
			O.C. 184th INFANTRY BRIGADE. Casualties NIL.	F.14.6
"	5		Do. Battalion and Company Training. No 13 Platoon 'D'	
			Company joined 184th Infantry Brigade School for instruction, relieving	4.13
			No 9 Platoon 'C' Company. Casualties NIL.	
"	6		Do. Battalion and Company Training. Casualties NIL.	F.14.0
"	7		Do. Do. Do.	F.14.0
"	8		Do. Battalion firing on the BUTTE DE TIR Range during the morning	
			Company and Specialist Training. Casualties NIL.	8.10
"	9		Do. Battalion relieved 2/4th WORCESTERS in right sub-sector.	App B.5
			Distribution. Right Front 'B';	
			Centre 'D', Left 'A', Support 'C'. Casualties NIL.	F.H.
CHEMICAL WORKS SECTOR	10		In Front line trenches. Patrols sent out by front line Companies, Wiring and	E.11.0

T2134. Wt. W708-776. 500000. 4/15. Sir J. C. & S.

Army Form C. 2118.

WAR DIARY
or
INTELLIGENCE SUMMARY.
(Erase heading not required.)

Instructions regarding War Diaries and Intelligence Summaries are contained in F. S. Regs., Part II. and the Staff Manual respectively. Title pages will be prepared in manuscript.

Place	Date 1917	Hour	Summary of Events and Information	Remarks and references to Appendices
CHEMICAL WORKS SECTOR	10		Improving trenches. Casualties 1 O.R. Wounded (gas).	G.H.Q.s
"	11		In front line trenches. Patrols and work as above. "B" Coy relieved "B" Coy on right. Special party of "B" Coy. were withdrawn for training behind the line. Casualties NIL	G.H.Q.s
"	12		Do. Patrols and work as above. Do.	G.H.Q.s
"	13		Do. Do. No.1 Platoon "A" Coy, relieved 18th Field School, No.13 Platoon "D" Coy. Casualties Captain R.F. CUTHBERT Wounded, 3 O.R. wounded (2 since died of wounds)	G.H.Q.s
"	14		Do. Patrols and work as above. Casualties NIL	G.H.Q.s
"	15		Do. Battalion relieved by 2/5th GLOSTERS and moved to support trenches. Casualties, 2/Lieut. G.C. GREEN Wounded, 1 O.R. wounded (at duty).	App B & G.H.Q.s G.H.Q.s
"	16		In support trenches. Working parties found day and night. Casualties NIL	G.H.Q.s
"	17		Do. Working parties as above. Do	G.H.Q.s
"	18		Do. Captain R.F. CUTHBERT rejoined. Do	G.H.Q.s
"	19		Do. The special party of "B" Coy. successfully raided part of the enemy trenches in accordance with Raid Order, with the exception	App B & G.H.Q.s

Army Form C. 2118.

WAR DIARY
or
INTELLIGENCE SUMMARY.
(Erase heading not required.)

Place	Date	Hour	Summary of Events and Information	Remarks and references to Appendices
CHEMICAL WORKS SECTOR	19		that the date originally fixed was altered from 14th to 19th. The following Officers took part :- Captain W.H. MOBERLY, D.S.O. (O.C. Raid), 2/Lieut. C.H. WALLINGTON and 2/Lieut. T.W. MALLETT. Orders, reports and sketches are attached (See App. B.8) Casualties :- Wounded (at duty) Captain W.H. MOBERLY, D.S.O. and 4 O.R. Casualties 1 O.R. wounded (at duty)	C/kw R/ms App B.9 9am
"	20		In Support trenches. Working parties as above.	C/kw
"	21		Do. Battalion relieved the 2/5th GLOSTERS in front line trenches. Distribution Right Front "C", Centre "B", Left "D", Support "A". No 4 Platoon "B" Coy. joined 181st Infantry Brigade School for instruction, relieving No 1 Platoon "A" Coy. Casualties NIL.	C/kw
"	22		In Front Line trenches. Patrols sent out by front line Companies. Wiring and improving trenches. Casualties NIL.	C/kw
"	23		Do. Patrols and Work as above. Casualties 1 O.R. wounded.	C/kw
"	24		Do. "A" Coy relieved "B" Coy in centre. Casualties, NIL.	C/kw
"	25		Do. Patrols and Work as above. Casualties, Killed, 2 O.R.	C/kw
"	26		Do. Do. Casualties NIL.	C/kw

Army Form C. 2118.

WAR DIARY
or
INTELLIGENCE SUMMARY.
(Erase heading not required.)

Instructions regarding War Diaries and Intelligence Summaries are contained in F.S. Regs., Part II. and the Staff Manual respectively. Title pages will be prepared in manuscript.

Place	Date	Hour	Summary of Events and Information	Remarks and references to Appendices
CHEMICAL WORKS SECTOR	27		In front line trenches. Patrols and Work as above. Casualties. Wounded 2 O.R.	G.John
"	28		Do. Battalion relieved by 1/8th K.O.S.B. and moved to billets in ARRAS. Casualties. NIL.	App B.10.
ARRAS	29		In Billets in Reserve. Battalion cleaning up and refitting. Casualties. NIL.	G.H.W.
"	30		Do.	G.H.W.
BERTINCOURT	30		The Battalion entrained at DAINVILLE at 9.50 A.M. and proceeded to BAPAUME where on detraining previous orders were cancelled and the Battalion was hurriedly entrained and conveyed to BERTINCOURT as a German Counter attack has taken place. The Battalion was billeted for the night at BERTINCOURT.	App B.11

[signature] Lt. Col.
Commanding 2/4 Oxford & Bucks L.I.

App. B.6

SECRET.   2/4TH BN. OXFORD AND BUCKS LIGHT INFANTRY.   Copy No. 5
                                                          8.11.17.
                    ORDER NO. 422.

Reference Map 51.B.N.W. and Trench Maps.
═══

1. The Battalion will relieve the 2/7th WORCESTERS in the right sub-Sector, CHEMICAL WORKS SECTOR, tomorrow.

2. Disposition of Coys.

   Right and   ) "B" Coy. OXFORDS relieves "C" Coy. WORCESTERS.
   "A" Strong Point.)

   Centre.   "D"   "   "   "   "B"   "   "

   Left and   ) "A"   "   "   "   "A"   "   "
   "B" Strong Point.)

   Support.   "C"   "   "   "   "D"   "   "

      In "A" and "B" Strong Points there will be a permanent garrison of not less than 1 Officer and 20 men.

3. Coys. will relieve in the order A, B, D, C.

4. Guides (1 per platoon) and 1 per Coy.H.Q.) will meet incoming units at Junction of NORTHUMBERLAND Lane and FAMPOUX Road at 4.45 p.m.

5. An Advance Party consisting of the following will move off at 9 a.m. and meet guides at above named junction at 11.30 a.m. Coy. Commanders will proceed independently.
   2/Lieut. WILTSHIRE will march the rest of the party.
   Coy. Commander.
   2/Lieut. WILTSHIRE.
   1 N.C.O. per platoon.
   No.1 of each Lewis Gun (without guns).
   4 H.Q. runners.
   2 runners per Coy.
   4 H.Q. Signallers.
   2 Signallers per Coy.
   4 Snipers.

6. "C" Coy. will detail the following Guard. They will move off at 8.30 a.m. with all kit, etc., and meet guides of the 183rd Brigade at Junction of PUDDING Trench (about 300x beyond CAM VALLEY) and FAMPOUX Road at 9 a.m.
   1 N.C.O. and 5 men as loading party at QUARRY.

7. Coys. will arrange parades at 7.45 a.m. for all men proceeding to the line (other than advance parties) for the purpose of carrying packs to the WHARF. The Adjutant will march the party, and one Officer per Coy. will be present. The men will carry nothing but their packs, except that 2 men per platoon will be fully armed (and carry haversack rations) and proceed by BARGE with the packs to ATHIES LOCK. 2/Lieut. LITTLE will proceed with this party and will report to the Adjutant for instructions at 4 p.m. today.

8. Lewis Guns and Drums will be loaded on limbers at PRISON by 11.30 a.m.

9. The Battalion will parade in full marching order (less packs), Jerkins optional, ready to move from Junction of RUE D'AMIENS and RUE DE LILLE (near "B" Coy's Officers' Mess) at 12.45 p.m. in the order H.Q., A, B, D, C with 200x between Coys.

10. Cookers will follow their Coys. Teas will be served in CAM VALLEY at 3 p.m. Dinners will be served at 11.45 a.m. One cook per platoon will go into the line.

11. Cookers will carry up empty petrol tins, which will be carried into the line as follows:-
    "A" Coy's Cooker.   17.
    "B"   "   "   13.
    "C"   "   "   10.
    "D"   "   "   8 plus 6 for H.Q.
    The Transport Officer will send these tins to the PRISON in the morning.

12. Rations will be brought to SINGLE ARCH at 10 p.m.

13. Snipers will parade with H.Q. and be attached to H.Q. for rations.

14. Billets will be inspected by the Adjutant at 12.30 p.m.
    One Officer per Coy. will be at Orderly Room at that hour to accompany him.

15. Sergeant KETTLE will arrange for the necessary number of dixies to be taken up to FAMPOUX by Transport.

16. All Valises, Stores, etc. for removal to Q.M.STORES will be collected by 3 p.m. "A" and "B" Coys. will each detail two Officers not proceeding to the line to report to the Adjutant at 4 p.m. tonight to receive instructions as to guarding these stores.

17. All blankets, neatly rolled and tied in tens, will be stacked in passage outside Recreation Room by 10 a.m.
    The greatcoats of any men who do not want to take them into the line will be labelled by platoons and stacked at same place and time.

18. The Coy.Sergt.Major of "A" Coy., the 4 N.C.O.s for instruction, L/Sgt.POCOCK, and Cpl.WILLIAMS and the 4 men per Coy. for L.G. instruction will parade at 2 p.m. and proceed to the Brigade School and report to the Commandant there.

19. The R.S.M., the C.S.M. "C" Coy., men detailed for boxing instruction, and the Buglers, will parade at 2.15 p.m. and proceed to Transport Lines.

20. Completion of Relief will be reported, the code being "GOLD".

21. Receipts for Trench Stores etc. will be sent to Battalion Orderly Room by 12 noon on 10th inst.

(sd) R.F.CUTHBERT,
Captain and Adjutant,
4 OXFORDS.

Battalion H.Q.
Issued at 3.10 p.m.

Copy 1 - 4. Companies.   7. Quartermaster.   10. 7th WORCESTERS.
     5. War Diary.   8. Transport Officer. 11. Medical Officer.
     6. 184th Bde.   9. R.S.M.   12. Battn.H.Q.

SECRET.   2/4TH OXFORD AND BUCKS LIGHT INFANTRY.   Copy No. 5

ORDER NO. 423.   14.11.17.

1. The Battn. will be relieved on 15th inst. by 2/5TH GLOSTERS.

2. Coys. will be relieved as under and in the order named.

OXFORDS.		GLOSTERS.
"A" Coy. (3 platoons)	by	"D" Coy.
"C" Coy. (3 platoons)	"	"A" Coy.
"D" Coy. (2 platoons)	"	"B" Coy.
"B" Coy. (3 platoons)	"	"C" Coy.

   1 platoone of OXFORDS "A" in B Strong Point will be relieved by 1 platoon of GLOSTERS "B".

3. Guides (1 per platoon and 1 per Coy. H.Q.) will meet incoming units at SINGLE ARCH at 4.30 p.m.

4. 1 officer per Coy., 1 N.C.O. per platoon, 2 Signallers, 2 runners per Coy. will arrive at Coy.H.Q. at 12 noon for taking over.
   Guides need not be sent for this party.
   B.Q. Signallers and runners will arrive at same time.

5. Numbers 1 of L.G. Teams in front line and representatives for O.P.s will arrive at their respective Headquarters at 2 p.m. Guides need not be sent.

6. Receipts for Documents, and Trench Stores handed over will be sent to Battalion H.Q. by 3 p.m. on day of relief.

7. All Trenches and Dugouts must be left thoroughly clean.

8. All Petrol Tins belonging to the Battn. (as distinct from those taken over in the line) will be brought out of the line. Also the hot food containers and Patrol Suits issued to "A" Coy.

9. Completion of Relief will be reported by wire, the code being ELIJAH.

10. On relief Coys. will take over the positions now occupied by the 2/5TH GLOUCESTERS as under.

OXFORDS.		GLOSTERS.
"A"	from	"D".
(1 platoon, Crete.)		
(1 platoon, Single Arch.)		
"B"	"	"C".
(PUDDING.)		
"C"	"	"B".
(FAMPOUX.)		
"D"	"	"A".
(PUDDING).		

11. Coys. will send 1 Officer per Coy. and 1 N.C.O. per platoon to take over quarters &c. by 12 noon on day of relief, and to return to SINGLE ARCH for purpose of guiding their Coys. on completion of relief.

12.   "C" Coy. will detail 2 parties of 25 men, and also 1 Officer, who will remain as a permanent R.E. working party while at FAMPOUX.   Orders in respect of these parties will be received direct from O.C. 479 Field Coy. R.E.

"C" Coy. will also detail 1 N.C.O. and 20 men to report daily at FAMPOUX DUMP at 5 p.m. for pumping water.

2 men to attend with this party on night of 14th to learn job.

13.   Details of other working and carrying parties will be notified later. Coys. to send in numbers available for work deducting the numbers detailed in para.12.

14.   RATIONS.

"A" Coy. rations to SINGLE ARCH at 8.15 p.m.

"C" "   "   to cross roads at H.17.d.6.8 at 8 p.m. where O.C. "C" Coy. will arrange to have a guide.

"A" & "C" Coys. rations can come up in the same limber.

"B" & "D" "   "   along ARRAS - FAMPOUX Road to Junction with YORK LANE at H.17.c.4.5 where guides will meet them at 8 p.m.

The limber that comes up to SINGLE ARCH will wait until loaded up with Orderly Room and Canteen stuff when it will be guided.

(sd) R.F.CUTHBERT,
Captain & Adjutant,
4 OXFORDS.

Issued at 8 p.m.

1 - 4.	Coys.
5.	War Diary.
6.	184 Bde.
7.	Quartermaster.
8.	Transport Officer.
9.	Medical Officer.
10.	File.

App B 8

Lt. Col. Wetherall. D.S.O. M.C.
2/4 Oxfds.
France. 20 Nov 1917

My dear Colonel
 Will you please convey to Capt Moberly, Lts Wallington & Mallet & all NCOs & men of B company who took part in last night's raid on the German trenches, my deep appreciation of their dashing & gallant exploit which adds credit to the already splendid record of the Bn who I am told made a successful attack. The raid was well planned & carried out.
It is most satisfactory to hear of the plucky conduct of all. Especially meritorious is the fine dash of Lt Wallington, & the grit shown by Pte Holt in sticking to the German machine gun all night.
Capt Moberly I regret to hear is wounded. He is already so well known as a gallant soldier, that his success was assured —
We are all very proud of the fine work of our comrades of the Oxfords
Yrs sincerely

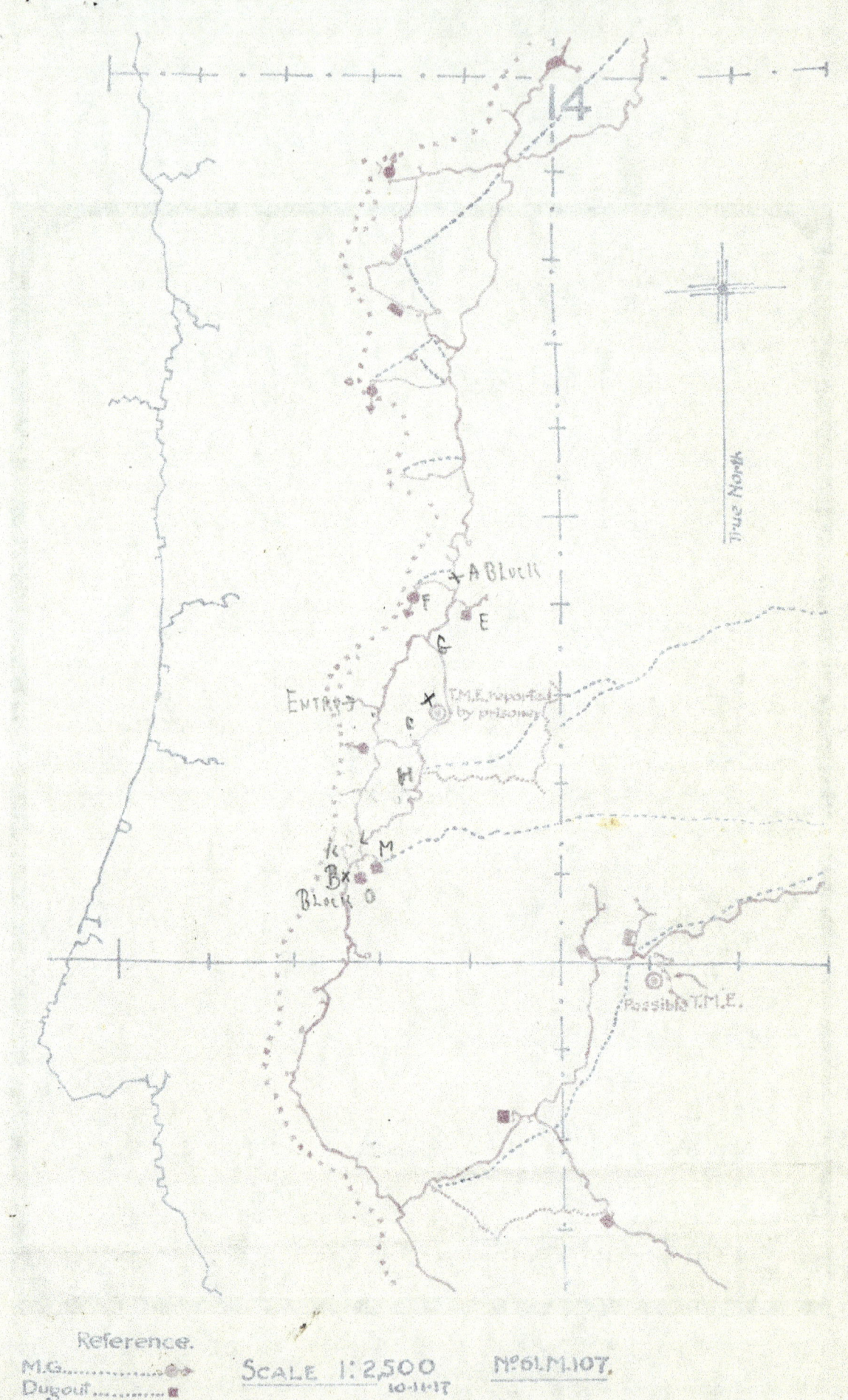

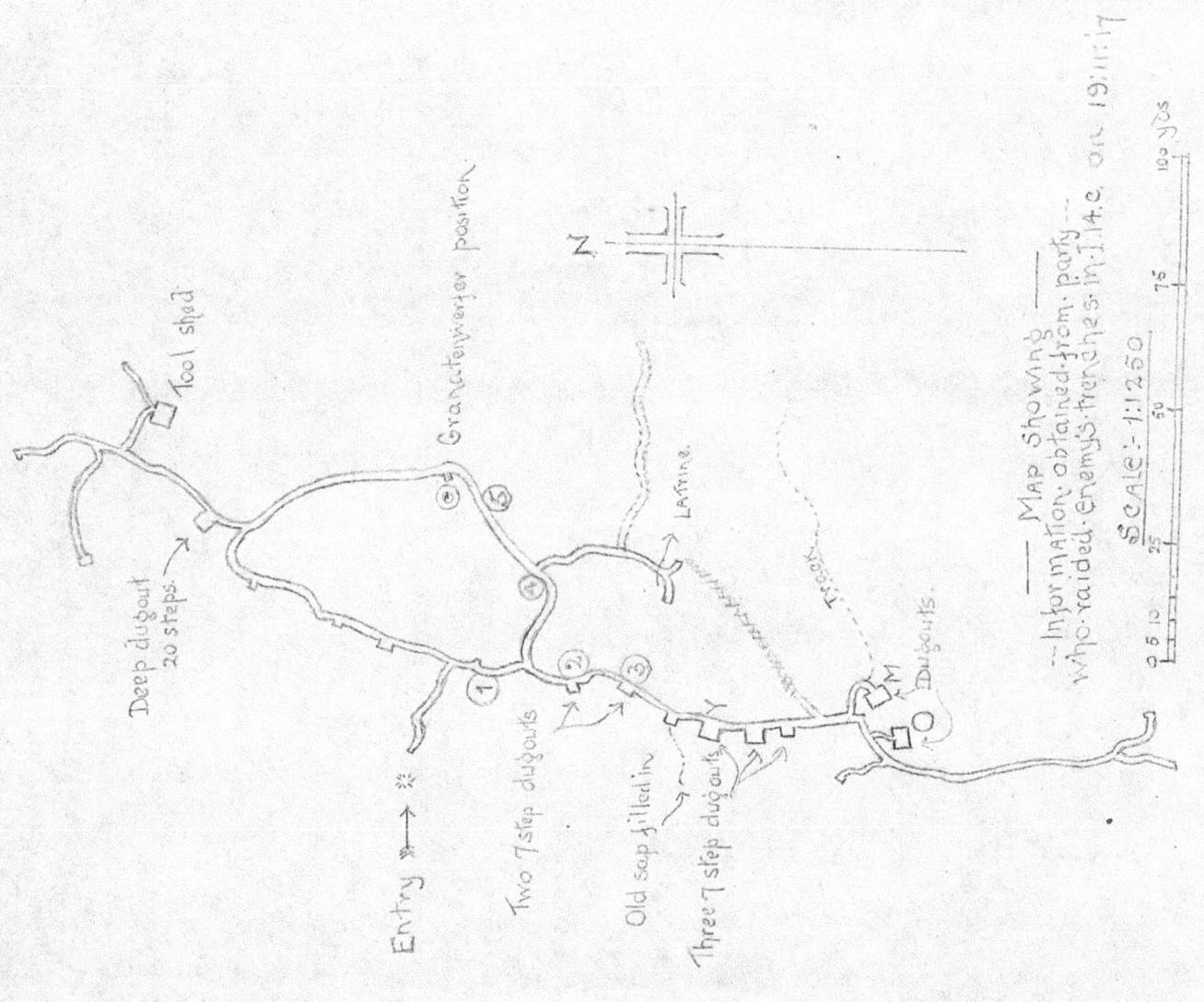

To Headquarters.
184th Infantry Brigade.

        I beg to forward the attached Report on our Raid.

20.11.17.

                       [signature] Lt. Col.,
              Commdg. 2/4th Oxford and Bucks L.I.

Report on Raid carried out by

2/4th Oxford and Bucks Light Infantry

on night of 19/20 November, 1917.

GENERAL. 1. The Raid was successfully carried out, the principal of using Gas answered very well as one party of 4 German Machine Gunners had their masks on and were standing at the bottom of the trench with no sentry, while others were in or near dug-outs evidently expecting no raid while gas shelling was in progress. It was evident that the Germans had no idea of the exact situation as no coloured lights of any sort were put up — not a round from either the German Artillery or Trench Mortars was fired, and only one Machine Gun was troublesome, this gun was silenced by a Stokes.

DETAILS. 2. The preliminary shelling with V.N. on the piece to be raided started at 10 p.m. and went on steadily to 10.30 p.m. when it lifted to other portions of the front line further North. 2/Lieut. RAWLINS, D307 Section of Howitzers shot extremely well in this important part of the programme.

At ZERO - 2 further shelling with V.N. near the piece to be raided, was carried out; from ZERO onwards hostile Trench Mortars were shelled with gas shells by 4.5 Howitzers; at ZERO the three 6" Stokes fired very accurately on our point of entry.

This was closely followed up by the Raiding Party. All parties entered the enemy trench successfully except "A" Storming Party which missed their gap and only found it when the Raid was nearly over, thus the part of the trench they were to have searched was hardly touched.

"B" Storming Party under 2/Lieut. WALLINGTON entered at the Sap which is obliterated except for an unoccupied shell hole post at the end.

The first party of 4 Germans were found at Point 1 on attached sketch. They had their gas masks adjusted, with a light Machine Gun on the parapet - this gun was brought in. This party bolted but one was shot dead in the head by 2/Lieut. WALLINGTON.

The next man found was in dug-out marked 2, he was sitting on the 3rd step and refused to move when ordered to surrender, he was also shot by 2/Lieut. WALLINGTON.

A German bomb was thrown at this party from near dug-out 3, in which another man was found who was promptly bayonetted by Corporal TAYLOR.

No more resistance was met with - dug-out N was bombed and also a gas bomb thrown down but nobody came up either at N or O.

2/Lieut. WALLINGTON then returned to the point of entry but finding it congested returned with 2 men along the trench, meeting one other German lying at the bottom of the trench who refused to get up so was bayonetted. Dug-out Y was blown up by an R.E. with a mobile charge. The Trench in this part was very clean, not sandbagged or revetted and had no trench boards - it was narrow.

"C" Storming Party entered at the Sap and acted according to scheme.

This party met one German at Point 4 who immediately, on seeing our men, laid down and refused to move – after much persuasion he had to be killed.

A Block of wire was found at Point 5, it was difficult to remove and this work was not finished when the order to withdraw was given.

The Trench covered by this party was deep and clean.

"D" Storming Party entered at the Sap and acted according to the scheme.

They met nobody, the trench erased on the sketch does not now exist it being levelled by T.M. fire.

All the dug-outs are as shown on map.

The Withdrawal was rendered more difficult by the failure of the tape men to run out the tape sufficiently far.

SUMMARY. 3. Our Party.

Strength actually in Trench, 2 Officers, 40 O.R.
In NO MANS LAND, 1 Officer, 22 O.R.

KILLED, or MISSING:- NIL.

WOUNDED:-
1 Officer (remaining at duty)
4 Men, very slightly.
Time of remaining in Trench, 15 minutes.

Germans.

PRISONERS:- NIL.

KILLED or WOUNDED:- 6.

1 Light Machine Gun captured.

Regiment Identified:- 458.

The Raiding Party was carefully drilled by Capt. MOBERLY and it was owing to the great trouble and energy shown in the training as well as his coolness during the raid, that its success is due.

2/Lieut. WALLINGTON - Corporal TAYLOR and Private HATT, form the subject of special recommendation.

20/11/17

Copy.

SECRET.   K.50.

To 184th Infantry Brigade.

PROPOSED RAID BY 2/4TH OXFORDS.

The following is a rough scheme for a raid to take place on night of 23rd/24th November, 1917.

The place of trench to be raided and the scheme for the Infantry to be the same as done by the 2/5th WARWICKS on the night of 14th/15th October, 1917.

As regards artillery, the following plan is suggested.

That on the night of the 22nd/23rd November, Field Howitzers fire gas shells on to known T.M. emplacements and on to piece of front line to be raided, and other selected targets in the vicinity.

On the night of the raid the 12 howitzers covering the Divisional Front to fire one round per gun on to the piece of trench to be raided using "V.N." gas shells, and to bombard the T.M. emplacements and other targets engaged the previous night with ordinary gas shells.

In addition our T.M.s may have to be employed in bombarding the German Sap which has been improved since the last raid.

The Corps Gas Officer has been approached and has agreed to supply 600 gas shells with a proper proportion of V.N.

The idea of this scheme is:-

(a) By employing gas shells instead of ordinary shells to avoid any intimation that a raid is imminent and thus to prevent the Germans from employing his usual tactics of evacuating his front line.

(b) To go in (without gas masks) 2 minutes after the Bombardment with V.N. shells, although the smell of gas still lingers, it is no longer dangerous, and so to catch the enemy wearing his masks.

I shall be glad if arrangements can be made as soon as possible for an aeroplane photograph of the trench concerned to be taken as soon as possible.

(sd) H.E.WETHERALL, Lieut.Colonel,
Commdg. 2/4th Oxf. & Bucks Lt.Infty.

9.11.17.

VERY SECRET.   Copy.   T.M.393.
                                                                13/11/17.

To O.C. 2/4th Oxfords.
   O.C. Right T.M. Group.

   61st Div.Art.)
   184 Inf. Bde.) For information.

PROGRAMME I. of MEDIUM TRENCH MORTARS in

Support of a Raid to be carried out on the

night 17/18th November, 1917, by the 2/4th

OXFORDS.

In the event of the Gas Bombardment on the night
16/17th Novr. being cancelled, Programme 1 will also
be cancelled and Programme 11 carried out.

No. of Mortar.	Position.	Target.	Time From	To.	Rate of fire.
6". A.1.	I.13.d.45.45.	I.14.c.80.32.	Zero.	Zero + 2.	4 rds. per min.
6". A.2.	I.13.d.45.45.	I.14.c.80.32.	Zero.	Zero + 2.	4 rds. per min.
6". A.3.	I.14.a.20.10.	I.14.c.85.45.	Zero.	Zero + 2.	4 rds. per min.
2". No.3.	I.14.a.20.10.	I.14.b.05.70.	Zero + 5	Zero + 20.	1 rd. per min. (T.M.C.G.).
2". No.5.	I.14.a.30.98.	I.14.b.30.85.	Zero + 5	Zero + 20.	1 rd. per min. (T.M.C.G.).

In addition to the above the following Mortars will stand by,
to fire on targets stated.
They will only fire on the order of an Officer who will be
stationed at each Emplacement.
The word to fire will be given in the event of Hostile T.M.s
or M.G.s dropping a barrage.

6". A.1.	I.13.d.45.45.	I.14.d.05.02.	When ordered.	2 rds. per min.
6". A.2.	I.13.d.45.45.	I.14.d.30.30.	When ordered.	2 rds. per min.
6". A.3.	I.14.a.20.10.	I.14.b.15.15.	When ordered.	2 rds. per min.

Delay action fuzes only will be used with H.E. Bombs.

PROGRAMME II.

In the event of the wind being unfavourable for Gas, Programme I. will be cancelled and the following carried out.

No. of Mortar.	Position.	Target.	Time from.	to.	Rate of fire.
6". A.1.	I.13.d.45.45.	I.14.c.84.26;	Zero.	Zero0+3.	4 rds. per min.
6". A.2.	I.13.d.4545	I.14.c.86.48.	Zero.	Zero+3.	4 rds. per min.
6". A.3.	I.14.a.20.10.	I.14.c.88.46.	Zero.	Zero+3.	4 rds. per min.
2". No.1.	I.14.c.40.67.	I.14.c.85.27.	Zero.	Zero+3.	1 rd. per min.
6". A.1.	I.13.d.45.45.	I.14.d.05.05.	Zero+3 Onwards.		1 rd. per min.
6". A.2.	I.13.d.45.45.	I.14.d.38.30.	Zerp+3 Onwards.		1 rd. per min.
6". A.3.	I.14.a.20.10.	I.14.c.80.71.	Zero+3 Onwards.		1 rd. per min.
2". No.5.	I.14.a.30.95.	I.14.b.40.85.	Zero+3 Onwards.		1 rd. per min.

On the Night 16/17 November 1917, a Gas Bombardment by 4.5 Hows and 2" T.M.s will be carried out at 11.0 p.m. in order to "accustom" the Enemy to the Gas Bombardment in support of the Raid on the night 17/18 November.

The Bombardment on the night 16/17 Novr. will be subject to the wind being favourable.

The following will be the targets for the 2" T.M.s firing T.M.C.G.

No. of Mortar.	Position.	Target.	Rate of fire.	No. of rds.
2". No.1.	I.14.c.40.67.	I.14.d.00.00.	1 rd. per min.	10.
2". No.2.	I.14.c.40.67.	I.14.d.40.80.	1 rd. per min.	10.
2". No.3.	I.14.a.20.10.	I.14.b.05.70.	1 rd. per min.	10.
2". No.5.	I.14.a.30.98.	I.14.b.30.85.	1 rd. per min.	10.

Please acknowledge.

(sd) G.L.R.WEBB,
Capt.
D.T.M.O. 61st Division.

RAID ORDER NO.1.   Copy No.
                                                    15th November, 1917.

Ref. MAP, Trench Map Chemical Works Sector and attached Sketch.

1.   "B" Company will raid the enemy front and support trenches
     between I.14.c.75.17 and I.14.c.88.46 on the 17th November.
     Objects of raid:-
          (a) To secure prisoners, wounded or unwounded, and to inflict
              casualties.
          (b) To collect papers, maps, and identifications.
          (c) To destroy any enemy machine guns, T.M., or dug-outs.

2.   Composition of parties:-
          O.C. Raid.   Captain MOBERLY.
          2 Signallers with telephone and duplicate wire of D.5 cable.
          2 wire cutters to improve passage in wire for exit.
          6 parapet men - 2 shovels to be carried by this party.
          2 Tape men.
          2 Lewis Gunners with gun and 3 drums.
          4 S.B. with 2 stretchers.
          4 men escort to prisoners.

          Four storming parties as follows:-
          A Party - 1 Officer, 6 Bayonet Men, 2 Intelligence Men,
                    1 R.E. with explosive.
          B   "   1 Officer, 10 Bayonet Men, 2 Intelligence Men,
                    1 R.E. with explosive.
          C   "   1 N.C.O., 6 Bayonet Men, 2 Intelligence Men.
          D   "   1 N.C.O., 6 Bayonet Men, 2 Intelligence Men.

          Rear Party in Front Line:-
          2/Lieut. TRUTCH and 8 O.R. for collection of stores and
               prisoners.

          Battalion Headquarters will be at Right Company Headquarters
     in COLOMBO. At Battalion Headquarters will be:-
          C.O.
          2 Signallers with telephone.
          F.O.O. and Signaller with telephone.

3.   DRESS.   *Without Tin Hats.*
     ~~Box Respirators in "alert" position.~~
     Rifle with bayonet fixed and magazine charged.
     20 rounds in right jacket pocket.
     2 Mills bombs (storming & parapet parties only).
     Faces blacked.
     White patches (size about 6 inches) sewn on back as follows:-
          No. A Storming Party - Square.
          "   B   ditto.   - Triangular.
          "   C   ditto.   -   "   upside down.
          "   D   ditto.   - Oblong.
          All Others.   - Circular.

     All Storming Parties except "B" to carry 4 No.27 bombs each.
     B Party to carry 8 No.27 bombs ~~each~~.
     Intelligence Men will also carry a sandbag slung over one
     shoulder by a sling, and an electric torch.

3. (contd.)
   Wire Cutters will carry 2 large wirecutters and red torch.
   R.E. men will carry a mobile charge.
   Parapet men and all leaders will carry whistles.
   No papers, pay-books, maps, or badges will be worn or taken.
   All bombs will be carefully cleaned and oiled.

4. Artillery programme as per Appendix "A".

5. Trench Mortar programme as per Appendix "B".

6. At Zero minus 90 the parties will arrive in our front line via CORFU AVENUE.
   At Zero minus 30 the parties will move over the parapet in position in front of the gaps specially cut in our wire.
   This assembly must be completed and all ranks lying flat before Zero minus 5.
   At Zero plus 3 the parties will dash forward through the gap and enter the German Trench in the following order:—
   No. A Storming Party.
   " B " "
   " C " "
   " D " "
   O.C. Raid.
   Signallers.
   Parapet Party.
   Wire Cutters.
   Tape men.
   Stretcher Bearers.
   Escort to Prisoners.

   No. A party via sap at I.14.c.76.35, remainder at I.14.c.79.30.

7. No. A storming party will go to the left on reaching the main trench and block at Point A, sending 2 men up Sap F and 2 to clear E — 2 men to be dropped at Point b.
   No. B storming party will go to the right from point of entry & block at Point B, dropping 2 men to clear Sap K — 2 men to dugout O — ditto to M — 2 to be dropped at L as sentries.
   No. C storming party will go straight on from point of entry turning to left at Point C, leaving 2 sentries there and going on to support No. A party at Point B, dropping 2 men to examine Point X.
   No. D storming party will go straight on from point of entry and turn to right at Point C, searching Point J and going on to support No. B party at Point L.
   All trenches will be cleared on the way and dugouts bombed, prisoners and heavy booty being handed up to the parapet party.
   The Intelligence men will follow their own parties and carefully search all dugouts and enemy dead for papers, maps, and shoulder-straps. They will report to O.C. Raid when their area is clear.
   R.E. men with parties will carry explosives to destroy any dugouts or any T.M.s or M.G.s it may not be possible to remove.
   Parapet men will line the enemy parapet and take over prisoners and salvage, working with A and B storming parties. They will (in conjunction with the Lewis Gunners) also see that the enemy do not come over the open in rear of their front line. Those near point of entry will shovel earth and push sandbags into the German trench to facilitate exit.

7. (Contd.)

Wire Cutters will immediately improve the gap in the enemy wire as soon as all parties are through. They will devote their attention to the track of the tape to facilitate the withdrawal. When the first golden rain rocket is fired they will shine their red torches at intervals to guide the parties back.

Stretcher Bearers will remain near O.C. Raid.

Tape men and signallers will act as per para.8. Both tape men will also act as parapet men after they have laid their tapes, and will, in addition, cut the tapes on their return just our side of the German wire.

"B" Coy's Lewis Gunners will cover the flanks of the raiders.

8. COMMUNICATION.

Two lines of D.5 cable will be connected with advanced Battalion H.Q. at Right Coy.H.Q. in COLOMBO, and carried out by the two signallers (one also having a telephone) who will be at least at 15 yds. interval and at least 20 yds. wide of all tape. They will both join up to O.C. Raid on the enemy parapet.

The two tape men will carry out two broad white tapes (one from front line near sap 1 and one from front line near sap 2) through the gap in our wire to the enemy parapet, where they will run outwards and lay them along the parapet as far as the storming parties have gone.

A pass-word will be communicated to all ranks immediately beforehand.

9. RETURN.

When all the Intelligence Men have reported, and when the O.C. Raid is satisfied that the area has been cleared, he will signal the withdrawal by blowing a whistle and ordering "C.I.", both being repeated by all parapet men. The signaller with O.C. Raid will signal "C.I." to our line. For 20 minutes after this signal a golden rain rocket will be sent up every minute from CORFU AVENUE near the CHALKPIT to assist in guiding back the parties.

When all the raiders are in, ~~blue rockets will be sent up from our line.~~

Order of return as follows:-
Nos. C and D storming parties.
"   A and B   ditto.
Parapet men (on order of O.C. Raid, "Parapet Party C.I.")
Signallers.
Stretcher Bearers.
Lewis Gunners.
O.C. Raid.

Every effort will be made to bring in casualties, but this duty will not be performed by any body except the stretcher bearers until after the signal to withdraw.

The parties will assemble in CORDITE RESERVE, where all leaders will check their parties and report to Sec.Lieut. WILTSHIRE.

A traffic control sentry will be posted by Sec.Lieut.WILTSHIRE at the junction of CORFU AVENUE and CORDITE RESERVE.

The command "RETIRE" is not to be used or obeyed.

10. The Advanced Regimental Aid Post will be established by the M.O. by the re-assembly point in CORDITE RESERVE.

11. Luminous watches will be carried by all leaders, and will be synchronised by the C.O. in Right Coy. H.Q. at 5 p.m.

12. Men with coughs and colds will not be taken.

13. ZERO hour will be notified later.

14. ACKNOWLEDGE.

                                                  Lieut.Col,
                     Commdg. 2/4th Oxf. & Bucks L.I.

Issued at

    Copies to:-
      No.1 to 184th Inf.Bde.
        2,3. C.O.
        4. Captain MOBERLY.
        5. Signalling Sergeant.
        6. 2/5th GLOUCESTERS.
        7. 184th L.T.M.B.
        8. Medium T.M.B.
        9. 307th Bde. R.F.A.
       10. War Diary.
       11. File.

SECRET.   2/4TH OXFORD & BUCKS LIGHT INFANTRY.   Copy No. 5
               ORDER NO. 424.   20.11.17.
Ref. Map 51.B.

1. The Battalion will relieve the 2/5TH GLOSTERS in the front system on the day of the 21st. The line comes under the Commanding Officer's command at 12 noon.

2. Coys. will relieve as under, the times mentioned means the times they will leave their present places:-
   "B" Coy. OXFORDS at 7 a.m. relieve "B" Coy. GLOSTERS in Front Centre.
   "C"   "   "   " 9.30 a.m.   "   "A" "   "   " Right Front
                                                            & "A" Strong Point.
   "D"   "   "   " 1 p.m.   "   "C" "   "   in Left Front &
                                                            "B" Strong Point.

   "A" Coy. OXFORDS move up to support in CORDITE at 3.30 p.m. The GLOSTER Coy. in CORDITE will not wait for relief. It is necessary for OXFORD "A" Coy. to be moving up at 3.30 p.m. as "C" Coy. GLOSTERS is moving down to SINGLE ARCH position.

3. Route for B and D Coys. down PUDDING to FAMPOUX ROAD, thence to X roads at B.17.c.4.4 to TRIPLE ARCH thence along railway to SINGLE ARCH from there up CORFU.
   "C" Coy. most covered way to SINGLE ARCH then up CORFU.
   All Coys. will move by posts, i.e. 1 N.C.O., 6 men - Support platoons and garrisons of A & B Strong Points by Sections.
   The distance between Sections depends on visibility but never less than 50ˣ.

4. No guides will be provided.

5. The only advance party as below:-
   H.Q. Signallers and Runners (except 2) to take over by 10 a.m., Battalion Ammunition Store by 12 noon.

6. "A" Coy. will find 3 men as Coffee Stall Guard at SINGLE ARCH to take over by 3.30 p.m. They will be rationed by "A" Coy.

7. Coys. will take the petrol tins which belong to the Battalion into the line.

8. Trenches must be left thoroughly clean, an Officer from B & D Coys. will report to Adjutant that they are so before moving off.
   "C" Coy. is to pay special regard to cleaning the FAMPOUX CELLARS.
   The cellars occupied by "B" Coy. will be inspected by an Officer before moving off, the report by "B" Coy. as above does not include these cellars.

9. Completion of relief will be reported by wire, the code being "SALONIKA".

10. The platoon of "A" Coy. now at Brigade School will report between 2 p.m. and 3 p.m. on 21st. O.C. "A" Coy. to have 4 guides at junction of PUDDING and FAMPOUX ROAD by 1.45 p.m. This platoon to be taken straight into new position in CORDITE which will be empty at that time.
    O.C. "B" Coy. will send No. 7 Platoon (strength 1 Officer & 27 O.R. to report to Brigade School, leaving PUDDING by 12.30 p.m.

11. RATIONS.

On night of 20/21st as usual except that "B" Coy. rations will be divided as follows:-

Breakfast Ration for whole Coy. at present place.

Rest of day's rations, except dinners for No.7 platoon, to go to SINGLE ARCH, to be stored in Bomb Stores, and looked after by "A" Coy. "B" Coy. to pick them up on way to line on 21st. Dinners for No.7 platoon to be delivered as at present.

Rations on night 21/22nd all at SINGLE ARCH at 5.30 p.m.

Mess cart to be at present Battn. H.Q. at 5.30 p.m. on 21st for purpose of moving Canteen and Orderly Room.

(sd) G.E.WILTSHIRE,
2/Lieut. & A/Adjt.,
4 OXFORDS.

Battn. H.Q.

Copies to:-
1 - 4.   O.C. Coys.
5.   War Diary.
6.   184 Inf. Bde.
7.   Quartermaster.
8.   Transport Officer.
9.   Medical Officer.
10.   File.
11, 12. Battn. H.Q.

App. B.10.

SECRET.   2/4TH OXFORD & BUCKS LIGHT INFANTRY.   Copy No.
                                                             27.11.17.
               ORDER NO.426.

1. The Battalion will be relieved on the 28th inst. by 7/8th K.O.S.B.s.

2. Coys. will be relieved as under and in this order named:-

   OXFORDS.   7/8th K.O.S.B.
       C   C
       B   By   A
       A   D
       D   B
   Posts and Strong points taken over as they stand.

3. GUIDES to report to 2/Lieut. WILTSHIRE.
   One per post, one each for A & B Strong points, one per Coy.H.Q. one for platoons in CORONA one for Battn. H.Q. at TRIPLE ARCH at 9 a.m.

4. Advance parties will be guided by H.Q. runners.

5. Receipts for documents and trench stores to be handed in to Orderly Room on arrival at ARRAS.

6. All trenches and dugouts must be left thoroughly clean.

7. The following articles will be left at Battn. Bomb Store at SINGLE ARCH.
   Lewis Gun Drums.   Hot Food Containers.   Battn. Petrol tins.
   Camp Kettles.   Patrol Suits.

8. The Lewis Guns and spare parts will be carried to CAM VALLEY, where a limber will be waiting. If limber is late each Coy. will detail one man to look after its four Lewis Guns and spare parts.
   Officers' chargers will be at the same place.

9. Completion of relief will be reported by wire the code being BLAST.

10. ROUTE.   C Coy. will come out via CEYLON. Other Coys. via CORFU.
    C and D Coys. will go via SINGLE and TRIPLE ARCH, FAMPOUX LOCK, CAM VALLEY.
    A and B Coys., if situation is quiet, through FAMPOUX to CAM VALLEY. Platoons to move to CAM VALLEY by sections at 50^x. There they will form up and march by platoons to the PRISON, ARRAS. Strict march discipline to be maintained after leaving CAM VALLEY. All movement through FAMPOUX to be as concealed as possible.

11. MEALS. Breakfasts served as early as possible. Another meal to be served before relief. The remainder of day's rations to be distributed amongst platoons and carried to CAM VALLEY, where it will be collected and put into limbers. One N.C.O. per Coy. to be detailed for this duty. "HIGH TEAS" will be served as soon as practicable on arrival.

                                        (sd) G.H.WILTSHIRE, 2/Lt.& A/Adjt.
Battn.H.Q.
Issued at 11.30 p.m.
   1 - 4 Coys.   6 184 Bde.   8 Quartermaster.
   5   War Diary. 7 Transport Officer.   9 Medical Officer.
                                              10 Office.

SECRET.   2/4th BN. OXFORD AND BUCKS LIGHT INFTY.   Copy No.
               ORDER NO. 428.   29.11.17.

1. The Battalion will parade for entraining at ARRAS.
   Order of March, H.Q, D, Bugles, C, B, A.
   Head of Battalion will pass Starting Point at 8.10 a.m.
   Starting Point:- Junction of Rue ST CLAIRE and Rue D'AMIENS.
   Intervals of 100^x will be kept between Companies.
   Dress:- Full Marching Order - full water bottles and one blanket will be carried. Steel hats to be worn.
   Journey will take about 1½ hours.

2. To-morrow 30th Inst.,
   Reveille will be at 5.45 a.m. Breakfasts, 6.30 a.m. After Breakfast each man will be issued with a cooked Dinner Ration.

3. One blanket per man will be rolled into bundles of 10 and will be ready stacked in the passage near Recreation Room at 7.30 a.m.
   The blankets must be tightly rolled to facilitate loading. One Officer per Coy. will supervise this. The blanket carried on the man will be collected at the detraining station and made up into bundles of 10. H.Q, and each Coy. to detail two men for this purpose.

4. Coy. Mess Boxes ready for loading on Cookers will be at the PRISON at 7.30 a.m.
   Valises will be stacked at PRISON and H.Q.Mess whichever is most convenient by 8 a.m.

5. Transport will pass Starting Point at 7.45 a.m.
   Starting Point:- Cross Roads, ST NICHOLAS.
   One cook will accompany each Cooker, the remainder will parade with the Battalion. Water Duty men to go with Transport.

6. One N.C.O. per COY. will report at Battn. H.Q.Mess at 7.45 a.m. They will report to Capt. MARCON. These N.C.O's will bring the Parade States of their Companies.

7. The PRISON to be left very clean. One Officer per Coy. to report to the Adjutant at the Orderly Room at 7.45 a.m. that this is so.

Battalion Hdqrs
Issued at 9 p.m.   (sd) G.H.WILTSHIRE,
                                                   2/Lieut and A/Adjt.

            Copy No. 1 - 4. Coys.
                        5. 184 Bde.
                        6. War Diary.
                        7. Quartermaster.
                        8. Transport Officer.
                    9 - 19. Office.

CONFIDENTIAL

WAR DIARY

*** of ***

2/4TH BATTALION, OXFORDSHIRE & BUCKINGHAMSHIRE LIGHT INFANTRY

From 1st December to 31st December, 1917

VOL. XX.
*****

Army Form C. 2118.

WAR DIARY
or
INTELLIGENCE SUMMARY.
(Erase heading not required.)

Instructions regarding War Diaries and Intelligence Summaries are contained in F.S. Regs., Part II. and the Staff Manual respectively. Title pages will be prepared in manuscript.

Place	Date 1917	Hour	Summary of Events and Information	Remarks and references to Appendices
BERTINCOURT	Dec 1st		Battalion marched at 3.30 a.m. and encamped at FINS, where they had been ordered to assemble at FINS. Casualties NIL.	G.H.W.
FINS	" 2nd		In Camp. Battalion marched at 10.30 a.m. to METZ, and were accommodated in huts and pumps. The Battalion was ordered to move at 10 p.m. to Divisional Reserve in HINDENBURG LINE N.E. of METZ, which it reached by marching in companies. Weather NIL. No note having been given. Casualties NIL.	G.H.W.
N.E. of METZ	" 3rd		In Reserve Trenches. Enemy attacked our Divisional Front at 6.30 a.m. and heavily shelled the positions we occupied, bringing no response from our artillery. "D" Coy moved further forward to support 182nd INFANTRY BRIGADE, returning same night to original position. Enemy artillery fire having slackened. Casualties. Wounded 1 O.R. (B Coy)	G.H.W.
"	" 4th		Do. "C" Coy moved further forward to support 182 INFANTRY BRIGADE. Casualties Killed 2 O.R. Wounded 11 O.R.	G.H.W.
"	" 5th		Do. "C" Coy returned to their original position. Battalion relieved 2/4th WORCESTERS in front line trenches, right on LA VACQUERIE Sector. Dispositions:- "B" Coy Left Front, "A" Coy Centre, "D" Coy Right Front, "C" Coy in support at CHALK PIT. Casualties Wounded 2 O.R. (includes 1 at duty)	G.H.W.
LA VACQUERIE Sector	" 6th		In front line Trenches. Wiring parties worked in front of our positions and Trenches improved	G.H.W.

T2134. Wt. W708-776. 500000. 4/15. Sir J. C. & S.

Army Form C. 2118.

WAR DIARY
INTELLIGENCE SUMMARY.
(Erase heading not required.)

Place	Date 1917	Hour	Summary of Events and Information	Remarks and references to Appendices
LA VACQUERIE Sector	Dec 6th (Contd.)		Two new trenches ("Piccadilly" and "Howard") dug. Casualties killed 10 O.R.	9/M
"	" 7th		In front line trenches. Wiring, improvement and digging of trenches continued. Casualties Wounded 10 O.R.	9/M
"	" 8th		Do. "C" Coy relieved "D" Coy in front line. Casualties NIL.	9/M
"	" 9th		Do. Casualties NIL.	9/M
"	" 10th		Do. Owing to great amount of wiring, duckboarding + new positions iones considerably strengthened. Battalion relieved at night by 2/7th Worcesters and marched to camp in HAVRINCOURT WOOD. Casualties NIL	9/M(N). App A 9/M
HAVRINCOURT WOOD	" 11th		In Reserve Camp. Resting and cleaning up. 2 hours gun fired for use against enemy aircraft, the latter shewing considerable activity in bombing the neighbourhood of the camp. Casualties NIL.	9/M
"	" 12th		Do. Company training	9/M
"	" 13th		Do. Do. Casualties Wounded 10 O.R. of duty.	9/M
"	" 14th		Do. Do. Casualties NIL	9/M
"	" 15th		Do. Do.	9/M
"	" 16th		Do. Battalion relieved 2/5th, 2/6th and 2/8th Warwicks in the left sector of Divisional front. Disposition: "D" Coy left front, "C" Coy Centre, N.W. of LA VACQUERIE.	App A.2 9/M 9/M

T2134. Wt. W708—776. 500000. 4/15. Sir J. C. & S.

WAR DIARY or INTELLIGENCE SUMMARY

Army Form C. 2118.

Place	Date 1917	Hour	Summary of Events and Information	Remarks and references to Appendices
	Dec 16th (contd)		"B" Coy Right front, "A" Coy Support	S.H.W.
N.W. of LA VACQUERIE	17th		In Front Line trenches. Wiring, digging and improvement of trenches. The Battalion front was considerably strengthened during the 3 days the Battalion held the line, wire being strengthened, and trenches improved. Casualties NIL. Casualties NIL.	S.H.W. S.H.W. App.A.3. S.H.W.
	18th		Do. Wiring, digging and improvement of trenches. Do.	S.H.W.
	19th		Do. Battalion relieved by DRAKE Battalion, 189TH INFANTRY BRIGADE and marched to Reserve Camp in HAVRINCOURT WOOD. Casualties Killed 'OR', Wounded 2.O.R.	S.H.W.
HAVRINCOURT WOOD.	20th		In Reserve Camp. Resting and cleaning up. Casualties NIL.	S.H.W.
	21st		Do. Company Training. Working parties found. Do.	S.H.W. App.A.4.
	22nd		Do. Battalion marched to billets near LECHELLE. Enemy aircraft active. Casualties NIL.	S.H.W.
LECHELLE	23rd		In Billets. Church Parade. Enemy aircraft at night. Do.	S.H.W. App.A.5
	24th		Do. Battalion entrained at ETRICOURT at 9.30.A.M. and detrained at PLATEAU about 11.A.M. Marched to huts and billets at SUZANNE, arriving about noon. Casualties NIL.	S.H.W.

WAR DIARY
or
INTELLIGENCE SUMMARY.
(Erase heading not required.)

Army Form C. 2118.

Place	Date 1917	Hour	Summary of Events and Information	Remarks and references to Appendices
SUZANNE	Dec 23rd		In huts + billets. Resting and holiday.	G.W.O
"	" 26th		Do. Battalion and Company training	G/102
"	" 27th		Do. Do.	G/102
"	" 28th		Do. Do.	G/102
"	" 29th		Do. Do.	G/102
"	" 30th		Do. Battalion held its Christmas dinner	G/102
"	" 31st		Do. Battalion moved by route march to CAIX starting at 9AM and arriving at 3:40AM. It was originally intended that the Battalion should billet at FRAMERVILLE, the destination however was altered at the last moment	APP A.B
			Casualties NIL	
			The following Officer and O.R were awarded the Military Cross and Military Medal respectively for gallantry and devotion to duty during a raid on the enemy's trenches at ARRAS on the night of 19/20th November. 2/Lt. C.H. WALLINGTON and No 203436 Pte T HATT	G/102

M. McTurrell
Lieut Colonel
C.C. 2/4th Oxf + Bucks L.I.

SECRET 2/4 Oxford & Bucks L Infty   Copy No 5
            Order No 431   10-12-17

1.   The Battalion will be relieved tonight
by 2/7 WORCESTERS in the following order

       OXFORDS   WORCESTERS
          C   C
          A   D
          B   B
          D   A

No 1 of Lewis Guns, Signallers etc may
arrive during daytime
Probable time of arrival of Relief 6.30 p.m.
                                    Coys; the same
2.   If they have returned to their ^ guides
that reported to Battn H.Q. this morning
for the purpose of guiding the relief up
will report again at 5 pm.

3.   Relief complete will be reported by
wire by code word RAIN. D Coy
will send a runner to report.

4.   On completion of relief the Battn will
move back by Companies to Q.15. Central.
Route VILLERS-PLOUICH & BEAUCAMP
At the E entrance to BEAUCAMP 1 Officer

and 1 man per Coy will meet the Coys & guide them to their billets.

5. All Lewis Guns, Lewis Gun drums & Rifle Grenade haversacks will be dumped in the CHALK PIT at R.20.a.2.2.9. under Corporal CARTER
If Coys do not know the CHALK PIT guides will be sent this afternoon to reconnoitre. The material must be carefully stacked.

6. All Hot food Containers and empty petrol cans will be sent down this afternoon to the CHALK PIT.

7. Trenches to be left as clean as possible.

8. Hot tea will be served on arrival in billets.

Battn. H.Q.   (Sd.) H. Whitehall Lt Col
Issued at 1 pm   Commdg 1/1 Oxford & Bucks L.I.

              Copy No 1 to Coys
                        5   War Diary
                        6   18th Bde
                        7   Amn. & Sd.
                        8   Battn H.Q.

SECRET.   2/4th OXFORD AND BUCKS LIGHT INFANTRY.   Copy No. 6
                 Order No. 434.   15.12.17.

1. The Battalion will relieve the 2/5, 2/6, WARWICKS in the front system and one Company of 2/8 WARWICKS in R.8.d.

2. From Right to Left Coys. relieve as follows :-

OXFORDS.	2/5 WARWICKS.
B.Coy.	S.Coy.
	2/6 WARWICKS.
C.Coy.	D.Coy.
D.Coy.	B. & C.Coys.
A.Coy.	A.Coy.

   One platoon of A.Coy to relieve one Coy. 2/8 WARWICKS in SUNKEN ROAD, R.8.d.

3. The Battalion will go in, in the following order, D, C, B, A, D.Coy will move off by platoons at 100^x interval from present position at 3.30 p.m., the other Coys. following in their turn.

   Guides (one per Battn. H.Q. and one per Coy. H.Q. and one per platoon) of the 2/6 WARWICKS and in the case of B.Coy, 2/5 WARWICKS, will meet Coys. at the E. end of BEAUCAMP (R.12.d.23.12) at 4 p.m. and will guide them by tape track passing to the N. end of VILLERS PLUICH.

   B.Coy will pick up fresh guides of 2/5 WARWICKS at Battn. H.Q., who will guide them up CORNWALL TRENCH.

   D. and C.Coys will go up NEW TRENCH.

4. Lewis Gun Limbers and cart for Orderly Room will be near B.Coy's Officers Hut at 2 p.m. for loading. At 3 p.m. these limbers will proceed to the same place where the guides are being met, where they will be unloaded by two men per Lewis Gun Section who will be detailed to accompany the limbers. Coys. will pick up their guns and Drums at this spot.

5. Blankets rolled in bundles of 10, Great Coats and any other article to be left out, will be stacked ready for loading at 10 a.m. in A. and B.Coy. Officers Huts.

6. MEALS AND RATIONS.
   Meals for tomorrow will be :-
   Breakfasts   8 a.m.
   Dinners   11.30 a.m.
   Teas   2.30 p.m.

   Before starting every man will be issued with his cooked bacon, fresh meat, and 1/3rd bread ration for consumption on the 17th inst.

   The remainder of the rations for the 17th will be brought up by Transport, to R.8.c.6.3. They will be there at 2 a.m. A.Coy. will carry the rations of C. and D.Coys. to the Junction of NEW and WELSH Trenches where C. and D. ration parties will carry them on. Two N.C.O's from A.Coy to be left in charge of these rations until place is cleared and receipt for number of packages received, obtained from C. and D.Coys parties.

   B.Coy's rations will be carried by A.Coy. to the Junction of CORNWALL and WELSH Trenches where the above procedure will be carried out.

   It will not be possible to send hot tea up to B, C, D.Coys. on the early morning of the 17th.

   10 Petrol cans per Coy. are being brought up by Transport - the well in VILLERS PLUICH is at present out of order.

7. The present camp will be left as clean as possible.

8. Completion of Relief will be notified by wire to Battn. H.Q. by code-word-"WOOD".

Battalion Headquarters (sd) G.H.WILTSHIRE,
Issued at 6.30 p.m. 2/Lieut. and A/Adjt.

            Copies 1 to 4.   Coys.
                     5.   Bde.
                     6.   War Diary
                     7.   Quartermaster.
                     8.   Transport Officer.
                     9.   2/5 WARWICKS.
                    10.   2/6. WARWICKS.
                    11.   2/8 WARWICKS.
                    12.   Office

App. A.4

Order No. 437   21.12.17

Orderly Officer – 2/Lt S.E. HERBERT

1. The Battn (less 40 men of "B" Coy) will march tomorrow to billet at LECHELLE.
Dress: Full Marching Order – Steel hats and jerkins to be carried on the pack as shown to Coy S.M's today.
Order of March: HQ, C, D, B, A.
HQ & C Coy will parade at 10.10 A.M. other Coys at intervals of 5 minutes. A distance of 200x will be maintained between Coys. There will be a 10 minute halt before each clock hour.

Cookers will follow their Coys.

One Lewis Gun Limber will follow D Coy & one B Coy. Mess Cart & Medical Cart will follow the Battn.

Transport at EQUANCOURT will not move from its present lines.

Meals for tomorrow:—
   Breakfast 7.45 A.M.
   Dinners on arrival in billets.

2. Lewis Guns & drums will be ready for loading near Cookers at 9 A.M.
Blankets rolled in bundles of 10 will be ready at same place at 9.30 A.M. Officers valises, Mess Boxes & Orderly Room boxes to be ready at the same hour.

3. An advance party of 1 Officer & 2 N.C.O's per Coy will parade at Batt. H.Q. under Capt. MARCON at 8 A.M. 1 N.C.O from H.Q. will also go.

4. 2/Lt. FLORY will report to the Adjutant at 9 P.M tonight for instructions as regards handing over the camp to the 6th GLOSTERS.

5. Camp to be left thoroughly clean.

6. Sick Parade at 7.30 A.M.

Batt. Hdqrs.
Issued at 6.30 P.M.

5th Bn Wiltshire
2/Lieut & A/Adjt.

1 – 4   Companies
5.   War Diary
6.   2nd in of Batt.
7.   Medical Officer
8.   Quartermaster
9.   Transport Officer
10.   R.S.M
11 & 12 Batt. H.Q

SECRET 1/4 Oxford & Bucks L.I. Copy No 3
Order No 435   19.12.16

In continuation of last nights orders

1. Arrangements for guiding in Relieving Battalion have been made verbally.

2. After Relief the Battn will go to HAVRINCOURT WOOD probably to the area previously occupied by the GLOSTERS in Q.15.a.
ROUTE The same as when entering

3. One man will be stationed at Road Junction Q.12.c.85.40. who will inform Coys of the site of Camp. Coys will find Guides on the TRESCAULT RD at Q.16.a.1.5. who will lead them to their tents

4. Lewis Guns & drums will be left under charge of 4/C WILKINS at the end of the RAVINE where rations are dumped.— they will be stopped at the correct place.— 2 men per Coy will be detailed for loading — Sgt LEWIS D Coy to be one of these men

5. Empty Petrol tins will be dumped at Battn H.Q. They will either be brought down when relieved or sent down before.

6... Relief complete to be sent by wire to Batt'n H.Q. code word being QUARRY.

Batt'n H.Q.　　　　　　　　　　(Sd) S.H. Williams
Issued at 2.30 p.m.　　　　　　　　　　Lt & Adjt

　　　　1-4　Coys
　　　　5　18th Bde
　　　　6　War Diary
　　　　7　Quartermaster
　　　　8　Transport Officer
　　　　9　Office.

SECRET: 2/4 Oxford & Bucks L.I.   Copy No 5
          Order No 440   23-12-17

1. The Battn: will parade at 7.15 am tomorrow between the Officers & mens huts for the purpose of entraining at ETRICOURT. The detraining place is PLATEAU and will be reached about 10.30 am. On the march an interval of 20ˣ will be kept between Coys.
DRESS. Full Marching order with Caps.
Order of March H.Q. DRUMS. A. B. C. D.

2. Officers valises, mens boxes, orderly room boxes & blankets (rolled in bundles of 10) will be stacked ready for loading by A Coys cooker by 7 am. Blankets must be tightly rolled, otherwise they take up too much room.

3. All No 1 Lewis Gunners & 2 Stretcher bearers per Coy will carry a shovel, which can be drawn from the Orderly Room.

4. An advance party of 1 NCO per H.Q. & 1 NCO per Coy will parade at 7 am under 2/Lt WALLINGTON M.C. for the purpose of marking the train. The NCO's must know his Coy parade state.

2/Lt WALLINGTON will report to the Adjutant tonight for further instructions.

5. One servant per HQ & one per Coy will go in a lorry with the mess boxes.

6. The Coys will report to the Adjt before moving off that their billets are left clean.

7. 2/Lt CORNISH and 65 men of D Coy will parade (apart from the Battn) in full marching order ready to move off at 7.15am. they will under the command of Captn ABRAHAM.

8. Breakfasts will be at 6 am. Before marching off each man will be issued with a dinner ration. Tea will be served on arrival in billets at SUZANNE

Battn H.Q. (Sd) G. H. Wiltshire
Issued at 4.30pm Lt & A/Adjt
    1-4 Coys
    5 War Diary
    6 Bde
    7 Qmr & T.O
    8 M.O.
    9-10 Office

SECRET.   2/4TH BN. OXFORD & BUCKS LT.INFTY.   Copy No. 5
              ORDER NO.447.   30.12.17.

1.   The Battalion will march to billets at FRAMERVILLE tomorrow.
     The Battalion will parade at 8.40 a.m. on the MERICOURT -
SUZANNE ROAD in the following order :-
     Headquarters, "C", Drums, "B", "D", "A".
     H.Q. will parade outside H.Q. Mess, "C" Coy.next, and so on.
     Dress:- Full Marching Order.
     50 yards interval to be kept between Coys.
     Route:- CAPPY - FROISSY (by roads along CANAL BANK) - PROYART.

2.   Transport will be ready to fall in behind the Battalion, (with
the exception of cookers, which will follow their Coys) at 9.5 a.m.
An interval of 200 yards will be divided kept between Battalion and
Transport and each group of 10 vehicles.
     Transport will be divided up into groups of 10 vehicles.
     O.C. "A" Coy. will detail 4 sections under an Officer to fall
out when passing the Transport. They will report to the Transport
Officer, and help the Transport over bad places on the road.

3.   Dinners will be served at 1 p.m.

4.   Officers' valises, Mess Boxes, Orderly Room Stores, and Blankets
(rolled tightly in bundles of 10) to be ready for loading by 8.30 a.m.
in HUT NO.5.
     One Officer's servant per H.Q. and Coy. to remain with above
and be brought along in lorry.

5.   All huts to be left clean. One Officer per Coy. to report to
Adjutant on parade that this has been done.

                                    (sd) C.N.WILTSHIRE,
                                         a/Lieut. & A/Adjt.,
                                         4 OXFORDS.

Battn. H.Q.,
Issued at 12.20 p.m.

              1 - 4   Coys.
              5.   War Diary.
              6.   184 Inf. Bde.
              7.   Q.M.
              8.   T.O.
              9.   M.O.
              10,11.   Battn. H.Q.

CONFIDENTIAL.

WAR DIARY.

of

2/4TH. OXFORDSHIRE & BUCKINGHAMSHIRE LIGHT INFANTRY.

From 1st.January 1918 - 31st.January 1918.

(Volumn XX1.)

Army Form C. 2118.

WAR DIARY
or
INTELLIGENCE SUMMARY.
(Erase heading not required.)

Place	Date 1919	Hour	Summary of Events and Information	Remarks and references to Appendices
CAIX	1st Jan		In Rest Billets. Battalion and Company Training. Casualties, Nil.	G.Ms.
"	2nd "		Do. Captain G.K. ROSE, M.C. proceeded to ENGLAND to attend Senior Officers' Course at ALDERSHOT. Casualties, Nil.	G.Ms.
"	3rd "		Do. Battalion and Company Training. Major H.J BENNETT proceeded on leave to ENGLAND. Casualties, Nil.	G.Ms.
"	4th "		Do. Battalion and Company Training. 2/Lieut. W.H. ENOCH joined for duty. Casualties Nil.	G.Ms.
"	5th "		Do. Battalion and Company Training. Casualties, Nil.	G.Ms.
"	6th "		Do. Church Parade Do.	2/Ms.
"	7th "		The Battalion moved by route march at 7.30 A.M. to billets at VOYENNES arriving at 4.30 P.M. 6 lorries of "D" Coy. were detailed to assist the Transport in getting over bad places, the differences and bad state of the roads making the going very difficult. The Commanding Officer (Lt.Col. H.E. de R. WETHERALL, D.S.O, M.C. and Captain W.H MOBERLY, D.S.O. and 2/Lieuts. W.H.ENOCH and B.O.WELLER proceeded to the GRICOURT Sector, to reconnoitre the part of the line to be taken over by the Battalion. Casualties, Wounded 2/Lt. B.O. WELLER	A85 A.Y. G.Ms.

WAR DIARY
or
INTELLIGENCE SUMMARY.

Army Form C. 2118.

Place	Date 1918	Hour	Summary of Events and Information	Remarks and references to Appendices
VOYENNES	8th Jan.		In Rest Billets. Battalion resting and cleaning up with the exception of "B" Coy who paraded in the morning for inspection by the G.O.C. 5th Army (General Sir H. de la P. Gough, K.C.B., K.C.V.O.) Captains K.E. BROWN, M.C. and A.J. ROBINSON and 2/Lieuts. H. TONES, M.C. and A.G. LEDGER proceeded to the GRICOURT Sector to reconnoitre the line. Casualties Nil.	G.W.
"	9th "		Do. Battalion moved by route march at 11 A.M. to hutments at ATTILLY, arriving about 4.30 P.M. The usual 6 sections were detailed to assist the transport over bad places, the roads still being in a very slippery condition making travelling difficult. 2/Lieuts. J. PETT ("A" Coy), C.H. WALLINGTON, M.C. ("B"), E. LITTLE ("C") and W.H. ENOCH ("D") proceeded in the morning to the GRICOURT Sector to take over French Stores &c and reconnoitre the positions to be held by their respective Companies. Casualties Nil.	App. A 8. G.W.
ATTILLY	10th "		In Reserve Hutments. Battalion relieved the FRENCH (6th Battalion, 21st Regiment) in the front line of GRICOURT Sector (Right sub sector of Divisional front). Wire was found to be strong. Disposition: "A" Coy Right, "C" Coy centre, "D" Coy left. "B" Coy in support at FRESNOY-LE-PETIT. Casualties Nil.	App A 9. G.W.

Army Form C. 2118.

WAR DIARY
or
INTELLIGENCE SUMMARY.
(Erase heading not required.)

Instructions regarding War Diaries and Intelligence Summaries are contained in F. S. Regs., Part II. and the Staff Manual respectively. Title pages will be prepared in manuscript.

Place	Date 1916	Hour	Summary of Events and Information	Remarks and references to Appendices
GRICOURT	11th Jan.		In front line trenches. Trenches improved and patrols sent out. Quartermasters Stores and transport moved from ATTILLY to MARTEVILLE	Casualties Nil. 9 p.m.
"	12th		Do. Trenches improved and patrols sent out	" Wounded 1 O.R. 5 p.m. 9 p.m.
"	13th		Do. Do.	" Nil. 9 p.m.
"	14th		Do. Battalion relieved at night in front line trenches by 2/5th GLOUCESTERS, and proceeded to support left trenches. Disposition: A & D Coys in OTTER COPSE, B in ESSLING REDOUBT, C in MAISSEMY. Notification received from Base Records that Captain R.P. CUTHBERT M.C. (Adjutant) had been struck off the strength of the unit on 28/12/14, pending Medical Board in ENGLAND. Casualties Wounded 10.R.	App. A.10 9 p.m. 9 p.m.
MAISSEMY	15th		In support trenches. Work of improvement of trenches, making firesteps & communication. Nil.	9 p.m.
"	16th		Do. Work as above. Old French gun positions near QUARRY N. of OTTER COPSE were subjected to a continuous shelling by the enemy from 1.30 p.m. to 5 p.m. Casualties Nil.	9 p.m.
"	17th		Do. Improvement of trenches, making firesteps &c. Casualties Nil.	9 p.m.
"	18th		Do. Battalion relieved 2/5th GLOUCESTERS, "D" Left, "C" in support at FRESNOY-LE-PETIT. Disposition "A" Right, "B" Centre, "D" Left, "C" in support at FRESNOY-LE-PETIT. Casualties Nil	App A.11 9 p.m.

WAR DIARY or INTELLIGENCE SUMMARY

Army Form C. 2118.

Place	Date	Hour	Summary of Events and Information	Remarks and references to Appendices
GRICOURT	19th Jan		In front line trenches. Improvement of trenches. Fighting patrols sent out. Major H.T. BENNETT reported from leave and resumed temporary command of 2/1st Bucks Battn. Casualties Nil.	2 mis
"	20th		Do. Work as above. Fighting patrols sent out. A line was observed in NO MAN'S LAND in front of "D" Coy (left of Battalion front). Cause unknown. A party of the enemy were observed trying to extinguish it and were dispersed by our Lewis gun fire. A message was received from 184* Infantry Brigade Headquarters that our listening sets had picked up an enemy message "To all ready for 4 A.M." Necessary precautions were taken but nothing unusual relieved. Casualties Nil.	9 mis
"	21st		Do. Work as above. Fighting patrols sent out from 4 P.M. to about 4.15 P.M. a display of coloured lights was seen all along the enemy front. No hostile artillery or machine gun fire followed. Casualties Nil. Battalion was relieved at night by 2/5* GLOUCESTERS and proceeded	9 mis
App A.12	22nd		Do. to dug-outs in support. Dispositions "A, C & D Coys at OTTER COPSE, "B" in QUARRY N.E. of FRESNOY-LE-PETIT. Casualties 1 O.R. Wounded	9 pm

Army Form C. 2118.

WAR DIARY
or
INTELLIGENCE SUMMARY.
(Erase heading not required.)

Instructions regarding War Diaries and Intelligence Summaries are contained in F. S. Regs., Part II. and the Staff Manual respectively. Title pages will be prepared in manuscript.

Place	Date 1918	Hour	Summary of Events and Information	Remarks and references to Appendices
FRESNOY-LE-PETIT	23rd Jan		In Support. Working parties found and trenches improved. Casualties Nil.	9/Nm
	24th		Do. Wiring "Strong Point" line especially at junction of BOUGEAUD and CHAMPAGNE trenches. The new system of defence was explained to all Officers and senior N.C.O.s by the Commanding Officer. Casualties Nil.	9/Nm
"	25th		Do. Work as above "	9/Nm
"	26th		Do. Battalion was relieved by 2/5th WARWICKS and marched to reserve billets in HOLNON WOOD. Casualties, Nil.	App A.13 9/Nm 9/Nm
HOLNON	27th		In Reserve. Bathing and cleaning up.	Do.
	28th		Do. Working parties found for digging new system of trenches under R.E. arrangements. Company and Musketry training, special attention being paid to the tactical handling of Lewis guns. Casualties Nil.	9/Nm
"	29th		Do.	9/Nm
"	30th		Do. Lt Col. H E de R WETHERALL, DSO, MC assumed Temporary command of the 184th Infantry Brigade. Major H J BENNETT rejoined from 2/1st Bucks Bn. and assumed command of the Battalion. Casualties Nil	9/Nm

Army Form C. 2118.

WAR DIARY
or
INTELLIGENCE SUMMARY.
(Erase heading not required.)

Instructions regarding War Diaries and Intelligence Summaries are contained in F. S. Regs., Part II. and the Staff Manual respectively. Title pages will be prepared in manuscript.

Place	Date	Hour	Summary of Events and Information	Remarks and references to Appendices
HOLNON	31st Jan 1918		In Reserve. Work as above.	Casualties Nil.
			The following honours and awards appeared in the New Years Honours List.	
			Awarded Military Cross: Captain R.F. CUTHBERT and Lieut. C.R. PARSONS	
			Mentioned in Sir Douglas Haig's despatch :-	
			Lt. Col. H E de R WETHERALL, D.S.O, M.C.	
			Captain A.J. ROBINSON.	
			" W.H. MOBERLY, D.S.O.	
			Lieut. W.H. ENOCH	
			201052 R.S.M. DOUGLAS, W.	
			200555 Sgt. LEATHERBARROW, J.	
			200895 " SHERWOOD, A	

H.J. Bennett.
Major,
Commdg 2/4th Bn Oxf & Bucks L.I.

SECRET.   2/4TH BN. OXFORD & BUCKS LIGHT INFANTRY.   Copy No. 5
                     ORDER NO. 454.   6/1/18.

Ref. Map AMIENS 1/100000.

1. The Battn. will march tomorrow under the command of Captain BROWN, M.C. to billets in VOYENNES. Route:- ROSIERES, LIHONS, CHAULNES; after this place route to be decided later.

2. The Battn. will parade in usual place at 7.30 a.m. in full marching order - steel hats to be carried - caps worn.   Order of march: H.Q., D, Drums, B, A, C (less 6 sections).   Distances will be as follows:- 200^x between units, 25^x between groups of 6 vehicles and Coys. Halts will take place 12 minutes before each clock hour.

3. Blankets will be tightly rolled in bundles of 10 and stacked near the two G.S. Wagons which will be parked in the yard by 6 a.m. Officers' valises, Mess boxes and Orderly room boxes to be ready by 6.15 a.m. and stacked either at Q.M. Stores or Bottom floor of Battn. billet whichever is most convenient. One servant per H.Q. and Coy. to be left behind to come on lorry.

4. Routine for tomorrow will be:- Reveille 5 a.m.; Breakfasts 6.15 a.m.; Dinners served on the road at 11.50 a.m. (Halt from 11.50 a.m. to 1 p.m. will be made for dinners.

5. Transport, less cookers which will follow their Coys., will march in rear of the Battn. divided into groups of 6 vehicles each. A rear guard of one Officer and 6 sections of "C" Coy. will report to the Transport Officer as the Transport passes the turning to the Battn. billet.

6. Lewis Gun limbers will be by the Cookers at 2 p.m. this afternoon. Coys. to load their Lewis Guns and drums as soon as limbers arrive.

7. As fresh units are going to occupy our present billets they are to be left scrupulously clean. One Officer per Coy. to report to Adjutant on parade that this has been done.

8. Sick parade at 6 a.m.

                                          (sd) G.H.WILTSHIRE,
Battn. H.Q.   2/Lieut. & A/Adjt.,
Issued at 12.40 p.m.   4 OXFORDS.

            1 - 4.   Coys.
            5.   War Diary.
            6.   184th Inf. Bde.
            7.   Quartermaster.
            8.   Transport Officer.
            9.   Medical Officer.
            10, 11.   Battn. H.Q.

App. A 8

SECRET.　　　　2/4th Bn. OXFORD & BUCKS LIGHT INFANTRY.　　Copy No. 5
　　　　　　　　　　　　　ORDER NO. 456.　　　　　　　　　　　8/1/18.

1. The Battn. will move tomorrow to Billets in BEAUVOIS Area.

2. The Battn. will parade by Companies.
   Order of March:- H.Q., B, Drums, A, C, D (less 2 sections).
   B Coy. to pass Brigade H.Q. at 11.10 a.m.
   Dress: Full Marching Order - Caps and leather jerkins to be worn.
   Great care to be taken that "Marching Order" is fitted as laid down by Brigade.
   Distances: 100ˣ between Units. 25ˣ between Coys. and each group of 3 vehicles. Halt
   15 minutes, before each clock hour.

3. Blankets tightly rolled in bundles of 10, will be stacked by Coys. in their own areas in one dump, where they will be collected by G.S. wagons at 10 a.m. Officers' valises, Orderly room boxes and Mess boxes to be ready at 10 a.m. at Coy. H.Q.
   One servant per H.Q. and Coy. to be left behind to come on lorry.

4. Routine for tomorrow will be:-
   　Reveille.　　　7.30 a.m.
   　Breakfasts.　　8 a.m.
   　Sick Parade.　 9 a.m.
   　Dinners served on the road at 12.40 p.m.

5. Transport, less Cookers which will follow their Coys., will march in rear of the Battn. divided into groups of 3 vehicles each. A rear guard of one Officer and 2 sections of D Coy. will report to the Transport Officer as the Transport passes the Brigade.

6. Billets to be left scrupulously clean. One Officer per Coy. to report to Adjutant on parade that this has been done.

　　　　　　　　　　　　　　　　　　　　(sd) G.H. WILTSHIRE,
　　　　　　　　　　　　　　　　　　　　　　　2/Lieut., A/Adjt.
Battn. H.Q.
Issued at 7.45 p.m.

　　　　　　　1 - 4.　Companies.
　　　　　　　5.　　　War Diary.
　　　　　　　6.　　　184th Inf. Bde.
　　　　　　　7.　　　Quartermaster.
　　　　　　　8.　　　Transport Officer.
　　　　　　　9.　　　Medical Officer.
　　　　　　10, 11.　Battn. H.Q.

SECRET   4/4 Oxford & Bucks L.I. Infty   Copy No 5
         Order No 158   9-1-18

1. Tomorrow the Battalion will relieve the
FRENCH 6th Battn 224 Regt in the
front system.

2. The Battn will parade at 3.40 pm
and proceed in the following order
H.Q. A.C.D.B. via MARTEVILLE to
MAISSEMY Cemetery where guides will
be met at 5.30 pm.
Teas will be served on the road.
Spare kit in Haversacks will be taken
to Q.M. Stores by 2 pm.
Cookers will follow their Coys.
All Lewis Guns and 12 drums per
gun (taken in 3 carriers) to be
loaded on limbers and will follow
the leading Coy.

3. An advance party of Signallers &
Runners & Observers will parade at
H.Q. hut at 9.30 am to proceed
to the line to take over.

4. Completion of relief to be sent by
wire - the Code word being VERMAND.
No speaking except in cases of great

SECRET. 2/4th Oxford and Bucks Light Infantry.   Copy No.

ORDER NO. 460.   13.1.18.

MAP REFERENCES :-   62 B, S.W. 1/20,000 and 62 C, 1/40,000.

1. The Battalion will be relieved on the night of the 14/15th by the 2/5 GLOSTERS in the following order from Right to Left,

OXFORDS.		GLOSTERS.
A.	by	A.
C.		D.
D.		B.
B.		C.

2. Signallers and No. 1 Lewis Gunners will arrive at 12.30 p.m. and will be guided to the Coys.

3. Guides for the Coys. as to place, time, etc. will be arranged direct between O's,C. Coys. concerned.
On receipt of these orders, Coys. are to report if this has NOT been done.

4. All petrol cans, gum boots, tools and hot food containers are be handed over and receipts obtained.

5. After relief Coys. will proceed to the following places :-
"A" and "D" Coys. to OTTER COPSE (M.32.b.) where "A" and "D" Coys. of the GLOSTERS are at present.
"B" Coy. to REDOUBT LINE in M.14.a. and d, where "C" Coy. of the Glosters are at present. "C" Coy. to near Support Battn. H.Q. in R.23.b.
Coys. will send one Officer, one guide per platoon and Coy. H.Q. to Battn.H.Q. by 10 a.m. tomorrow, when they will be guided to the various places.
All arrangements as regards cooking, water supply, &c. are to be found out. Also the work that the GLOSTERS are now doing, which will be continued by the respective Coys.
"A" Coy. will take over the post of 1 N.C.O. and 10 men in CHAMPAGNE TRENCH at present found by "A" Coy. of the GLOSTERS.

6. Lewis Guns and drums, camp kettles, &c. will be carried to the new places and no limbers will be provided for this purpose.

7. Relief complete will be notified by wire, code word being NAMELESS

8. Rations and Water carts tomorrow will arrive at new Coy. H.Q. at 11 p.m.

Battn. H.Q.
Issued at 6.30 p.m.

(sd) G.H.WILTSHIRE,
2/Lieut. and A/Adjt.

Copy No.1 - 4. Coys,
5. BdeM
6. War Diary.
7. 2/5 GLOSTERS.
8. Quartermaster.
9. Transport Officer.
10. Office.

SECRET.   2/4th Oxford and Bucks Light Infantry.   Copy No.

ORDER NO. 462.   17.1.18.

Map References :-   62B,S.W. 1/20,000 and 62C, 1/40,000.

1. The Battalion will relieve on the night of the 18/19th the 2/5 GLOSTERS in the following order from Right to Left,.

OXFORDS.	GLOSTERS.
A.	A.
B.	D.
D.	B.
C. (in reserve)	C.

   The only Coy. to have guides is "B" Coy. The GLOSTER guides will be at Reserve Coy. H.Q. at 5.45 p.m. No Coy. will move forward before 5.15 p.m.

2. Signallers and Observers will take over by 3 p.m. If "B" Coy. requires guides for the Signallers they are to call at the GLOSTER H.Q. No.1 Lewis Gunners will go with this party.

3. All petrol cans, gum boots, tools, hot food containers are being left in the line by the GLOSTERS. Camp kettles will be taken into the line.

4. Parties of the GLOSTERS will arrive to take over during the course of the day. Receipts for stores to be obtained and sent to Orderly Room.

5. Blankets will be collected by the Transport. They are to be left rolled ready for loading in a dry place. "A" Coy. will detail a man to look after their blankets. This man to proceed to the Transport Lines with the limber taking the blankets. "B" Coy. will leave the Shoemakers in charge. "C" and "D" will leave their Coy. barbers.

6. Rations will arrive for H.Q. and "C" Coy. at 6 p.m. Other Coys. at 6.30 p.m.

7. Relief complete will be reported by wire code word being 'STICKY'

Battn. H.Q.   (sd) G.H.WILRSHIRE,
Issued at 6.30 p.m.   2/Lieut. and A/Adjt.

         1 - 4.   Coys.
             5.   War Diary.
             6.   184 Bde.
             7.   GLOSTERS.
             8.   Quartermaster.
             9.   Transport Officer.
            10.   Officer

SECRET.   4th Oxford & Bucks L.I.   Copy No. 6
Ref. Maps   Order No. 464   25.1.18
Trench Map 62B. S.W.
           62 C.

1. The Battalion will be relieved on the night of the 26/27th by
   the 2/5 WARWICKS as under:—

        OXFORDS   WARWICKS
          A   by   C
          B   "   D
          C   "   A
          D   "   B

   Time of arrival of relief is not known.

2. Guides will only be required by WARWICKS D Coy. These
   will be detailed by O.C. B Coy.
       The Guides will meet the WARWICKS D Coy at the Quarry
   and will guide them into FRESNOY.

3. Limbers will arrive at present ration dumps at 5.30 P.M.
   to take:—
        (a) Blankets — which must be rolled tightly in bundles of 10.
        (b) Lewis Guns
        (c) Valises, Mess Boxes and Orderly Room Boxes.
   If the limbers have not arrived when relief is complete Coys. will
   detail one man to remain behind in charge of (a) (b) and (c)
   respectively.

4. All Trench Stores, including tools and washing tubs to be handed
   over, receipts obtained being sent to Orderly Room.

5. After relief Coys. will proceed to dug outs in HOLNON WOOD
   (X.11.a. B.10.) now occupied by 2/7 WARWICKS
    X.11.d.1.1.

6. An Advance party of 1 Officer and 3 O.R. per Coy. will
   be detailed from the Transport to proceed to HOLNON WOOD
   (X.11.d.1.1.)
   (X.11.a. B.10.)
       They will meet Capt. MARCON at 2/7° WARWICKS Batt H.Q. there
   at 2 P.M.
       After finding out where the various Coys are to go they
   will reconnoitre the route to KEEPERS HOUSE (R.35.d.65.35)
   where they will meet the Coys at 6 P.M. and guide them
   in.

7. Relief complete will be notified by wire, code word
   being "CATHEDRAL".

Batt. Hdqrs   Copies 1 – 4. Coys
Frained at 3 P.M.   5.   R.E.
                                     6.   War Diary
                                     7.   2/5 WARWICKS Bd) G.H Wiltshire
                                     8.   Q.M.   1/West 48/Arft.
                                     9.   T.O.
                                    10.   Office

SECRET   2/4 Oxford & Bucks Lt Infty   Copy No 8
            Order No 463   21·1·18

Map Refs:-
French Map 62B S.W. 1/20000.
     and 62C 1/20000

1. The Battalion will be relieved on the night of the 22nd/23rd by the 2/5 GLOSTERS in the following order from Right to Left:-

OXFORDS		GLOSTERS
A	by	C
B	by	D
D	by	B
C (Reserve)	by	A

2. Sig ullrs, Observers and Hot Water Runners with guides before 3 p.m.

3. Guides will only be required by GLOSTERS 'C' Coy. O/C A Coy will arrange for guides to be at THE MONUMENT at 5·30 p.m.

4. All petrol cans, gum boots, tools, hot food containers and coding tubes, besides all FRENCH STORES to be handed over, receipts obtained being sent to Orderly Room.

5. After relief Coys will proceed to the following places:-

A. C & D Coys to OTTER COPSE (M.32 b)
(1 Officer per Coy to meet Captn MARCON at
Battn H.Q. at 3 pm who will allot the
accommodation) where A. C & D of the
GLOSTERS are at present.
B Coy and part of Battn H.Q. (as detailed)
to ATTILLY where B Coy of the GLOSTERS
are at present.
Battn H.Q. will be near Brigade H.Q.
MAISON DE GARDE
B Coy will send an advance party of
1 Officer and 3 O.R. to report at GLOSTER
H.Q. at MAISON DE GARDE at 2 pm. They
will be shown the best way to ATTILLY.
After seeing accommodation they will return
and meet their Coy by the Reserve Coy
H.Q. in FRESNOY.
A limber will be found at about
M. 27. a 6. 2. into which they will put
their Lewis Guns and Drums.

6. Relief complete will be notified by wire
Code word being "WIRELESS"

Battn H.Q.   (Sd) G.H. Hilchins
formed at 3 pm   Lt. & Adjt
    1 - 4 Coys   7 5/ GLOSTERS
    5 184 Bde   8 Quartermaster
    6 War Diary   9 Transport Officer
                   10 Office

CONFIDENTIAL

WAR DIARY

*** of ***

2/4TH BATTALION, OXFORDSHIRE & BUCKINGHAMSHIRE
LIGHT INFANTRY

From 1st Feb. 1918 to 28th Feb. 1918.

VOLUME XXII.

*****

WAR DIARY
or
INTELLIGENCE SUMMARY.

Army Form C. 2118.

Place	Date	Hour	Summary of Events and Information	Remarks and references to Appendices
HOLNON	FEB 1st		In reserve. 2 hours Training. Digging of Battle Zone line in afternoon. Casualties 2 O.R. Wounded accidentally; while rapid loading. Being practiced with live rounds. CAPT. W.H. MOSELEY S.S.O. on leave.	edwM.
"	2nd		In reserve. 2 hours training in morning. Free afternoon — Rota — nance of Div.l "PIERROTS" at V.A.Bx attended by percentage of Battalion.	edwM.
"	3rd		In reserve. Battalion relieved 2/4 GLOSTERS in left subsector of Right sector — on night 3/4 TH. Relief complete at 8.50½ pm. Disposition as follows:— "C" Coy. (Left front) — "B" Coy (Right front), "A" Coy (Counter attack) "D" Coy. in Keypoint — at ENGHIEN REDOUBT — Batt. HQRS in FAYET. CAPT. BROWN M.C. acting as 2nd in command. CAPT MARCON acting as Adjutant vice 2/Lieut WILTSHIRE (sick)	? edwM. edwM.
FAYET	4TH		In the line. Quiet day. Some M.G. fire (enemy) during night. Intermediate station for SOS signals established.	edwM.
"	5TH		In the line. Quiet day.	edwM.
"	6TH		In the line. Quiet day. FAYET Château grounds lightly shelled during morning. 20.11.09 CSM OSBORNE. BMT awarded Belgian Croix de Guerre.	edwM.

WAR DIARY
or
INTELLIGENCE SUMMARY.
(Erase heading not required.)

Army Form C. 2118.

Place	Date	Hour	Summary of Events and Information	Remarks and references to Appendices
FAYET	FEB 7TH		In the line. — Battalion relieved by 2/5 GLOSTERS on night 7/8TH — Moving into support in QUARRY in HOLNON WOOD. — Batt. HQRS — A.B.C. COYS in Quarry. D. Coy in Sunken Road E. of HOLNON. Casualties 1 O.R. wounded.	Appx 1 & S.W.M
HOLNON	8TH		In Support. Cleaning up, inspection by COYS. Work on ENGHIEN REDOUBT by A.B.C. COYS at night. D. Coy working in FAYET under orders of 2/5 GLOSTERS. — 13 Offrs. 300 O.R. (including 3 Oxfords)	& W.M
"	9TH		In support. Cleaning up, inspection in morning. Work at night as on 8TH. Capts Brown, McIntyre.	& W.M
"	10TH		In support. Work as on previous day. Lt ENOCH — as acting Adjutant.	& W.M
"	11TH		In support. Draft from 2/5 Oxfords joined Battalion. — marching from VMY. Battalion relieved 2/5 GLOSTERS in ENGHIEN REDOUBT.	Appx 3 & W.M
"			To MARTEVILLE: being billeted near transport. Batt. HQ in QUARRY at ENGHIEN REDOUBT. C. (Centre front); D (Right front); C (Counter Attack); B. (in left sub-sector right sector.). A (Left front). COYS disposed as follows: — Relief complete 10 p.m. — Quiet night. ENGHIEN REDOUBT.)	
FAYET	12N		In front line. Quiet day. — GEN. MAXSE (XVIII Corps) inspected Batt. in the line in morning. Intermediate S.O.S. put up owing to fog which Batt. front patrolled 4 times during night	& W.M
"	13TH		In front line. Quiet day & night. —	& W.M
"	14TH		In front line.	& W.M
"	15N		In front line. Battalion relieved by 2/5 GLOSTERS & moved to support in Quarry in HOLNON WOOD. Batt HQ. A.C.D. in Quarry B. Coy in SUNKEN ROAD E. of Batt. Lt L.M. EBERLY D.S.O. returned from leave.	A & W.M

Army Form C. 2118.

WAR DIARY
or
INTELLIGENCE SUMMARY.
(Erase heading not required.)

Instructions regarding War Diaries and Intelligence Summaries are contained in F. S. Regs., Part II and the Staff Manual respectively. Title pages will be prepared in manuscript.

Place	Date FEB	Hour	Summary of Events and Information	Remarks and references to Appendices
HORION	16th		In Support. Cleaning up; inspection by COys in morning; Altering and wiring at night, in ENGHIEN REDOUBT (A.E.D.COYS); wiring by B.Coy. under E/Lt OTTERS. Routine when in support - Breakfast 8 am. Ord. Room 10 am. Sick Parade 10 am. Dinner 12.45 p.m. Tea 4 p.m. - Baths 6	CWJM
"	17th		In Support. Works above. Football matches played by COYS at Transport lines MARTEVILLE. Baths at MARTEVILLE.	CWJM
"	18th		In Support. Works as above.	Appex 51 CWJM
"	19th		In Support. Battalion relieved by 2/6 R.WARWICKS into Div. Reserve at VAUX. Men billetted in huts.	CWJM
VAUX	20th		In Reserve. Cleaning up; Inspection in morning. Recreation in afternoon. PROLIX - VAUX. Band performance at evening performance. 6th Def. draft joined unit	CWJM
"	21st		In Reserve. Re-organisation of COys - absorption of 6th Def. draft taking place in the afternoon. Special performance of the "FROLICS" for the Battalion at night.	CWJM
"	22nd		In Reserve. Battalion relieved 2/8 WORCESTERS & 1/9 N.R. SCOTTS in front area (Centre area) - RILOT COMPLETE 11.15 P.M. Disposition: B (Left front) C (Right front) D (Counter attack) A (Anthony point) Ellot in OTTER COPSE. HQ in FRESNOY QUARRY. Near distribution of Divisions/Bdes. in depth.	CWJM Appex 52
FRESNOY QUARRY	23rd		Infantine. Quiet day. Got alarm at night but no infantry action. Lieut CUNNINGHAM Airborne duties of act. adjutant vice 2/LT FINCH (sick)	L.I.O.R. killed: 4 O.R. wounded (1 at Ally).
"	24th		In further. Quiet day.	CWJM

Army Form C. 2118.

WAR DIARY
or
INTELLIGENCE SUMMARY.

(Erase heading not required.)

Place	Date	Hour	Summary of Events and Information	Remarks and references to Appendices
FRESNOY QUARRY	FEB 25		In front line. Quiet day on whole, some aerial activity. Raid by Can. Corps on left.	C.S.M.
"	26th		In front line. Quiet day on whole — B. Coy HQrs & area round some shelled intermittently. Inter-company relief — A & D relieving B & C respectively.	C.S.M
"	27th		In front line. Some hostile shelling in front of line of resistance. C. Coy's HQrs moved to OTTER COPSE.	C.S.M
"	28th		In front line. Quiet day on whole.	

H.H. Bennett
Major Comdg
2/4 Oxf & Bucks L.I.

SECRET.   2/4TH BN. OXFORD AND BUCKS LIGHT INFANTRY.   Copy No. 5
          ORDER NO. 471.   2/2/18.

Ref. Maps 1/20000 62.B.S.W. and 62.C.S.E.

1. The Battalion will relieve the 2/4TH GLOSTERS in left sub-sector of Divisional Right Sector on night of 3/4th.

2. Coys. will relieve as follows:-

OXFORDS.		GLOSTERS.
B	relieve	D (Right front).
C	"	A (Left ").
A	"	B (Counter-attack Coy in FAYET).
D	"	C (Passive defence Coy in Quarry at S.4.c.1.7).

3. GUIDES will meet the Battn. at Churchyard at Western end of FAYET at 6.30 p.m. and take them to Battn. Hdqrs. where further guides will take forward the Coys. holding the outpost line.
   No guides will be found for "D" Coy. who will march direct to the QUARRY by the SELENCY - FAYET road.

4. Coys. will move in the following order with 200x between platoons - C,B,A,H.Q.,D, moving off from X.11.d.3.4 at 5 p.m.
   DRESS. Full Marching Order with greatcoats - less haversacks in the case of B and C Coys.

5. Officers' valises, Medical room and surplus Orderly room boxes and all blankets (rolled in tens) to be ready for loading by 11 a.m. in the field to the E. of the quarry. Lieut. MITCHELL will supervise the loading of the above.

6. Limbers will be at Battn. H.Q. at 2 p.m. for loading Lewis gun drums and Coy. mess boxes. 1 limber will follow C Coy. with Lewis guns, magazines and mess boxes of C and B Coys, and will offload guns and magazines at the entrance to FAYET, after which it will take the mess boxes to their respective Coy. Hdqrs.
   1 limber will take Lewis guns, magazines and mess boxes of A, H.Q. Coys. and will follow "A" Coy. The Lewis guns and magazines will be offloaded at the entrance to the village and the remainder taken to Battn. H.Q. 1 limber will follow "D" Coy. & take their Lewis guns & magazines & mess boxes direct to the Quarry.

7. Advanced parties as follows:-
   "A" Coy. 1 Officer, an N.C.O. per platoon, to report to 2/4th GLOSTERS Battn. H.Q. at 3 p.m.

7. (contd.)

    H.Q. Coy.   1 N.C.O., 4 Signallers, & 2 Observers to report at 2/4th GLOSTERS Battn. H.Q. at 3 p.m.

    D Coy.   1 Officer, an N.C.O. per platoon, and 1 per Coy. H.Q. will report at the Quarry at 3 p.m.

8.   2/Lieut. STOWELL will report at Battn. H.Q. at 11 a.m. and be prepared to hand over billets and stores to a representative of the 2/4th GLOSTERS.

9.   Details to be left out of the line to parade at 2 p.m. under Lieut. MITCHELL in field above Quarry. Tea ration to be carried.

10.   Receipts for all trench stores to be forwarded to Battn. H.Q. by 8 a.m. 4th inst.

11.   Billets to be left clean before Coys. move off.

12.   Code name for relief will be "PRESTIGE" - to be sent by wire.

                                                    (sd) G.R.WILTSHIRE,
                                                          2/Lt. & Acting Adjt.

Battn. H.Q.
Issued at 7.45 p.m.

                1 - 4.   Coys.
                5.   War Diary.
                6.   184th Inf. Bde.
                7.   Quartermaster.
                8.   Transport Officer.
                9.   Medical Officer.
              10,11.   Office.
               12.   R.S.M.

SECRET.   2/4TH BN. OXFORD & BUCKS LT.INFTY.   Copy No. 5
                      ORDER NO.472.   6.2.18.

Ref. Maps 62 B.S.W.
& 62 C.S.E.

1. The Battalion will be relieved on night 7/8th by 2/5 GLOSTERS and
    will move into Support - H.Q.,A,B & C Coys. to QUARRY in X.12.a.6.3
    (marching by platoons by SELENCY - HOLNON - ATTILY, guides meeting
    them on road near QUARRY) and D Coy. to Sunken Road running through
    S.3.a.

2. Relief as follows:-
    OXFORDS.   GLOSTERS.
        B   relieved by   D
        C   "   "   A
        A   "   "   C
        D   "   "   B
    This order holds good in the relief in Support.

3. GUIDES. A,B,C Coys. will send 1 guide per Coy. H.Q. and 1 guide
    per platoon to report Battn.H.Q. in FAYET at 6.15 p.m. & afterwards
    to meet incoming unit at Cemetery at S.5.a.0.6. O.C. B & C Coys.
    to arrange for guides for each post in front line to be at their
    Coy.H.Q. at 6.15 p.m.

4. ADVANCE PARTIES.
    (a) A,C & D Coys. of 2/5 GLOSTERS will send 1 Officer, 2 Runners,
    1 Signaller per Coy. and 1 N.C.O. per platoon to report at Battn.
    H.Q. at 3 p.m. on 7th. These parties will take over billets,
    trench stores, etc. Receipts for these Stores and for all documents
    & maps duly signed, will be sent to Battn.H.Q. by 4.30 p.m. on 7th
    inst.
    (b) 1 Officer from A,B, & C Coys. respectively will report to
    Capt. ROBINSON at D Coy's H.Q. in QUARRY at 10.15 a.m. on 7th before
    proceeding to reconnoitre ground in support area.
    (c) A party under Lt.ENOCH will take over from the 2/5 GLOSTERS
    reporting at their H.Q. at 2.30 p.m. Receipts for stores taken over
    to reach Battn.H.Q. at 9 a.m. on 8th.

5. 1 limber for B & C Coys. and 1 limber per H.Q. and A Coys. will
    call at Battn. & Coy. H.Q. at 8 p.m. to load L.G.s and drums,
    Mess boxes and Orderly room box. These will be dumped at their
    respective H.Q. and a guard of 1 N.C.O. and 2 men left in charge.
    ½-limber will call at D Coy's H.Q. at 6 p.m.

6. Relief complete to be sent over the wire. The code words
    will be names of respective Coy.Commanders.
                                              (sd) C.S.W.MARCON,
Battn.H.Q.   Capt. for Adjt.,
Issued at 6.15 p.m.   4 OXFORDS.
              Copies 1 - 4. Coys.
                     5.   War Diary.
                     6.   184 Bde.
                     7.   2/5 GLOSTERS.
                     8.   Quartermaster.
                     9.   Transport Officer.
                    10.   Office.

SECRET.   2/4TH BN. OXFORD AND BUCKS LIGHT INFANTRY.   Copy No. 6

ORDER NO. 475.   10/2/18.

Ref. Map 82.B.S.W. 1/20000.

1. The Battalion will relieve the 2/5TH GLOSTERS in Left Sub-Sector on the night 11/12th inst.

2. DISPOSITIONS.
   Left Front Coy. "A" Coy. OXFORDS relieve "A" Coy. GLOSTERS.
   Right   "   " "D" "   "   " "D" "   "
   Counter-Attack " "C" "   "   " "C" "   "
   Strong Point   " "B" "   "   " "B" "   "

3. GUIDES.
   5 Guides for each of A, C and D Coys. will be at CEMETERY, W. of FAYET, S.5.a.9.6, at 6.30 p.m. Each guide will have written slip shewing number of platoon he is to guide.

4. ORDER OF MARCH.
   D Coy., A Coy., C Coy., H.Q., B Coy., B Coy. will move at 5.15 p.m., D Coy. at 5.45 p.m.
   A distance of 200 yds. will be maintained between platoons.

5. ROUTE.
   HOLNON - SELENCY - FAYET Road - except for D Coy.

6. ADVANCE PARTY.
   An Advance Party of 1 Officer and 1 Signaller per Coy., 1 N.C.O. per platoon, Sgt. PAGE, 4 Battalion Runners & 4 Battalion Signallers will report as follows:-
   A, C, & D Coys. at Old Battn. H.Q. in FAYET at 3 p.m.
   Battn. H.Q. & B Coy. at QUARRY N.4.c.1.7 at 3 p.m.
   "A" Coy. will send two men to take over O.P. in FAYET at 3 p.m.

7. WATER.
   Water for A, C & D Coys. from Tanks in FAYET ; for B Coy. & H.Q. from water cart at Battn. H.Q.

8. RATIONS.
   The Medical Officer, his staff, 2 water-men and 1 canteen man will be rationed with C Coy.

9. Officers' valises, and blankets rolled in tens will be dumped by Coys. on track near watercart by 11 a.m. tomorrow.

10. TRANSPORT.
    One limber with rations, will report at D Coy's H.Q. at 5.30 pm. and will pick up Mess Boxes. D Coy. will leave one man to guide limber. Valises will be picked up by returning limber.
    One limber for Lewis guns and Mess boxes of A & C Coys., and one limber for B Coy. & H.Q. will report at 3.30 p.m.
    Companies must arrange to load Lewis Guns at once.
    Lewis Guns will be offloaded at CEMETERY, Mess Boxes being taken on to respective Coy. H.Q.

11. List of Trench Stores taken over will be sent to Battn. H.Q. by 6 a.m. 12th inst.

                                                          OVER.

12. Completion of relief will be wired to Battn. H.Q., code word being names of Coy. Commanders concerned.

(sd) W.H. ENOCH,
Lieut. & A/Adjt.,
4 OXFORDS.

Battn. H.Q.
Issued at 7.30 p.m.

Copies:-

1 - 4.   Os.C. Coys.
   5.   War Diary.
   6.   184th Inf. Bde.
   7.   Quartermaster.
   8.   Transport Officer.
   9.   Medical Officer.
10, 11. Battn. H.Q.

Secret.   2/4TH BN. OXFORD & BUCKS LIGHT INFANTRY.   Copy No.
                       ORDER NO.476.   14.2.18.

Ref. Maps
62 B.S.W. and 62C S.E. 1/20000.

1.   The 2/5 GLOSTERS will relieve the Battn. in the left sub-sector on the night 15/16th inst.

2.   DISPOSITIONS.
       Right Front Coy.   C Coy. GLOSTERS relieve D Coy. OXFORDS.
       Left   "   "   B "   "   " A "   "
       Counter-Attack "   A "   "   " C "   "
       Strong Point "   D "   "   " B "   "

3.   GUIDES. A,C & D Coys. will each send 5 guides to be at CEMETERY W of FAYET, S.5.a.0.6 at 6.30 p.m.

4.   BILLETS. On relief the Battn. will move into SUPPORT. Battn.H.Q. A,C & D Coys. to dugout in QUARRY X.12.a.8.2 and B Coy. to SUNKEN RD. through S.3.a.

5.   ROUTE. FAYET - SELENCY - HOLNON Rd. Guides will meet Coys. on road near QUARRY.

6.   ADVANCE PARTIES.
       (a) 2/5 GLOSTERS will send following Advance Parties:-
Representatives of Front Line Lewis Gun Teams to report this evening.
       One Officer and one Signaller per Coy. and 1 N.C.O. per platoon, 4 Battn. Signallers and 4 Battn. Runners to report by 3 p.m. tomorrow.
       (b) 2/4 OXFORDS will send 1 Officer and 1 N.C.O. per Coy. and 1 Officer and 2 Signallers for Battn. H.Q. to take over at 3 p.m.
       Coys. will take over from respective Coys. relieving them.

7.   TRANSPORT.
       One limber for C Coy. and Medical Boxes will be at AID POST at 7 p.m.
       One limber for A and D Coys. will be at AID POST at 8 p.m.
       A and D Coys. will send 1 N.C.O. and 1 man to AID POST to supervise loading of Lewis Guns and Drums, which will be dumped at this spot. C Coy. will make their own arrangements.
       One half limber at Battn.H.Q. for B Coy's Mess boxes at 6.30 P.M. This limber will proceed to B Coy's new Headquarters and return to pick up Battn.H.Q. Mess boxes and Orderly room boxes.
       B Coy. will arrange to carry their Lewis Guns.

8.   RATIONS.
       Rations and water will be sent for Battn.H.Q. and 3 Coys. to QUARRY in HOLNON WOOD at 5 p.m. and for B Coy. at 6 p.m.

9.   Receipts for Trench Stores handed over and taken over will be forwarded to Battn.H.Q. by 9 a.m. 16th inst.

10.   Completion of relief will be wired to Battn.H.Q. code word being names of Coy. Commanders concerned.

11.   ACKNOWLEDGE.

                                               (sd) W.H.ENOCH,
Battn.H.Q.   Lieut. & A/Adjt.
Issued 8.30 p.m.   1 - 4.Coys.   6. War Diary.   8. Medical Officer.
                    5. GLOSTERS.   7. 184 Inf.Bde.   9. Transport.
                                               10. Office.

SECRET.   2/4TH BN. OXFORD & BUCKS LIGHT INFANTRY.   Copy No.
Ref. Map   ORDER NO. 481.   18.2.18.
ST. QUENTIN 18 1/100000.

1.   The Battalion will be relieved tomorrow the 19th inst. by the 2/6th ROYAL WARWICKS and will move into Divisional Reserve at VAUX.

2.   On relief, Coys. will move by platoons at 1000 yards distance. Lewis Gun limbers will move in rear of Coys. "B" Coy. will move at 6 p.m.

3.   ROUTE. HOLNON - ATTILY - ETREILLERS - VAUX Road.

4.   Advance Parties.
       (a) The 2/6th WARWICKS will send 1 Officer per Coy. and 1 N.C.O. per platoon to take over at 3 p.m. tomorrow.
       (b) The 2/4 OXFORDS will send 1 Officer, Coy.Q.M.S. and 1 N.C.O. per Coy. and 1 Officer and 1 N.C.O. for Battn.H.Q. to report at VAUX at 12 noon tomorrow.
       2/Lieuts. WALLINGTON and STOWELL will be detailed by the Transport Officer to take over for B and D Coys. respectively.

5.   GUIDES. Guides will meet Coys. on road at entrance to VAUX.

6.   TRANSPORT.
       One limber for H.Q. Mess Boxes and Orderly Room boxes and one G.S. wagon for Officers' valises at 4 p.m.
       One limber for Lewis guns, Blankets and Mess boxes for each of A, C and D Coys. at 5.30 p.m.
       One limber for Mess Boxes and Lewis guns will report at "B"Coy's H.Q. at 6.30 p.m. O.C. "B" Coy. will detail party to remain behind to load.

7.   Blankets (rolled in tens), Lewis guns and Mess boxes will be dumped by Coys. near track at entrance to QUARRY at 5 p.m. Coys. will detail party to load immediately limbers arrive.
       Officers' valises will be dumped at same place by 3.30 p.m.

8.   TRENCH STORES.
       Companies will forward to Orderly Room by 12 noon tomorrow, list of stores they will hand over.
       Receipted lists of stores both handed over and taken over will be sent to Orderly Room by 9 a.m. 20th instant.

9.   Completion of relief will be notified to Battn.H.Q. by runner.

                                        (sd) W.H.ENOCH,
                                        Lieut. & A/Adjt.,
Battalion H.Q.   2/4th Oxf. & Bucks Lt.Infty.
Issued at 8 p.m.

          Copies:- 1 - 4. O.C. Coys.   8. Transport Officer.
                    5.   War Diary.   9. M.O.
                    6.   184th Inf.Bde.   10,11 Battn.H.Q.
                    7.   Quartermaster.

SECRET. 2/4TH BN. OXFORD & BUCKS LIGHT INFANTRY. Copy No. 5
ORDER NO. 483. 21.3.18.

Ref. Maps 62.B. S.W. and 62 C. S.E. 1/20000.

1. The Battalion will relieve the 2/8TH WORCESTERS and the 9TH ROYAL SCOTS in the centre Sub-Sector on the night 22nd/23rd inst.

2. DISPOSITIONS.
"C" Coy. Right Front Coy. relieve "B" Coy. 8th WORCESTERS in posts known as 17, 18, & 20 and two posts in WARWICK TRENCH. Also relieve "A" Coy. ROYAL SCOTS in Posts 1, 2, 3 & 4.
"B" Coy. Left Front Coy. relieve "A" Coy. ROYAL SCOTS in Posts 5, 6, 7, & 8 and "D" Coy. ROYAL SCOTS in Posts 9 and 10.
"D" Coy. Counter-attack Coy. Nos. 13 & 16 platoons relieve "B" Coy. 8th WORCESTERS in SUNKEN ROAD, M.34.D, Coy.H.Q. & Nos. 14, 15 platoons in bank at S.2.B.8.7.
"A" Coy. Strong Point Coy. relieve 1/5th GORDONS in dugouts at OTTER COPSE.

3. GUIDES.
(a) C Coy. From 2/8th WORCESTERS for posts 17, 18 & 20 and Line of Resistance at CEMETERY, FAYET at 7.30 p.m.
From "A" Coy. 9th ROYAL SCOTS, one per post and one for Coy. H.Q. at MONUMENT at 7.30 p.m.
(b) "B" Coy. From "A" Coy. 9th ROYAL SCOTS, one per post and one for Coy. H.Q. at MONUMENT at 7.30 p.m.
No other guides will be supplied.

4. ADVANCE PARTY.
(a) "C" Coy. 1 Officer, also 1 N.C.O. per platoon report at H.Q. 8th WORCESTERS in FAYET by 3 p.m.
1 Officer, also 1 N.C.O. per platoon report H.Q. "A" Coy. ROYAL SCOTS, M.28.d.9.2 by 1 p.m.
(b) "B" Coy. 1 Officer per Coy. and 1 N.C.O. per platoon report H.Q. "A" Coy. ROYAL SCOTS, M.28.d.9.2 by 1 p.m.
(c) D Coy. 1 N.C.O. per platoon (Nos. 13 & 16) report H.Q. "B" Coy., 8th WORCESTERS at FAYET by 3 p.m.
1 Officer, also 1 N.C.O. per platoon take over from 5th GORDONS billets at S.2.B.8.7 by 4 p.m.
(d) "A" Coy. 1 Officer and 1 N.C.O. report Coy. H.Q. 5th GORDONS at OTTER COPSE by 4 p.m.
(e) Battn.H.Q. Sgt. PAGE and 1 runner report at QUARRY, M.27.c.8.5 at 4 p.m.

5. ORDER OF MARCH.
B Coy., C Coy., Nos. 13 & 16 platoons D Coy., move at 2.30 p.m. via ETREILLERS - SAVY - HOLNON - SELENCY. A halt for tea will be made off the road just W. of SAVY. The cookers of B Coy. & C Coy. will march with their Coys., returning to Transport lines after tea.
The SAVY - HOLNON WOOD ROAD will not be passed before 6.30 p.m.
H.Q. A Coy., D.Coy.H.Q. & Nos. 14 & 15 Platoons move at 2.45 p.m. via ETREILLERS & ATTILY to X.4.d.2.4, where a halt for teas will be made, march being resumed at 6.15 p.m.
The Cookers of A & D Coys. will follow column.

6. Blankets and haversacks will be dumped by Coys. on road near billets by 11 a.m.
Officers valises, surplus Mess Boxes, and Orderly Room boxes by 2 p.m.

OVER.

7. TRANSPORT.
1 limber for Lewis Guns & Mess boxes of B & C Coys. will follow B Coy.
One half limber with Lewis Guns will follow Nos. 13 & 16 platoons D Coy.
One half limber for Lewis Guns and Mess Box will follow A Coy.
One limber for Battn. H.Q. and Lewis Guns and Mess Box of D Coy. will follow D Coy.
L.G.s will be loaded by 12 noon.

8. RATIONS.
(a) B Coy. will be dumped at 8.30 p.m. near dugout at M.28.c.3.3 where they will be met by 2 guides from B Coy.
(b) C Coy. & Nos. 13 & 16 platoons D Coy. will be dumped at Cookhouse near MONUMENT at 8 p.m.

9. List of Trench Stores and documents taken over will be forwarded to Battn. H.Q. by 8 a.m. 23rd inst.

10. Completion of relief will be wired to Battn. H.Q. at QUARRY M.27.c.0.3 , code words being names of Company Commanders concerned.

11. ACKNOWLEDGE.

(sd) W.H.ENOCH,
Lieut. & A/Adjt.,
2/4th Oxf. & Bucks L.I.

Battn.H.Q.
Issued at 9.30 p.m.

Copies:-
1 - 4.   Os.C. Coys.
5.   War Diary.
6.   184th Inf. Bde.
7.   Q.M.
8.   T.O.
10,11.   Bn.H.Q.
12.   5th GORDONS.
13.   9th ROYAL SCOTS.
14.   8th WORCESTERS.

CONFIDENTIAL.

WAR DIARY

- of -

2/4TH BATTALION, OXFORDSHIRE & BUCKINGHAMSHIRE LIGHT INFANTRY.

From 1st March 1918 to 31st March, 1918.

VOLUME XXIII.

****

CONFIDENTIAL.

War Diary

of

2/4th Battalion Oxfordshire & Buckinghamshire Light Infantry.

from 1st March, 1918, to 31st March, 1918.

(Volume XXIII).

WAR DIARY
or
INTELLIGENCE SUMMARY.
(Erase heading not required.)

Army Form C. 2118.

Instructions regarding War Diaries and Intelligence Summaries are contained in F. S. Regs., Part II. and the Staff Manual respectively. Title pages will be prepared in manuscript.

Place	Date 1918	Hour	Summary of Events and Information	Remarks and references to Appendices
FRESNOY QUARRY	1st March		In front line. Improvement of trenches. Fighting Patrols sent out. Some hostile shelling in front of resistance. Bn Coy Headquarters and area round sunk shelled intermittently. Casualties NIL.	App.?! BEB
"	2nd "		Do. Battalion relieved at night by 2/5th GLOUCESTER Regiment and marched to Reserve Billets at UGNY. Casualties NIL.	BEB
UGNY	3rd "		In Reserve billets. Battalion resting and cleaning up. Do.	BEB
"	4th "		Do. Company and Specialist training. Do.	BEB
"	5th "		Do. Do. Do.	BEB
"	6th "		Do. D Coy moved to dig outposts in Battle Zone for work on dumping cables. Casualties NIL	BEB
"	7th "		Do. A,B,C Coys Company and Specialist training. D Coy as for 6th. Do.	BEB
"	8th "		Do. Battalion and Company training. D Coy digging. Do.	BEB
"	9th "		Do. A demonstration of the use of near Master S.O.S. Signals given by the Brigade Bombing Officer. Casualties NIL Summer Time came into force and W.ENOCH took over duties of Adjutant.	BEB
"	10th "		Do. Battalion relieved the 2/4th ROYAL BERKS in the Battle Zone. Dispositions: 'B' Right Front Coy. 'D' Left Front Coy. 'A' Counter attack Coy. 'C' Strong Point Coy. Before taking over billets in ATTILLY HUTS, battle positions were manned. Casualties, NIL	Map P.2 BEB

Army Form C. 2118.

WAR DIARY
or
INTELLIGENCE SUMMARY.

(Erase heading not required.)

Instructions regarding War Diaries and Intelligence Summaries are contained in F. S. Regs., Part II. and the Staff Manual respectively. Title pages will be prepared in manuscript.

Place	Date 1918	Hour	Summary of Events and Information	Remarks and references to Appendices
ATTILY	11th March		In Huts in Battle Zone. Working parties day and night found by A,B,C Coys for improvement of trenches and bivouac table under R.E's. "D" Coy carried out Company training. Casualties NIL	6916
"	12th "		Do. Do.	6916
"	13th "		Do. Do.	6916
"	14th "		Do. Major H.T. BENNETT assumed temporary command of the Battalion vice Lt. Col. H.E. DE R. WETHERALL, D.S.O., M.C., temporarily commanding 184th Infantry Brigade. Casualties NIL	6916
"	15th "		Do. Work and training as above. Lieut. W. HENOCH left Unit to take up appointment of Adjutant to 1st Battalion Oxford and Bucks Light Infantry. Casualties NIL	6916
"	16th "		Do. Work and training as above. Do.	6916
"	17th "		Do. Do.	6916
"	18th "		Do. Battalion relieved the 2/4th ROYAL BERKS. in the Forward Zone. Dispositions: "C" Right front Coy; "B" Left front Coy; 2 Platoons "A" in Sunken Road near the NEEDLE (Mounted attack Coy); H.Q. and 2 Platoons "A" at the WILLOWS; M.26.c.1.5 (Ref Map 62.B.S.W.), D.H.Q. and Battalion Headquarters at ENGHIEN REDOUBT. Casualties NIL	App 2.A. 6916 6916 6916
FAYET.	19th "		In forward zone. Wiring and improvement of trenches. Fighting patrols sent out. Casualties NIL	6916

WAR DIARY or INTELLIGENCE SUMMARY

Army Form C. 2118.

Place	Date 1918	Hour	Summary of Events and Information	Remarks and references to Appendices
FAYET	20th March	In Forward Zone	Wiring and improvement of trenches. Fighting patrols sent out. Casualties NIL	BAB
	21st		Our positions were subjected to a severe enemy bombardment commencing at 4.30 A.M. Gas being freely used on our back areas and ridges. At 9 A.M. under a heavy smoke barrage a strong enemy attack was launched penetrating the Forward Zone and surrounding BIB HEM REDOUBT the garrison of the latter, D Coy and Battn Headquarters held at till 4 P.M. at which time owing to casualties they attempted to fight their way out the remainder of the Battalion and Headquarters of 2/5th GLOUCESTERS. Casualties:- Officers Missing:- Capt K.E.BROWN M.C., Capt C.E.P.FORESHEW M.C., Capt F.T.CAHILL M.R.C.U.S.A. 2/Lieuts R.OSTLER, T.PET, C.H.WALLINGTON M.C. V.C.GRAY, J.C.CUNNINGHAM, T.W.MALLETT, F.A.NAYLOR, G.SHELLEY, G.V.ROWBOTHAM N.S. C.H.LEACH, P.T.SIMMS. Missing believed Killed:- Lieut G.E.BASSETT, 2/Lieuts R.G.HGOUGH, W.H.FLORY, C.O.HALL. Wounded and Missing:- 2/Lieut E.LITTLE. Other Ranks: Killed 5, Wounded 32, Wounded and Missing 31, Missing 494.	
ATTILLY	22nd		During this day the Battalion held one of the lines in the Battle Zone until they were given the sig. in strong enemy attack about 1.30 P.M. when it withdrew in good order to a prepared position in front of BEAUVOIS. At night an enemy attack penetrated the positions on our right our position however remained intact. Casualties:- Other Ranks Missing 5, Wounded 1, Wounded and Missing 1.	BAB

Army Form C. 2118.

WAR DIARY
or
INTELLIGENCE SUMMARY.
(Erase heading not required.)

Instructions regarding War Diaries and Intelligence Summaries are contained in F. S. Regs., Part II. and the Staff Manual respectively. Title pages will be prepared in manuscript.

Place	Date 1918	Hour	Summary of Events and Information	Remarks and references to Appendices
BEAUVOIS	23rd March		The Battalion withdrew at 3 A.M. to billets at BILLANCOURT, where it was reinforced by details of 61st Durham Battalion. At night marched to billets at LANGUEVOISIN, on return to 20th Division. Casualties 2/Lt G. GEFFALL killed in action. 6 O.R. Wounded	B.R.6
LANGUEVOISIN	24th		The Battalion moved at 11 A.M. and occupied high ground in front of HOMBLEUX. At 3 P.M. it withdrew to position along road back from BREUIL-QUIQUE, which was held during the night. Casualties: O.R. Killed 1, Wounded 12, Wounded 17.	B.R.6
HOMBLEUX	25th		The Battalion were relieved at night by FRENCH troops after withdrawing slightly during the day. Casualties: Capt. A. H. MOBERLY, D.S.O. Wounded; 2/Lt A. ROWLERS in Missing. O.R. 2 Killed 2 Wounded	B.R.6
FRESNOY- LA -CHAUSSEE	26th		The Battalion marched to billets at FRESNOY-LA-CHAUSSEE in the morning, and to MEZIERES in the afternoon, which village was placed in a state of defence. At 11 P.M. moved forward to billets at LE QUESNIL to fire for e of enemy attack. Casualties 2 O.R. Wounded.	B.R.6
LE QUESNIL	27th		Prepared defences of LE QUESNIL & took up position at 3 P.M. O.P. 10 P.M. The Battalion was relieved by FRENCH troops embracing 4th MEZIERES and many points up to MARCELCAVE at 4 A.M. Casualties LT.COL. H. F. DE R. WETHERALL D.S.O. Wounded.	B.R.6
MARCELCAVE	28th		The Battalion took part in Decisive attack on LA MOTTE-EN-SANTERRE but owing to heavy hostile machine gun and rifle fire, objective was not gained.	B.R.6

Army Form C. 2118.

WAR DIARY
or
INTELLIGENCE SUMMARY.
(Erase heading not required.)

Instructions regarding War Diaries and Intelligence Summaries are contained in F. S. Regs., Part II. and the Staff Manual respectively. Title pages will be prepared in manuscript.

Place	Date 1918	Hour	Summary of Events and Information	Remarks and references to Appendices
MARCELCAVE	28th (contd)		Battalion occupied reserve trenches to N. of MARCELCAVE but withdrew at 8 P.M. to W. of MARCELCAVE and dug in. Casualties: Wounded 2/Lieuts A.H.LEWIS and B.A.GARRAUD. O.R. Wounded 2.	
"	29th		Quiet day. Casualties Nil.	
"	30th		Enemy attack on our front in the afternoon was beaten off by rifle fire with severe losses to the enemy. Casualties: Major H.T.BENNETT, O.R. Wounded 20. Missing Major H.T.BENNETT.	
"	31st "		The Battalion was relieved at 4 A.M. by AUSTRALIAN Troops and moved back to billets at GENTELLES.	

E.C.Rose Captain
Commdg 2/4 Bn Oxford & Bucks L.I.
10/4/18

SECRET App. P.1 2/4 Bn Oxford & Bucks Lt Infy   Copy No 5
              Order No 484   2 March 1918

1. The Battn will be relieved on the night of 2/3 inst by the 2/5 GLOSTER Regt and proceed to billets at UGNY

2. Following is the order of Relief:

   OXFORDS   by   GLOSTERS
     D Coy   A
     A   D
     C   C
     B   B

3. An advance party of 2/5 GLOSTERS comprising 2 Signallers from Bn H.Q. & 1 per Coy and 2 runners from Bn H.Q. by 3 pm. One officer per Coy and 1 Sergt per platoon will also report by 3 pm to take over.

4. Guides for Right posts, line of resistance (1 guide per platoon) and Coy H.Q. will be detailed by O.C. D Coy to meet the incoming parties at the MONUMENT at 7.15 pm. Guides for left posts and line of resistance (1 guide per platoon) and Coy H.Q. will be detailed by O.C. A Coy to be at point on road 200 yards below Bn H.Q. at 7 pm. O.C. "C" Coy will arrange a guide for the 2 platoons in SUNKEN RD to be at the Cellar in FAYET at 7 pm. Also a guide for the platoon in CHAMPAGNE TR to be at OTTER COPSE at 7 pm.

5. All Trench Stores must be carefully checked and handed over & receipted list to be sent to this office by 5 pm. Relief complete to be notified by code "Your B2 received." Dugouts to be thoroughly cleaned and inspected before handing over.

6. After Relief Battn will march out as follows H.Q. B & C Coys will march to UGNY via ATTILLY, BEAUVOIS, LANCHY. A halt will be made at X9d27 (62c S.E.) where hot cocoa will be served from Cooker. A & D Coys will march to Transport Football ground at MARTEVILLE where cocoa will be served and will then entrain for FORESTE from which place they will march to UGNY.
Lt PETT will meet these Coys at MARTEVILLE with directions as to entrainment.

7. **Transport.** 1 limber for B Coy & 2 platoons of "C" at OTTER COPSE 6.30 pm. 1 limber for H.Q. at 6.30 pm.
1 limber for D Coy & 2 platoons of C at D Coys Cookhouse 7.30 pm (pick up 30 petrol tins)
1 limber for A Coy at WILLOWS at 7 pm, pick up 20 petrol tins. A & D Coy by tram from MARTEVILLE 11.30 pm.

Battn H.Q.
Issued at 7.45 am

(Sd) J.C Cunningham
Lt & A/Adjt for
Major Cudg 7/R Oxf & Bucks L.I.

Copy Nos 1-4 O/c Coys
5 War Diary
6 Transport Officer
7 Q.M.
8 Medical Officer
9 184 Inf Bde
10 Office

Routine for March 3rd.

Rouse   8.15 am
Breakfast   9 am
Sick Parade   10 —

Coys will be at disposal of Coy Commanders for cleaning up and organisation.

(Sd) J.C Cunningham
Lt & A/Adjt
for Major Cudg

2-3-18

S E C R E T.   2/4TH BN. OXFORD & BUCKS LT.INFTY.   Copy No. 5
                     ORDER NO.493.   9.3.18.

Ref. Maps 62.C.S.E., 1/20000 and ST.QUENTIN 1/100000.

1. The Battalion will relieve the 2/4TH ROYAL BERKS in the BATTLE ZONE tomorrow 10th inst.
   Before taking over billets in ATTILY HUTS, Battalion will man the battle positions.

2. DISPOSITIONS.
   "B" Coy.   Right Front Coy.
   "D" "   Left   "   "
   "A" "   Counter-Attack Coy.
   "C" "   Strong Point Coy.

3. ADVANCE PARTIES.
   One Officer from each Company and 1 N.C.O. from each Platoon will parade at 8 a.m. under the Senior Officer and march to the H.Qrs. of the ROYAL BERKS at the ATTILY Huts where guides will be found to shew them the routes to the Posts from the Huts. They will later join the Battalion on arrival and guide them to the Battle Positions. Lieut. CUNNINGHAM, Cpl. Mew, and 4 runners will represent H.Qrs. The runners will reconnoitre to all Coy. H.Qr.s   The Advance Parties will take over billets and Trench Stores.

4. ORDER OF MARCH.
   H.Q., A Coy., B Coy., C Coy.   March by Coys. at 300 yards distance. Bugle Band will march in front of A Coy. and after 40 minutes will halt at the side of the road and pick up B Coy. After a further 40 minutes it will pick up C Coy.
   The Cookers will follow their Coys., H.Q. being supplied by A Coy.

5. ROUTE.
   LANCHY - BEAUVOIS and track through W.18.c & d to the ATTILY - VILLEVECQUE Road.
   Companies will halt at the edge of ST.QUENTIN WOOD in X.4.d. where teas will be served.

6. At 5.30 p.m. Coys. will pile their packs in their huts, if vacated by ROYAL BERKS at that time, otherwise outside huts, leaving a sentry over the packs of each platoon. Platoons will then be lead by their guides to their battle positions.
   When in position Coy.Commanders will report by runner to Battn. Battle H.Q. at R.34.d.8.2, sending two messages with an interval of 5 minutes. This will ensure four runners knowing the way to Battn.H.Q. When these runners have been despatched, Coys. will return to billets without further orders.

7. Battalion will move off from road in front of Battn.H.Q. at 2 p.m.

8. Blankets of H.Q., A & C Coys. will be rolled in bundles of ten and stacked on grass by road in front of Bn.H.Q. by 11 a.m.
   Blankets of B Coy. will be stacked at Q.M.Stores by same time.
   Officers' valises will be dumped at Q.M.Stores by 11.30 a.m.
   Those of H.Q. Officers outside H.Q. Hut by same time.

                                                       OVER.

8. (contd).

H.Q. Mess Boxes and Orderly Room Boxes will be outside H.Q. Hut by 1.30 p.m. Mess Boxes will be dumped at Q.M. Stores by 1 p.m.
Officers' surplus kit will be at Q.M. Stores by 12 noon.
Lewis Gun limbers of A & C Coys. & Bn.H.Q. will be brought into the huts for loading by 10 a.m.
Lieut. COOMBES will arrange for a party to load the H.Q. guns.
B Coy. will load their guns at the Transport Lines.
Lewis Gun limbers will follow their Coys. on the march.

9. List of trench stores taken over will be forwarded to Bn.H.Q. by 8 a.m. 11th inst.

10. ACKNOWLEDGE.

W. H. ENOCH (sd)
Lieut. & A/Adjt.
2/4th Oxf. & Bucks L.I.

Battalion Headquarters.
Issued at 8 p.m.

Copies:-
1 - 4. Companies.
5. War Diary.
6. 184th Inf. Bde.
7. Quartermaster.
8. Transport Officer.
9. 2/4TH ROYAL BERKS.
10, 11. Battalion H.Q.

SECRET.   2/4TH BN. OXFORD & BUCKS LIGHT INFANTRY.   Copy No. 5
                         ORDER NO. 500.   17th March, 1918.
Ref. Map 62.B.S.W.

1. The Battalion will relieve the 2/4th ROYAL BERKS in the Forward Zone on the night 18/19th. The Officers and Details left out of the line will march back to the Transport Lines under Captain W.H. MOBERLY, D.S.O. at 2.30 p.m. 2 limbers for Officers' kits & blankets will accompany.

2. Dispositions.
   Right Front Coy.   "C".
   Left   "   "   "B".
   Counter-attack Coy.   2 platoons "A" in Sunken Road near the Needle.
   H.Q. and 2 platoons "A" at the Willows M.28.c.1.5.
   ENGHIEN REDOUBT.   "D" Coy.
   Battalion Headquarters. ENGHIEN REDOUBT.
   The platoons of "D" Coy. will occupy the posts in the Redoubt before settling into their dug-outs.

3. ORDER OF MARCH.
   "C" and 2 platoons "A" via HOLNON - SELENCY - FAYET, The NEEDLE.
   "D" Coy.   HOLNON Crucifix (S.2.d.85.30), The Four Trees.
   Battalion H.Q.   Same Route.
   "B" Coy. & H.Q. & 2 platoons "A".   MAISON DU GARDE - OTTER COPSE.

4. Starting Point.   ATTILLY HUTS.   Time 7.30 p.m.

5. GUIDES.
   1 per post in the Outpost Line and 1 per platoon for "C" Coy. at the NEEDLE at 8.30 p.m.
   Same number of guides for "B" Coy. at junction of valley with OTTER COPSE Road, M.26.d.0.25. There will be no guides for "A", "D", & Battn.H.Q.

6. ADVANCE PARTIES.
   "A" Coy.   1 Officer, 1 N.C.O. per platoon.
   "B" & "C", 1 Officer per Coy., 1 N.C.O. per platoon, 2 signallers.
   "B" Coy. will also send Nos.1 & 2 of the Lewis Gun of their left platoon in OXFORD TRENCH.
   "D" Coy.   1 Officer, 1 N.C.O. per platoon, 2 signallers.
   Battalion H.Q. R.S.M., Cpl. Mew, and 5 Signallers.
   These parties will report in the line at 3 p.m.

7. COOKING.
   "C" Coy. and 2 platoons of "A" will cook in the cookhouses near the NEEDLE.   "B" Coy. near Coy. H.Q.   H.Q. and 2 platoons of "A" near Dug-outs at the WILLOWS.
   Battn.H.Q. & "D" Coy.   ENGHIEN REDOUBT.
   Each Coy. will take up 6 Camp Kettles.   Battalion H.Q. 4.
   WATER.
   "A", "B" & "C" Coys. will have 20 full tins each brought up with the rations on the night of 18th. After which these Coys. will fetch their water from FAYET or FRESNOY as convenient.
   Battn.H.Q. and "D" Coy. will draw from water-cart in the REDOUBT.
   RATION DUMPS.
   "A", "B", & "C" at the Cookhouses at the NEEDLE.
   Battn. H.Q. & "D" at the REDOUBT.

                                                              OVER.

Officers' valises, blankets and men's haversacks will be dumped at the edge of the wood below the R.S.M's hut by 10.30 a.m. The R.S.M. will arrange for a policeman to take charge. Lewis Guns, H.Q. Messboxes, Coy. Messboxes, Orderly Room box & Camp kettles to be ready at the same place for loading at 6.30 p.m.

9. **TRANSPORT.**

1 limber for "C" Coy. and 2 platoons of "A" will follow "C" Coy. & 1 limber for "B" Coy., H.Q. & 2 platoons of "A" Coy. will be at the WILLOWS for offloading at 8.30 p.m.

1 limber for Headquarters, and Medical Cart for "D" Coy.

A receipt will be given by each Lewis Gun leader to the Transport Driver when the Lewis Guns and magazines are offloaded.

10. Receipts for handing over and taking over to reach Battn.H.Q. by 3.20 a.m. on the 19th.

The billets in ATTILLY WOOD must be left scrupulously clean.

11. Completion of relief to be notified to Battn.H.Q. by code words "YOUR NOTE RECEIVED".

(sd) J.C.CUNNINGHAM,
Lieut. & A/Adjt.,
2/4th Oxf. & Bucks Lt. Infty."

Battn.H.Q.
Issued at 4.30 P.M.

Copies:-
1 - 4. Companies.
5. War Diary.
6. 184 Inf.Bde.
7. Quartermaster.
8. Transport Officer.
9. 2/4TH ROYAL BERKS.
10,11. Battn.H.Q.

NOTE.

A party of 1 Officer and 40 O.R. will report to 479 Field Coy. at 5 p.m. for work and will be billeted in M.D.1 Dugout. Further orders and details follow.

184th Brigade.

61st Division.

2/4th BATTALION

OXFORD & BUCKS LIGHT INFANTRY

APRIL 1918.

Army Form C. 2118.

WAR DIARY
or
INTELLIGENCE SUMMARY.

(Erase heading not required.)

Instructions regarding War Diaries and Intelligence Summaries are contained in F. S. Regs., Part II. and the Staff Manual respectively. Title pages will be prepared in manuscript.

Place	Date 1918.	Hour	Summary of Events and Information	Remarks and references to Appendices
GENTELLE.	April 1st.		Capt. ROBINSON in command of the Battalion. Day spent in putting village in state of defence. Intermittent enemy shelling all day. Casualties:- O.R.:- Killed 1, wounded 1.	Apps
GENTELLE.	2nd.		Day spent as on previous day. Casualties:- O.R.:- Wounded 1.	Apps
GENTELLE.	3rd.		The Battalion marched to LONGUEAU and thence proceeded by bus to MERICOURT. The Transport left CAGNY at 12-30 A.M. and marched by road (37 miles). Casualties:- O.R.:- Wounded 6.	Apps
MERICOURT.	4th.		Day spent in bathing and refitting. Casualties:- Nil.	Apps
MERICOURT.	5th.		Day spent as on previous day. Casualties:- Nil.	Apps

Army Form C. 2118.

WAR DIARY
or
INTELLIGENCE SUMMARY.
(Erase heading not required.)

Instructions regarding War Diaries and Intelligence Summaries are contained in F.S. Regs., Part II. and the Staff Manual respectively. Title pages will be prepared in manuscript.

Place	Date 1918.	Hour	Summary of Events and Information	Remarks and references to Appendices
MERICOURT.	April 5th.		Day spent in re-organising the Battalion. Capt. G.K.ROSE, M.C. joined for duty and assumed temporary command of the Battalion. Casualties:- Nil.	CRC
AVESNE.	7th.		The Battalion marched to AVESNE and went into billets. The 2/1ST. BUCKS (25th. Entrenching Battn.) has been amalgamated with the Battalion, which keeps its former name. A draft of 431 Other ranks joined the Battalion. Casualties:- Nil.	CRC CRC CRC
AVESNE.	8th.		Day spent in re-organising. Casualties:- Nil.	CRC
AVESNE.	9th.		Day spent in re-organising. Warning order for a move by the Division North received. Casualties:- Nil.	CRC
AVESNE.	10th.		Battalion Drill and Company Training in the morning. Tactical exercise for Officers in afternoon. Orders for the Battalion to entrain early the following day received. Casualties:- Nil.	CRC
In the train.	11th.		The Battn. (less "D" Coy. who were attached for purposes of train accommodation to 2/5 GLOUCESTERS) marched to HANGEST, where a delay of several hours occurred owing to change of destination necessitated by German attack at ARMENTIERES. Between CANDAS and DOULLENS the train broke in half, no accident but further delay resulting. Casualties:- Nil.	App.1.
ROBECQ.	12th.	3 A.M.	Orders were received immediately on the train's arrival at STEENBECQUE for the Battalion to march forward at once and take up a defensive position along the line of the NOE RIVER, it being reported that the Germans had broken through our battle positions and were threatening MERVILLE. The 51ST.DIVISION was reported to be holding a line East of CALONNE and B.de PACAUT.	App.2.

Army Form C. 2118.

WAR DIARY
or
INTELLIGENCE SUMMARY.
(Erase heading not required.)

Instructions regarding War Diaries and Intelligence Summaries are contained in F. S. Regs., Part II. and the Staff Manual respectively. Title pages will be prepared in manuscript.

Place	Date	Hour	Summary of Events and Information	Remarks and references to Appendices
ROBECQ.	April 12th. (contd)		Operation Order No. 1. was thereupon issued. Special instructions were left at the Station for "D" Coy.	

After the breakfast halt 7 - 8 A.M. on roadside W. of HAVERSKERQUE the C.O. and three Company Commanders rode forward through ST.VENANT to LES AMUSOIRES and found the situation to be critical.

A message to the Battalion despatched from the Brigade at 8-25 A.M. stated that the enemy had broken through the 51ST.DIV. in front and was nearing the NOE RIVER, which was not held by any of our troops.

By 9 A.M. hostile patrols had reached CARVIN and BAQUEROLLES FME. and our artillery having withdrawn early in the morning to West of the LA BASSEE CANAL were putting down a light barrage between LES AMUSOIRES and the ROBECQ - CALONNE Road. In addition a large Ammunition Dump along the ST. VENANT - ROBECQ Road was on fire, proving a serious menace to the Battalion's right flank if manoeuvre was required. After reporting these facts to Brigade and an interview with G.O.C. 182 BDE. the C.O. decided to be prepared to press an attack at once in order to gain the S.E. bank of the NOE RIVER. Companies accordingly moved forward in column of fours with intervals of 50 yards between Platoons along the ST. VENANT - LA HAYE - LES AMUSOIRES Road in the order "C", "B", "A". - "C" Coy. finding the Advanced Guard.

The Companies debouched from LES AMUSOIRES and advanced across open ground to 200 yards N. of the ROBECQ - CALONNE Road, where the advance was stopped on the left ("C" Coy) owing to the inability of the 182 BDE. on their left to make good the line of the Road. The C.O. decided to disregard the danger of an exposed left flank in favour of seizing the bridge-head at Q.14.c.8.2. and at 11 A.M. ordered all three Coys. to cross the ROBECQ - CALONNE Road and establish a line across the NOE RIVER. By 12 noon "A" and "B" Coys. had accomplished this task after slight enemy opposition, but "C" Coy. had to fight hard for the bridge-head at Q.14.c.8.2. losing Capt. BUTTFIELD, M.C. and 2/Lt. BENNETT (both wounded) and 30 Other ranks before BAQUEROLLES FME. and the houses at Q.14.c. Central were in our hands and the position secured. All was

(A7093). Wt. W1839/M1293 75,000. 1/17. D. D. & L., Ltd. Forms/C.2118/14.

Army Form C. 2118.

WAR DIARY
or
INTELLIGENCE SUMMARY.

(Erase heading not required.)

Instructions regarding War Diaries and Intelligence Summaries are contained in F.S. Regs., Part II. and the Staff Manual respectively. Title pages will be prepared in manuscript.

Place	Date	Hour	Summary of Events and Information	Remarks and references to Appendices
ROBECQ.	April. 12th. (contd)		quiet by 7 P.M. During the afternoon "D" Coy. rejoined and was ordered into reserve at LES AMUSOIRES. In gaining the line of the NOE RIVER free use was made of Lewis Guns and snipers from house roofs. The enemy resistance was not considerable except on the left at BAQUEROLLES FME. and houses at Q.14.c.Central. Enemy artillery shelled the ROBECQ - CALONNE Road during the afternoon and a heavy T.M. of long range fired on CARVIN and the houses in P.24.b. when "A" Coy. first occupied them. It was silenced by concentrated Lewis Gun and Rifle fire. During the night the position CARVIN - BAQUEROLLES FME. was consolidated. Casualties:- CAPT. L.F.BUTTFIELD, M.C. and 2/Lt. T.D.BENNETT wounded. O.R.:- Killed 10. Wounded 19. Missing 4.	
ROBECQ.	13th.		At 7-50 A.M. at the moment of a thick fog the enemy attacked the frontage occupied by the 183 BDE. (1000 yds. to the Battalion's left), at the same time enfilading the ROBECQ - CALONNE Road with his artillery, some of which had been moved up in the fog to very close range. Owing to the exposed condition of the Battalion's left flank at Q.14c.5.5. and to guard against risk that an enemy attack delivered in strength down the CALONNE - ROBECQ Road might isolate the three Companies S. of the River, "D" Coy. was ordered to form a defensive flank to "C" Coy. and remained in position until 10 A.M. when all was quiet. Between 12 noon and 5-30 P.M. the troops holding the line of the CALONNE - ROBECQ Road on the left of "C" Coy. were heavily shelled by the enemy and, in spite of the control and example shewn by 2/Lt. LODGE who twice went up to their position, eventually withdrew to the line of the road through Q.15.b. facing East, giving up the houses along the CALONNE - ROBECQ Road as far S. as Road junction	

Army Form C. 2118.

WAR DIARY
or
INTELLIGENCE SUMMARY.
(Erase heading not required.)

Instructions regarding War Diaries and Intelligence Summaries are contained in F. S. Regs., Part II. and the Staff Manual respectively. Title pages will be prepared in manuscript.

Place	Date	Hour	Summary of Events and Information	Remarks and references to Appendices
ROBECQ.	April. 13th. (contd)		at Q.14.c.3.4. This move obliged "C" Coy. to withdraw from the houses at Q.14.c.5.3. and the farm S. of the NOE RIVER at Q.20.a.5.8. As these houses, especially that at Q.14.c.5.3., constituted the key to the line of the NOE RIVER, orders were given for the re-capture by "C" Coy. both of the buildings from which withdrawal had been obliged and of the houses on each side of the road at Q.14.c.4.6. At 7-30 P.M. two Platoons of "C" Coy. attacked and captured the three houses at Q.14.c.5.3. and 4.6. taking a Machine gun and killing a good number of the enemy. Two L.T.M'ts manned by personnel of the Battalion assisted in this operation. The houses at Q.14.c.4.6. were re-occupied by the WARWICKS at nightfall. Casualties:- O.R.:- 11 wounded.	
ROBECQ.	14th.		At 6-30 A.M. in continuation of the policy of the previous day, "C" Coy., assisted by the L.T.Ms occupied the Farm at Q.20.a.5.3. and also drove the enemy out of the house at Q.14.c.8.2. During the morning it appeared that the houses about Q.20.Central were not held by the enemy, civilians being seen moving among them and no fire being directed at our aeroplanes from this area. A Battle Patrol consisting of a Platoon of "A" Coy. was accordingly sent to find out whether the ground was held by the enemy, with orders to reach the road running through Q.20.b. and d.if only slight opposition was met, when our line would have been advanced to include the houses and enclosures in Q.20. The Patrol reached the road immediately W. of the houses without opposition, but came under M.G. and rifle fire from the houses E. of the HENNEBECQ, when further advance was attempted. After a short fire fight the Patrol withdrew covered by Lewis Gun fire from the farm at Q. 20.a.5.8. × RIEZ du VINAGE was attacked and captured by the 4TH.DIVISION right operating on the Battalion's left during the afternoon, in consequence of which "A" Coy. swung its right forward S. E. of CARVIN in order to join up with the left flank of the 1ST.HANTS.	

Army Form C. 2118.

WAR DIARY
or
INTELLIGENCE SUMMARY.
(Erase heading not required.)

Place	Date	Hour	Summary of Events and Information	Remarks and references to Appendices
ROBECQ.	April 14th. (contd)		Casualties:- Lieut. H.C.BANTON wounded. O.R.:- Killed 5, Wounded 22, missing 1.	
ROBECQ.	15th.		The day passed quietly, our artillery and L.T.Ms carrying out registration. At 7 P.M. the enemy, after a brisk bombardment of our line, developed an attack against "C" Coy., moving in extended order from Q.14.d. against BAQUEROLLES FME. This attack was beaten off by rifle fire. Soon afterwards a report was received that large numbers of the enemy were collecting in the houses in Q.14.b. and d. Our artillery heavily shelled this target and the enemy must have lost heavily. At 7-30 P.M. "B" Coy. (Capt.STANLEY) carried out an attack on the houses in Q.20. in accordance with Operation Order No. 2. The operation was entirely successful and by 9 P.M. the objectives had been captured. Unfortunately the 4th.DIVISION, which had been relied on to co-operate on the right did not affect a junction with "B" Coy's right flank and the enemy, who were in large numbers along the Road E. of the HENNEBECQ and being strongly reinforced from LA PIERRE AU BEURE, commenced to counter-attack at 9-30 P.M. and threatened to envelop "B" Coy's flank in the houses at Q.20.d.0.6 and 3.7. Orders were then given, at 10-15 P.M., for "B" Coy. to withdraw to their original position. All our wounded were brought in. LA PIERRE AU BEURE, Q.20. and Q.14.b. and d. were shelled by our Artillery during the night. A German prisoner was taken by "B" Coy. during the day. Casualties:- 2/Lt.S.F.KEMP and 2/Lt.G.W.COUCHER Killed. O.R.:- Killed 2, Wounded 18, Missing 1.	
ROBECK.	16th.		Considerable shelling by the enemy occurred at times during the day. In the evening the Battn. was relieved by 2/5 GLOUCESTERS and went into billets at ST. VENANT. Relief was not complete	

Army Form C. 2118.

WAR DIARY
or
INTELLIGENCE SUMMARY.
(Erase heading not required.)

Instructions regarding War Diaries and Intelligence Summaries are contained in F. S. Regs., Part II. and the Staff Manual respectively. Title pages will be prepared in manuscript.

Place	Date	Hour	Summary of Events and Information	Remarks and references to Appendices
ROBECQ.	April 16th. (contd)	until 2 A.M.	The Battalion came under the orders of G.O.C. 183rd BDE. Casualties:- Capt.A.F.L.SHIELDS (R.A.M.C.) and 2/LT. A.C.STOWELL Wounded at duty. O.R.:- Killed 2, Wounded 25, Missing 5.	CRE
ST.VENANT.	17th.		The village was frequently shelled by the enemy during the day, without causing casualties, nearly all the men being accommodated in cellars. "B"Coy. were out working at night on Support trenches East of ST.FLORIS. Lt.Col. C.R.C.BOYLE, D.S.O. joined the Battn. and took over command, Capt. ROSE, M.C. taking duties of 2nd. in command. Casualties:- O.R.:- Wounded 1.	CRE
ST.VENANT.	18th.		Quiet day, except for some enemy shelling of the village. In the afternoon, "B" and "C" Coys. found a working party on reserve trenches covering the CANAL BRIDGE N. of ST.VENANT. Casualties occurred from enemy shelling. At night "A" Coy. worked on Reserve trenches W. of ST.FLORIS. Casualties:- O.R.:- Wounded 4.	CRE
ST.VENANT.	19th.		In the evening the Battn. relieved the 2/5 GLOUCESTERS, taking over the frontage previously occupied by the Battn. with the exception of Farms at Q.19.b.8.6. and at Q.20.a.5.8. which had remained in the hands of the enemy after an otherwise unsuccessful attack upon 2/5 GLOUCESTERS during night of April 18th/19th. Dispositions of Coys:- "A" Coy. on right, "B" Coy.Centre, "D" Coy. left, "C" Coy. in Reserve, BATTN. H.Q. LES AMUSOIRES. Casualties:- O.R.:- Killed 1, Wounded 5.	CRE
ROBECQ.	20th.		Quiet day. The night spent in improving posts and putting out wire, special attention being paid to the defence of "D" Coy's front which runs	

Army Form C. 2118.

WAR DIARY
or
INTELLIGENCE SUMMARY.
(Erase heading not required.)

Instructions regarding War Diaries and Intelligence Summaries are contained in F. S. Regs., Part II. and the Staff Manual respectively. Title pages will be prepared in manuscript.

Place	Date	Hour	Summary of Events and Information	Remarks and references to Appendices
ROBECQ.	April 20th. (contd)		from BAQUEROLLES FME. along W. bank of CLARENCE RIVER, including all the houses about Q.14.c.4.5., thence crossing ROBECQ - CALONNE Road at Q.14.c.5.9. and joining with 2/7 WORCESTERS at Q.14.c.0.1. Casualties :- O.R.:- Killed 1.	(ORE
ROBECQ.	21st.		At dawn "B" Coy. (Capt. STANLEY) occupied Farm at Q.19.b.8.6. without opposition and established a post there. A quiet day, with little enemy shelling on front line. During the afternoon Battn.H.Q. was shelled for twenty minutes with 5.9"s., no damage resulting. During the night 4TH.DIV. on the right attacked PACAUT WOOD. Casualties:- O.R.:- Killed 2, Wounded 2.	ORE ORE
ROBECQ.	22nd.		Quiet day. Casualties:- O.R.:- Wounded 1.	
ROBECQ.	23rd.		At 4-30 A.M. the 2/5 GLOUCESTERS, who had assembled in the area between CARVIN and "A" Coy.H.Q. at Q.19.c.5.9., carried out an attack upon the houses and enclosures in Q.20., with their final objective the road running S.E. through Q.20.b. The 4TH. DIV. co-operated on the right. "B" and "D" Coys. assisted the advance by Lewis Gun and Rifle fire. The attack was completely successful, nearly a hundred prisoners and several machine guns being taken by the GLOUCESTERS. In addition 45 prisoners surrendered to "D" Coy., being brought in by A/C.S.M. MOSS who went out to reconnoitre two hours after the attack had taken place. During the day and following night 5 machine guns were taken by "D" Coy., one having been brought in by the prisoners and the rest found in posts South and West of BAQUEROLLES FME. from which the enemy had been driven by the attack. During the afternoon and night hostile artillery was active against the GLOUCESTERS' new front, and "D" Coy's left flank which now prolonged the new line northwards. "A" & "B" Coys. remained in their positions, which ceased to be front line after the attack. Casualties:- O.R.:- Wounded 2.	ORE

Army Form C. 2118.

WAR DIARY
or
INTELLIGENCE SUMMARY.

(Erase heading not required.)

Instructions regarding War Diaries and Intelligence Summaries are contained in F. S. Regs., Part II. and the Staff Manual respectively. Title pages will be prepared in manuscript.

Place	Date	Hour	Summary of Events and Information	Remarks and references to Appendices
ROBECQ.	April 24th.		At 5 A.M. enemy shelling set fire to BAQUEROLLES FME, causing "D" Coy. H.Q. to move into trenches until the fire died down. At 6-30 A.M. the enemy attacked the GLOUCESTERS on their new front. The attack was defeated with loss. 70 prisoners were taken by the GLOUCESTERS. The Battn. was relieved in the evening by the 2/4 R.BERKS and withdrew to billets, H.Q.; "C" and "D" Coys. to the LUNATIC ASYLUM, ST.VENANT, "A" and "B" Coys. to LA BRASSERIE N. of ROBECQ. Companies reached billets about midnight. Casualties:- Nil.	CRE
ST.VENANT.	25th.		At 7-15 A.M. a large aeroplane bomb fell 30 yds.from Battn.H.Q. causing no damage. Day spent in cleaning up, bathing and general re-organisation. Casualties:- Nil.	CRE
ST.VENANT.	26th.		Some training was carried out in the morning. "A" and "C" Coys.supplied working parties on reserve trenches at night. Casualties:- O.R.:- Wounded 1.	CRE
ST.VENANT.	27th.		Training and Working parties as for 26th. Casualties. NIL.	CRE
ST.VENANT.	28th.		Battn.H.Q. was shelled at 2-30 P.M.for ten minutes. In the evening the Battn.relieved the 2/4 R.BERKS in the front line, now a two-Coy. frontage, astride the ROBECQ - CALONNE Road. Disposition of Coys; "B" on the right, "A" on the left, "C" in support, "D" in Reserve. Battn.H.Q. at Q.19.c.5.9. being in the same farmhouse as on Nov. 1st, 1916. Casualties:- O.R.:- Wounded 3 (one at duty).	CRE

(A5092). Wt. W12839/M1293. 75,000. 1/17. D. D. & L., Ltd. Forms/C.2118/14.

Army Form C. 2118.

WAR DIARY
or
INTELLIGENCE SUMMARY.

(Erase heading not required.)

Instructions regarding War Diaries and Intelligence Summaries are contained in F. S. Regs., Part II. and the Staff Manual respectively. Title pages will be prepared in manuscript.

Place	Date	Hour	Summary of Events and Information	Remarks and references to Appendices
ROBECQ.	April 29th.		Enemy shelled fairly heavily during the day. Casualties:- O.R.:- Killed 1, Wounded 2.	
ROBE CQ.	30th.		Fairly quiet day. Enemy artillery paid more attention to back areas. Casualties:- Wounded: 2/Lieut. R.W.E. CRADDOCK. 2/Lieut. H.JONES, M.C. (at duty). O.R. 3.	

Lieut.Col.
Commanding 2/4th.Batt'n.Oxford & Bucks Light Infantry.

SECRET.   Copy No. _1_

2/4TH. BATTN. OXFORD & BUCKS LIGHT INFTY.

ORDER NO. 509.   10th. APRIL, 1918.

1. The Battalion will march to HANGEST tomorrow 11th. inst. and entrain.

2. The Battalion, less "D" Coy., will form up at the Starting Point in the order, H.Q., "A", "B", "C" Coys. at 4-10 A.M.

3. Starting Point:- Main cross roads 400 yds. W. of A. in AVESNE.

4. H.Q. will pass the Starting Point at 4-15 A.M.

5. Cookers will march in rear of Companies.

6. Intervals of 100 yds. will be maintained between Companies.

7. There will be a halt of 10 minutes before each clock hour.

8. There will be a halt from 5-30 A.M. to 6-15 A.M. for breakfasts.

9. The Transport will march independently under the Transport Officer, arriving at HANGEST STATION by 7-40 A.M.
Route:- BELLOY - WARLUS - TAILLY - LE QUESNOY - SOUES - HANGEST.

10. Blankets will be dumped at the Q.M.Stores by 6 P.M. today.

11. Officers' Valises will be dumped at Q.M.Stores by 6 P.M. today.

12. Officers' Riders will not be available.

13. Billets will be cleaned, and inspected at 7 P.M. tonight.

14. "D" Coy. will march independently to WARLUS, passing the Starting Point at 7-30 A.M.
On arrival at WARLUS they will halt short of cross roads and report to O.C. 2/5 GLOCTERS.
Breakfast will be at 6 A.M. and Cooker will then proceed to WARLUS, reporting to GLOSTER Transport Officer at 8 A.M.

15. Dinners will be issued at the Station.

ACKNOWLEDGE.
ISSUED AT 3-15 P.M.
                                                   Capt.& Adjutant,
                                         2/4th. Battn. OXFORD & BUCKS L.I.

Copies:-   No.1. War Diary.   2. C.O.   3. Adjutant.
           4. 184 Bde.   5. "A" Coy.   6. "B" Coy.
           7. "C" Coy.   8. "D" Coy.   9. T.O.
           10. Q.M.   11. M.O.   12. File.

SECRET 4/1 Oxford & Bucks Lt Infty Copy No 9
OPERATION ORDER No 2

Ref Map Sheet 36ᴬ S.E.   15 April 1918
1/20,000

1. <u>Information</u>   The 4th Div yesterday
captured RIEZ du VINAGE. The
ENEMY still hold the houses
and enclosures about Q.20 central
and are in LA PIERRE AU
BEURE.

2. <u>Intention</u>   B Coy will attack and
occupy the road and houses lying
S of BAQUEROLLES FME. and
between the COURANT DE HENNE-
BECQ on the EAST and the
BAQUEROLLES FME – RIEZ DU
VINAGE ROAD on the West.
        Southern limit of the
advance will be Road junction
at Q.20.C.9.6. At this point
B Coy will link up with the
1st HANTS who are going to
advance simultaneously from
RIEZ du VINAGE along the Road
to BAQUEROLLES FME.
        A line will be dug and
held on the general line of

the BAQUEROLLES FME - RIEZ DU VINAGE Road with posts holding all the houses in the area attacked.

3. **Detail** (a) Zero will be 7.30 pm
(b) Men of B Coy moving Southwards will use bombs and rifle grenades. On no account will any wild rifle shooting be done.
Due warning will be given of the cooperation by 1st HANTS.
(c) Sufficient tools will be carried forward in the advance
(d) Prisoners or M.G. captured will be sent direct to Battn H.Q. under sufficient escort.

4. **Artillery T.M. M.G.** All details have been arranged personally
Forward control of operations will be by O.C. B Coy at BAQUEROLLES FME.

5. **REPORTS. R.A.P.** As at present. Present Disposition of Companies will continue until further orders.

Battn H.Q.   J.K. Ross Capt. & Adjt
Issued 5.15 pm   2/4 OXF & BUCKS L.I.

1. 184 Inf Bde   4. O/C B Coy   7. File
2. 1st Hants   5. "   C Coy   8. LTMB
3. "   "   6. War Diary   9. Offrs & OCs

SECRET April 5   Copy No 4

2/4TH BN. OXFORD & BUCKS L.I.
OPERATION ORDER NO 1.
             12th April 1918.

Ref:- Map issued

1.

INFORMATION. The Germans are believed to have captured ARMENTIERES and are threatening MERVILLE.
Part of our 51st Div are holding a line running roughly through Q.6 - 11 - 17 - 23 - 29.

2.

INTENTION. The Battn will take up a defensive line along the River NOE. Limits of frontage - P.24 d on right to Q.14 c on left (including Bridge).
The GLOSTERS will continue the line on our right - the 182 BDE on our left.
The line of the River NOE will be defended at all costs.

3.

DETAIL. Coys will be disposed as follows:-
    'A' Coy on right.
    'B'   in centre.

- 2 -

'C' Coy on Left.
Points of division between Coys will be pointed out by the C.O. on the ground if possible.
In any event 'A' & 'C' Coys will be responsible that their outer flanks are correctly situated and are in touch with neighbouring troops; and all Coys. will be responsible that no gap exists between each other.

(b) 'D' Coy will be in Reserve. Orders will be given later as to this Coy's location.

(c) The Line of Resistance will be on main ROBECQ – GALONNE Road.
It is impressed on all ranks that the enemy must not be allowed to cross the River.

Special Orders regarding defence of the Bridge in Q.14.c. will be given to 'C' Coy.

-3-

4. Coys will report situation of their HQ on all occasions throughout forthcoming operations.

5. LIAISON. 'A' & 'C' Coys will each detail an Officer or good N.C.O. and 6 reliable men to maintain liaison with Batt HQ & 2/5 GLOSTERS and with Batt HQ of Battn on our left respectively.
These Officers will keep the C.O. informed of occurrences on the flanks.
NO VERBAL ORDER TO THE EFFECT THAT OTHER TROOPS ARE RETIRING WILL EITHER BE PASSED OR ACCEPTED

6. REPORTS. Battn HQ will be on ROBECQ - CALONNE Road about Q.13.d.3.2.
Position of R.A.P will be handed later

-4-

State SOP orders regarding Transport Rations, dumps ac Field Sain issued orally.

ACKNOWLEDGE

Issued at STEENBECQ STN at 3.30 A.H. by Orderly.

J. Rose
Captain
Comdg 2/4th BN
OXF & BUCKS L.I.

CONFIDENTIAL.

WAR DIARY

OF

2/4th. BATTALION OXFORDSHIRE AND BUCKINGHAMSHIRE LIGHT INFANTRY.

FROM 1st. MAY 1918 to 31st. MAY 1918.

(VOLUME XV)

Army Form C. 2118.

WAR DIARY
or
INTELLIGENCE SUMMARY.
(Erase heading not required.)

Instructions regarding War Diaries and Intelligence Summaries are contained in F. S. Regs., Part II. and the Staff Manual respectively. Title pages will be prepared in manuscript.

Place	Date	Hour	Summary of Events and Information	Remarks and references to Appendices
Robecq	May 1		Quiet day. At night work carried on the SUPPORT line (Front System) also wiring in front of posts. Casualties:- O.R.:- Wounded 1	CRE
Robecq	" 2		Ditto. Shelling has not been considerable in front area during last 4 days. During the night the Battn. was relieved by 2/5 GLOUCESTERS, and moved back into Support, D Coy to MARQUOIS, C Coy to the Breastworks south of LES AMUSOIRES, A & B Coys to LA BRASSERIE, Battalion H.Q. went to ST. VENANT -- but moved the next morning to the lonely Estaminet on the ROBECQ Road. Casualties:- O.R.:- Wounded 2	CRE
ROBECQ	" 3		Quiet day, the Battalion found a working party for work on Reserve trenches during the night. Casualties:- Nil.	CRE
ROBECQ	" 4		Ditto " Casualties:- Nil.	CRE
ROBECQ	" 5		Ditto. No working party. "	CRE
ROBECQ	" 6		In the evening the Battalion moved back into Reserve, A & B Coys to houses along the BUSNES -- ST. VENANT Road, (East of CANAL) C & D Coys and H.Q. to the Lunatic Asylum ST. VENANT. Casualties:- Nil	CRE
ST. VENANT	" 7		Day spent in bathing and reorganisation. Mess' Men's Packs which had been brought from dump behind STD. ORDER, were issued to them again. During the morning a 5.9" hit the door of the ORDERLY ROOM, at a time when everyone was out. A & C Coys found a working Party in the evening. Casualties:- 1 Wounded	CRE
ST. VENANT	" 8		Quiet day. A little training carried out. A Coy held a BOXING Contest at their billets in the evening. Working Party found by B & D Coys. Casualties:- Nil	CRE

(A70921) Wt. W1289/M1293. 75,000. 7/17. D. D. & L., Ltd. Forms/C.2118/14.

Army Form C. 2118.

WAR DIARY
or
INTELLIGENCE SUMMARY.
(Erase heading not required.)

Instructions regarding War Diaries and Intelligence Summaries are contained in F. S. Regs., Part II. and the Staff Manual respectively. Title pages will be prepared in manuscript.

Place	Date	Hour	Summary of Events and Information	Remarks and references to Appendices
ST. VEN ANT	May 9		The Enemy were expected to be about to make an attack, involving the Brigade's front, with BETHUNE as their objective. In consequence special orders were given by the C.O. and certain precautions taken. The Enemy had been very quiet the last few days and weather conditions favoured an attack, the probability of which was declared by captured prisoners. Between 10 & 11 p.m. the enemy shelled the area on both sides of the CANAL West of ROBECQ but became quiet before midnight. No attack developed. Casualties:- Nil.	ENG
ST.VENANT	MAY 10		The day was quiet. The BATTALION has been hardly shelled at all during the last 4 days the BATT—ALION has been in reserve. The billets of A & B Coys have also been im—mune --- along the ST.VENANT-BUSNES Road. ST.VENANT was persistently shelled during this morning and afternoon. In the evening the BATTALION relieved the 2/4 R. BERKS in the front line, which has not altered materially since last occupied by the BATTALION. Dispositions:- D Coy on Right, C Coy on Left, B Coy in Support, A Coy in Reserve. BATTN. H.Q. in CARVIN, the previous H.Q. having been vacated by the R. BERKS in consequence of shelling. Casualties:- Nil.	ENG
ROBECQ	" 11		A quiet day. Wiring and trench improvement carried out at night. Casualties:- Nil.	ENG
ROBECQ	" 12		The day passed quietly. Hostile Artillery became active between 9.45 and 11 p.m. on the front line and supports, causing 17 O.R. casualties. Casualties:- Killed 8 O.R. Wounded 9 O.R.	ENG
ROBECQ	" 13		A successful raid was carried out by C Coy during the night (See Appendices P 9 and P 10). Under cover of an effective Artillery barr—barrage 2nd Lieut. ROWLERSON with 25 O.R. of NO. 12 platoon cut their w way through the wire which the Enemy had put up round his posts in the Orchard at Q14.d 7.4. and afterwards cleared both the posts and the farm.	ENG

(47023). Wt. W12830/M1293 75,000. 1/17. D. D. & L., Ltd. Forms/C.2118/4.

Army Form C. 2118.

WAR DIARY
or
INTELLIGENCE SUMMARY.
(Erase heading not required.)

Place	Date	Hour	Summary of Events and Information	Remarks and references to Appendices
ROBECQ	May 13 contd.		Two prisoners were captured and our party suffered no casualties. Retaliation by the Enemy's Artillery was slight. A message of congratulation was sent upon this operation was received from the Corps Commander. Casualties:- Nil.	GMR
ROBECQ	" 14		The day passed quietly. In the evening the Battalion was relieved by the 2/5 GLOUCESTERS, and moved back to Support, A Coy to MARQUOIS, B Coy to the Breastworks south of LES AMUSOIRES, C & D Coys to IN BRASSERIE, H.Q. to the solitary Estaminet on the ST.VENANT-ROBECQ Road. During the relief the Enemy shelled our Trenches, possibly as a form of retaliation for the previous night's raid. Casualties:- Wounded:- 6 O.R.	GMR
ROBECQ	" 15) " 16) " 17)		In Support. The period passed quietly without special interest and without any casualties.	GMR
ROBECQ	" 18		At night the Battalion was relieved by the 2/5 GLOUCESTER REGT. and moved back into Reserve, C & D Coys and H.Q. to the LUNATIC ASYLUM S.E. of ST.VENANT, A & B Coys to houses along the ST.VENANT-BUSNES Road. Casualties:- Nil.	GMR
ST.VENANT	" 19		Quiet day. Weather very warm. During the last three nights AIRE and the neighbourhood of the Transport lines at LA LACQUE have been heavily bombed by Enemy aeroplanes. Casualties:- Wounded:- 1 O.R.	GMR
ST.VENANT	" 20		In the early morning a few shells fell round the ASYLUM buildings. The day was spent in bathing and administration. D Coy held a boxing contest in the evening. Capt. ABRAHAM met with a riding accident and had to go to hospital. Casualties:- Wounded:- 1 O.R.	GMR

Army Form C. 2118.

WAR DIARY
or
INTELLIGENCE SUMMARY.
(Erase heading not required.)

Instructions regarding War Diaries and Intelligence Summaries are contained in F.S. Regs., Part II. and the Staff Manual respectively. Title pages will be prepared in manuscript.

Place	Date 1918	Hour	Summary of Events and Information	Remarks and references to Appendices
ST. VENANT	May 21		Between 7 and 10 a.m. the ASYLUM was rather heavily shelled by an Enemy Battery of 5.9" guns. A shell pierced the roof of the house occupied by C & D Coys H.Q. and after glancing off the inside of the reverse wall of the building fell through the ground floor into the cellar where it exploded. 2nd.Lieut. LODGE (O.C. Coy) and Capt. ROBINSON (C.C. D Coy) were wounded by this shell and casualties also to 4 O.R. were caused. C Coy had two casualties in the Men's billets during the same bombardment. 2nd. Lieut. LODGE died on his way to hospital and was buried the same evening in GUARBECQUE. The rest of the day was quiet. The Commanding Officer carried out a kit inspection of Companies. Casualties:- Died of Wounds:- 2nd. Lt. T. LODGE. Wounded:- Capt. A.J. ROBINSON. Killed:- 2 O.R. Wounded:- 4 O.R.	EAG EAG EAG EAG EAG EAG
ST. EVANT	" 22		In the evening the Battalion relieved the 2/4 ROYAL BERKSHIRE REGT. in front line. Disposition of Coys:- B Coy on right, A Coy on Left, C Coy in Reserve, with B.H.Q. at GLOUCESTER FARM, D Coy in AMUSOIRES Line with H.Q. at MARQUIS. BATTN. H.Q. at CARVIN as before. Casualties:- Nil.	
M OBECQ.	" 23		Quiet day. Some shelling round Battn. H.Q. Casualties:- Nil.	
ROBECQ.	" 24		Ditto. Weather consistently fine and warm. Casualties:- O.R.:- Killed 1. Wounded 1.	
ROBECQ.	" 25		At night inter Company relief was carried out. Casualties:- Nil.	

Army Form C. 2118.

WAR DIARY
or
INTELLIGENCE SUMMARY.
(Erase heading not required.)

Place	Date 1918	Hour	Summary of Events and Information	Remarks and references to Appendices
ROBECQ.	May 26		Quiet day. No special incident. Casualties Nil.	EAE
ROBECQ.	" 27		Transport lines at LA LACQUE came in for attention by a heavy H.V. gun during the morning. At night Hostile Artillery showed much increased activity both upon the Front line and upon the area round Battn. H.Q. Casualties:- O.R.:- Wounded 1.	EAE
ROBECQ.	" 28		No incident to record beyond increased Artillery Activity. About midnight the Enemy put down a heavy barrage, particularly round CARVIN FM. and along the CAUCHY-ROBECQ Road and AUBIGNY line. During the night also LA LACQUE was shelled by the Enemy H.V. gun, probably 19". The Battalion Band, 28 strong, previously belonging to the 5th. Battn. of the Regt. joined for duty. Casualties:- Nil.	EAE
ROBECQ.	" 29		At night the Battalion was relieved by the 2/5 GLOUCESTER REGT. and moved back to Support Billets at LA PIERRIERE. During the relief the Enemy shelled the roads and tracks North and West of ROBECQ, somewhat heavily but caused no casualties. One Platoon of A Coy was attacked and Bombed by a low-flying Enemy Aeroplane but suffered no casualties damage. Casualties:- O.R.:- Killed 7. Wounded 5.	EAE
LA PIERRIERE	" 30		Quiet day spent in usual cleaning up and organisation. Casualties:- Nil.	EAE
LA PIERRIERE	" 31		Ditto. Weather continuing fine and warm. Casualties:- Nil.	EAE

Commdg. 2/1 Battn. Oxf. & Bucks Lt. Infty.
Lieut. Colonel,

Q

14 15

2 guns A b55

Tracing taken from Sheet..............................

of the 1:.................... map of...............................

Signature............................... Date..............

SECRET   OPERATION ORDER NO 17.   App Pg   Copy No 2
                By Lieut. Col. C.R.C. Boyle D.S.O.
            Commdg. 2/4th Oxf. and Bucks Lt. Infty.   13/5/18.

1. C Coy will carry out a raid to-night 13th/14th with the intention
   (1) of obtaining identifications
   (2) of inflicting casualties on the enemy

2. Strength - 1 Officer and 25 O.R's with 1 Lewis Gun.

3. Zero will be at 11.55 p.m.

4. Objective - house and enclosure at Q.14.d.7.4.

5. As soon as party secures a prisoner it will return to its own lines.

6. The 2nd ESSEX Regt. will co-operate with L.G. and M.G. fire on the right flank.

7. Artillery programme -
   From zero to zero plus 4 mins barrage will stand with its front edge on a line from Q.14.d.0.6. to Q.14.d.7.0. to house at Q.21.a.00.45.
   This will lift at zero plus 4 mins and from zero plus 4 to zero plus 29 becomes a box barrage with its front edge on a line from Q.14.d.1.5 to Q.15.c.0.5 to Q.15.c.20.25 to house at Q.21.a.00.45.
   4.5" Hows. will fire on roads and selected targets in rear from zero to zero plus 29 mins.

8. M.G. programme attached.

9. Raiders will be formed up in front of our wire at 11.40 p.m. and at zero plus 4 mins will advance on the objective.

10. No man will carry any papers or badges (including red circles) or other means of identification.
    Men will not wear their identity discs: special discs will be issued.

11. O.C. C Coy will arrange to mark gaps in the wire to enable the returning party to find them quickly.

12. Raiding party will carry wire cutters.

13. Prisoners will be sent at once to Battn H.Q.

14. Watches will be synchronised at 9 p.m. at C Coy's H.Q.

15. Reports will be sent to Battn. H.Q. as soon as possible.

16. All working and ration parties will be under cover by 11.30 p.m. until 1 a.m.

17. O.C. C Coy will arrange to vacate forward post at Q.14.d.00.45. and reoccupy when all is quiet.

Battn. H.Q.   ~~Adjutant~~   Captain.
Issued at 4.30 p.m.   Adjutant 2/4th Oxf and Bucks Lt. Infty.

Copies to - No. 1 File   5 B Coy.
               2 War Diary   6 D Coy.
               3 C Coy   7 2nd ESSEX Regt.
               4 A Coy   8 Battn. H.Q.

Operation Order No 4 Secret   Copy No. 6
by Major R.R. Will Cmdg 256 Bde R.F.A.

13th May 1918

(1) 184 Inf. Bde are raiding the enemy tonight in house and orchard adjoining Q14.d.7.4 at Zero hour.

(2) This will be supported by 255 and 256 Brigades R.F.A.

(3) As per attached tracing —

(a) A/255 will enfilade with 2 guns the railway track (running through Q15.d.) from Q15.c.65.00 to Q15.b.65.00.

(b) B/255 will barrage along road from house (inclusive) at Q20.b.99.45 to X Roads at Q15.c.25.70.

(c) C/255 will barrage road from Q14.c.25 to X Roads at Q14.b.65.20.

(d) D/255 will search road and houses and orchards adjoining from Q15.c.25.70 to X Roads at Q9.d.25.50.

(e) D/256 will search road and houses and orchards adjoining from Q14.b.65.20 to X Roads at Q9.d.25.50.

(f) A/256 will barrage from house at Q20.b.99.45 to Q14.d.8.0 to Q14.d.60.15.

(g) C/256 will barrage from Q14.d.60.15 to river at Q14.d.0.6.

(h) B/256 will devote all its guns to house and orchard to be raided Q.14.d.7.4.

(i) A, B and C/256 will lift to the line Q15.c.3.2 – Q15.c.0.5 to river at Q14.b.38.12.
A. Batting on the right, C. on the left and B superimposed.

Zero to Zero plus 29
Zero + 4 Zero + 14
Zero + 4 Zero + 29

(4) Rate of Fire.
18 pdrs
Zero to Zero + 4   4 rds per gun per minute
Zero + 4 to Zero + 15   3 "   "   "   "   "
Zero + 15 to Zero + 29   2 "   "   "   "   "

4.5" Hows. Half the above rates.

(5) Ammunition
18 pdrs will use Shrapnel throughout with a corrector calculated to give 70% on graze.

(6) Watches will be synchronised by 256 Bde at Inf. Bde. H.Q. at 8 pm.

(7) Zero hour will be 11.55 pm.

(8) Acknowledge.

Major R.R.
Comdg 256th Bde R.F.A.

Copies No. 1 A/256   5 255 Bde R.F.A.
          2 C/256   6&7 184 Inf. Bde
          3 B/256   8 16th D.A.
          4 D/256   9 File

SECRET.   Copy No. 1
          "C" Coy 61st Batt: M.G.C. Operation Order No. 80.
Ref Map: 1/20000 Sheet 36A.S.E.   13-5-18

1. The 2/4TH Oxfordshire & Buckinghamshire Light
    Infantry will carry out an operation on the night
    May 13/14th in order:-
      (1) To obtain identifications.
      (2) To inflict casualties on the enemy.

2. The Objective is the farm and enclosure at
    Q14d.7.4 (ORCHARD FARM)

3. From zero to zero plus 4 mins, the
    Artillery barrage will stand with its front
    edge on a line from Q14d.0.6 to Q14d.70 to
    House at Q21a.00.45.
       This lifts at zero plus 4, and from zero
    plus 4 mins: to zero plus 29 mins becomes a
    box barrage with its front edge on the line
    from Q14d.15 to Q14b.55.00 to Q15c.0.5 to Q15c.20.25
    to House at Q21a.00.45.
       4.5 Howitzers on roads and selected points
    in rear from zero to zero plus 29

4. This Company will co-operate as follows:-
(a) Two Guns No. 4 Sect: Q19b.65.46.
    Two Guns No. 1 Sect: Q19d.22.94
      Barrage Area:- Q21a.05.70, Q20b.90.80.
                    Q15c.28.18, Q15c.10.30.
      Rate of Fire - zero to zero plus 15 - Medium
                    zero plus 15 to zero+29 - Slow.
(b) One gun No. 4 Sect. under 2/Lieut Cox at Q20d.64.90.
    will move forward at dusk to post in
    Q14c.8&10, & will fire on road from Q14d.37.75
    to Q14d.60.57.
      Rate of fire - zero to zero plus 15 - Medium
                    zero plus 15 to zero plus 29 :- As
Distribution   situation demands

Issued at 4.30 P.M. Zero Hour 11.55 P.M.
  Copies No. 1 2/4 Ox' and Bucks.
         2   184 Inf Bde   Jno. Sbaffield Lieut
ACKNOWLEDGE 3   Section Officers   for OC "C" Coy 61 B" M.G.C.
         5   No. 2 Sect "D" Coy for inf.

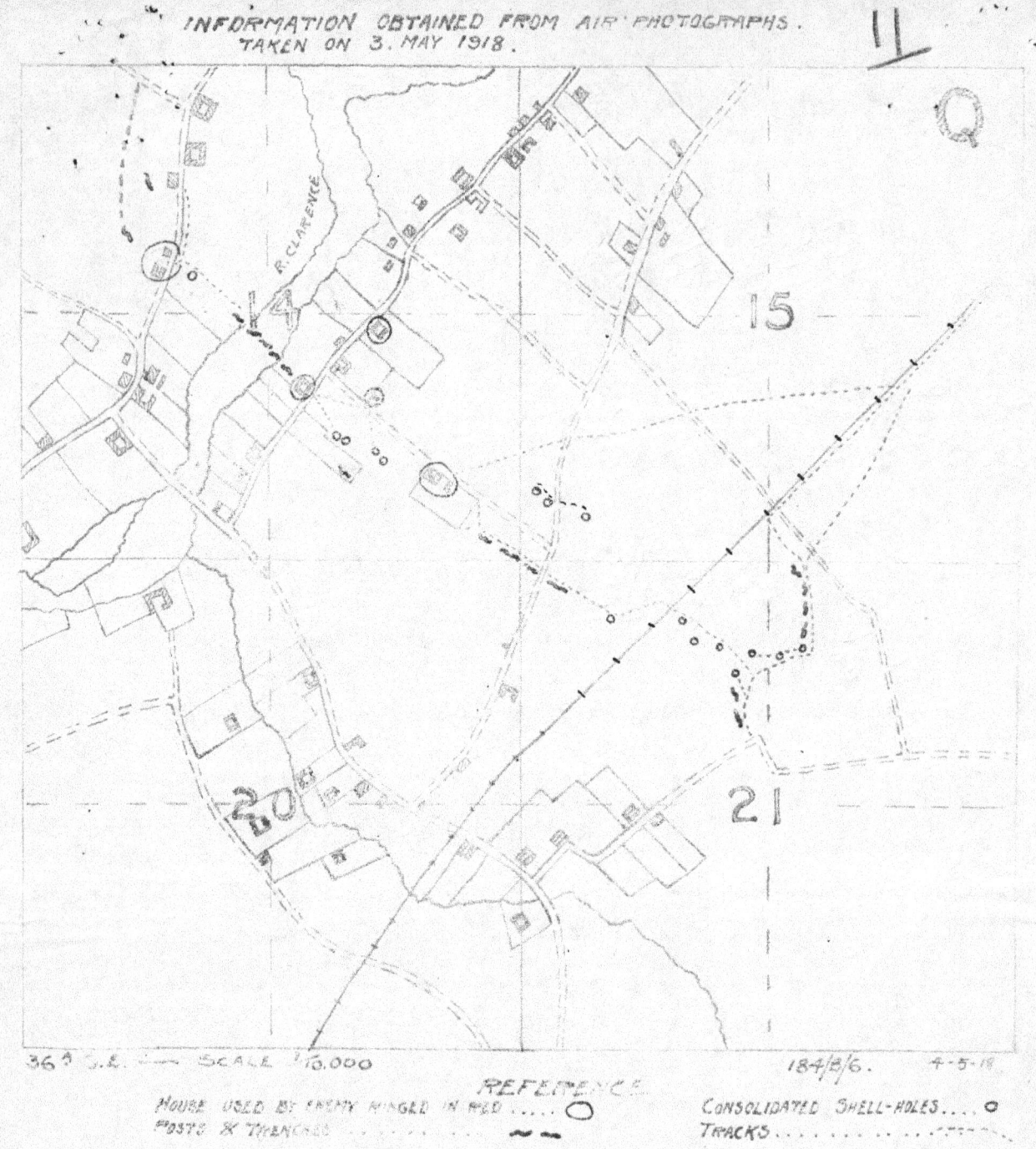

```
   36          576
   33         1188
  ---         1008
  108         ----
  108         2772
 1188         18 are
              4 Selver  4 6 2

   36          36
   16          28
  ---         ---
  216         288
   36          72
  ---        ----
  576.       1008
```

App. P.10

Report on Raid carried out by 1 Officer and 25 O.R. of No. 12 Platoon 2/4th Oxf & Bucks Lt. Infty. on the night of 13/14th May, 1918 on Farm at Q.14.d.7/4.

Object

To obtain identification and inflict casualties on the enemy.

The Raiding Party left its line at 11.40 P.M. and formed up on the other side of our wire, in three small columns, at about 10 paces interval.

1 N.C.O. and 3 men on the right, the Officer and 14 O.R. in the centre, and 1 N.C.O. and 6 men on the left, the party on the right having a Lewis Gun.

After the barrage had started, we closed up under it and directly it lifted over the farm, doubled forward towards our objective

The ground was free from obstacles as far as the enemy wire, with the exception of a ditch across the front, which can easily be jumped.

Having arrived at the wire, we passed along it a short distance, looking for gaps, but none were found.

The wire is low, but very strongly put up, and the party had considerable difficulty

(2)

in getting through it. It took over 10 minutes to get the whole party through.

When everybody was through the Lewis Gun got into position about 20 yds to the right of the right hand corner of the hedge, with orders to fire if any opposition came from the right. Meanwhile the two other parties had formed up. On the order to push, the Officer's party made for the right hand corner of the hedge, and ran along the S.E. side in the direction of the road in rear of the house. About half way along was a gap which the party entered followed by the third party under the Sergeant.

On getting into the Orchard we split up into small parties and started to search the whole place. Not much attention was paid to the house as we expected to find posts in the orchard. The Officer looked about the ground floor but saw nothing.

Two main posts were found just inside the hedge, one on the right and one on the left, but both were empty when the party arrived.

The two prisoners were found lying in a shell-hole which had been converted into a small post and which had a large gap in the hedge in front of it.

By this time the barrage was timed to finish, so on a signal by whistle the party withdrew from the Orchard and getting through the wire, marched on a compass bearing back to our own lines.

A white sheet which had been fixed up at the gap in our wire was a good guide and enabled us to find the gap without difficulty.

The party returned to its post having incurred no casualties.

The only opposition met with was from a M.G. on the left of the farm but this was silent after a short time.

(sd) G.A. ROWLERSON,
2/Lieut.,
Officer i/c Raiding Party

14/5/18

CONFIDENTIAL

WAR DIARY

OF

2/4TH BATTALION OXFORDSHIRE AND BUCKINGHAMSHIRE LIGHT INFANTRY

FROM 1ST JUNE 1918 TO 30TH JUNE 1918.

VOLUME XXVI

Army Form C. 2118.

WAR DIARY
or
INTELLIGENCE SUMMARY.
(Erase heading not required.)

Instructions regarding War Diaries and Intelligence Summaries are contained in F. S. Regs., Part II. and the Staff Manual respectively. Title pages will be prepared in manuscript.

Place	Date 1918	Hour	Summary of Events and Information	Remarks and references to Appendices
LA PIERRIERE.	June. 1st.		In the evening A and D Coys. held a Boxing Competition in Orchard behind Headquarters. Casualties:- NIL.	
"	2nd		At night the Battn. relieved the 2/4th R.BERKS in the Left Battalion Sector. Disposition of Coys. - A on Right, B on Left, D in Support, C in AMUSOIRES Line. Battn.H.Q. in LES AMUSOIRES in a different house to that occupied in April as H.Q., the latter having been seriously ruined by shelling. Casualties,NIL.	
ROBECQ.	3rd		Fairly quiet. A thorough programme of work consisting principally of wiring and revetting was started. Casualties, NIL.	
"	4th		Weather fine and dry. The characteristics of the present sector held by the Battalion are as follows. The Front Line is a chain of detached posts sufficiently ill dug, between which no movement by day is possible. On taking over, the front line wire was so scanty as to be non-existent as an obstacle. The Support Company, which is accommodated in what is properly described as the Reserve Line (of the front	

Army Form C. 2118.

WAR DIARY
or
INTELLIGENCE SUMMARY.
(Erase heading not required.)

Instructions regarding War Diaries and Intelligence Summaries are contained in F.S. Regs., Part II. and the Staff Manual respectively. Title pages will be prepared in manuscript.

Place	Date 1918	Hour	Summary of Events and Information	Remarks and references to Appendices
ROBECQ.	June. 4th.		system) has some liberty of movement in day-time as its line is intended to be continuous. The entire area occupied by the four Coys. is entirely flat, open and devoid of any features. Casualties, NIL.	
"	5th		Quiet day. Usual working and petrolling at night. Casualties, Wounded O.R. 3.	
"	6th		Quiet. Each night there is some shelling of TRIPPS FARM (Q.18.a.2.5) and on the roads leading up to LES AMUSOIRES. Supply of rations to Companies is by Pack Mules from TRIPPS FARM. Casualties, Wounded O.R. 4.	
"	7th		During the night there was lively shelling of TRIPPS FM. which was set on fire and burnt down, and on the tracks leading forward. Casualties NIL.	
"	8th		Quiet. Weather continuing warm and fine. Casualties, Wounded 2 O.R.	
"	9th		Considerable amount of illness has broken out among Off-	

T/134. Wt. W708-776. 500000. 4/15. Sir J.C. & S.

Army Form C. 2118.

WAR DIARY
or
INTELLIGENCE SUMMARY.
(Erase heading not required.)

Instructions regarding War Diaries and Intelligence Summaries are contained in F.S. Regs, Part II. and the Staff Manual respectively. Title pages will be prepared in manuscript.

Place	Date 1918. June.	Hour	Summary of Events and Information	Remarks and references to Appendices
ROBECQ.	9th		-icers and O.R. of the Battalion H.Q. The illness resembles influenza. Casualties Wounded 20.O.R.	[sig]
"	10th		At night the Battalion was relieved by 2/5th GLOUCESTERS and returned to LA PIERRIERE. Casualties Wounded 5 O.R.	[sig]
LA PIERRIERE	11th		Battalion bathing and cleaning up. Casualties, NIL.	[sig]
"	12th		C.O.s inspection of Companies. Casualties, NIL.	[sig]
"	13th		Some training carried out, including Firing of Lewis Guns at extemporised range, along the Railway Embankment near the Village. Casualties, NIL.	
"	14th		The Commanding Officer and 2nd in Command went sick, following the Adjutant and Signalling Officer. Major G. CHRISTIE MILLER from 2/5th GLOUCESTERS temporarily took command of the Battn, which relieved the 2/4th R. BERKS in the Right Battn. Sector of Front Line during the night. During the progress of the relief the Enemy shelled the Roads and Tracks rather heavily	[sig]

T2134. Wt. W708—776. 500000. 4/15. Sir J. C. & S.

Army Form C. 2118.

WAR DIARY
or
INTELLIGENCE SUMMARY.

(Erase heading not required.)

Instructions regarding War Diaries and Intelligence Summaries are contained in F. S. Regs., Part II. and the Staff Manual respectively. Title pages will be prepared in manuscript.

Place	Date 1918 June.	Hour	Summary of Events and Information	Remarks and references to Appendices
LA PIERRIERE	14th.(continued.)		causing several casualties.	
			Disposition of Companies:- C Coy. on right, D Coy on left, B Coy. in Support, A Coy. in Reserve, Battalion Hqrs at CARVIN	
			Casualties:- O.R.:- Killed 2. Wounded 4.	
RO BECQ.	15th.		Quiet. Usual wiring and patrolling carried out. Casualties :- Nil.	
ROBECQ.	16th.		Usual conditions. Fairly Quiet. Casualties :- Nil.	
ROBECQ.	17th.		Usual conditions. Fairly Quiet. Casualties :- O.R. Killed 1.	
ROBECQ.	18th.		At night an inter-Company relief took place "A" and "B" Coys going up to Front Line, "C" returning to Support, and "D" to Reserve. Casualties :- Wounded 1 O.R.	
ROBECQ.	19th.		Lieut. Col. WETHERALL returned from Hospital and re-assumed command. Casualties :- Wounded 1 O.R.	
ROBECQ.	20th.		Usual Routine. Quiet. Casualties :- Nil.	

Army Form C. 2118.

WAR DIARY
or
INTELLIGENCE SUMMARY.
(Erase heading not required.)

Place	Date 1918	Hour	Summary of Events and Information	Remarks and references to Appendices
ROBECQ.	June. 21st.		Weather became windy and cloudy. Enemy quiet except for a certain amount of registration shooting. Casualties :- Wounded 1 O.R.	RB
ROBECQ.	22nd.		Reasonably quiet. Wiring and Patrolling has been carried on nightly during the last week although work has been much handicapped by illness (P.U.O.) through the Battalion and changes in Company Officers necessitated. At night the Battalion was relieved by the 2/5 GLOUCESTER REGT, the relief being specially quiet and easy. Casualties :- Nil.	RB
LA-PIERRIERE	23rd.		Cleaning up and bathing. Casualties :- NIL.	RB
LA-PIERRIERE	24th.		Ditto. Ditto.	RB
LA-PIERRIERE	25th.		On Thursday the Battalion should have moved back to the LINGHEM area in company with the remainder of the Brigade but in consequence of the amount of sickness among the relieving Brigade (182nd.) the Battalion was kept in	

Instructions regarding War Diaries and Intelligence Summaries are contained in F. S. Regs., Part II. and the Staff Manual respectively. Title pages will be prepared in manuscript.

Army Form C. 2118.

WAR DIARY
or
INTELLIGENCE SUMMARY.
(Erase heading not required.)

Instructions regarding War Diaries and Intelligence Summaries are contained in F. S. Regs., Part II. and the Staff Manual respectively. Title pages will be prepared in manuscript.

Place	Date 1918.	Hour	Summary of Events and Information	Remarks and references to Appendices
	June.			
LA PIERRIERE	25th.		(continued) LA PIERRIERE in reserve to that Brigade. Casualties :- Nil.	R.B.
LA PIERRIERE	26th.		Training Programme commenced. This consists of Battalion Parade in the morning followed by Platoon Training and a certain amount of Range work (using the BERGUETTE-ST.VENANT Railway embankment for this) and Counter - Attack practice. Casualties :- Nil.	R.B.
LA PIERRIERE	27th.		Training. The following reorganisation has been carried out ---- Each Platoon into three Sections, being two rifle Sections and one double Lewis Gun Section (i.e. a Section armed with two Lewis Guns, strength 11 O.R.) 12 O.R. are now also attached to Battalion Headquarters to man the 4 A.A. Lewis Guns. A successful Battalion Concert, in open air, was held in the evening. Casualties :-Nil.	R.B.
LA PIERRIERE	28th.		In the morning the G.O.C. Brigade (Brig. General PAGAN, D.S.O)	R.B.

Army Form C. 2118.

WAR DIARY
or
INTELLIGENCE SUMMARY.

(Erase heading not required.)

Instructions regarding War Diaries and Intelligence Summaries are contained in F. S. Regs., Part II. and the Staff Manual respectively. Title pages will be prepared in manuscript.

Place	Date 1918.	Hour	Summary of Events and Information	Remarks and references to Appendices
LA PIERRIERE	June. 28th.		(continued) inspected the Battalion which was drawn up in Quarter Column in "D" Company's Orchard. After a very thorough inspection the Brigadier General complimented the Battalion on its excellent turn-out. In the afternoon the Brigadier General also inspected the Battalion 1st. Line Transport at OBLOIS, when he congratulated Lieut. KIRK, Transport Officer on its very satisfactory condition. A Tactical Scheme for Officers and Platoon Commanders was held in the evening. Casualties :- Nil.	RB RB RB
LA PIERRIERE	29th.		Training continued. The Second Round in the Battalion Inter-Section Football Competition was completed. This competition is between Section teams of 6 each which play ten minutes each way. Casualties :- Nil.	
LA PIERRIERE	30th.		No occurrence of consequence. Casualties :- Nil.	

W. M. .... Lieut. Col.,
2/4th Oxf. & Bucks Lt. Infty.

CONFIDENTIAL.

WAR DIARY

of

2/4TH. BN. OXFORDSHIRE & BUCKINGHAMSHIRE
LIGHT INFANTRY.

FROM.

1st. JULY, 1918.

TO.

31st. JULY, 1918.

(VOLUME 27.)

Army Form C. 2118.

WAR DIARY
or
INTELLIGENCE SUMMARY.
(Erase heading not required.)

Instructions regarding War Diaries and Intelligence Summaries are contained in F. S. Regs., Part II. and the Staff Manual respectively. Title pages will be prepared in manuscript.

Place	Date	Hour	Summary of Events and Information	Remarks and references to Appendices
La PIERRIERE	1/7/18.		Training continued.	
do.	2/7/18.		Training carried on. Battalion Parade each morning in "D" Coys. Orchard.	SKR
do.	3/7/18.		Training, including Platoon attacks upon a house and rifle bombing carried on.	
do.	4/7/18.		Training continued.	
do.	5/7/18.		The Final of the Inter-Section Football Competition resulted in victory for "A" Coy. "A" Coy. also providing the runners up.	SKR
do.	6/7/18.		Training as usual. Preliminary rounds in Brigade Boxing Competition took place at LINGHEM in the afternoon.	
do.	7/7/18.		The G.O.C. Division inspected the Battalion after Church Parade. In the afternoon Brigade Sports, including Boxing, took place at LINGHEM. The Battalion easily won the Brigade Challenge Cup.	
do.	8/7/18.		Battalion Sports held, lasting all day. Battalion H.Q. won most points in Inter-Company Competition. In the evening the "Frolics" gave an entertainment in "A" Coy's yard. A slight thunderstorm accompanied by rain occurred at nightfall.	
do.	9/7/18.		Orders to move up into the Line were cancelled, pending Divisional relief.	
do.	10/7/18.		Battalion marched to HAM-EN-ARTOIS and was thence conveyed by bus to LIETTRES. Heavy rain fell during the evening.	SKR
LIETTRES	11/7/18.		Day spent in improving the Billets and getting settled. Three Companies are in an old P.O.W. Camp, one Company in a Farm.	

Army Form C. 2118.

WAR DIARY
or
INTELLIGENCE SUMMARY.
(Erase heading not required.)

Instructions regarding War Diaries and Intelligence Summaries are contained in F. S. Regs., Part II. and the Staff Manual respectively. Title pages will be prepared in manuscript.

Place	Date	Hour	Summary of Events and Information	Remarks and references to Appendices
LIETTRES.	12/7/18.		Heavy rain nearly all day. No training carried out in consequence.	S.M.R.
do.	13/7/18.		Battalion march to LINGHEM for training.	
do.	14/7/18.		Some rain fell. Voluntary Church Parade. Inter-Platoon Football matches commenced.	
do.	15/7/18.		The Battalion marched to CUHEM in the morning and practised the attack against a wood situated near FLECHINELLE. During the night a severe thunderstorm occurred.	S.M.R.
do.	16/7/18.		Training was restricted owing to a warning order to move having been received.	
do.	17/7/18.		The Battalion paraded at 9.35.a.m. and march via LINGHEM and FONTES to COTTES, a small village adjoining ST.HILAIRE. Usual farmhouse billets.	S.M.R.
COTTES.	18/7/18.		Day spent in interior economy and reconnaisance of Training grounds.	
do.	19/7/18.		The Battalion moved again, marching to WARNE, N.W. of AIRE, about 9 miles.	S.M.R.
WARNE.	20/7/18.		A most severe thunderstorm visited the neighbourhood in the afternoon. Battalion is in good but scattered billets. Q.M.Stores had mostly to be erected for the third time in ten days, out of material carried here.	
do.	21/7/18.		Day spent in reconnoitring new Training areas and preparation of Training Programmes.	
do.	22/7/18.		The Battalion marched via ROQUETOIRE to PONT ASQUIN near WARDRECQUES and went into bivouacs in a field. Battalion has left XI Corps and	S.M.R.

WAR DIARY
INTELLIGENCE SUMMARY.

(Erase heading not required.)

Army Form C. 2118.

Place	Date	Hour	Summary of Events and Information	Remarks and references to Appendices
WARNE.	22/7/18. (cont'd.)		5th.Army and is now in XV Corps and 2nd.Army. The Division is still in G.H.Q. Reserve.	
PONT ASQUIN.	23/7/18.		A very wet morning. The C.O. and Company Commanders visited the Battle Positions N. of HAZEBROUCK which the Battalion may have to occupy in case of Enemy attack on this Sector.	
do.	24/7/18.		Weather became fine again. Battalion drill in the morning. During the night hostile aeroplanes visited the neighbourhood and dropped bombs. Two men of the Battalion were slightly wounded by our anti-aircraft defences.	
do.	25/7/18.		In the afternoon the Brigade was inspected by General Plumer, commanding 2nd.Army.	
do.	26/7/18.		Heavy showers of rain fell during the day. "A" and "D" Coys. attacked "B" and "C" Coys. in a scheme near the Camp.	
do.	27/7/18.		At the XI Corps Horse Show the Battalion Tug-of-War team gained the victory. Continuance of unsettled weather.	
do.	28/7/18.		The weather became finer. The Battalion played and lost a Rugby Football match against Brigade Headquarters.	
do.	29/7/18.		Range work by the Battalion during the morning. Weather fine and warm.	

Army Form C. 2118.

WAR DIARY
or
INTELLIGENCE SUMMARY.
(Erase heading not required.)

Instructions regarding War Diaries and Intelligence Summaries are contained in F. S. Regs., Part II. and the Staff Manual respectively. Title pages will be prepared in manuscript.

Place	Date	Hour	Summary of Events and Information	Remarks and references to Appendices
PONT ASQUIN.	30/7/18.		Companies training in the attack on Training Area south of the Canal de NEUF FOSSE.	S.u.R.
do.	31/7/18.		The Battalion paraded at 9.P.M. for Brigade Route March to SR.HILAIRE area. Route was through RAQUINGHEM - AIRE - FONTES. Distance 13 miles. Reached Billets in COTTES at 3.A.M. Accommodation the same as last time.	S.u.R.
			A list of Officers who have joined and quitted the Battalion during the month is attached.	App 'A'

Lieut.Col.
Commanding 2/4th.Oxford & Bucks Lt.Infty.

2/4th. Oxford & Bucks Lt.Infty.   APPENDIX "A"

Officers who have joined the Battalion during
           July, 1918.
_____

    2/Lieut.S.W.Bown,   12th.
    2/Lieut.F.V.Ponder,   16th.
    Lieut.G.W.Woodford,M.C. 16th.
    Lieut.R.L.McConnell,   20th.
    Major.H.J.Cupper,   22nd.
    Capt.J.W.Shilson,   23rd.
    Lieut.J.E.Ellis,   27th.

Officers who have quitted the Battalion during
           July, 1918.
_____

    2/Lieut.W.E.Franklin.
    2/Lieut.T.G.L.Harris.

    To England 14/7/18 for posting to
    the R.A.F.

_____

CONFIDENTIAL.

War Diary

of

2/4th Battalion Oxfordshire & Buckinghamshire Light Infantry.

1st August, 1918 to 31st August, 1918.

(Volume XXVIII).

Army Form C. 2118.

WAR DIARY
or
INTELLIGENCE SUMMARY.
(Erase heading not required.)

Instructions regarding War Diaries and Intelligence Summaries are contained in F. S. Regs., Part II. and the Staff Manual respectively. Title pages will be prepared in manuscript.

Place	Date 1918.	Hour	Summary of Events and Information	Remarks and references to Appendices
COTTES.	Aug. 1st.		Late Reveille. Day spent in resting and improvements to billets. Casualties:- Nil.	G.M.
"	2nd.		Rain interfered with Training. The Battalion beat 2/5th GLOUCESTERS at Football by 6 - 0. Casualties:- Nil.	G.M.
"	3rd		Company Training and Ranges. Casualties:- Nil.	
"	4th		In the afternoon the Battalion moved at short notice by lorries to THIENNES, where it relieved 2nd K.O.S.B. in billets and bivouacs. Casualties:- Nil.	
THIENNES.	5th		At night the Battalion relieved the 1st EAST SURREYS in the front line (Right Battalion, ARREWAGE Sector). The move up to the line was by Light Railway and the relief passed off quietly. Battalion Transport and Q.M. Stores moved to STEENBECQUE. Casualties:- Wounded 2 O.R. (1 at duty).	G.M.
ARREWAGE.	6th		Disposition of Companies is as follows:- B Coy. on Right, A on Left, D Right Support, C Left Support, Battalion H.Q. at CAUDESCURE STATION. During the day C Coy. were heavily shelled and had several casualties. Conditions otherwise were quiet. Casualties:- Killed 5 O.R. Wounded 4 O.R.	G.M.
"	7th		Very quiet day. Enemy Artillery shewing practically no activity. At 7 p.m. A and B Companies carried out an attack organised at very short notice against the German Front line between HAZEBROUCK - MERVILLE ROAD and BONAR FARM. Objectives were carried after some opposition, the line was consolidated and posts pushed forward to keep touch with the Enemy whose retirement on MERVILLE had been forecast by the Staff but did not take place. About 12 casualties occurred altogether in the attacking Companies. [illegible] O.R.	

Army Form C. 2118.

WAR DIARY
or
INTELLIGENCE SUMMARY.

(Erase heading not required.)

Instructions regarding War Diaries and Intelligence Summaries are contained in F.S. Regs., Part II. and the Staff Manual respectively. Title pages will be prepared in manuscript.

Place	Date	Hour	Summary of Events and Information	Remarks and references to Appendices
ARREWAGE.	7th (contd)		Four Prisoners of the 189th Infantry Regiment and one Machine Gun were captured. The night passed quietly in the front line. The area round Battalion H.Q. was heavily gassed during the night. Casualties:- Killed 2 O.R. Wounded 2/Lt. A.R.MOORE and 12 O.R.	
"	8th		Intermittent Artillery activity occurred during the day. Lieut. Col. F.M.WOULFE-FLANAGAN, D.S.O., E.SURREY REGT. having been posted to the Battalion for Acting Command assumed command from Lieut.Col. WITHERALL, D.S.O., M.C. who was suffering from effects of gas. During the night a Farm-house occupied by B Coy. as an advanced post was set alight by a German Very Light and had to be temporarily evacuated. It was re-occupied at dawn. Casualties:- Killed.5 O.R. Wounded 4 O.R. Gassed Captain R.F. SYMONDS, Lieut. J.KIRK, and 2/Lieut.W.C.M.CUBBAGE. 38 O.R.	
"	9th		During the night the Battalion was relieved A,C,D Coys by R.BERKS, B Coy, who held line S. of BOURRE RIVER by 182nd Bde. Relief was delayed owing to breakdown in telephones and the double nature of the operation, and was not completed until 4 a.m. Between 11 p.m. and 3 a.m. the Enemy heavily bombarded the Eastern edge of NIEPPE FOREST with Gas Shell. After the relief the Battalion occupied Support Trenches in rear of the Brigade Front with Battalion H.Q. at CHAPELLE BOOM. Casualties:- Wounded:- Lieut. R.THOMAS and 1 O.R.	
"	10th		In Support. Casualties:- Nil.	
"	11th		At dawn the R.BERKS and GLOUCESTERS attacked German Posts opposite them and endeavoured to cross the PLATE BECQUE N. and S. of RENNET MI. This attack was not successful. The R.BERKS succeeded in crossing the BECQUE in one place, while the GLOUCESTERS did the same in the case of one platoon, which returned later with prisoners and two Machine Guns.	

Army Form C. 2118.

WAR DIARY
or
INTELLIGENCE SUMMARY.
(Erase heading not required.)

Instructions regarding War Diaries and Intelligence Summaries are contained in F. S. Regs., Part II. and the Staff Manual respectively. Title pages will be prepared in manuscript.

Place	Date	Hour	Summary of Events and Information	Remarks and references to Appendices
ARREWAGE.	11th (contd)		At night the Enemy shelled area round Battalion H.Q. Rather heavily between 10 and midnight. Casualties:- Wounded 1 O.R.	
"	12th		In Support. Casualties:- Nil.	
"	13th		In Support. Casualties:- Nil.	
"	14th		At night the Battalion was relieved by the 5th Suffolk Regt. (183rd Inf. Bde) and went back into Reserve at SPRESIANO CAMP in NIEPPE FOREST. The relief was accomplished fairly quietly and was complete by 11 p.m. Casualties:- Nil.	
SPRESIANO CAMP.	15th		Usual baths and cleaning up. Casualties:- Wounded Lieut. K.G.E. RAMAGE.	
"	16th		Ditto. Casualties:- Nil.	
"	17th		Battalion engaged harvesting crops round LE PARC. Casualties:- Nil	
"	18th		Quiet day. Hostile H.V. shelling of STEENBECQUE and STEENBECQUE - ST. VENANT Road has ceased. Casualties:- Nil.	
"	19th		Harvesting. Casualties:- Nil.	
"	20th		Battalion moved forward on short notice to support the 183rd Inf. Bde., which had advanced the line about 2000 yards during the preceding day and night. The Battalion crowded into what vacant trenches and other accommodation it was possible to find about the CHAPELLE BOOM area. Casualties:- Nil.	
CHAPELLE BOOM.	21st		Remained in same position. Battalion H.Q. moved to old R.A.P. in FLANK FARM. Casualties:- Wounded 1 O.R.	

Army Form C. 2118.

WAR DIARY
or
INTELLIGENCE SUMMARY.
(Erase heading not required.)

Instructions regarding War Diaries and Intelligence Summaries are contained in F. S. Regs., Part II. and the Staff Manual respectively. Title pages will be prepared in manuscript.

Place	Date	Hour	Summary of Events and Information	Remarks and references to Appendices
CHAPELLE BOOM.	22rd		Lieut. Col. WOULFE-FLANAGAN departed on a course and Major ROSE assumed temporary command. Area occupied by Battalion shelled during the night by enemy Long Range 4-in. and 6-in. guns. Casualties:- Nil.	
"	23rd		Some shelling again took place of the CHAPELLE-BOOM - DENE FARM area, our Artillery Position having moved forward into the Battalion Area. Casualties:- Wounded Lieut. J.E. ELLIS and 1 O.R.	
"	24th		At night the Battalion relieved the 5th Suffolks in the Outpost Line in front of NEUF BERQUIN. Relief was complete by midnight. Disposition of Companies:- A on Right, B Centre, C Left, D in Reserve. The outposts are found by 6 platoons, 2 from each front Company, and the Picquet Line is manned by a like garrison. During the night the ITCHIN - BONAR FM area was shelled constantly by 5.9s firing a proportion of Blue Cross Shell. The front area was moderately quiet. Casualties:- Nil.	
NEUF BERQUIN.	25th		Positions organised. The Battalion Commander is in command of the following detachments of other arms, - 1 Battery R.F.A.; 1 Sec. M.G., 1 Sec. L.T.M.B.; 1 Sec. R.E. Casualties O.R. K.5, W.5. D Coy. at BRONCO FARM do carrying of Rations for forward Coys. Rations come up as far as BRONCO FM. by pack mules.	
"	26th		Shelling during the day not considerable, but severe at night against all roads and tracks leading up to the Front. Casualties:- O.R. Killed 1, Wounded 3.	
"	27th		A quiet day with some rain. Hostile howitzers active against gun positions E. of NIEPPE FOREST all day. Casualties:- Nil.	
"	28th		In accordance with orders received the previous night, the Battalion carried out an attack against the German Positions astride the NEUF BERQUIN - ESTAIRES Road.	See App. M.1.

WAR DIARY
or
INTELLIGENCE SUMMARY.

(Erase heading not required.)

Army Form C. 2118.

Place	Date	Hour	Summary of Events and Information	Remarks and references to Appendices
NEUF BERQUIN (contd)	28th		B and C Coys. who commenced to advance at 11.30 a.m. under cover of a creeping barrage, pushed forward a distance of 500 yards, but were unable to cross the LAUDICK BROOK owing to M.G. fire from BOWERY COTTAGES, which the 40th Division operating on the Battalion's left, failed to capture. The enemy afterwards held the houses about RUE MONTIGNY strongly, and further progress having become impossible, the original outpost line was resumed at dusk. South of the NEUF BERQUIN - ESTAIRES Road A Coy., by means of Patrols, occupied the German wired position East of the SKELTER CROSS - OBOS COTTAGE Road in two places and held on all day. At dusk the enemy, with half a Company, moved up from the enclosures at SKELTER CROSS and commenced to take these patrols in the rear, whereupon they withdrew after treating the Germans with Lewis Guns. During the night A Coy. held its previous outpost positions East of HEMERIE CHAPEL. During the attack hostile artillery did not retaliate with much vigour, but during afternoon and evening the NEUF BERQUIN - ESTAIRES and NEUF BERQUIN - ROBERMETZ Roads as well as all tracks and approaches to the village were severely harassed. C Coy. who held the ground E. of COCHIN CORNER received much attention from hostile T.M. Casualties: Killed 4 O.R.; Wounded 2/Lt. W.A.H.GOODMAN and 22 O.R. Wounded & Missing 1 O.R.	C in R (?) SinR SinR C in R C in R
"	29th		During the day B and C Coys., guided by instructions which had been rendered void by an 11th hour barrage table of the Division on the Left, successfully advanced their lines as far as the RUE PROVOST - RUE MONTIGNY Road, occupying all the farms and enclosures along this road with slight opposition. B Coy. also moved forward along the ESTAIRES Road a distance of 300 yards and A Coy. established themselves along the East side of the SKELTER CROSS - OBOS COTTAGE Road. During the night the Battalion was relieved by 2/5th GLOUCESTER REGT. North of the NEUF BERQUIN - ESTAIRES Road, and by the 2/4th R.BERKS South of it, and withdrew into Support Trenches West of the VIERHOUCK - MERVILLE Road. Battalion H.Q. went into TANKARD FM. Relief was completed by 3 a.m.	

Army Form C. 2118.

WAR DIARY
or
INTELLIGENCE SUMMARY.

(Erase heading not required.)

Instructions regarding War Diaries and Intelligence Summaries are contained in F.S. Regs., Part II. and the Staff Manual respectively. Title pages will be prepared in manuscript.

Place	Date	Hour	Summary of Events and Information	Remarks and references to Appendices
NEUF BERQUIN.	29th (contd)		Lieut. Col. WOULFE-FLANAGAN having rejoined the Battalion re-assumed command. ESTAIRES, DOULLIEU, LA GORGUE burning vigorously. Casualties:- Wounded 2 O.R.	
LES PURESBECQUES.	30th		During the day the Battalion was warned to be prepared to move forward in support of 2/5th GLOUCESTERS who had advanced a mile during the day. Definite orders were received during the night by telephone. Casualties:- Nil.	
"	31st	9 a.m.	At 9 a.m. the Battalion moved up to NEUF BERQUIN, A and B Coys. to PULLET FM., C and D Coys. to COCHIN CORNER areas, Battn H.Q. HUTTON MILL. Later in the afternoon A Coy. was moved forward to RUE MONTIGNY and D Coy. to RUE PROVOST. Some rain fell in the night. NEUF BERQUIN was slightly shelled during the night by long range 4.2s. Casualties:- O.R. Killed 1 O.R., Wounded 3 O.R.	

Lieut. Colonel,
Commdg. 2/4th Oxf. & Bucks Lt. Infty.

M.O. **OPERATION ORDERS** by
Major G.K. Rose M.C.
Commanding 2/4 Oxf Bucks Lt Infty

SECRET. REF. MAP 36 A. N.E. 1/20000

1. **Information.** The enemy is holding the line BOWERY COTTAGES LAUDICK FARM RUE MONTIGNY.

2. **INTENTION.** B &
   B and C Companies will attack tomorrow 27th and will occupy the line RAILWAY CRATER road N. in NEUF BERQUIN E of RUE MONTIGNY dump and enclosures at L.9.c.5.4. S.W. Corner of enclosures at L.9.A.4.b.
   120th Brigade will attack on the left. A Company will operate as detailed below on the right. 119th Brigade will attack on left of 120th Brigade.

3. **DETAIL.**
   (a) Division of frontage.
       C Company's left flank will include the light railway which runs NE from NEUF BERQUIN.
       B Company's left flank will include NEUF BERQUIN - RUE MONTIGNY road. Right flank of D Company will remain in present position as a pivot

(b). Zero hour on 27th will be notified later. Watches will be synchronised by an Officer of B and C Companies, and representatives from 184 T M B and Machine Gun Section at C Company Headquarters at 8.15 a.m 27th inst

(c) Artillery co-operation. Artillery fire consisting of a creeping barrage will commence on the front of the 119th Brigade at zero. The 119th Brigade will advance behind this until it has reached the line PRINCE FARM RUE PROVOST BOWERY COTTAGES. 119th Brigade will reach this line by zero plus 90

(d) Between zero and zero plus 90 the Artillery will put down a standing barrage on the line of the LAUDICK. At zero, under cover of this barrage B and C Companies will commence to trickle forwards in section columns but no troops will be within 600 yards of the LAUDICK BROOK until zero plus 60. This barrage will commence to creep forward at zero plus 90 at the following rate:-

Zero plus 90 Lifts 100 yards

Zero plus 84 lifts 100 yards
Zero plus 97 lifts 100 yards.
Afterwards lifting 100 yards every three minutes. At zero plus 127 the creeping barrage will become a protective barrage 300 yards in front of objective until zero plus 145.

B Company, C Company and 120th Brigade will advance simultaneously commencing at zero plus 90. The rate of advance of B and C Coys platoons will vary with the distance they have to go.

The wire in front of LAUDICK BROOK if not already cut will be cut with wire cutters between zero plus 60 and zero plus 90.

(D) FORMATION

C Company will attack with two platoons in front and two in support. B Company will attack with two platoons in front and one in support, one remaining stationary to hold the CRATER and the posts on either side of it. The stationary platoon will assist the operations by keeping down any hostile fire from the direction of TROMPE BRIDGE.

(4) CONSOLIDATION. The 1st objectives will become the line of resistance and will be organ in depth. On receipt of orders the attack, D Company may be required to move two platoons to COTCHIN CORNER and two platoons to PULLET FARM.

(5) MACHINE GUNS
Two Vickers Guns will support C Company in the advance. Two Vickers guns in A Company area will assist by neutralizing any enemy machine guns along or south of the NEUF BERQUIN-ESTAIRES ROAD.

(6) LIGHT TRENCH MORTARS
One gun will support each of B and C Companies. O.C. M.G. Section and Light Trench Mortars will respectively meet Os. C. B and C. Coys an arranged plan of co-operation.

(7) R.E.
One R.E. N.C.O. and 1 Sapper will be attached to each B and C Coys in order to locate "booby traps" and assist in consolidation

(8) LIAISON
C Coy will maintain liason with

120th Brigade Light Coy throughout

9. DUMPS

Ammunition, water, etc will be at Hutton Mill.

10. PRISONERS

To ITCHIN FARM Escort 1 per ten men captured.

11. REPORTS.

Advanced Battalion H.Q. will open at C. Coy H.Q. L 12 D.9.1. at 8 a.m. tomorrow 27th inst. All reports will be sent there.

On reaching their objectives the front platoons of B and C Coys will fire 3 White Very Lights in quick succession.

ACTION of A COY

At zero plus 90 A Coy will commence to push forward fighting patrols each consisting of two sections under an officer in the direction of OBUS COTTAGE and SKELTER CROSS. If reached by these patrols this line will be held and will become part of the line of resistance. O.C. A Coy will arrange cooperation with left Coy Royal Berks

R.A.P. 300 yards east of ATOM FARM.

26-8-18.

Col. J.W. Shulson,
Capt & Adjt
For Major Commanding
2/4 Oxf & Bucks Lt Infty.

DISTRIBUTION

B. C. A. D Coys & File

CONFIDENTIAL.

WAR DIARY
of
2/4TH. BATTALION
OXFORDSHIRE & BUCKINGHAMSHIRE LIGHT INFANTRY.

From.
1st. September, 1918.

To.
30th. September, 1918.

{ VOLUME 29. }

Army Form C. 2118.

WAR DIARY
or
INTELLIGENCE SUMMARY.
(Erase heading not required.)

Instructions regarding War Diaries and Intelligence Summaries are contained in F. S. Regs., Part II. and the Staff Manual respectively. Title pages will be prepared in manuscript.

Place	Date	Hour	Summary of Events and Information	Remarks and references to Appendices
RUE MONTIGNY.	Sun. 1/9/18.		Battalion Headquarters and "B" and "C" Companies moved forward to RUE MONTIGNY and RUE PROVOST. Remaining two Companies in same position. Casualties:- 1.O.R. Wounded.	K.W.S
CHAPPELLE DUVELLE.	Mon. 2/9/18.		Brigade relief. Battalion in CHAPPELLE DUVELLE. Casualties :- Nil.	K.W.S
"	Tues. 3/9/18.		Cleaning up and improving quarters. Casualties :- Nil.	K.W.S
ESTAIRES.	Wed. 4/9/18.		Battalion moved to Estaires area. "C" and "D" Companies at TROU BAYARD, "A" and "B" Companies at ESTAIRES. Casualties:- Nil.	K.W.S
"	Thur. 5/9/18.		G.O.C. 184 Brigade addressed officers in the morning. Inspection and Platoon drill. Casualties :- Nil.	K.W.S
"	Fri. 6/9/18.		Training in attack over open country. Casualties:- Nil.	K.W.S
"	Sat. 7/9/18.		Training continued: Baths. Casualties :- Nil.	K.W.S
"	Sun. 8/9/18.		Church Parade morning. Casualties :- Nil.	K.W.S
"	Mon. 9/9/18.		Training in Billets owing to heavy rain. Casualties :- Nil.	K.W.S
"	Tues. 10/9/18.		Training started, but cancelled owing to warning order to go into line. Company Commanders reconnoitred new line. Battalion relieved 1ST. EAST LANCS REGT. Casualties:- Capt. G.R. GLUTSON. (wounded).	K.W.S
LAVENTIE.	Wed. 11/9/18.		Right Front Battalion. "A" and "G" Companies front line. "D" Company in support. "B" Company in Reserve. Battalion Headquarters in LAVENTIE. Casualties :- Nil.	K.W.S
"	Thur. 12/9/18.		The Battalion carried out an attack on JUNCTION POST. Two platoons of "C" Company, three platoons of "A" Company were employed.	K.W.S

Army Form C. 2118.

WAR DIARY
or
INTELLIGENCE SUMMARY.
(Erase heading not required.)

Instructions regarding War Diaries and Intelligence Summaries are contained in F. S. Regs., Part II. and the Staff Manual respectively. Title pages will be prepared in manuscript.

Place	Date	Hour	Summary of Events and Information	Remarks and references to Appendices
LAVENTIE.	Thur. 12/9/18.	(cont'd)	Zero 5.15.a.m. The wire was successfully crossed and the objective nearly reached on both flanks: on the right "A" Company put four enemy Machine Guns out of action; but owing to very heavy rain movement was very difficult,and Rifles and Lewis Guns became clogged with mud. The enemy offered strong resistance, and compelled the right to withdraw. No news was received of two parties on the left, and remainder were forced to withdraw at dark. Casualties:- 2/Lieut.J.F.GEORGE, wounded. 2/Lieut.H.CLAYTON, wounded. 2/Lieut.G.A.ROWLERSON, missing. O.R. Killed 7, wounded 22. Missing 18. Wounded and missing 1. Total, 48.	
"	Fri. 13/9/18.		"B" and "D" Companies relieved "C" and "A" Companies respectively, night of 12th./13th. Battalion relieved by 2/4th.ROYAL BERKS REGT. Casualties :- Nil.	
SAILLY.	Sat. 14/9/18.		Behind Sailly. Re-organisation of Companies. Battalion relieves 2/7TH.ROYAL WARWICKS. Casualties :- Nil.	
"	Sun. 15/9/18.		Behind Sailly. Training and repair of Billets. Casualties:- Nil.	
"	Mon. 16/9/18.		Training: improvement and repair of billets. Casualties :- Nil.	
"	Tues.17/9/18.		Battalion moved to LINGHEM for work on CORPS SCHOOL; entrained at GREVE FARM; marched from LA LACQUE to LINGHEM. Casualties:- Nil.	
LINGHEM.	Wed. 18/9/18.		Work, digging, tarring of huts etc. Casualties :- Nil.	
"	Thur. 19/9/18.		Work as before. Casualties :- Nil.	
"	Fri. 20/9/18.		Work. Baths. Casualties :- Nil.	
"	Sat. 21/9/18.		Work as before. Casualties :- Nil.	

Army Form C. 2118.

WAR DIARY
or
INTELLIGENCE SUMMARY.
(Erase heading not required.)

Instructions regarding War Diaries and Intelligence Summaries are contained in F. S. Regs., Part II. and the Staff Manual respectively. Title pages will be prepared in manuscript.

Place	Date	Hour	Summary of Events and Information	Remarks and references to Appendices
LINGHEM	Sun 22/9/18		Work in morning. Casualties nil.	
"	Mon. 23/9/18		Work as before. Casualties nil.	
"	Tues. 24/9/18		Battalion moved back to LE CRUSECBEAU entraining at LA LACQUE, detraining at GREVE FARM. Casualties nil.	
LE CRUSECBEAU	Wed. 25/9/18		Some training carried out in morning. Improvement of billets. Casualties nil.	
"	Thurs. 26/9/18		Line reconnoitred by Company Commanders. Training in morning. Casualties nil.	
"	Fri. 27/9/18		The Battalion relieved 1st.Battalion E.LANCS in right front sector. "D" and "B" Companies in Front Line. Casualties Nil.	
LAVENTIE.	Sat. 28/9/18		2/4th. ROYAL BERKS relieved "B" Company on our left and "C" Company in Left Support. Front line held by 2 platoons of "B" & two of "D" Company. "C" Company S of SAILLY STATION, "A" Company behind NOUVEAU MONDE. Active patrolling by "D" Company. Casualties :- O.R. Killed 1, Wounded 3. (1 at duty).	
"	Sun. 29/9/18		Daylight patrol arranged to reconnoitre JUNCTION POST, but came in contact with enemy daylight patrol at starting point. Casualties :- Missing 2/Lieut.P.E.CRADDOCK. (believed Prisoner).	
"	Mon. 30/9/18		2/5th.GLOUCESTERS attacked JUNCTION POST through the Battalion. Objectives reached but considerable opposition met. Inter-Company relief. Casualties:- Nil.	

Shaula Haragan Lieut.-Col.
Commanding 2/4th. Bn. Oxford & Bucks Light Infantry.

CONFIDENTIAL.

WAR DIARY

** of **

2/4TH BATTALION, THE OXFORDSHIRE & BUCKINGHAMSHIRE LIGHT INFANTRY

From 1st Oct. 1918 to 31st Oct. 1918.

VOL. XXX.
*****

Army Form C. 2118.

WAR DIARY
or
INTELLIGENCE SUMMARY.
(Erase heading not required.)

Instructions regarding War Diaries and Intelligence Summaries are contained in F.S. Regs., Part II. and the Staff Manual respectively. Title pages will be prepared in manuscript.

Place	Date	Hour	Summary of Events and Information	Remarks and references to Appendices
LAVENTIE EAST.	Tues. 1.10.18.		2/5th Gloucestershire Regiment withdrawn night 1st/2nd, the Battalion front being held by A.Company on the left in Junction Post area - with C.Company on the right. Casualties O.R. Killed 1, Wounded 5.	
ROUGE DE BOUT	Wed. 2.10.18.		2/4th Royal Berks attacked and captured Bartlette Farm. Zero 5.45. Enemy withdrew along the whole divisional front, A. and C. Companies were immediately ordered to follow him up, which they did with little opposition. All objectives reached. Battalion Headquarters moved to ROUGE DE BOUT. Casualties O.R. Wounded 1.	
CROIX MARECHAL	Thurs. 3.10.18.		Pursuit continued by A. and C. Companies. Old British front line trenches taken and passed - line established just East of Old German front line system and handed over to 2/6th Durham Light Infantry on relief. Battalion relieved by 2/6th Durham Light Infantry - 59th Division, a slow and difficult relief. On relief the Battalion marched to ROUGE DE BOUT cross roads and was conveyed thence by bus to THIENNES. Casualties nil.	
THIENNES	Fri. 4.10.18.		Companies employed in washing and cleaning up. Casualties Nil.	
"	Sat. 5.10.18.		Quiet day. Casualties Nil.	
"	Sun. 6.10.18.		Battalion entrained THIENNES Railway Station at 0247 hours and travelled to ROSEL Station - and marched thence to BEAUVAL to billets. A. Company travelled by train leaving THIENNES 1217 hours. Casualties nil.	
BEAUVAL	Mon. 7.10.18.		Company training. Casualties nil.	
"	Tues. 8.10.18.		Company training. Casualties nil.	
"	Wed. 9.10.18.		The Battalion marched to DOULLENS and entrained at Doullens Railway Station at 1230 hours, and proceeded by train to HERMIES Railway Station, & thence by march route to an area about MOEUVRES - GRAINCOURT	

Army Form C. 2118.

WAR DIARY
or
INTELLIGENCE SUMMARY.
(Erase heading not required.)

Instructions regarding War Diaries and Intelligence Summaries are contained in F.S. Regs., Part II. and the Staff Manual respectively. Title pages will be prepared in manuscript.

Place	Date	Hour	Summary of Events and Information	Remarks and references to Appendices
BEAUVAL.	Wed. 9.10.18.		No accomodation whatever was available. Casualties nil.	
HERMIES.	Thurs. 10.10.18.		The Battalion marched from the area MOEUVRES - GRAINCOURT to a camp 1 Mile W. of Bourlon Wood. Casualties Nil.	
W. OF BOURLON WOOD.	Fri. 11.10.18.		Company training. Casualties nil.	
"	Sat. 12.10.18.		Battalion training. A scheme of attack by the Battalion on a 2 Company frontage was carried out. Objectives HEIDER Trench E.15.b.3.4. to E.15.b.9.9. Map 57c N.E. Second objective the Copse E.9.b.3.5. to E.10.a.1.1. Map 57c N.E. Casualties nil.	
"	Sun. 13.10.18.		Company training 1100 to 1300. Casualties nil.	
"	Mon. 14.10.18.		All Small Box Respirators inspected and tested in a gas chamber. Company training. Casualties nil.	
"	Tues. 15.10.18.		Company training. A. and D. Companies allotted Bourlon Wood Range from 0930 to 1300 hours. Casualties nil.	
"	Wed. 16.10.18.		Battalion Route March from Camp to Sugar Factory on main Cambrai - Bapaume road - Graincourt - Cantaing - Fontaine Notre Dame - Camp. About 10 miles. Casualties nil.	
"	Fri. 17.10.18.		The Battalion marched from Camp 1 mile W. of Bourlon Wood to CANTAING to camp vacated by 9th Northumberland Fusiliers. Casualties nil.	
CANTAING.	Sat. 18.10.18.		The Battalion marched from Camp at CANTAING to billets at CAGNOCLES, vacated by 8th Queen's Regiment (24th Division) Casualties nil.	

Army Form C. 2118.

WAR DIARY
or
INTELLIGENCE SUMMARY.
(Erase heading not required.)

Instructions regarding War Diaries and Intelligence Summaries are contained in F. S. Regs., Part II. and the Staff Manual respectively. Title pages will be prepared in manuscript.

Place	Date	Hour	Summary of Events and Information	Remarks and references to Appendices
CAGNOCLES	Sun.20.10.18.		Quiet day. Church Parade. Casualties nil.	
"	Mon.21.10.18.		Battalion Parade and Company training carried out. Casualties nil.	
"	Tues.22.10.18.		Battalion Parade and Company Training carried out. Casualties nil.	
"	Wed. 23.10.18.		The Battalion marched to ST. AUBERT Casualties nil.	
ST. AUBERT.	Thurs.24.10.18.		At 0600 hours the Battalion marched out of billets and took up a support position in the open country E. of HAUSSY. The Division had taken over in the front line from 19th Division the previous night, the 183rd Infantry Brigade holding the outpost position W. of the HARPIES RIVER during the night 23rd/24th October. On the morning of 24th 183rd Infantry Brigade carried out an attack against the high ground N.E. of BERMERAIN and secured the line of LE ROGNEAU RIVER. At 1600 hours the Battalion moved forward through the villages of ST. MARTIN and BERMERAIN which were heavily shelled and attacked the enemy positions along the ridge N.E. of ROGNEAU RIVER. B Company attacked on the right, D. on the left with A. in support and C. in reserve. The 2/5th Gloucesters on the Battalion's left attacked LA JUSTICE. The attack was completely successful against considerable hostile opposition. One enemy officer and one O.R. and two Machine guns were captured, also considerable enemy war material. Heavy casualties were inflicted on the enemy in the fighting. At dusk the position astride the LARBLIN - LA CROISETTE Road was consolidated by B. and D. Companies. Battalion Headquarters were established at LA FOLIE FARM. No enemy counter-attack took place. Casualties Wounded: 2/LIEUT. J. ABBOT, Other Ranks Killed 5, Wounded 14.	
BERMERAIN	Fri. 25.10.18.		At 0930 hours Battalion Headquarters moved to LARBLIN where they afterwards remained. At 1430 hours B. and D. Companies continued the advance across	

Army Form C. 2118.

WAR DIARY
or
INTELLIGENCE SUMMARY.

(Erase heading not required.)

Instructions regarding War Diaries and Intelligence Summaries are contained in F. S. Regs., Part II. and the Staff Manual respectively. Title pages will be prepared in manuscript.

Place	Date	Hour	Summary of Events and Information	Remarks and references to Appendices
BERMERAIN	Fri. 25.10.18.		the VALENCIENNES - LE QUESNOY RAILWAY and successfully forced the passage of the PRECHELLES stream and stormed the high ground on its Eastern side in face of Enemy's Machine Guns which fired from the direction of MARESCHES. A line was established at dusk a thousand yards east of SEPMERIES, with the 1ST ROYAL BERKS (2nd Division) on the Battalion's right and the 2/4TH ROYAL BERKS on its left. During the night 25th/26th Oct. the position remained unchanged. A. Company moved two platoons forward in support of each of B. and D. Companies. C. Company remained in reserve immediately West of the VALENCIENNES - LE QUESNOY RAILWAY (S.E. of PARQUAUX). Casualties O.R. Killed 5. Wounded 22.	
SEPMERIES.	Sat. 26.10.18.		The Battalion continued to occupy the positions gained the previous day. Enemy artillery shewed much increased activity all day. At night the Brigade was relieved by the 183rd Infantry Brigade. The Battalion after relief by the 11TH SUFFOLKS moved back to BERMERAIN where Headquarters and all companies were accomodated in billets. In the course of the day Transport, Q.M.Stores and details also moved up to BERMERAIN Casualties Other Ranks Killed 1, Wounded 12.	
BERMERAIN	Sun. 27.10.18.		Rest and cleaning up. Weather fine and warm. Casualties nil.	
"	Mon. 28.10.18.		Bathing under Battalion arrangements. Interior economy carried on with until midday when orders were received for the Battalion to take over as part of the garrison of the CORPS line, N.E. of VENDEGIES. The Battalion relieved the 2/6th ROYAL WARWICKS in the evening in this line, A. and C. Companies being in front, B. and D. in support and immediately N.E. of VENDEGIES. Battalion Headquarters were in VENDEGIES. Transport, Q.M.Stores and Details remained where they were in BERMERAIN. Casualties nil. During the night VENDEGIES was rather heavily shelled by Enemy High Velocity Guns, many yellow cross shells falling in the vicinity of Battalion Headquarters. No gas casualties resulted. BERMERAIN was also treated with attention from the enemy's high velocity guns.	

Army Form C. 2118.

WAR DIARY
or
INTELLIGENCE SUMMARY.
(Erase heading not required.)

Instructions regarding War Diaries and Intelligence Summaries are contained in F. S. Regs., Part II. and the Staff Manual respectively. Title pages will be prepared in manuscript.

Place	Date	Hour	Summary of Events and Information	Remarks and references to Appendices
VENDEGIES.	Tues.29.10.18.		In the morning the Transport moved from its proximity to BERMERAIN and numerous batteries to ground S.W. of ST. MARTIN. In the evening the Battalion left its positions taken up on the 28th and returned to BERMERAIN, with dispositions the same as on the last occasion. Casualties O.R. Wounded 1.	
BERMERAIN	Wed.30.10.18.		Training was carried out under Company arrangements. BERMERAIN was shelled by High Velocity Guns at intervals during the day and night. Casualties O.R. Wounded 1.	
"	Thurs.31.10.18.		Training was carried out under Company arrangements. The General Officer Commanding 184th Infantry Brigade inspected a platoon from "A" Company at 1430 hours and a platoon from "B" Company at 1500 hours. Slight enemy shelling of BERMERAIN by High Velocity Guns. Casualties Nil.	

(signature) Lieut. Colonel
Commanding 2/4th Oxf. & Bucks Lt. Infty

2/4TH OXF. & BUCKS LT. INFTY.

APPENDIX "A".

OFFICERS WHO HAVE JOINED THE
BATTALION DURING OCTOBER, 1918.
-:-:-:-:- :-:-:-:-:-:-:-:-:-:-:-:-

Captain A. C. Jee.   4.10.18.
Lieut. F. M. Passmore.   4.10.18.
2/Lieut. W. I. Parkinson.   7.10.18.
Lieut. J. M. Rolleston.   21.10.18.
Lieut. A. N. Hunt.   25.10.18.
2/Lieut. A.J.R.McAnsh   25.10.18.
2/Lieut. A. R. Price.   25.10.18.
Captain G.C.Miller,M.C.   26.10.18.

CONFIDENTIAL

WAR DIARY

** of **

2/4TH BATTALION, OXFORDSHIRE & BUCKINGHAMSHIRE LIGHT INFANTRY.

From 1st Nov.1918 to 30th Nov.1918.

VOL. XXXI.

WAR DIARY
or
INTELLIGENCE SUMMARY.

(Erase heading not required.)

Army Form C. 2118.

Place	Date	Hour	Summary of Events and Information	Remarks and references to Appendices
BERMERAIN.	Friday 1/11/18.		182nd Infty. Bde. carried out an attack on the line St.Hubert river in L.33.b. (51A) Zero 0515 hours. The Battalion acted as Reserve Battalion of Reserve Brigade, and stood to at 0515 hours. Orders were received at 1215 hours for the Battalion to occupy Corps Line of Resistance in front of VENDEGIES. This move was carried out: but orders were received immediately on its completion for the Battalion to move forward and take up positions West of MARESCHES, with Battalion Headquarters at house at L.30.b.7.1. (51A) (Joint Headquarters with 2/4th Gloucesters). This move was completed by 1930 hours. There was heavy enemy shelling during the evening on ARTRES and between the river and railway from Artres to SEPMERIES. In the morning the 182nd Infantry Brigade had reached its objectives, but during the day was driven from ST. HUBERT by enemy counter attacks, supported by tanks. At 1930 hours the 2/5th Gloucesters carried out an attack with two Companies, on the ST. HUBERT cross roads, but failed to reach their objective, and established a line along the ridge running N.W. of MARESCHES through L.25.b., L.19.c. A. and C. Companies 2/4th Oxfordshire and Buckinghamshire Light Infantry relieved 2/4th Gloucesters in this position about 2300 hours. The G.O.C. 184th Infantry Brigade visited the Battalion Commander, and gave instructions for the Battalion to carry out an attack on the morning of the 2nd. Casualties: Lieut. G. W. WILLIS wounded. Other Ranks Killed 1, wounded 13.	App.
MARESCHES.	Sat. 2/11/18.		At 0530 hours the Battalion attacked the SAINT HUBERT cross-roads with A. and C. Companies in the front line, B. Company in support and D. Company in reserve. Two Companies 2/5th Gloucesters attacked on our right and the 4th Division attacked simultaneously on our left. The attack was preceded by a creeping barrage, which was followed up very closely by the Infantry.	App.

Army Form C. 2118.

WAR DIARY
or
INTELLIGENCE SUMMARY.
(Erase heading not required.)

Instructions regarding War Diaries and Intelligence Summaries are contained in F. S. Regs., Part II. and the Staff Manual respectively. Title pages will be prepared in manuscript.

Place	Date	Hour	Summary of Events and Information	Remarks and references to Appendices
MARESCHES.	Sat. 2/11/18.		Resistance was met with from enemy Machine Guns, particularly at L.20.d.7.5; but the assault was pushed forward with such speed & energy by both Companies, that the enemy resistance became completely demoralized, and large bodies surrendered all along the line.	½ R.B.
		0630 hours	The cross roads at SAINT HUBERT was in our possession by 0630 hours and two enemy tanks fell into our hands on the ridge North West of SAINT HUBERT. The enemy could be seen retiring, over the rising ground in L.16, in the direction of JENLAIN. The Battalion pushed on to a line L.14.central - L.15.central thence southwards towards the river at L.33.a.1.4., many enemy machine guns being captured.	
			B. Company moved up with 2 platoons to a line between SAINT HUBERT and MARESCHES cemetery. The other 2 platoons formed a protective flank to A. Company.	
			On our left we were in touch with 1st Seaforth Highlanders, 4th Division. 2/5th Gloucesters came up into position on our right. In the evening A. Company occupied the road junction in L.27.a. During the morning between 0600 hours and 1000 hours there was very heavy enemy shelling on the area between MARESCHES and the front line, both inclusive.	
			In this successful operation, the following captures were made by the Battalion:- Machine Guns Light 37, Machine Guns heavy 6. Trench Mortars Light 8, Trench Mortars heavy 2., Tanks 2, Field Guns 2 Anti-tank rifles 4, prisoners 550.	
			On the night 2/3rd Companies of 1/4th Shropshires, Cheshires and Staffords took up positions in the area held by the Battalion. On completion of these moves Companies withdrew to BERMERAIN. Owing to the complicated relief C. Company six and 2 platoons of B. Company did not reach their billets until 0800 hours on 3rd inst.	
			Casualties: 2/LIEUT. S. W. BOWN wounded. Other ranks Killed 6 Wounded 34, wounded at duty 3.	
BERMERAIN.	Sun. 3/11/18.		The Battalion marched at 1100 hours to AVESNES-LEZ-AUBERT -	½ R.B.

Army Form C. 2118.

WAR DIARY
or
INTELLIGENCE SUMMARY.
(Erase heading not required.)

Instructions regarding War Diaries and Intelligence Summaries are contained in F. S. Regs., Part II. and the Staff Manual respectively. Title pages will be prepared in manuscript.

Place	Date	Hour	Summary of Events and Information	Remarks and references to Appendices
BERMERAIN	Sun. 3/11/18.		route being cross roads Q.14.d.8.2. (51A) - CHAUSSEE BRUNEHAUT SAULZOIR - MONTRECOURT - ST. AUBERT - AVESNES-LEZ-AUBERT. No-one fell out on route. Casualties nil.	
AVESNES-LEZ-AUBERT.	Mon. 4/11/18.		Company inspections. Baths under Battalion arrangements. Weather fine. Casualties nil.	
"	Tues.5/11/18.		The Battalion marched to BERMERAIN. Very wet weather. No-one fell out on route. Casualties nil.	
BERMERAIN.	Wed. 6/11/18.		Company training. Casualties nil.	
"	Thurs.7/11/18.		Company training. Casualties nil.	
"	Fri. 8/11/18.		Company training from 0900 hours to 1030 hours. The Battalion marched at 1200 hours to MARESCHES. Casualties nil.	
MARESCHES.	Sat. 9/11/18.		Company training. Casualties nil.	
"	Sun.10/11/18.		Church parade 1030 hours. Casualties nil.	
"	Mon.11/11/18.	09.00 hours.	News that armistice had been signed received at Battalion at This was announced on Battalion parade which was held on the same ground as had been the scene of the SAINT HUBERT battle of the 1st and 2nd of the month. Three cheers were given for the KING and the National Anthem played by the Band. The morning's programme, a scheme repeating the attack of the previous week was then carried out. Casualties: LIEUT. V. S. WILKINS died (influenza).	
"	Tues.12/11/18		The Battalion was inspected by the General Officer Commanding	

Army Form C. 2118.

WAR DIARY
or
INTELLIGENCE SUMMARY.
(Erase heading not required.)

Instructions regarding War Diaries and Intelligence Summaries are contained in F. S. Regs., Part II. and the Staff Manual respectively. Title pages will be prepared in manuscript.

Place	Date	Hour	Summary of Events and Information	Remarks and references to Appendices
MARESCHES	Tues.12/11/18.		184th Infantry Brigade on Battalion Parade Ground between MARESCHES AND ARTRES.	
"	Wed. 13/11/18.		The Battalion was employed repairing the railway near SEPMERIES	
"	Thurs.14/11/18.		The Battalion marched to billets at HAUSSY.	
HAUSSY	Fri. 15/11/18.		The Battalion marched to billets at CAGNONCLES.	
CAGNONCLES.	Sat. 16/11/18.		The Battalion marched to CAMBRAI and was billeted at the HOPITAL PARMENTIAIRE (in barracks).	
CAMBRAI.	Sun. 17/11/18.		Church Parade at 1030 hours in Battalion Barracks. Award of the VICTORIA CROSS to No. 285242, L/Cpl. WILCOX, A. for gallantry in attack on JUNCTION POST on the 12th September, came through to the Battalion.	
"	Mon.18/11/18.		Battalion parade in morning and company training. Baths in afternoon.	
"	Tues.19/11/18.		Battalion parade and training. Retreat played by massed bands of the Brigade in the PLACE DES ARMES.	
"	Wed.20/11/18.		Battalion parade and training.	
"	Thurs.21/11/18.		Battalion parade and training.	
"	Fri. 22/11/18.		Salvaging in CAMBRAI area.	
"	Sat. 23/11/18.		Salvaging in CAMBRAI area. Transport left for BERNAVILLE area.	
"	Sun. 24/11/18.		Church Parade in Barracks. Lieut. Col. E. M. Woulfe-Flanagan, D.S.O. proceeded on leave: command of the Battalion taken over by Major G. K. Rose, M.C.	

Army Form C. 2118.

WAR DIARY
or
INTELLIGENCE SUMMARY.
(Erase heading not required.)

Instructions regarding War Diaries and Intelligence Summaries are contained in F. S. Regs., Part II. and the Staff Manual respectively. Title pages will be prepared in manuscript.

Place	Date	Hour	Summary of Events and Information	Remarks and references to Appendices
CAMBRAI	Mon.25/11/18.		The Battalion was under orders to entrain at 1600 hours but owing to delay in railway transportation this did not happen. The Battalion remained in billets for the night.	NDR
"	Tues.26/11/18.		The Battalion remained in its own billets at short notice to entrain. A day's rations were drawn and meals were provided as well as possible under the uncertain circumstances and with the facilities still available in the Barracks.	NDR
"	Wed. 27/11/18.		The Battalion entrained at CAMBRAI VILLE Station at 1300 hours and commenced the journey at 1430 hours. After a certain amount of slow progress the train stopped at LOURQUES and remained stationary in a siding the whole night.	NDR
LOURQUES	Thurs.28/11/18.		The train started from LOURQUES at 0930 hours and proceeded through DOUAI and BREBIERES to ARRAS where a wait of several hours occurred. Iron rations were eaten by the whole Battalion during the journey. At 2000 hours the train had reached FREVENT where it remained in a siding until past midnight.	NDR
DOMART.	Fri.29/11/18.		After its four hours' wait the train left FREVENT siding at 0015 hours and ran to CONTEVILLE with only one stop (at AUXI-LE-CHATEAU). Detrainment took place at CONTEVILLE in rain and darkness and was completed by 0200 hours. After a meal in an adjoining field the Battalion marched to its billets at DOMART-EN-PONTHIEU, which was reached at 0630 hours. The journey from CAMBRAI, delays in which were explained by the transport through DOUAI and ARRAS of repatriated British prisoners, had altogether occupied 40 hours from the time of actual starting and 86 hours from the originally scheduled time of departure.	NDR
"	Sat.30/11/18.		Day spent in rest and organization.	NDR

WAR DIARY
INTELLIGENCE SUMMARY.
(Erase heading not required.)

Army Form C. 2118.

The following awards have been made during the month.

OFFICERS.

SECOND BAR TO THE MILITARY CROSS.

CAPTAIN H. JONES: M.C.

THE MILITARY CROSS.

Captain J. STANLEY.
Lieut. F. M. PASSMORE.
2/Lieut. E. J. R. McANSH.

OTHER RANKS.

VICTORIA CROSS.

285242, Cpl. WILCOX, A.

DISTINGUISHED CONDUCT MEDAL.

9663, C.S.M. CUNNINGHAM, R.

THE MILITARY MEDAL.

202123, Cpl. ROSSER, L.R.
265994, Pte. (L/c) WARD, F.C.
266962, Pte. (L/c) STRANGE, H.R.
34633, Sgt. MADDICK, T.

E. M. Rose Major,
Commanding 2/4th Oxf. & Bucks Lt. Infty.

COPY.

DIVISIONAL ROUTINE ORDERS
by
Major-General F.J.DUNCAN, C.M.G., D.S.O.
Commanding 61st Division.

------oOo------

Headquarters, 18th November, 1918.

3267. HONOURS AND AWARDS.

His Majesty the King has been graciously pleased to award the VICTORIA CROSS to:-

No. 285242 L/Cpl. A. WILCOX, Oxford & Bucks L.I.

During a local operation on the morning of September 12th 1918, in front of LAVENTIE, the flank platoon of "A" Company, 2/4th Bn. Oxford and Bucks Light Infantry was held up by heavy and persistent Machine Gun fire from a trench about 70 yards distant. Finding it impossible to advance L/Cpl. WILCOX crawled towards the trench with 4 men, bombed it, and finally rushed the gun nearest to him, disposed of the gunner and being unable to take the gun along with him, put it out of action.

He then worked his way up the trench, bombed the next gun position, (during which action two of his Section were wounded) and himself again rushed the gun, killed the gunner in a hand to hand struggle and put the gun out of action.

In spite of the reduced number of his party, this N.C.O. continued his advance up the trench. Bombing the gun positions he killed 1 gunner, wounded another, and put two more guns out of action (it still being impossible to dispose of them otherwise) and successfully reached his objective.

Having by this time only 1 man with him, L/Cpl. WILCOX was obliged to withdraw when the Germans counter-attacked in strength. Besides being so extremely outnumbered, he was without fire weapons, rifles being clogged up with mud, owing to the fact that the weather during and before the operations was very bad. In spite of the very superior numbers against him, he withdrew successfully.

------oOo------

SPECIAL ORDER OF THE DAY

By

MARSHAL FOCH
COMMANDER-IN-CHIEF OF THE ALLIED ARMIES.
---------------------oOo---------------------

G.Q.G.A. le 12 Novembre, 1918.

OFFICIERS, SOUS-OFFICIERS, SOLDATS DES ARMEES ALLIEES.

Après avoir résolument arrêté l'ennemi, vous l'avez, pendant des mois, avec une foi et une énergie inlassables, attaqué sans répit.

Vous avez gagné la plus grande bataille de l'Histoire et sauvé la cause la plus sacrée : la Liberté du Monde.

Soyez fiers.

D'une gloire immortelle vous avez paré vos drapeaux.

La Postérité vous garde sa reconnaissance.

(Signed) F. FOCH,

Le Maréchal de France,

Commandant en Chef les Armées Alliées.

(Translation).

OFFICERS, NON-COMMISSIONED OFFICERS, and SOLDIERS OF THE ALLIED ARMIES.

After bringing the enemy's attack to a stand by your stubborn defence, you attacked him without respite for several months, with inexhaustible energy and unwavering faith.

You have won the greatest battle in history and have saved the most sacred of all causes, the Liberty of the World.

Well may you be proud!

You have covered your standards with immortal glory, and the gratitude of posterity will ever be yours.

(Signed) F. FOCH,

Marshal of France,

Commander-in-Chief of the Allied Armies.

2/4TH OXF. & BUCKS LT. INFTY.

OFFICERS WHO HAVE JOINED THE BATTALION DURING NOVEMBER, 1918.
------------------oOo------------------

    CAPTAIN C. S. S. MATTHEWS.   Rejoined 29th.
    2/LIEUT. W. H. MULLARD.   Joined 7th.
    2/LIEUT. H. C. AVERY.   Joined 24th.

OFFICERS WHO HAVE LEFT THE BATTALION DURING NOVEMBER, 1918.
------------------oOo------------------

LIEUT. G. W. WILLIS - To England wounded 11th.
LIEUT. E. H. FAWCITT - To England sick 4th.
LIEUT. V. S. WILKINS.   died (influenza) 11th.

CONFIDENTIAL.

WAR DIARY

of

2/4TH BATTALION

OXFORDSHIRE AND BUCKINGHAMSHIRE LIGHT INFANTRY.

From   To
1st December, 1918   31st December, 1918.

{ Volume }
{   32   }

Army Form C. 2118.

WAR DIARY
or
INTELLIGENCE SUMMARY.

(Erase heading not required.)

Instructions regarding War Diaries and Intelligence Summaries are contained in F. S. Regs., Part II. and the Staff Manual respectively. Title pages will be prepared in manuscript.

Place	Date	Hour	Summary of Events and Information	Remarks and references to Appendices
DOMART	Sun. 1st Dec.		Church Parade in Theatre.	
"	Mon. 2nd "		Battalion parade: training for an hour and a half. Cleaning up and organisation of billets. Education scheme commenced.	
"	Tues. 3rd "		Battalion parade: training as before.	
"	Wed. 4th "		Very wet. Company parades and billet organisation.	
"	Thurs. 5th "		Wet: inspection of billets.	
"	Fri. 6th "		Battalion parade and training.	
"	Sat. 7th "		Battalion parade and training.	
"	Sun. 8th "		Church parade in theatre.	
"	Mon. 9th "		Battalion parade and training till 12.30. Football match against 179 Field Company R.E.	
"	Tues. 10th "		Battalion parade and training. Football match "A" Company v. "A" Company of Royal Berks at FRANQUEVILLE.	
"	Wed. 11th "		Very wet. Billet inspection. Lieut. Col. E. M. WOULFE-FLANAGAN, D.S.O. resumed command of Battalion on returning from leave.	
"	Thurs. 12th "		Battalion parade. Practice of ceremonial. Football matches "B" Company v. "D" Company of GLOUCESTERS. "C" Company v. "A" Company of GLOUCESTERS, both played at DOMQUER.	
"	Fri. 13th "		Very wet. No training.	

Army Form C. 2118.

WAR DIARY
or
INTELLIGENCE SUMMARY.
(Erase heading not required.)

Instructions regarding War Diaries and Intelligence Summaries are contained in F. S. Regs., Part II. and the Staff Manual respectively. Title pages will be prepared in manuscript.

Place	Date		Hour	Summary of Events and Information	Remarks and references to Appendices
DOMART	Sat.	14th		Route March: ST. LEGER - VIGNACOURT - BERTAUCOURT.	
"	Sun.	15th		Church parade in Theatre.	
"	Mon.	16th		Battalion parade and training.	
"	Tues.	17th		Battalion parade and training. Football match "B" Company against "D" Company GLOUCESTERS.	
"	Wed.	18th		Very wet. Company parades. Inter-platoon football competition started.	
"	Thurs.	19th		Wet. Company parades. Inter-platoon football competition.	
"	Fri.	20th		Battalion parade. Football in afternoon.	
"	Sat.	21st		Battalion parade. Football in afternoon.	
"	Sun.	22nd	c	Church parade in Theatre.	
"	Mon.	23rd		Battalion parade. Football in afternoon.	
"	Tues.	24th		Battalion muster parade.	
"	Wed.	25th		Some frost. Weather fine and clear. Christmas dinners in Theatre and "A" Company billet.	
"	Thurs.	26th		Holiday.	
"	Fri.	27th		Wet. Company parades.	
"	Sat.	28th		Wet. Short route march.	

Army Form C. 2118.

WAR DIARY
or
INTELLIGENCE SUMMARY.
(Erase heading not required.)

Instructions regarding War Diaries and Intelligence Summaries are contained in F. S. Regs., Part II. and the Staff Manual respectively. Title pages will be prepared in manuscript.

Place	Date	Hour	Summary of Events and Information	Remarks and references to Appendices
DOMART	Sun. 29th		Church Parade in Theatre.	
"	Mon. 30th		Battalion parade and training.	
"	Tues. 31st		Battalion parade. Fete in afternoon for children of DOMART.	

Sherrill Harcourt, Lieut. Colonel,
Commanding, 2/4th Oxf. & Bucks Lt. Infty.

2/4TH OXF. & BUCKS LT. INFTY.

OFFICERS WHO HAVE JOINED THE BATTALION DURING DECEMBER, 1918.

—————————————oOo—————————————

Lieut. J. W. BENNETT	Joined 15th.
2/Lieut. G. Ashplant.	Joined 19th.
2/Lieut. C. ELICK.	Joined 19th.
Lieut. J. W. ROWLEY.	Joined 24th.

OFFICERS WHO HAVE LEFT THE BATTALION DURING DECEMBER, 1918.

—————————————oOo—————————————

Captain W. G. MURRAY.	Left 1st.
Captain J. H. D. FAITHFULL.	Left 10th.
Lieut. J. C. CURTIS.	Left. 12th.

CONFIDENTIAL.

WAR DIARY

of

2/4TH BATTALION OXFORDSHIRE AND BUCKINGHAMSHIRE
LIGHT INFANTRY.

{ VOLUME }
{ 33 }

From   To

1st January, 1919   31st January, 1919.

Army Form C. 2118.

WAR DIARY
or
INTELLIGENCE SUMMARY.
(Erase heading not required.)

Instructions regarding War Diaries and Intelligence Summaries are contained in F. S. Regs., Part II. and the Staff Manual respectively. Title pages will be prepared in manuscript.

Place	Date	Hour	Summary of Events and Information	Remarks and references to Appendices
DOMART	Wed. 1/1/19		Battalion parade. Football in afternoon. Platoon Competition.	100
"	Thurs. 2/1/19		Route March. "D" Company marched to ABBEVILLE for three days.	108
"	Fri. 3/1/19		Battalion parade. Football in afternoon. Platoon competition.	109
"	Sat. 4/1/19		Muster parade. Ceremonial. Practice for trooping of colours.	110
"	Sun. 5/1/19		Church parade in Theatre.	
"	Mon. 6/1/19		Presentation of colours. First party for demobilization left.	106
"	Tues. 7/1/19		Battalion parade. Football in afternoon.	107
"	Wed. 8/1/19		Battalion parade. Football, platoon competition in afternoon.	
"	Thu. 9/1/19		Route march.	
"	Fri. 10/1/19		Battalion parade. Football in afternoon.	110
"	Sat. 11/1/19		Battalion muster parade.	
"	Sun. 12/1/19		Church parade in Theatre.	
"	Mon. 13/1/19		Battalion parade. Football in afternoon.	
"	Tues. 14/1/19		Battalion parade and cross country run. Semi-final Divisional Group competition.	108
"	Wed. 15/1/19		Battalion parade. Platoon competition in afternoon.	
"	Thurs. 16/1/19		Battalion parade. Semi final of platoon competition.	109
"	Fri. 17/1/19		Route March.	102

Army Form C. 2118.

WAR DIARY
or
INTELLIGENCE SUMMARY.

(Erase heading not required.)

Instructions regarding War Diaries and Intelligence Summaries are contained in F. S. Regs., Part II. and the Staff Manual respectively. Title pages will be prepared in manuscript.

Place	Date	Hour	Summary of Events and Information	Remarks and references to Appendices
DOMART	Sat.18/1/19		Company parade. Final of Divisional Group football competition played at COCTEVILLE 184th Infantry Brigade defeated by 61st D.A.C. : 9 - 2.	
"	Sun.19/1/19		Church parade in Theatre. Lantern service in the evening. "B" Company marched to ABBEVILLE for three days.	
"	Mon.20/1/19		Battalion parade.	
"	Tues.21/1/19		Battalion Parade. Re-play of semi-final Platoon competition.	
"	Wed.22/1/19		Battalion parade. Range. Battalion match v. Brigade.	
"	Thu.23/1/19		Route march. Final of platoon competition won by Battalion Headquarters.	
"	Fri.24/1/19		Battalion parade. Very hard frost.	
"	Sat.25/1/19		Battalion muster parade. Physical Training demonstration.	
"	Sun.26/1/19		Church parade in Concert Hall.	
"	Mon.27/1/19		Battalion parade.	
"	Tues.28/1/19		Battalion parade and short route march. A fall of snow.	
"	Wed.29/1/19		Battalion parade. Football and basket ball in morning. Orders received to prepare to move for Base Duties at LE HAVRE.	
"	Thurs.30/1/19		Company parades and training.	

Army Form C. 2118.

WAR DIARY
or
INTELLIGENCE SUMMARY.

(Erase heading not required.)

Instructions regarding War Diaries and Intelligence Summaries are contained in F. S. Regs., Part II. and the Staff Manual respectively. Title pages will be prepared in manuscript.

Place	Date	Hour	Summary of Events and Information	Remarks and references to Appendices
DOMART	Fri. 31/1/19		Day spent in organization prior to move. Transport left DOMART at 11.00 hours for ETAPLES.	
	31/1/19.		[signature] Lieut. Colonel, Commanding 2/4th Oxf. & Bucks Lt. Infty.	

2/4TH OXF. & BUCKS LT. INFTY.

OFFICERS WHO HAVE JOINED THE
BATTALION DURING JANUARY, 1919

Captain R. I. ABRAHAM.   1/1/19.
2/Lieut. G. F. MURDEN.   13/1/19.

OFFICERS WHO HAVE LEFT THE
BATTALION DURING JANUARY, 1919.

Captain H. T. CROSTHWAITE	For Demobilization	12/1/19
Captain E. F. V. DEYNS.	ditto	22/1/19
Captain G. C. MILLER, M.C.	ditto	19/1/19
Lieut. J. M. ROLLESTON.	ditto	20/1/19
Lieut. G. W. WOODFORD, M.C.	ditto	15/1/19
Lieut. W. H. MILLARD.	ditto	6/1/19
Lieut. B. J. NEWBERY.	ditto	21/1/19
Lieut. J. W. BENNETT.	ditto	26/1/19
2/Lieut. A. E. G. BENNETT.	ditto	27/1/19

CONFIDENTIAL.

WAR DIARY

OF

2/4TH BATTALION OXFORDSHIRE & BUCKINGHAMSHIRE LIGHT INFANTRY.

1ST FEBRUARY, 1919 to 28TH FEBRUARY, 1919.

(VOLUME XXXIV).

Army Form C. 2118.

WAR DIARY
or
INTELLIGENCE SUMMARY.
(Erase heading not required.)

Instructions regarding War Diaries and Intelligence Summaries are contained in F. S. Regs., Part II. and the Staff Manual respectively. Title pages will be prepared in manuscript.

Place	Date	Hour	Summary of Events and Information	Remarks and references to Appendices
DOMART - EN - PONTHIEU.	1/2/19.		Battalion marched to CONTEVILLE and entrained for ETAPLES. Arrived at ETAPLES after a three hour journey. Marched to Camp at CUCQ.	T.S.P.B
CUCQ.	2/2/19.		Arrangement of Camp.	T.S.P.B
"	3/2/19.		Guard duties commence. "A" Coy. moves down to ETAPLES. Transport arrives.	T.S.P.B
"	4/2/19.		Battalion parade. Guards in ETAPLES.	T.S.P.B
"	5/2/19.		Battalion parade. Guards in ETAPLES. Considerable fall of snow.	T.S.P.B
"	6/2/19		Battalion moved into Camp in ETAPLES at "E" Depot.	T.S.P.B
ETAPLES	7/2/19.		Battalion parade. Arrangements for running Demobilisation Reception Camp. B and D Coys. to run Reception Camp, "A" Coy. Officers' Reception Camp, "C" Coy. duty Company for guards. 1st train arrived during night of 7/8th.	T.S.P.B
"	8/2/19.		Demobilisation and Embarkation work under 184th Infantry Brigade H.Q. The Brigade made up by 2/7th Warwicks and 1/5th D.C.L.I. both of whom run dispersal camps. Two more trains in. Very hard frost.	T.S.P.B
"	9/2/19.		Work continued. CANDAS and VALENCIENNES trains due in each night except WEDNESDAY and THURSDAY.	T.S.P.B
"	10/2/19.		Work in Reception Camp. All guards in town supplied by "C" Coy. Frost continues very severe.	T.S.P.B
"	11/2/19.		Demobilisation work as before. From 20 to 30 P.O.W. supplied each day for labour.	T.S.P.B

Army Form C. 2118.

WAR DIARY
or
INTELLIGENCE SUMMARY.
(Erase heading not required.)

Instructions regarding War Diaries and Intelligence Summaries are contained in F. S. Regs., Part II. and the Staff Manual respectively. Title pages will be prepared in manuscript.

Place	Date	Hour	Summary of Events and Information	Remarks and references to Appendices
ETAPLES.	12/2/19.		No trains in at night. Day spent in medical inspection and despatch of parties as usual.	
"	13/2/19.		General cleaning up of Camp.	
"	14/2/19.		Battalion Parade. Baths.	
"	15/2/19.		CANDAS and VALENCIENNES trains in in early morning. Frost goes, weather much milder.	
"	16/2/19.		No trains in.	
"	17/2/19.		Work in demobilisation camp. CANDAS train in.	
"	18/2/19.		No trains in.	
"	19/2/19.		Battalion parade and route march.	
"	20/2/19.		Cleaning up in camps.	
"	21/2/19.		Battalion parade. Inspection, marching order.	
"	22/2/19.		Work in Camp.	
"	23/2/19.		Train in afternoon.	
"	24/2/19.		Delousing of men arrived 23rd. TOURNAI train in in afternoon.	
"	25/2/19.		Work in Camp and at DELOUSER. TOURNAI train in in afternoon.	

Army Form C. 2118.

WAR DIARY
or
INTELLIGENCE SUMMARY.
(Erase heading not required.)

Instructions regarding War Diaries and Intelligence Summaries are contained in F. S. Regs., Part II. and the Staff Manual respectively. Title pages will be prepared in manuscript.

Place	Date	Hour	Summary of Events and Information	Remarks and references to Appendices
ETAPLES.	26/2/19.		Ordinary Camp Routine. Train in about 17.00 hours. From this date men received and deloused in afternoon direct from Concentration Camp, ETAPLES.	15/23
"	27/2/19.		Work in Camp. No train in.	13/23
"	28/2/19.		Cleaning up of camps. Inspection of billets and Reception Camps by Commanding Officer. Baths in afternoon.	15/23

Signed,

Lieut. Colonel,
Commdg. 2/4th Oxf. & Bucks Lt. Infty.

2/4TH BN. OXF. & BUCKS LT. INFTY.

JOINED 6/2/19.

2/Lieut. P.T. SEAR.
  "   R.G. SEAR.

QUITTED.

Captain R.L. ABRAHAM.   18/2/19.
2/Lieut. A.G. STEWART. 15/2/19.

AWARD.

Captain C.R. CLUTSOM, 3rd Bn. Wiltshire Regt.

CHEVALIER DE L'ORDRE DE LEOPOLD WITH PALM and THE
BELGIAN CROIX DE GUERRE.

CONFIDENTIAL.

WAR DIARY

of

2/4TH BATTALION OXFORDSHIRE AND BUCKINGHAMSHIRE LIGHT INFANTRY

From
1st March, 1919

To
31st March, 1919.

(VOLUME)
(XXXV.)

Army Form C. 2118.

WAR DIARY
or
INTELLIGENCE SUMMARY.
(Erase heading not required.)

Instructions regarding War Diaries and Intelligence Summaries are contained in F. S. Regs., Part II. and the Staff Manual respectively. Title pages will be prepared in manuscript.

Place	Date	Hour	Summary of Events and Information	Remarks and references to Appendices
ETAPLES.	1/3/19.		Demobilization Camp work. Company work for Companies not employed. Summer time came into force.	
"	2/3/19.		Sunday routine.	
"	3/3/19.		Work in Demobilization Camp.	
"	4/3/19.		Draft of 5 Officers and 102 Other Ranks arrived from 16th (R.D.Y.) Bn. Devonshire Regiment.	
"	5/3/19.		Draft of 5 Officers and 157 Other Ranks arrived from 12th (W.S.Y.) Bn. Somerset Light Infantry.	
"	6/3/19.		Company inspections of new drafts.	
"	7/3/19.		Company parades.	
"	8/3/19.		Billet inspection by the Commanding Officer.	
"	9/3/19.		Church Parade Service in the Church Army Hut.	
"	10/3/19.		Battalion Parade. Headquarter Company disbanded. All men sleep and eat with their Companies. Captain A. C. JEE assumed command of "C" Company. Draft of 2 Officers and 117 Other Ranks arrived from 6th Bn. Wiltshire Regiment.	
"	11/3/19.		Battalion Parade.	

Army Form C. 2118.

WAR DIARY
or
INTELLIGENCE SUMMARY.
(Erase heading not required.)

Instructions regarding War Diaries and Intelligence Summaries are contained in F. S. Regs., Part II. and the Staff Manual respectively. Title pages will be prepared in manuscript.

Place	Date	Hour	Summary of Events and Information	Remarks and references to Appendices
ETAPLES.	12/3/19.		Battalion Parade and Training.	
"	13/3/19.		Battalion Parade.	
"	14/3/19.		Battalion took over a large number of Guards from the 2/7th Royal Warwickshire Regiment who were leaving ETAPLES.	
"	15/3/19.		Battalion Parade and Physical Training under instruction of Gymnastic Staff. Guards now found daily by the Battalion numbered 120 all ranks.	
"	16/3/19.		Church Parade at Church Army Hut.	
"	17/3/19.		Battalion Parade and Physical Training.	
"	18/3/19.		Captain R. E. M. YOUNG having proceeded for demobilization. Lieut. F. W. PASSMORE, M.C. assumed command of "B" Company.	
"	19/3/19.		Battalion Parade. Warning of a move received. Day spent collecting stores of the Reception Camp.	
"	20/3/19.		Battalion Parade.	
"	21/3/19.		Battalion Parade. Battalion still find a large number of guards.	

Army Form C. 2118.

WAR DIARY
or
INTELLIGENCE SUMMARY.
(Erase heading not required.)

Instructions regarding War Diaries and Intelligence Summaries are contained in F. S. Regs., Part II. and the Staff Manual respectively. Title pages will be prepared in manuscript.

Place	Date	Hour	Summary of Events and Information	Remarks and references to Appendices
ETAPLES.	22/3/19.		Inspection of Camp by the Commanding Officer. Inspection cut short by an outbreak of fire in an adjoining camp lately vacated by the 1/5th Duke of Cornwall's Light Infantry. No damage done to the Battalion Camp.	
"	23/3/19.		Relieved of half the number of guards by 1/6th Battn. Cheshire Regiment. Advance party proceeded to LE TREPORT.	
"	24/3/19.		Battalion Parade.	
"	25/3/19.		Battalion Parade. 2/Lieut. E. C. A. CORNISH promoted Lieut. 2/Lieut. T. D. BENNETT promoted Lieut.	
"	26/3/19.		Battalion Parade.	
"	27/3/19.		Orders to move to LE TREPORT received.	
"	28/3/19.		Transport moved to LE TREPORT by road, staying at COLLINI BEAUMONT night of 28/29th. 2/Lieut. E. J. R. McANSH, M.C. promoted Lieut.	
"	29/3/19.		Battalion entrained at 10.10 hours to proceed to LE TREPORT in a snow storm. Camp taken over by 2/14th London Scottish. The train left New Siding ETAPLES at. 11.58 hours and arrived at LE TREPORT at 16.30 hours. Battalion marched up to the Camp,	

Army Form C. 2118.

WAR DIARY
or
INTELLIGENCE SUMMARY.

(*Erase heading not required.*)

Instructions regarding War Diaries and Intelligence Summaries are contained in F.S. Regs., Part II. and the Staff Manual respectively. Title pages will be prepared in manuscript.

Place	Date	Hour	Summary of Events and Information	Remarks and references to Appendices
ETAPLES.	29/3/19 (cont'd.)		lately No. 16 General Hospital, (Philadelphia). Very good quarters indeed. Transport stayed at ST. VALERY night of 29/30th.	
LE TREPORT	30/3/19.		Day spent in settling into billets and cleaning up. Church parade at 11.00 hours. Transport arrived at 15.30 hours, having had a good journey.	
"	31/3/19.		Companies at disposal of O.C. Companies. Draft of 1 Officer and 8 Other Ranks arrived from the 2nd Battalion Royal Berkshire Regiment.	

31/3/1919.

[signature]
Lieut. Colonel
Commanding 2/4th Oxf. & Bucks Lt. Infty.

2/4TH BN. OXF. & BUCKS LT. INFTY.

OFFICERS WHO HAVE JOINED THE BATTALION DURING MARCH, 1919.

2/Lieut. R. J. WILLOUGHBY,	(Devon Regt.)	4/3/19.
Lieut. R. J. P. McINTOSH.	(Devon Regt.)	4/3/19.
2/Lieut. E. J. RAMSEY.	(Devon Regt.)	4/3/19.
2/Lieut. C. G. B. EDDOWES	(Devon Regt.)	4/3/19.
Lieut. J. F. W. CARSWELL.	(Devon Regt.)	4/3/19.
2/Lieut. A. H. B. BISHOP.	(Wilts Regt.)	5/3/19.
2/Lieut. C. L. TABOR.	(Somerset L.I.)	5/3/19.
2/Lieut. W. E. PARKER, M.M.	(Wilts Regt.)	5/3/19.
2/Lieut. J. E. DORAN.	(Somerset L.I.)	5/3/19.
2/Lieut. C. E. PEARCE.	(Wilts Regt.)	5/3/19.
Captain L. D. MARTIN.	(Devon Regt.)	10/3/19.
Lieut. J. A. GALLEY.	(Wilts Regt.)	10/3/19.
Lieut. J. W. PAVEY.	(R. Berks Regt.)	31/3/19.

OFFICERS WHO HAVE QUITTED THE BATTALION DURING MARCH, 1919.

Major G. K. ROSE, M.C.	For demobilization	14/3/19.
Captain R. E. M. YOUNG.	ditto	17/3/19.
Captain H. JONES, M.C.	ditto	29/3/19.
Lieut. B. O. WELLER.	ditto	26/3/19.
Lieut. G. ASHPLANT, M.M.	ditto	17/3/19.
2/Lieut. T. D. BENNETT.	ditto	17/3/19.
2/Lieut. A. R. PRICE.	ditto	3/3/19.
2/Lieut. P. T. SEAR.	To England sick	31/3/19.

CONFIDENTIAL.

WAR DIARY
of

2/4TH. BATTALION OXFORDSHIRE & BUCKINGHAMSHIRE LIGHT INFANTRY.

From 1st. April, 1919............ 30th. to April, 1919.

{ VOLUME XXXVI. }

Army Form C. 2118.

APRIL 1919.

2/4th. Oxford & Bucks Light Infantry.

WAR DIARY
or
INTELLIGENCE SUMMARY.
(Erase heading not required.)

Instructions regarding War Diaries and Intelligence Summaries are contained in F. S. Regs., Part II. and the Staff Manual respectively. Title pages will be prepared in manuscript.

Place	Date	Hour	Summary of Events and Information	Remarks and references to Appendices
Le Treport.	1st.		Battalion Parade and Training.	
	2nd.		Battalion Parade and Training.	
	3rd.		Battalion Parade, Training and Baths.	
	4th.		Battalion Parade, Training and Baths. Drafts from 6th. Battn. Dorset Regiment and 4th. Battn. Bedford Regiment arrived.	
	5th.		Battalion Parade and Training. Baths for men of Draft.	
	6th.		Church Parade in Church Hut. Inspection of Draft by Commanding Officer.	
	7th.		Battalion Parade and Training. Hours 09.30 to 12.15. 14.00 to 15.00.	
	8th.		Battalion Parade. Prospective N.C.Os. Class commences.	
	9th.		Battalion Parade and Training.	
	10th.		Battalion Parade. Transport Inspection by Commanding Officer.	
	11th.		Battalion Parade. Hockey Match against Div. R.E. in afternoon.	
	12th.		Battalion Parade. Football Match against Tank Corps in afternoon.	
	13th.		Church Parade in Church Hut.	
	14th.		Strong wind and rain. Training in Huts. Education & Signalling Classes commenced.	
	15th.		Advance Guard Scheme. Bad weather continues.	
	16th.		Battalion Parade.	

Army Form C. 2118.

Page 2.
April, 1919.

WAR DIARY
or
INTELLIGENCE SUMMARY.

(Erase heading not required.)

Instructions regarding War Diaries and Intelligence Summaries are contained in F.S. Regs., Part II. and the Staff Manual respectively. Title pages will be prepared in manuscript.

Place	Date	Hour	Summary of Events and Information	Remarks and references to Appendices
Le Treport.	17th.		Battalion Parade and Company Training. Major G.E.Swinton,M.C., E.Surrey Regiment, joined for duty as Second in Command.	13/2/3
	18th.		Good Friday. Church Parade in morning. No training.	13/2/3
	19th.		Inspection of Companies by Commanding Officer. Full Marching Order. Camp Inspection.	13/2/3
	20th.		Easter Sunday. Church Parade in morning.	13/2/3
	21st.		Company Parades and Training till 10.45 hours. Inter-platoon football competition commenced.	13/2/3
	22nd.		Company Parades and Training.	13/2/3
	23rd.		Company Parades and Training in morning.	13/2/3
	24th.		Company Parades and Training.	13/2/3
	25th.		Battalion Parade.	13/2/3
	26th.		Inspection by Divisional Commander postponed. Lecture by Brigade Commander on Battalion's forthcoming move to Egypt. Men under 20 left for 2/5th. Gloster Regiment.	13/2/3
	27th.		Church Parade in Church Hut. Lt.-Col. E.M.Woulfe-Flanagan, D.S.O. goes on leave, and Major G.E.Swinton,M.C. takes over Command of Battalion.	13/2/3
	28th.		Heavy rain. Training indoors. Draft arrives from 2/5th. Gloster Regiment.	13/2/3
	29th.		Weather continues bad. Training indoors.	-do-
	30th.		Training as per programme for week. Football in afternoon.	13/2/3

G. E. Swinton
Major,
COMDG. 2/4TH. OXFORD & BUCKS LIGHT INFANTRY.

2/4TH. OXFORD & BUCKS LIGHT INFANTRY.

APRIL, 1919.

NOMINAL ROLL OF OFFICERS JOINED.

4.4.19.	From 4th. Bn. Bedford Regiment............	Lieut. G. Theed.
"	" "	2nd. Lt. W. Holmes.
"	" "	2nd. Lt. K. E. Eyles.
"	" 6th. Bn. Dorset Regiment............	Capt. V. S. Hebbert.
"	" "	2nd. Lt. G. V. Sturgeon. (R. Sussex Regiment).
"	" "	Lieut. M. Sorley.
"	" "	2nd. Lt. T. W. Prismall.
7.4.19.	" 2nd. Bn. R. Berkshire Regiment.......	2nd. Lt. W. J. V. Tanner.
12.4.19.	" 4th. Bn. Bedford Regiment............	2nd. Lt. A. W. H. Oakman, M.C.
"	" 6th. Bn. Dorset Regiment............	Capt. C. F. Harrison, M.C.
"	" "	2nd. Lt. H. E. Camidge.
"	" "	Capt. H. C. T. Robinson. (R. Sussex Regiment).
17.4.19. 29	" 5th. Bn. East Surrey Regiment.......	Major G. E. Swinton, M.C. (E. Surrey Regiment)
29-4-19.	" 9th. Northumberland Fusiliers.......	2nd. Lt. G. Bestford.

OFFICERS QUITTED.

4-4-19.	To England for Demobilization............	Captain A. C. Jee.
	do.	Capt. C. S. S. Matthews.
	do.	Lt. R. J. P. McIntosh. (Devon Regiment.)
	do.	2nd. Lt. W. I. Parkinson.
12.4.19.	do.	Captain J. Stanley, M.C. (Hunts Cyclists).
26.4.19.	To 2/5th. Bn. Gloster Regiment..........	Captain L. D. Martin. (Devon Regiment).
	do.	2nd. A. W. H. Oakman, M.C. (Bedford Regiment)